Writing Add-ins for Visual Studio .NET

LES SMITH

APress Media, LLC

Writing Add-ins for Visual Studio .NET
Copyright © 2002 by Les Smith
Originally published by Apress in 2002

ISBN 978-1-59059-026-3   ISBN 978-1-4302-1101-3 (eBook)
DOI 10.1007/978-1-4302-1101-3

Technical Reviewer: Bob Flickinger
Editorial Directors: Dan Appleman, Peter Blackburn, Gary Cornell, Jason Gilmore, Simon Hayes, Karen Watterson, John Zukowski
Managing Editor: Grace Wong
Project Manager and Development Editor: Tracy Brown Collins
Copy Editor: Nicole LeClerc
Production Manager: Kari Brooks
Compositor: Impressions Book and Journal Services, Inc.
Indexer: Ron Strauss
Cover Designer: Kurt Krames
Manufacturing Manager: Tom Debolski
Marketing Manager: Stephanie Rodriguez

Writing a book is not an easy job. Living with a person who is writing a book can be even harder. I dedicate this book to my loving wife, Ellen, who has stuck by me and encouraged me, not only during the months that it took to write this book, but also through the many years of laboring in software development, gaining the experience that led to the writing of this book. She encouraged me to keep going when the research I had to do did not seem to yield the data that I needed to continue. She stuck by me as I wrote, hour after hour, night after night, on a seemingly endless task. I thank her for her patience, understanding, inspiration, and love.

Brief Contents

Contents

Foreword

Like it, tolerate it, or do it yourself—that's what dealing with developer tools used to be. You either liked what you were given, managed with what you were given, or had to write not only the part you liked yourself, but also those features you thought were lacking. When it comes to something as complex as the Visual Basic IDE, that would be a large development effort just to duplicate what Microsoft gave you. Besides, who wants to reinvent the wheel by writing yet another editor?

Programming technology has been developed to componetize our applications and objects such that we can provide open access to other developers to enhance the feature set or functionality of the code without actually having to distribute source code. So now when we get the latest toy from Microsoft, if we find it lacks functionality or a feature that would be beneficial, we can simply write a chunk of code and add it to the application as seamlessly as though the feature were there since day one. As simple as that sounds, it is still no small task.

I'm sure I could write pages about Les Smith's decades of programming experience and knowledge. But this book isn't about programming practices. It's about writing add-ins and what you need to know to get your code connected and running in the IDE. What I can tell you about Les is that he has been writing add-ins to the IDE since Microsoft introduced it in VB 5.0. When it comes to add-ins, Les has been there, done that, and has product on the market. He already knows what works and what doesn't.

I have written add-ins before, so I know the basic ins and outs of them. I also know how frustrating it is to try to find answers to what I consider common questions when it comes to how to do something with an add-in. So, I knew what topics Les had to address in this book. This is very much a roll-up-your-sleeves-and-dive-into-it type of book. Each chapter properly builds on the previous ones. Les does a great job of taking you step by step through the process and pointing out the things to look out for.

Get it up and running—that's what it's all about. You don't have time to pore over page upon page of "noise" in MSDN to try to figure out what would take 5 minutes for someone to show you. Les has done all that work for you and has broken it down into a clear, concise, step-by-step process. This is a book you'll refer back to time and again as you write add-ins to improve on a good start.

Bob Flickinger
VP/COO
BeCubed Software, Inc.

About the Author

Les Smith is an independent software developer. Having worked with computers for over 30 years, he has seen computers shrink from the room-filling behemoths of the early years to the small handhelds of today. His experience ranges from developing operating systems for mainframes to developing applications to developing developer tools. He has worked for a mainframe manufacturer and has made technical sales presentations to top information technology management in many of the largest corporations in America. He has had project lead responsibilities in numerous commercial and government entities, including several NASA installations.

He now contracts in application development, having specialized in Visual Basic for the past 10 years. He is also president of HHI Software, and he is the developer of such products as VBCommander and VBXRef2000. He is in the process of rewriting these products (add-ins) in Visual Basic .NET.

You can visit his Web site at http://HHISoftware.com or send him an e-mail at hhisoftware@wctel.net.

About the Technical Reviewer

BOB FLICKINGER attended the University of Central Florida and earned a degree in physics. He has been working with computers since before the Apple II. He has worked with various programming languages, including FORTRAN, BASIC, assembly language, and C/C++, and he's been working with Microsoft's Visual Basic since its initial version 1.0 release. In 1993, Bob was hired by MicroHelp, Inc., to manage their technical support team and later worked as the senior developer for MicroHelp's UnInstaller. In 1996, Bob and other developers from MicroHelp left to form BeCubed Software, Inc., where they continue to develop component tools for Windows developers.

Acknowledgments

ALTHOUGH THIS BOOK bears my name as the author, no one writes a book and gets it published by himself. Many long hours have been spent, not only by me as the author, but also by many others.

First of all, I want to thank Dan Appleman for giving me the opportunity to write this book. I've appreciated Dan's books for years. When I submitted an outline and introduction to the book, Dan, without knowing me, said, "Let's do it!" For that chance, I am grateful.

I want to thank my project manager, Tracy Brown Collins, for her patience in trying to limit my long sentences and in teaching a technician how to make a book readable.

I want to thank my technical reviewer, Bob Flickinger from BeCubed Software, Inc. Bob has been a friend for years, and I thank him for checking the code and the book, for critiquing me when I needed it, and for making suggestions for changes and additions to the book.

I want to thank Nicole LeClerc, my copy editor, who has tirelessly and without complaint corrected my grammar, spelling, and sentence structure.

I want to thank a number of people at Apress, whom I do not know, who are responsible for getting this book to press.

Finally, I want to thank you, the readers, for buying this book. I truly hope that it will be of help to you. After all, if we go through this life without being a help to others, why do we live?

Introduction

THIS BOOK WAS WRITTEN for the experienced Windows developer who wants to take advantage of the extensibility functionality of Visual Studio .NET. Extensibility has been around for several versions of Visual Studio. *Extensibility* is a big word for the way Visual Studio.NET allows developers to extend the functionality of the integrated development environment (IDE). Prior to the advent of .NET, Visual Studio had one IDE for C++ and a different one for Visual Basic (VBIDE). Now, as you probably already know, Visual Studio's IDE accommodates Visual C++, Visual Basic, and the new kid on the block, Visual C#, along with provisions for future languages. Consequently, add-ins can now be written in any of the three afore-mentioned languages, and the resulting add-ins can support the other languages, regardless of the language in which the add-in was created.

Some of you may be asking, "What's an add-in?" That's okay, you don't have to be experienced in writing, or even using, add-ins in order to benefit from this book. An add-in is a tool. Actually, it's a special type of DLL (.NET assembly) that you can create and compile using Visual Studio .NET's extensibility object model to extend and customize Visual Studio's IDE. The primary aim in writing an add-in is to automate tasks in the IDE that are difficult, repetitive, and tedious to accomplish without such a tool. Chapter 1 provides a detailed description of an add-in.

Why Do I Need to Write an Add-in?

Many of you reading this introduction are corporate developers. Many of you are contractors or consultants. Regardless of whether you are a corporate employee, contractor, consultant, or you have your own company (I am both a consultant and have my own company to write add-ins for commercial consumption), you get paid for production. I've found add-ins to be one of the best ways for me to increase my own productivity. When I can create an add-in that saves me time or makes me more productive, the company for which I am consulting or develop-ing gets their applications done quicker, which saves them money. When companies save money, they make money. We've all heard the old saying, "A penny saved is a penny earned." However, now when you save a few minutes, you save a few dollars. Therefore, by saving dollars, you are making dollars for your employer.

Not only will add-ins allow you to save time, but also when you write an add-in that automates tasks you would normally do manually, the add-in does the job for which it was written and does it accurately every time. The add-in, if written properly, works just like any other well-written and debugged program. It does not make mistakes!

Just recently, I wrote an add-in that creates "wrapper" code around the XML DOM. The feature converts any number of class properties to and from an XML string. This allows the passing of one parameter, an XML string, instead of many parameters. I was moving code from the modules of a "fat client" client/server application to DLLs for use on an application server. Several forms had over 100 controls, and the prospect of marshalling 100-plus properties across DCOM was daunting. Because I had numerous forms to convert, I needed a tool to automate the creation and parsing of the parameters to and from XML. I spent 5 hours creating a new add-in that eliminated 30 to 40 hours of drudgery, not to speak of the errors that I would have introduced had I done the job manually.

Now, if you can write an add-in that automates tasks flawlessly and even generates error-free code, you have become more valuable to your employer. In my case, as a consultant, or contract programmer, I get paid for production. I get rewarded with extended contracts for above-average performance. Therefore, add-ins have been a great boon to my career for years.

Add-ins are a great way to enforce standards and consistency across a development team. For example, in one of the commercial add-ins that I have developed, VBCommander, there are numerous features that ensure consistency across a project. One instance of this is the Property Prompter. This feature displays a dialog box every time a control is dropped on a form. The Prompter automatically determines the type of control being placed and enters a predetermined prefix into a text box on the Prompter's dialog box, positioning the cursor just beyond the prefix so that the developer can directly enter the rest of the control's name. Depending on the type of control—a command button, for example—the Caption property (Text in .NET) may be automatically created and the first character of the caption will be preceded by an ampersand (&), causing it to be underlined on the command button when it appears on the form. These and other properties that the developer would have to go to the property page and enter manually are automatically prompted for and in some cases suggested or supplied.

Another important feature that is used constantly is block commenting. The add-in not only comments a block of code (the IDE obviously has this feature), but it also encapsulates the selected block with a header and footer that includes the developer's name and the date of the change. There are several options in the Comment menu of the add-in that not only allow you to comment a block, but also enable you to surround a change or an addition of code with a header and footer. Subsequently, a complementing feature of the add-in allows a developer to search a file or the whole project for changes made by programmer and date, thus producing a list of changes made by a programmer or all changes made on a certain date or time frame.

By now you should be able to see, if you are new to add-ins, the business case for writing add-ins.

Who Should Read This Book?

This book is for intermediate to advanced VB programmers who may or may not have previous experience writing add-ins. It will be helpful if you have written add-ins in VB 5.0 or VB 6.0, but this is not a prerequisite for using this book. If you have only used add-ins and wondered how they were created, this book will teach you to write them in Visual Studio .NET. If you are faced with moving add-ins from VB 5.0/6.0 to .NET, this book will show you what must be changed.

How This Book Is Organized

The object of this book is to take you from the basics of simply creating your first add-in to building some fairly complex features into an add-in. With this in mind, each chapter covers a new facet of extensibility. As you learn new material in each chapter, you will add new functionality to your add-in. Although you will build several add-ins in the course of this book, you will also add functionality to the basic add-in that you create in Chapter 2.

What This Book Does Not Do

This book does not rehash the theory behind programming practices, nor does it give you an example of the use of every method, property, and constant in the extensibility model. There are currently 500 topics that appear in the Search Result window of the MSDN help file if you search on the word "extensibility." The book does not teach you how to use every one of the methods; nor does MSDN, for that matter. The extensibility model exposes many objects that you probably won't need in writing many practical, timesaving add-ins.

Most important, this book is not an introduction to Visual Studio .NET. This book assumes that you are already developing programs in Visual Studio .NET, and therefore it does not attempt to explain the basics of Visual Studio .NET. Add-ins are not meant for beginning programmers, in any version of Visual Basic, and that is especially true of writing add-ins for Visual Studio .NET. If you are not already programming in .NET, I strongly suggest that you get a good introductory book on the subject and spend a good amount of time working with basic Visual Studio .NET programming before you tackle add-ins.

What This Book Does

It is not enough just to teach you how to create an add-in. The Add-in Wizard can do that for you without you writing a line of code. The problem is that it won't do anything! This book will teach you how to create the user interface (UI) to the add-in. In other words, it will show you how to get your menu(s) and tool buttons on the Visual Studio .NET UI. That has always been the hardest part of learning to write add-ins for me. This book will also teach you how to debug an add-in. This is always challenging, no matter how good a programmer you are. In addition, it will show you how to manipulate code in Windows and controls on forms.

Chapter 10 deals with the subject of handling multiple languages in an add-in. In that chapter you will see an add-in created in Visual C#. That add-in will call a DLL written in Visual Basic .NET. You will see that it is easy to write an add-in in multiple languages that can manipulate projects that are being developed in one or more different languages.

In addition to teaching you the basics of writing an add-in, this book illustrates how to write some real, usable, timesaving features, which to me is the main purpose of add-ins. You will find as you examine some of my code that I am a pragmatist, not a purist. You may not agree with that philosophy, but again, as a self-employed consultant I am paid for producing, not theorizing, philosophizing, or trying to squeeze the last, unneeded line of code from a procedure. Some developers spend needless hours examining, and usually rewriting, other people's code simply because they don't like the way it's written. Many times, I've supervised this type of developer and found that they not only didn't improve the code, they broke it, simply because they did not take time to "understand all they knew" about the code. This type of developer is afflicted with an NIHS (Not In His or Her Shop) mentality. In other words, if the NIHS developer didn't write it, it can't be any good. We've all met this type of developer. Please don't be one!

About the Code in This Book

Code in this book for the most part will be in Visual Basic; therefore, the sample code for this book will for the most part be in Visual Basic. The reason for this is obvious: Visual Basic continues to be the single most popular programming language. However, I avoid most Visual Basic–specific commands so that you will find it trivial to migrate the code in this book to C#. The methods and properties referenced in the sample code apply to VB .NET, C#, and other .NET languages.

Most of the code supplied for this book is in the form of add-in projects or solutions. They consist of whole solutions, including all of the files for all of the projects in the solution. Normally, there is a solution (.sln) with two projects. There is a project for the add-in and a setup project for the solution. The easiest way to run the add-in on your machine is to load the add-in solution into Visual

Studio .NET. You then need to build and install the add-in. This causes the proper registry entries to be created.

 **NOTE** *The Add-in Wizard will normally create the proper registry entries when an add-in is created initially. When an add-in is moved to another computer, as will be the case for the code for this book, the registry entries will not automatically be in the registry of the destination computer. This is true even when you try to start the add-in in debug mode.*

In order for the add-in to run, it must be registered and the Add-in Manager must be able to see it. Building and installing the add-in will create the required registry entries for you. For information on how to build and install an add-in, please see the "Installing the New Add-in" section in Chapter 2. This subject is covered again in Chapter 13. In that chapter you will see a procedure for manually registering and creating the Add-in Manager registry entries.

You can download the code from this book from the Downloads section of the Apress Web site (http://www.apress.com). I trust that you will download the code from there, rather than typing it in from the book. There are two reasons for this. First, typing it in is a time-consuming and error-prone process. Second, there is a lot of code involved in one add-in, and there is at least one add-in in each of the chapters from Chapter 2 through Chapter 12.

What Is an Add-in?

"Your footsteps are easier to follow than your advice."
—Author Unknown

AN *ADD-IN* IS A TOOL that you create programmatically by using objects, methods, properties, collections, and events in .NET's extensibility object model. These objects and their respective methods, properties, and events enable you to automate difficult and tedious tasks within the Visual Studio integrated development environment (IDE). These tasks are usually accomplished in response to an event, such as the mouse being clicked, a form being added to a project, or a control being added to a form. The action may or may not be visible to the developer.

I'm not sure why Microsoft calls this functionality "add-in" instead of "add-on" or "extender." However, it is interesting to note that if you take the letters *a* and *i* from "add-in," it could be an abbreviation for artificial intelligence (AI). Without being presumptuous, certain add-in features act like AI. For example, consider the form prompter dialog box, which pops up when you add a form to a project. The dialog box asks you for certain required properties, such as form name, text (caption in earlier versions of Visual Basic), and other properties, such as sizing options and whether the form should stay on top (TopMost) of other forms. The add-in has jumped ahead of the developer and reminded him to fill in certain required information, without his having to bring up or search through the property window. It also keeps him from having forms named Form1, Form2, and so forth.

As is the case with ActiveX components, several third-party software vendors write complex add-ins for Visual Studio. I have developed and marketed commercially three major add-ins: VBCommander, VBXRef, and VBCommander/Pro.

What Is Extensibility?

An add-in extends the functionality of the Visual Studio IDE. *Extensibility*, therefore, is the mechanism exposed to the add-in developer that provides the ability to enhance and extend the functionality of the IDE. *Automation* refers to user-created code and tools that automate tasks in the environment and programmatically drive the IDE. Extensibility basically exposes the IDE internal functions to the add-in developer. The creative developer can programmatically invoke almost all of the tasks, which can be performed using the multitude of menu options, tool buttons, and shortcut keys in the IDE. Add-ins are literally limited only by the imagination and creativity of the developer.

You can use the Visual Studio .NET automation model to create custom tools for taking the time-consuming drudgery from mundane development tasks. You can create a tool to help other programmers create their applications. This is the ultimate goal in writing add-ins. The *automation model* was known in earlier versions of Visual Studio as the *extensibility object* (and the terms "automation model" and "extensibility object" are used interchangeably). It is a programming interface that gives you access to the underlying routines that drive the IDE. The automation model allows you to customize, manipulate, and automate the IDE. For example, you can programmatically create projects and project items, including classes, forms, and methods, and you can even automate the project build and deployment processes.

You can access the automation model in one of two environments. The first, and obviously the easiest, is through macros. Visual Studio .NET introduces the macro recorder and accompanying Macros IDE. These features are completely new to Visual Studio, and I cover them in detail in Chapter 8 of this book. The second, more complex, yet infinitely more rewarding method is to create extensions to the IDE by writing add-ins. Add-ins are compiled applications that manipulate the development environment and automate tasks.

Add-ins can be invoked in a variety of ways, including through the Add-in Manager, toolbar commands or buttons, the development environment (devenv) command line, and events such as IDE start-up. A variety of add-in and macro examples are available in the samples/automation directory of the third Visual Studio CD.

In addition to the common automation object model provided by Visual Studio to all of its languages, tools, and packages, individual Visual Studio development languages can also offer their own unique additions to the automation object model to support their specific features and components. As a result, you can create an add-in that works equally well with any Visual Studio language or one that is tailored to support the special features of a particular language, such as Visual Basic, Visual C#, or Visual C++.

The Extensibility Object Model for Visual Basic and Visual C# Projects

Visual Studio .NET provides a general extensibility model for all languages sharing the IDE. Additionally, it provides a specific object model that pertains only to Visual Basic and Visual C#. The VSLangProj namespace provides the ability to manipulate project attributes, which are found only in Visual Basic and Visual C#.

DTE Object

DTE stands for *Development Tools Extensibility*. The DTE object is the most important object in extensibility because it is the root object. It is literally a pointer to the IDE through which all other objects that are exposed by the IDE are referenced. An instance of the DTE object is passed to the OnConnection method that you implement when you create an add-in. The DTE object is the Application object in VBA. The OnConnection method will be described in Chapter 2 and explored again in Chapter 3. When the Add-in Wizard, which is described in detail in Chapter 2, creates an add-in project, one of the objects that it references is the EnvDTE namespace. In the declarations section of the file Connect.vb, you will see the following code:

```
Imports EnvDTE
```

The Add-in Wizard will add a reference to the file DTE.OLB, which is the object library for the DTE. Including this object library in your add-in project allows you access to all of the methods, properties, and events exposed by the IDE. If you have never written an add-in before, the code snippets in this chapter may not mean a lot to you. If that is the case, do not be alarmed. The code will make sense as you get into the details of coding in later chapters. The code shown in Listing 1-1 is just a small example of how the DTE object will be used once it is passed into the add-in. This subroutine will comment the block of code selected in the active code window (or active document, as it is known in .NET).

Listing 1-1. Comment Selected Block

```
Sub CommentSelected Block
    Dim sel As TextSelection = DTE.ActiveDocument.Selectioon()
    Dim stPtr As EditPoint = sel.TopPoint.CreateEditPoint()
    Dim endPtr TextPoint = sel.BottomPoint
    Dim commentChar As String = "'***"

    Try
        Do While (stPtr.LessThan(endPtr))
            stPtr.Insert(commentChar)
            stPtr.LineDown()
            stPtr.StartOfLine()
        Loop
    Finally
            ' we could insert code here for undoing if an error were encountered
    End Try
End Sub
```

NOTE *The subroutine in Listing 1-1 was extracted from sample macro code, and references to the DTE object would be made by a reference to the application variable in an actual add-in. Chapter 3 illustrates this process in detail.*

Exploring the DTE Object

Because access to everything in the extensibility model begins at the DTE, or root object, you can begin there and drill down a level or two in the model to look at some of the components of the DTE object. Obviously, this is neither the time nor the place to examine the whole DTE object. If you search for the word "extensibility" in MSDN, the search will return around 500 topics. Additionally, if you search for the word "DTE," the search will return around 400 topics. The DTE object is truly huge.

Let's explore a few of the DTE's basic properties to give you a feel for what's available at the root level. In order to do that, you'll start two instances of Visual Basic (VB) .NET. One will have the add-in that you're debugging, and the other will use the add-in. The second copy of VB .NET will have another project open, a new Windows application. Connecting to the add-in, which you're debugging, allows you to stop in the add-in to examine objects within the IDE. Please don't be concerned with what the add-in is doing or how it was created and run. You'll deal with this in detail in Chapter 2. Suffice it to say that at this point you have two copies of VB .NET running, just as you would in the debugging of a COM DLL. You've stopped the add-in with a breakpoint in the Click Event method of its menu option. This allows you to display as many properties as you like before allowing the Click Event to continue.

NOTE *I don't show images to illustrate the demonstration in this section, as I cover the Add-in Wizard and step through a basic add-in in Chapter 2.*

For example, you will just print some of the properties from the Command (Immediate) window. Remember that the pointer to the DTE was passed to you in the OnConnection method as the parameter "application." The code in that method has typecast the parameter to type EnvDTE.DTE with the following code:

```
Dim applicationObject As EnvDTE.DTE
applicationObject = Ctype(application, EnvDTE.DTE)
```

> **NOTE** *As you are probably already aware of .NET, you no longer use the Set command to set an object. Rather, you just use the syntax shown in the preceding example:* `obj = object`.

Displaying DTE Basic Properties

Now you can use the applicationObject to qualify any reference to a component of the IDE. The code in Listing 1-2 simply displays several basic properties of the applicationObject (DTE). In each case, a print command (?) will be followed by the value echoed back from the IDE.

Listing 1-2. Displaying DTE Properties

```
?applicationObject.Name
    "Microsoft Development Environment"

?applicationObject.Mode
vsIDEModeDesign
' response above indicates we are in design mode

' display the number of add-ins listed with the Add-in Manager
?applicationObject.Addins.Count
3

' display the ActiveDocument Name
?applicationObject.ActiveDocument.Name
"Form1.vb"

' display the ActiveDocument path
?applicationObject.ActiveDocument.Path
"E:\VSProjs\WindowsApplication1\"

' display the ReadOnly property of the document
?applicationObject.ActiveDocument.ReadOnly
False

' there are two documents open in the project that the add-in is
' connected to, verify it
?applicationObject.Documents.Count
2
```

```
' display the fullname of the development environment exe
?applicationObject.FullName
"E:\Program Files\Microsoft Visual Studio.NET\Common7\IDE\devenv.exe"

' display the IDE MainWindow Caption
?applicationObject.MainWindow.Caption
"WindowsApplication1 - Microsoft Visual Basic.NET [design] - Form1.vb"
```

The displays shown in Listing 1-2 are the result of a simple exercise to demonstrate how you use the DTE object to access the components of the IDE. It would be difficult to go much further in this context. Drilling down into the multitude of objects, methods, and events requires the creation of objects. One of the sad things that you'll discover (if you haven't already) as you begin debugging in VB .NET is that the powerful features of editing, changing, and executing the changed code in the IDE are no longer possible in Visual Basic .NET. I believe that this is due to the fact that VB and C# are compiled to Microsoft intermediate language (IL), and the just-in-time (JIT) compiler compiles the code just before it's executed. C++, on the other hand, initially compiles to native code, and there's no such limitation in the C++ debugger. This is real negative for VB developers, but it appears that we're stuck with it. In any case, you can't insert new code and execute it (the new code) without rebuilding the application. However, depending on the Debug option settings, you can change code and continue debugging; you just can't execute the changed code until the project is rebuilt.

Another method of exploring and executing methods in the extensibility model is to use the Macros IDE. This new feature is an excellent way to learn how to manipulate the objects of the IDE. You'll explore this new functionality in Chapter 8 of this book.

The Automation Object

The automation object model consists of a few distinct, but related, groups of objects that provide the major functionality of the IDE. To understand the model, you must understand how these functional groups work.

All of these functional groups are fully outlined in the Visual Studio .NET Automation Object Model chart, which you can find in the Visual Studio Help file. Some of these groups are as follows:

- Solution- and project-related objects

- Tool window objects, such as the Task List, Output window, and Toolbox

- Code editor objects

- Debugging objects

- Code manipulation objects

- Window and document manipulation objects

- Event objects

- Add-in management objects

Each functional group consists of one or more objects, collections, and interfaces that comprise a component's functionality. For example, the primary function of the event objects group is to provide access to events occurring in the IDE. You can monitor such things as files being saved, new files being added, and so forth.

One such object in this group is the TaskListEvents object, which allows you to respond to events that occur in the Task List. Another object in this group is the BuildEvents object, which allows you to respond to events that occur in a build operation, such as when a build begins or completes.

The TaskList object represents the Task List and has associated objects that allow you to add and remove items from it. The Project object represents items in a project, and objects in its functional group allow you to add, remove, and save items in projects, as well as obtain information about them, such as the paths and names of all of the files in the project and the number of files.

Other New Features of .NET

In addition to the rather drastic changes to the Visual Basic language, as well as extensibility, there are a number of new .NET features that aid the add-in developer. These are highlighted in the following sections.

Recording Macros

You can automate repetitive tasks using the macro-recording features. The macros are stored as VB .NET procedures that you may edit using the Visual Studio .NET Macros IDE. The Macros IDE allows developers to edit macros and even use macros to learn about the extensibility object model.

Writing Macros

For more complex situations, you can write macros using VB .NET. You can use all the features of VB .NET in macros, including inheritance, structured error handling, and the .NET Framework.

Organizing Macros

The Macro Explorer in the Visual Studio .NET Macros IDE provides a hierarchical view of the available macros, which are organized into modules contained in macro projects. From this window, you can organize, edit, and run macros.

Manipulating Code Without Parsing

The project-neutral extensibility model, called the *general extensibility model*, provides access to the individual code files of your project. You can drill down to the level of an individual variable declaration and modify it without having to parse the code. Go straight to the code element you want to modify using the CodeModel object, get its location in the Document object, and modify your code.

Add-ins

As noted previously, add-ins are not new in .NET, but they certainly are different and enhanced. Add-ins are extensions to the IDE. They are compiled applications that manipulate the environment and automate tasks. Because they are compiled, add-ins are more powerful, more versatile, and more deployable than macros. Add-in projects implement the IDTExtensibility2 interface. The power of add-ins rests in the following facts:

- You have access to all the features of .NET to modify the IDE.

- You can write add-ins using any of the Visual Studio .NET languages.

- Add-ins are compiled; therefore, your code is not exposed as it is in macros.

- Add-ins are easy to distribute because they are compiled.

The Add-in Wizard is provided to create skeleton add-in projects. Chapter 2 discusses and demonstrates the use of the Add-in Wizard.

Wizards

Wizards are simplified add-ins that implement the IDTWizard interface. These applications lead users through a task step by step.

Visual Studio Integrator Program

Most users of Visual Studio .NET will find that their needs are met by the use of add-ins, macros, and wizards. Some users may find that they need to go beyond these capabilities. For example, someone might want to introduce a new programming language into the Visual Studio IDE, which could possibly create a need for a new project type, a new or customized text editor, and possibly new debugging features.

The Visual Studio Integrator Program (VSIP), although not a topic of this book, was created to allow this kind of custom extensibility. The VSIP provides you with tools and information that will facilitate the integration of custom products into the Visual Studio .NET environment. You can find out more about the program at http://msdn.microsoft.com/vstudio/vsip/default.asp.

Making a VB 6.0 Add-in Work in .NET

If you are new to add-ins, you can ignore this section. If you are used to writing add-ins in VB 6.0, you may be asking, "Are all of my add-ins broken?" The answer to this question is, in a practical sense, "Yes!" What I mean here is that .NET provides a completely new and totally different automation model. It is referenced by implementing IDTExtensibility2, whereas VB 6.0 implemented IDTExtensibility. These two models are as different as night and day. It turns out that both models exist in .NET. However, upon trying to connect one of my VB 6.0 compiled add-ins via COM interoperability, I have found that it will not load, even though I have succeeded in getting it listed in the Add-in Manager dialog box. I receive an error message that says, "No such interface exists." This means that .NET does not recognize the VB 6.0 compiled IDTExtensibility interface. I explore the use of the VB 6.0 model in .NET in Chapter 13, where I discuss the migration of VB 6.0 add-ins to .NET.

There is one small exception to the declaration that VB 6.0 add-ins are broken. Add-in toolbars, tool buttons, and menus are not really so much a part of Visual Studio automation as they are Microsoft Office. For example, if you had an add-in that was launched from VB only because you added a toolbar, tool button, or menu to the IDE's toolbar, that add-in will still probably work. A good example of this is VisData. VisData was really a stand-alone executable, which allowed you to launch it from the IDE. It had functionality that allowed you to add it to VB IDE as an add-in. All this meant was that it could add a picture button menu to the Add-in menu in the VB 6.0 IDE. Once launched, it had no interaction with the IDE, and it required no interaction with the extensibility model.

NOTE *The fact that you could add VisData to the Add-in menu in VB 6.0 does not now imply that VisData can be run as an add-in in .NET. The Connect class would have to be changed to implement IDExtensibility2 to use the new interfaces to .NET.*

Therefore, if you have VB 6.0 add-ins that require no interaction with the IDE other than to add a UI to the IDE, you can still compile them under VB 6.0 with a minor modification to the Connect class, and then connect them to Visual Studio .NET, placing your UI on its toolbar.

If you look on the third CD of Beta 2 in the \Samples\Automation\cmdBrowse directory, you'll find a sample add-in (cmdBrowser.vbp), which you can compile under VB 6.0 and connect to Visual Studio .NET. I've done it, and it works fine. Why does this add-in work and mine doesn't? The answer is that this add-in doesn't implement IDTExtinsibility. Rather, it's a special type of add-in that exposes special OnConnection and OnDisconnection methods that are still recognized by .NET.

NOTE *This book is based on the release version of Visual Studio .NET. I made a reference to the Beta 2 CD in the preceding paragraph simply because the automation samples were available on that CD. You can also download these samples from the Microsoft Web site.*

The sample add-in is quite handy, in that it will search through the registry, find all of the commands in the Visual Studio .NET IDE (menus, tool bars, and tool buttons), and place them in a tree view. Furthermore, because the UI of the add-in launches an ActiveX document rather than a VB form, it is a dockable tool window. You can actually learn several things from examining this sample add-in in detail.

In order to make your old add-in interface work, you must add a reference to DTE.OLB to your VB 6.0 project references. Then, you need to replace the OnConnection and OnDisconnection methods in the Connect class. The code in Listing 1-3 is incomplete and is not meant to work by itself. It is included here as an illustration of how to connect a simple VB 6.0 add-in to .NET, and it is therefore not included with the code of this chapter. You can find an entire project using code similar to this on the third CD of the Beta 2 release.

Listing 1-3. VB 6.0 Add-in Code

```
Option Explicit
Public FormDisplayed As Boolean
Public oVB As EnvDTE.DTE
Dim mcbMenuCmdBar As Office.CommandBarControl
Dim gwinWindow As EnvDTE.Window
Dim DismDisplay As Object
Public WithEvents MenuHandler As CommandBarEvents   'command bar event handler
Attribute MenuHandler.VB_VarHelpID = -1


'--------------------------------------------------------
'this method adds the add-in to VS
'--------------------------------------------------------
Private Sub AddinInstance_OnConnection(ByVal Application As Object, _
                    ByVal ConnectMode As AddInDesignerObjects.ext_ConnectMode, _
                    ByVal AddInInst As Object, custom() As Variant)
    On Error GoTo ErrH

      'save the vb instance
    Set oVB = Application

    ' place the menu on the Tools Menu
    Set mcbMenuCommandBar = AddToToolsMenu("My VB6 Add-in")
    ' set up event handler for click event
    Set Me.MenuHandler = _
            oVB.Events.CommandBarEvents(mcbMenuCmdBar)
    Exit Sub
ErrH:
    MsgBox Err.Description
End Sub

'this method removes the add-in from VS
Private Sub AddinInstance_OnDisconnection(ByVal RemoveMode As _
        AddInDesignerObjects.ext_DisconnectMode, custom() As Variant)
    On Error Resume Next
     'delete the command bar entry
    mcbMenuCmdBar.Delete
End Sub

Private Sub IDTExtensibility_OnStartupComplete(custom() As Variant)
' this does nothing but must be available to the IDE
End Sub
```

```
'this event fires when the menu is clicked in the IDE
Private Sub MenuHandler_Click(ByVal CommandBarControl As Object, _
            handled As Boolean, CancelDefault As Boolean)
    ' Here you might load a form or Shell and executable
    ' you just can't reference anything in the Extensibility Object
End Sub


Function AddToToolsMenu(rsMenuCaption As String) As Office.CommandBarControl
    Dim cbMenuCmdBar As Office.CommandBarControl   'command bar object
    Dim cbMenu As Object

    On Error GoTo AddToToolsMenuErr

    'see if we can find the add-ins menu
    Set cbMenu = VSInstance.CommandBars("Tools")

    'add it to the command bar
    Set cbMenuCmdBar = cbMenu.Controls.Add(1)
    'set the caption
    cbMenuCommandBar.Caption = rsMenuCaption
    Set AddToAddInCommandBar = cbMenuCommandBar
    Exit Function

AddToToolsMenuErr:
    Err.Clear
End Function
```

Obviously, this add-in Connect class does nothing but add a menu to the Tools menu in the IDE, but it does illustrate how to connect a VB 6.0 compiled add-in to Visual Studio .NET. The interface to the command bar interface is the same in .NET as it is in VB 6.0 because the toolbars in the respective IDEs are both derived from the Microsoft Office 8 object model. As you can see, the only difference between the illustrated Connect class and a VB 6.0 Connect class is the name that precedes the OnConnection and OnDisconnection methods, as shown here:

- *VB 6.0 interface:* IDTExtensibility_OnConnection

- *.NET interface:* AddinInstance_OnConnection

- *VB 6.0 interface:* IDTExtensibility_OnDisconnection

- *.NET interface:* AddinInstance_OnDisconnection

Obviously, this has been a slimmed-down, simple example. If you would like to see a real VB 6.0 add-in that even docks a Tool window in the Visual Studio .NET IDE, try the sample (cmdBrowser) project. You will need to compile the DLL under VB 6.0. Next, you will need to register the add-in in the proper place for Visual Studio .NET to find it and list it in its Add-in Manager dialog box. In the directory where you find the cmdBrowser project, you will also find a registration file named cmdbrws70.reg. The contents of the file are shown in Listing 1-4.

Listing 1-4. Creating a Registry Entry

```
REGEDIT4
 [HKEY_LOCAL_MACHINE\SOFTWARE\Microsoft\VisualStudio\7.0\Addins]
 [HKEY_LOCAL_MACHINE\SOFTWARE\Microsoft\VisualStudio\7.0\Addins\
    CmdBrowser.Connect]
"FriendlyName"="Command Browser"
"Description"="View information about Visual Studio commands."
"LoadBehavior"=dword:00000005
"CommandLineSafe"=dword:00000000
```

To run this registration file and register the add-in, double-click the file in Windows Explorer. The next time you start Visual Studio .NET, the add-in will appear in the Add-in Manager dialog box. Open the dialog box, click the check box to the left of the cmdBrowser add-in, and also click the StartUp check box. The add-in will start when you close the Add-in Manager dialog box.

Summary

In this chapter you discovered that there are some really good reasons for taking the trouble to learn to write add-ins. You learned that a lot of things have changed, not only in extensibility, but all over Visual Basic. Obviously, if you have done any work in .NET, you have already found this out the hard way. You looked at some elementary examples of the use of the DTE object. Finally, you saw that it is still possible to connect a simple VB 6.0 add-in to Visual Studio .NET.

In Chapter 2, you will use the Add-in Wizard to create your first add-in. Although you will keep the first add-in simple, it will get you into some real add-in code.

Getting Started with the Add-in Wizard

"Even if I knew that tomorrow the world would go to pieces,
I would still plant my apple tree."
—Martin Luther

ALTHOUGH YOU COULD CREATE an add-in by creating the necessary classes and methods yourself, it is much easier and faster to use the Add-in Wizard provided by Visual Studio .NET.

There are several reasons for using the Add-in Wizard, even if you're an experienced add-in developer. First, the wizard creates two projects and inserts them into the solution (.sln) project. The first is an add-in project and the second is a setup project. Creating a setup project isn't an intuitive process and I much prefer to have the wizard do it for me. Without a setup project, you won't be able to debug your add-in. The wizard also creates a .reg file for registering your new add-in. Finally, the wizard creates a globally unique identifier (GUID) for your add-in and ensures that every required method is included in the Connect class. It's very easy to forget, and it might seem a minor detail, but if something is missing, you could spend hours trying to determine the meaning of some of the cryptic diagnostics that emit from Visual Studio. The wizard guarantees that you don't get caught in that trap.

In this chapter, I show you how to use the Add-in Wizard to create your first add-in. Then you'll modify the add-in to cause it to actually respond to a click on its menu option. Finally, you'll explore the more important methods of the add-in Connect class.

Creating an Add-in Using the Add-in Wizard

To create the add-in, the Add-in Wizard guides you through a series of steps in which you're prompted to choose from several options. These options determine some of the features that the wizard puts in the add-in's code. First, you must select an add-in project type, which causes the Add-in Wizard to be executed. Once you've completed all of the steps in the wizard, the add-in project is automatically created and saved, and is ready for testing.

When you first open a new instance of Visual Studio .NET, you'll see the start page. You have three options here. First, you can select a project from the recent projects list, assuming that you've worked on one or more projects before. Second, you can click the Open Project button to browse for a project. Third, you can click the New Project button to create a new project.

Selecting the Project Type

To create an add-in, click the New Project button. The New Project dialog box appears, as shown in Figure 2-1. The New Project dialog box offers you a choice of languages in which you can create a project. At present, these languages are limited to Visual Basic, C#, and C++, but Microsoft has intimated that there may be many others. Under the Other Projects folder are several types of projects, including extensibility projects.

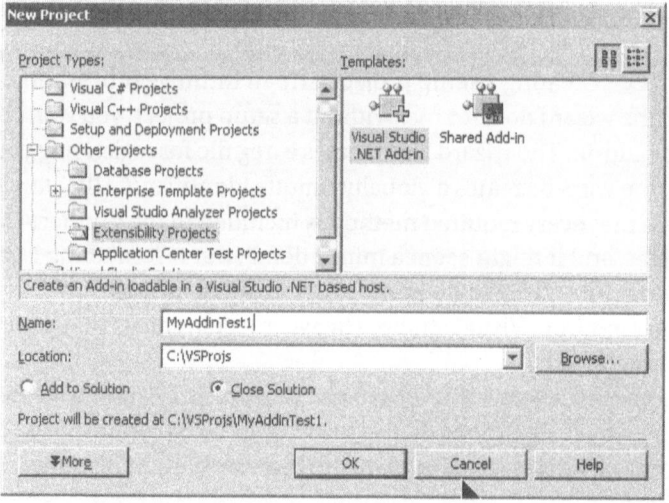

Figure 2-1. Selecting the project

Click the Extensibility Projects folder under the Other Projects folder. At this point, it might seem natural to double-click the add-in icon in the Templates window of the New Projects dialog box. Don't be tempted to do that here. If you do, the wizard will automatically give the add-in a default name and store the project files in a default directory. If you don't already know where Visual Studio stores projects by default, you'll then have to search for the project. Instead of double-clicking the add-in icon, change the name of the project from the default MyAddin1 to something more meaningful. Also, use the Browse button to select the directory in which you want the add-in files stored.

Once you've selected the name and directory, click the OK button to start the Add-in Wizard. At this point, the wizard's welcome window appears, as shown in Figure 2-2.

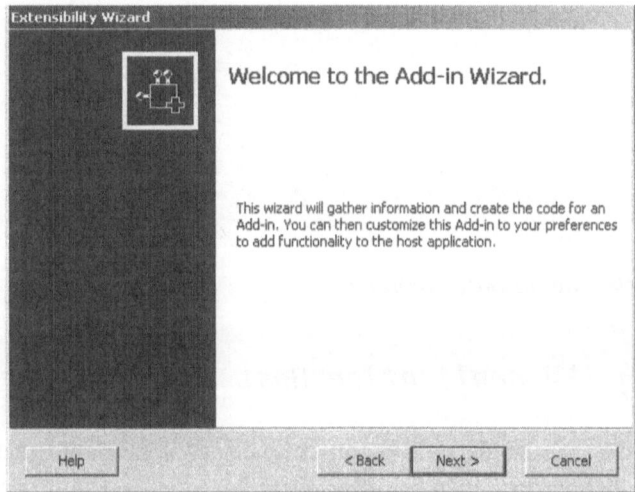

Figure 2-2. The Add-in Wizard's welcome window

Selecting the Add-in's Base Language

Click the Next button in the welcome window to proceed to Step 1 of the wizard (see Figure 2-3). Here, you select the Visual Studio language the code of the add-in will be generated in, and in which you will write the code. Because most of the code in this book will be in Visual Basic, select the "Create an Add-in using Visual Basic" option.

If you were to select Visual C# or C++, the code for the basic add-in Connect class would be created in that language. I encourage you to try this on your own, just to see the code generation for the different languages. This is especially helpful if you are adept at programming in multiple languages. Actually, you will do just that in Chapter 10, which covers handling multiple languages in an add-in. Now that you have selected the language for the add-in, click the Next button to proceed to Step 2.

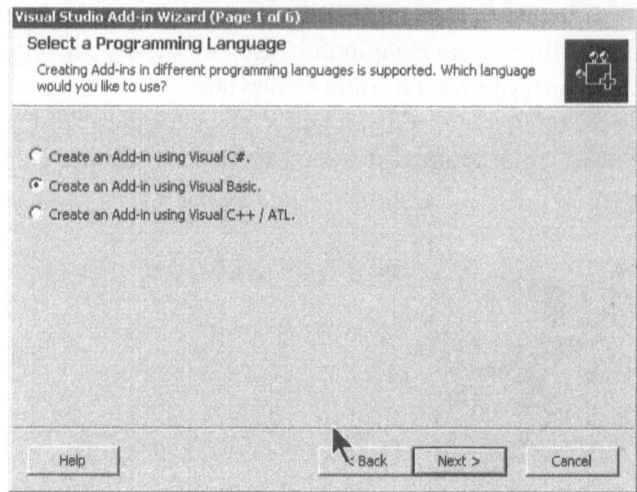

Figure 2-3. Selecting the base language

Selecting the Application Host

Step 2 of the wizard (see Figure 2-4) contains a list of all available host applications, such as Microsoft Visual Studio .NET, that can host the add-in. To select or clear a host, click its check box. You can select more than one host if more than one is listed. Changing the host changes how the deployment project's resulting .msi file registers the add-in.

For this add-in, check the Microsoft Visual Studio .NET option and deselect any other hosting options. This will allow the add-in to be used only in the Visual Studio .NET IDE. Click the Next button to proceed to Step 3 of the wizard, where you will enter the name and description of your add-in.

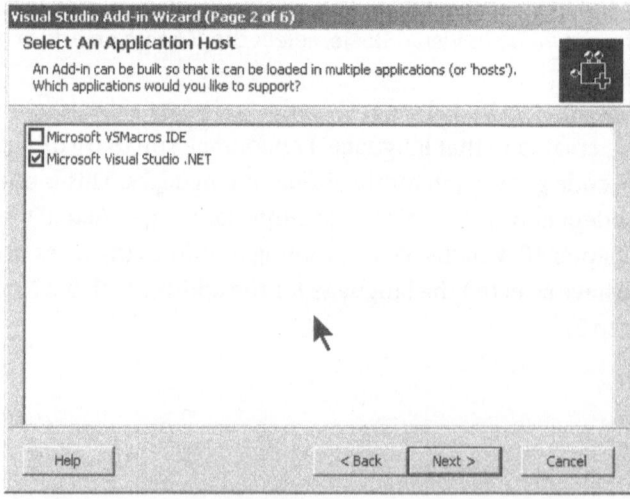

Figure 2-4. Selecting a host application

Entering a Name and Description

You may think you already entered a name for your add-in in the New Projects dialog box shown in Figure 2-1. You're right—but that was the *internal name* for the add-in. The name you enter in Step 3 is different. This name, often referred to as the *friendly name* in the Visual Studio .NET documentation, is the name by which the user will know the add-in.

Step 3 allows you to enter a friendly name and description for your new add-in. This name appears in the Add-in Manager dialog box's Available Add-ins list and gives the user a short description of what the add-in does.

Two questions are asked in this step's dialog box, as shown in Figure 2-5. Give thought to what you enter into the two text boxes, as the text you input will appear from now on in the Add-in Manager dialog box.

1. *What is the name of your Add-in?* Enter the name that you want the add-in to display in the Add-in Manager dialog box's Available Add-ins list. This is generally referred to as the friendly name of the add-in. This is also the external name by which the add-in will be known.

2. *What is the description for your Add-in?* This brief description appears next to the Name box in the Description box of the Add-in Manager dialog box. If you make this description longer than the space provided, it probably won't display in its entirety in the Description box.

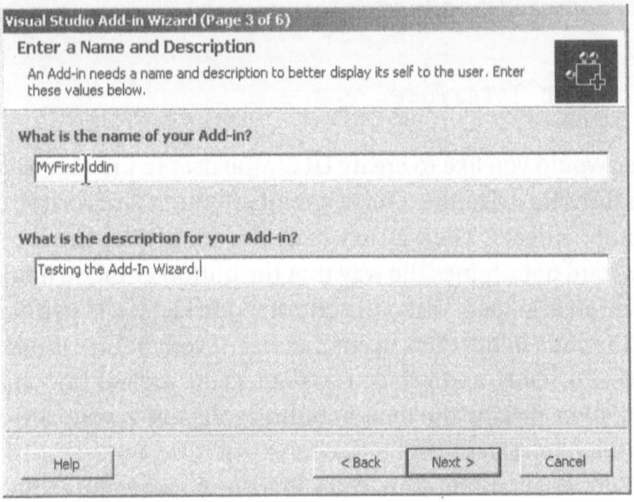

Figure 2-5. The Enter a Name and Description dialog box

Click the Next button to proceed to the next step, where you will be prompted to customize your add-in.

Choosing Add-in Options

Step 4 of the Add-in Wizard (see Figure 2-6) presents you with several options for customizing the add-in. Here, you can elect to have the wizard create a user interface (UI) for you. Please note that this will be a very simple, one-menu-item user interface. However, the code will demonstrate how to add a menu to the IDE for your add-ins. Also, you will be able to select when the add-in loads and who is able to use the add-in.

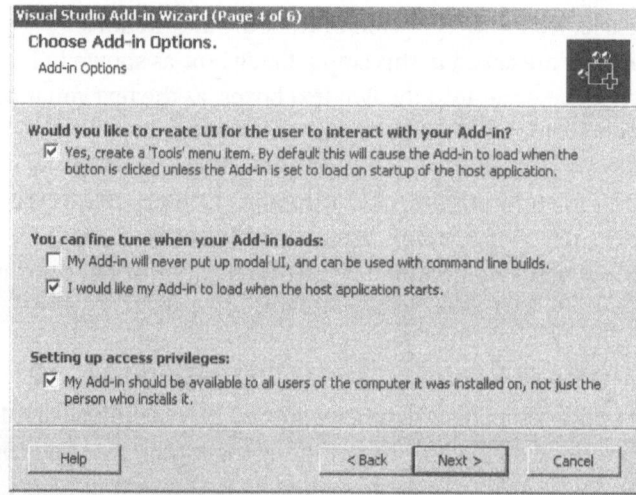

Figure 2-6. Customizing the add-in

Creating a User Interface

Selecting the "Would you like to create UI for the user to interact with your Add-in?" option causes the wizard to create a toolbar button and accompanying menu item automatically. The way in which you modify the Connect class generated by the wizard determines the way that the button or menu item reacts.

If your add-in is loaded, when the button is clicked it will perform the action specified by the code in the Click event handler. If your add-in is not set up to load when the IDE loads, and you do not remove the toolbar button in your disconnect code, then clicking the toolbar button will launch your add-in and transfer control to the Click event handler.

If you do not select this option, you will have to create the code manually to place the UI buttons and/or menu items on the appropriate toolbar. This is probably what you will do as you develop more complex add-ins. For now, let the wizard create the button for you. Please note that although the wizard will create a Click event handler for the button, it will not place any code in the handler to give a visible response that you have clicked the button. I discuss how to do that later in this chapter, once the Connect class has been generated.

Determining When the Add-in Loads

Step 4 also allows you to fine-tune when your add-in loads; this prompt indicates that you tell the wizard about the operation of your add-in. The "You can fine tune when your Add-in loads" option prompts you to select one of two options. These options describe how you plan for your add-in to behave with respect to displaying modal UI and add-in start-up.

Selecting the first check box specifies that your add-in will never display a modal dialog box. For most complex add-ins, this isn't practical. What this means is that your add-in can run from the command line, and it will never stop execution to prompt a user for input. In the documentation, this type of add-in is called *command line safe*. Generally, I don't foresee personally writing this kind of add-in. Any add-in that I've ever written has had many, many modal dialog boxes forcing interaction with the user. In my opinion, a macro, which can operate without user intervention, is better suited for a command line–safe operation. Even for your simple wizard test, you won't select this option, because you'll display a modal message box.

Selecting the second check box specifies that the add-in will be loaded when the IDE is started. You can also program your add-in to behave either way, depending on how it's loaded. When the IDE loads an add-in, it tells the add-in what the connection mode is. Your add-in could launch its UI in its OnConnection method when it's loaded normally, or it could avoid that UI when it's loaded for a command line build operation.

Setting Up Access Privileges

Selecting the "Setting up access privileges" check box specifies who can use the add-in. It can be shared with all users of the computer on which it is installed, or you can limit its use to only the person that originally installed the add-in.

Creating an About Box

Step 7 will normally allow you to create an About box for your add-in. Although I discuss this briefly, the Add-in Wizard in the initial release version of Visual Studio .NET ignores this option. Even if you select the option, the wizard will not create the About box. In reality, you will probably want to create your own About box somewhere other than in the Connect class, which is the only real code module that the wizard creates for you.

The window for Step 7 (shown in Figure 2-7) prompts you to create an About box for your add-in that displays version information, support information, licensing information, and so forth. If you don't want to create an About box for your add-in, leave the check box unchecked and click the Next button. Because the wizard won't create the code for the About box I bypass this step.

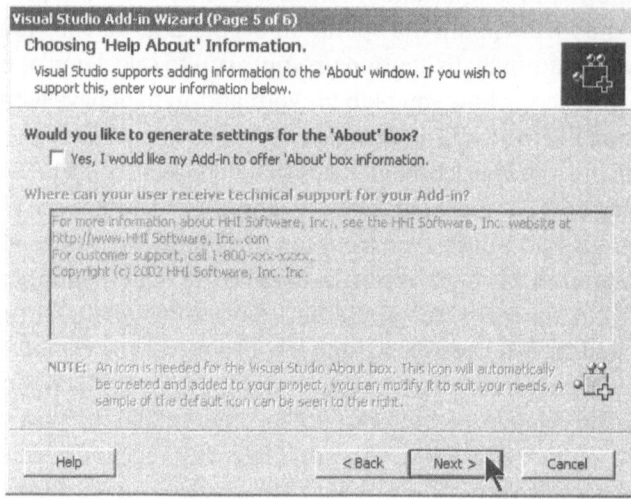

Figure 2-7. Creating an About box

Viewing a Summary of Options Selected

Click the Next button to proceed to the last step in the Add-in Wizard, where you are shown a summary of the options you have selected for your new add-in. Figure 2-8 displays this summary.

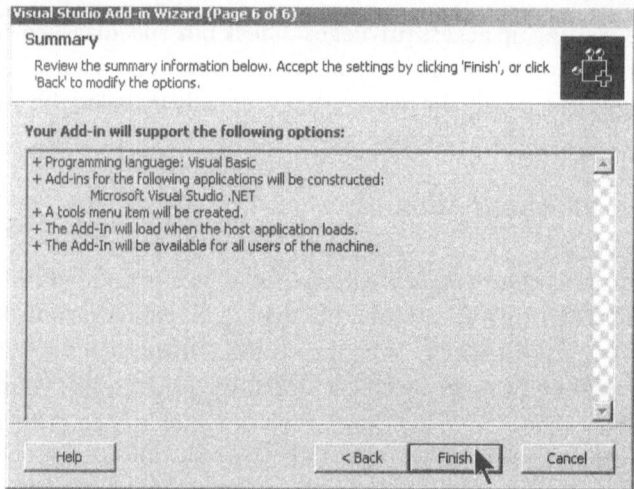

Figure 2-8. Summary of selected options

The page in Figure 2-8 summarizes the choices you've made for constructing your add-in. All of the options that you specified in the earlier panels are listed here, including the following:

- Programming language

- Application host(s)

- Whether the add-in appears as a command on the Tools menu

- Add-in load options

- Add-in availability

- Whether the add-in is command line safe

If any of these options are not what you meant to select, you may click the Back button and correct them. Note that any step that you "back" over will have to be redone. After you correct the incorrect option(s), click the Next button until you return to the Summary screen, and then click Finish to create the add-in.

Once the Add-in Wizard has generated the new add-in, it is placed in the directory you selected in the New Projects dialog box (see Figure 2-1).

Automatic Registration of Your Add-in

The Add-in Wizard automatically performs registration for you. The add-in shows up in your registry with the key hierarchy, as shown in Figure 2-9.

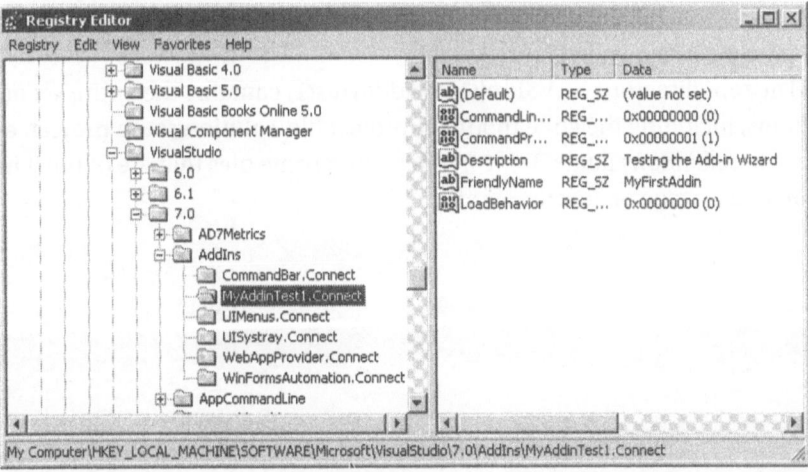

Figure 2-9. Registry entry for your add-in

Directory Hierarchy Created by the Wizard

In addition to registering your add-in when you click the Finish button in the final step of the wizard, the project and the solution setup will be saved in a rather complex directory structure, as shown in Figure 2-10.

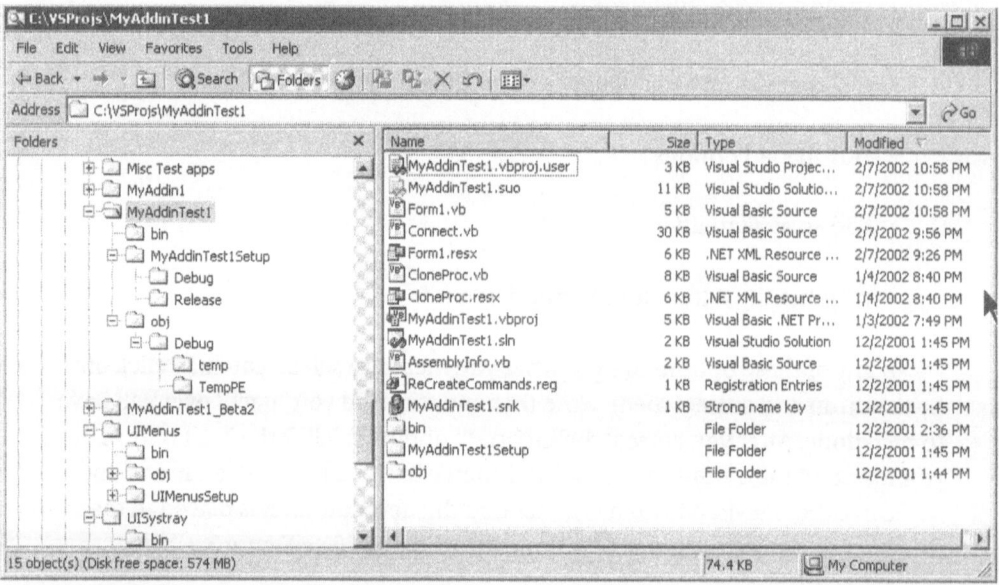

Figure 2-10. Directory hierarchy

The wizard creates an entry in the registry, which causes Visual Studio .NET to list your add-in in the Add-in Manager dialog box. For those of you who wrote add-ins in an earlier version of Visual Basic, the add-ins used to be listed in VBADDINS.INI. In Visual Studio .NET, they are listed in the registry, in the structure previously shown in Figure 2-9.

The root directory, E:\VSProjs\MyAddinTest1, contains the entire set of project items, including the code modules, project file, solution setup project, and other miscellaneous items. Table 2-1 describes some files that are of most interest to you at this stage of development.

Table 2-1. Description of Main Files Created by the Wizard

FILE	DESCRIPTION
Connect.vb	The Connect class contains the code for connecting and disconnecting the add-in.
MyAddinTest1.vbproj	Project file for the add-in (corresponds to .vbp in Visual Basic 6.0).
MyAddinTest1.sln	Solution setup project (new in .NET) used in installation of the add-in.

Manually Connecting with the Add-in Manager

On the Tools menu in the IDE is an entry for the Add-in Manager. If you click that menu item, the Add-in Manager dialog box displays, as shown in Figure 2-11.

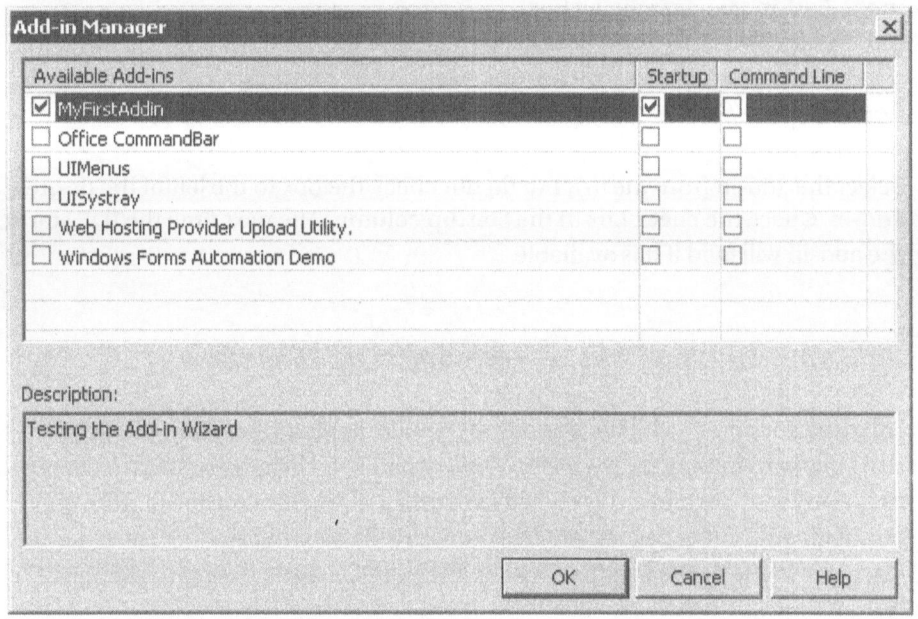

Figure 2-11. Add-in Manager dialog box

The Add-in Manager presents the dialog box shown in Figure 2-11 for loading and unloading add-ins. The dialog box also allows the user to dictate add-in load behavior. Once the dialog box is displayed, it lists all currently registered add-ins. You can set the following options:

- You can have the add-in load immediately or load when the environment (in this case, the Visual Studio IDE) starts.

- Optionally, you can have the add-in load only when the environment is started through the command line, such as a build operation.

Loading an Add-in Immediately

Select this option by checking the check box to the left of the desired add-in. Click the check box in the Startup column, and then click OK. Because your add-in has a user interface, it will appear on the Tools menu when you click OK. Because your add-in has a message box coded in the OnConnection method, it will display the "On Connection" message as it is loaded. If you attempt to load an add-in that cannot be either located or loaded, the IDE will ask if you would like to remove the add-in from its list of registered add-ins. If you respond positively, the add-in will be removed from the registry, and it will no longer be listed in the Add-in Manager dialog box.

Loading an Add-in at (Next) Environment Start-up

Select the add-in from the list, but do not check the box to the left of the desired add-in. Check the check box in the Startup column. The next time the IDE starts, the add-in will load if it is available.

Options in the Add-in Manager Dialog Box

You can experiment with the options in the Add-in Manager dialog box to see what happens in the registry. For example, open Regedit and go down to the registry entry for your add-in, as shown in Figure 2-9. Unchecking the Startup check box in the Add-in Manager dialog box causes the LoadBehavior to change to (0). Checking it causes the LoadBehavior in the ProdID Registry entry to change to (1).

MyAddinTest1 Displayed in the Add-in Manager Dialog Box

As you can see, the Add-in Wizard has added your add-in to the list of available add-ins. This dialog box is only slightly different from the Visual Basic 6.0 Add-in Manager dialog box. In .NET, add-ins can be run from a command line. Because you did not select the option that would allow you to run from the command line, that check box is not checked. The dialog box shows that you want your add-in loaded when the .NET IDE loads.

Reviewing the Code Generated by the Wizard

The main file of interest that the wizard created for you is Connect.vb. As described earlier, this file contains the code for connecting and disconnecting the add-in. Although you will explore the Connect class in detail in Chapter 3, you will look at the code briefly here. You do this in order to make some minor changes and additions to the generated code; you must add some code or the add-in will not do anything but run. For example, as the wizard generated the code to create a menu and button, it did not generate any code to respond to a click of the button.

First, you look at the code the wizard generated, and then you make some minor modifications. Listing 2-1 shows what the wizard generated.

Listing 2-1. Wizard Generated Code

```
Imports Microsoft.Office.Core
imports Extensibility
Imports System.Runtime.InteropServices
Imports EnvDTE


#Region " Read me for Add-in installation and setup information. "
' When run, the Add-in wizard prepared the registry for the Add-in.
' At a later time, if the Add-in becomes unavailable
' for reasons such as:
'    1) You moved this project to a computer other than the one it was
'       originally created on.
'    2) You chose 'Yes' when presented with a message asking if you
'       wish to remove the Add-in.
'    3) Registry corruption.
'       you will need to re-register the Add-in by building the
'         MyAddinTest1Setup project
'         by right-clicking the project in the Solution Explorer,
'          then choosing install.
#End Region
```

```
<GuidAttribute("C4C6993D-080F-414E-982C-7846C7E5AF0E"), _
              ProgIdAttribute("MyAddinTest1.Connect")> _
Public Class Connect

    Implements Extensibility.IDTExtensibility2
    Implements IDTCommandTarget

    Dim applicationObject As EnvDTE.DTE
    Dim addInInstance As EnvDTE.AddIn

    Public Sub OnBeginShutdown(ByRef custom() As Object) _
            Implements IDTExtensibility2.OnBeginShutdown
    End Sub

    Public Sub OnAddInsUpdate(ByRef custom() As Object) _
            Implements IDTExtensibility2.OnAddInsUpdate
    End Sub

    Public Sub OnStartupComplete(ByRef custom() As Object) _
            Implements IDTExtensibility2.OnStartupComplete
    End Sub

    Public Sub OnDisconnection( _
            ByVal RemoveMode As ext_DisconnectMode, _
            ByRef custom() As Object) _
            Implements IDTExtensibility2.OnDisconnection
    End Sub

    Public Sub OnConnection(ByVal application As Object, _
            ByVal connectMode As ext_ConnectMode, _
            ByVal addInInst As Object, _
            ByRef custom() As Object) _
            Implements IDTExtensibility2.OnConnection

        applicationObject = CType(application, EnvDTE.DTE)
        addInInstance = CType(addInInst, EnvDTE.AddIn)
        If connectMode = ext_ConnectMode.ext_cm_UISetup Then
            Dim objAddIn As AddIn = CType(addInInst, AddIn)
            Dim CommandObj As Command
```

```vb
        'IMPORTANT!
        'If your command no longer appears on the appropriate
        ' command bar, you add a new or modify an existing
        ' command, or if you would like
        ' to re-create the command, close all instances of Visual
        ' Studio .NET and double-click the file
        ' ReCreateCommands.reg'
        ' in the folder holding the source code to your Add-in.
        ' IMPORTANT!
        Try
            CommandObj = _
                applicationObject.Commands.AddNamedCommand(objAddIn, _
                "MyAddinTest1", _
                "MyAddinTest1", _
                "Executes the command for MyAddinTest1", _
                True, 59, Nothing, 1 + 2) _
                '1+2 == vsCommandStatusSupported+vsCommandStatusEnabled
            CommandObj.AddControl( _
                        applicationObject.CommandBars.Item("Tools"))
        Catch e As System.Exception
        End Try
    End If
End Sub


Public Sub Exec(ByVal cmdName As String, _
                ByVal executeOption As vsCommandExecOption, _
                ByRef varIn As Object, _
                ByRef varOut As Object, _
                ByRef handled As Boolean) _
                Implements IDTCommandTarget.Exec
    handled = False
    If (executeOption = _
        vsCommandExecOption.vsCommandExecOptionDoDefault) _
        Then
        If cmdName = "MyAddinTest1.Connect.MyAddinTest1" Then
            handled = True
            Exit Sub
        End If
    End If
End Sub
```

```
            Public Sub QueryStatus(ByVal cmdName As String, _
                    ByVal neededText As vsCommandStatusTextWanted, _
                    ByRef statusOption As vsCommandStatus, _
                    ByRef commandText As Object) _
                    Implements IDTCommandTarget.QueryStatus
        If neededText = _
           EnvDTE.vsCommandStatusTextWanted.vsCommandStatusTextWantedNone _
           Then
           If cmdName = "MyAddinTest1.Connect.MyAddinTest1" Then
               statusOption = _
               CType(vsCommandStatus.vsCommandStatusEnabled + _
               vsCommandStatus.vsCommandStatusSupported, _
               vsCommandStatus)
           Else
               statusOption = vsCommandStatus.vsCommandStatusUnsupported
           End If
        End If
    End Sub
End Class
```

The code in Listing 2-1 will run but it will not do anything but sit there. It will place a menu item with accompanying button on the Tools menu of the IDE, but again, clicking the menu item will not cause the add-in to respond.

Making Minor Changes to the Add-in

At this point, let's make some minor changes to allow you to follow the progress of the add-in as it connects and disconnects. You'll cause the add-in to respond when you click its menu item. You'll add code to the OnDisconnection method, which will remove the add-in's menu item when the add-in is unloaded. Last, but certainly not least, you'll add some error-handling code to trap any error that may be encountered. I'll say this again and again throughout this book: *Don't be stingy with error-handling code*. Never leave anything to chance, hoping that your code won't fail. Murphy was an optimist when he said, "Anything that can fail, will fail, and it will fail at the worst time and place possible."

Changes to the Scope of the CommandObj

In order to remove the CommandObj when you disconnect, you have to change the scope of the object by moving it from the OnConnection method to the declarations section of the Connect class, as shown in Listing 2-2. This will make the object global to the class and make the object visible to the OnDisconnection method.

Listing 2-2. Moving the CommandObj to Module Level

```
Public Class Connect

    Implements IDTExtensibility2
    Implements IDTCommandTarget

    Dim applicationObject As EnvDTE.DTE
    Dim addInInstance As EnvDTE.AddIn
    ' **** moved to module level so OnDisconnect can see it *****
    Dim CommandObj As Command
```

Changes to the OnConnection Method

In Listing 2-3, I make a few minor changes to the OnConnection method. The lines that I change appear in bold. First, I change the test for the ConnectMode argument to ext_ConnectMode.ext_cm_Startup. This will guarantee that the User Interface menu item is not added unless the add-in is really being connected for use at the time the IDE is started. Visual Studio .NET has a default option of placing an add-in's UI in the IDE and leaving it there all of the time, even when the add-in is not running. I do not recommend that you follow this method of operation. I use many add-ins from time to time, but some are used so infrequently that I certainly would not want their menus cluttering the IDE if I had no intention of using them for some period of time.

Next, I comment the original CommandObj Dim statement, so that you can see the point from which I moved it.

Finally, I add a couple of message boxes to trace my progress through the connection process and to inform me of any possible error encountered in placing the tool button.

Listing 2-3. Changes to the OnConnection Method

```
Public Sub OnConnection(ByVal application As Object, _
            ByVal connectMode As ext_ConnectMode, _
            ByVal addInInst As Object, _
            ByRef custom() As Object) _
            Implements IDTExtensibility2.OnConnection
    applicationObject = CType(application, EnvDTE.DTE)
    addInInstance = CType(addInInst, EnvDTE.AddIn)
    ' changed test of connectmode from
    ' ext_ConnectMode.ext_cm_UISetup
    If connectMode = ext_ConnectMode.ext_cm_Startup Then
```

```
                    Dim objAddIn As AddIn = CType(addInInst, AddIn)
                    ' moved to module level so OnDisconnect can see it
                ' Dim CommandObj As Command
                MsgBox("On Connection")
                    Try
                        CommandObj = _
                            applicationObject.Commands.AddNamedCommand(objAddIn, _
                            "MyCommand1", _
                            "Click Me", _
                            "Executes the command for MyAddinTest1", _
                            True, 59, Nothing, 1 + 2)
                        CommandObj.AddControl( _
                                applicationObject.CommandBars.Item("Tools"))
                    Catch e As System.Exception
                    MsgBox("Can't place toolbutton, error: " & _
                            e.Message, MsgBoxStyle.Critical, _
                            "MyAddinTest1")
                    End Try
                End If
        End Sub
```

Now I add the code to the OnDisconnection method to remove the
CommandObj (menu item) once the add-in is unloaded. These changes appear
in bold in Listing 2-4.

Listing 2-4. Changes to the OnDisconnection Method

```
    Public Sub OnDisconnection( _
                ByVal RemoveMode As ext_DisconnectMode, _
                ByRef custom() As Object) _
                Implements IDTExtensibility2.OnDisconnection
            Try
                ' display a message to tell what we are about to do
                MsgBox("Disconnect, remove Tool Button", _
                    MsgBoxStyle.Information, "MyAddinTest1")
                ' remove the add-in command button
                CommandObj.Delete()
            Catch e As System.Exception
                ' if we should fail to remove the button, display the error
                MsgBox("Error in Disconnect: " & _
                    e.Message, _
                    MsgBoxStyle.Critical, _
                    "MyAddinTest1")
            End Try
        End Sub
```

Running the Add-in

When you create an add-in using the Add-in Wizard and then run it, another instance of Visual Studio .NET starts, allowing you to test and debug the resultant add-in. Normally, one or more commands for the add-in are placed on one or more menus, such as the Tools menu. When you finish debugging the add-in and then close this second instance of Visual Studio .NET, the command information is saved. When you eventually close the first instance of Visual Studio .NET, however, the command information that was written by the second instance of Visual Studio .NET is overwritten. The effect is that when you restart Visual Studio .NET, your new add-in command no longer appears on the menu. To restore commands to menus, you can run an included registry (.reg) file that is generated by the Visual Studio .NET Add-in Wizard.

Having said this, you will recall that you put code in the OnDisconnection method of the Connect class to remove your add-in menu item. I believe that it should be the responsibility of the add-in developer to place and remove the add-in's menus or tool buttons as the add-in is loaded and unloaded. To leave an add-in's menus in the IDE, even though the add-in is not running, is confusing to the application developer using the add-in.

I discuss the debugging process in detail in Chapter 4. For now, you have two ways of running the add-in.

First, you could do a full build followed by an installation of the add-in. From that point, the next time you start the .NET IDE, the add-in will be loaded and connected. When the IDE is unloaded, the add-in will be disconnected.

Alternately, you can simply press F5 or click the Run button on the main toolbar. The add-in will go through the build process, and if the build is successful (has no errors), a second copy of .NET will be loaded automatically. As it loads, it will load and connect your add-in.

 **TIP** *If your add-in does not connect when the second instance of Visual Studio .NET is started, go to the Add-in Manager dialog box and check both check boxes for the add-in. When you close the dialog box, the add-in should connect and display its user interface.*

If you had placed breakpoints in the code of the Connect class, for example, in the OnConnection method, your code would be stopped at the breakpoints.

Regardless of the method of execution, the add-in will be loaded and connected. As the IDE loads, your add-in will be started. You will recall that you placed a MsgBox display in the OnConnection method of the Connect class. When Visual Studio starts the add-in, it will call the OnConnection method and you will see the MsgBox displayed with the "On Connection" message.

If you click the Tools menu, you will see the add-in's tool button at the top of the Tools menu, as shown in Figure 2-12. Your add-in's menu text is "Click Me" and it is highlighted.

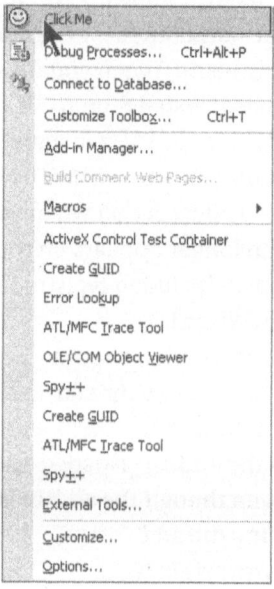

Figure 2-12. Add-in menu item

If you now click the selected menu item, the add-in will display a box with the message "You rang?"

Registering the Add-in

Once an add-in is created, it must be registered as a COM component with Microsoft Windows. As described earlier in this chapter, the Add-in Wizard automatically performs this registration for you. Obviously, I have used the wizard to create the add-in for me, and it has registered the add-in. If you choose to run the code for this chapter, or any chapter in this book, without using the Add-in Wizard, you will need to register the add-in.

To register the add-in, load the solution for the add-in into Visual Studio and follow the instructions in the next section, "Installing an Add-in." After an add-in is registered, the Visual Studio IDE recognizes it. To list it in the Add-in Manager dialog box, there must be as set of registry keys for it, as shown in Listing 2-5.

It is sometimes useful to know what the registry keys the Add-in Wizard creates look like. The Add-in Wizard and the Installation Wizard create a unique programmatic ID (ProgID) for each add-in and insert it into the registry. A ProgID consists of the name of the project followed by a period and the name of the class module, such as MyAddinTest1.Connect. As shown earlier in Figure 2-9, Visual Studio stores this registry information in the following keys.

CAUTION *In the release documentation, the key for this is listed as HKEY_ CURRENT_USER, but in reality, the key is generated in HKEY_LOCAL_ MACHINE. Obviously, the documentation or the root key will probably change in a future update of the system.*

Listing 2-5 shows the registry key structure for the registered add-in.

Listing 2-5. Registry Keys for the Add-in

```
HKEY_LOCAL_MACHINE
    SOFTWARE
        MICROSOFT
            VISUAL STUDIO
                7.0
                    ADDINS
                        MyAddinTest1 (ProgID-Internal Name of Add-in)
```

Each ProgID contains the following name/value pairs:

- *Friendly name:* The name that appears in the Add-in Manager's Available Add-ins list. This value is optional, but it should be used.

- *Description:* A string that displays at the right of the Add-in Manager dialog box. This value is optional, but it should be supplied.

- *LoadBehavior:* A DWORD bit field with the following optional values:

    - ID_UNLOADED – 0: The add-in should be unloaded immediately.

    - ID_STARTUP – 1: The add-in should be loaded at IDE startup.

    - ID_COMMAND_LINE – 4: The add-in should be loaded via the devenv command line.

- *CommandPreload:* A Boolean value that indicates whether it is the first time that Visual Studio has started since the add-in was loaded. "0" specifies that Visual Studio has started more than once since the add-in was loaded. "1" specifies that Visual Studio has not started since the add-in was loaded. When Visual Studio starts, you can pass ext_cm_UISetup to its OnConnection method's ConnectMode argument, provided these conditions are met: You either load an add-in, or it is marked to load at start-up, and its CommandPreload setting is 1. After that, you can check to see if the type of connection is ext_cm_UISetup. If it is, you can perform whatever task you want, such as putting a command on the toolbar, or using Commands.AddNamedCommand or Command.AddControl.

- *CommandLineSafe:* Indicates whether the add-in was designed to avoid displaying a UI when invoked by the development environment command line.

- *SatelliteDllPath:* If present, the value is a string that is a full pathname to a directory, ending with a backslash (\). The Add-in Manager looks for the concatenation of SatelliteDllPath, the locale ID of the installed machine, the backslash, and SatelliteDllName.

- *SatelliteDllName:* The value is a string that names a file. The directory containing the file is either the directory containing the DLL that constitutes the add-in or the computed directory described for SatelliteDllPath.

Installing the Add-in

After you've debugged your add-in (debugging an add-in is the subject of Chapter 4), you can do a build and installation of your add-in.

NOTE *If you create an add-in using the Add-in Wizard, and you only want to run it on your computer, you don't have to worry about installation. The Add-in Wizard will make all of the registry entries and so forth. However, if you give your add-in to someone to use on another computer, she will have to go through an installation to get all of the registry entries to make it run and to get it listed in the Add-in Manager dialog box.*

Although you probably won't see any difference in the registry, I'll illustrate how to do a complete build followed by an installation. To create an installation and install the new add-in on your computer, do the following:

1. Click the Build menu item in the Build menu. You can follow the progress of the build in the Immediate window, just below the main code window. If there are no errors, a series of success messages will be displayed in the window. If there are build errors, they will be listed in the window, and you will have to correct the errors and rebuild the application. If coding errors are encountered, they will be listed in the window. Double-clicking the error will cause the IDE to position to the error in the respective code window.

2. If the build is successful, go to the Solution Explorer and right-click the MyAddinTest1 solution project. From the pop-up menu, select Install. The Setup Wizard will be invoked and display its welcome window, as shown in Figure 2-13.

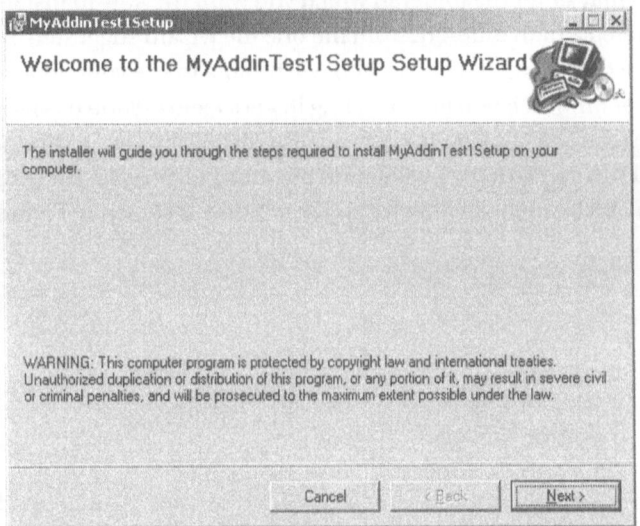

Figure 2-13. Setup Wizard welcome window

3. Click the Next button to proceed with the setup. The Setup Wizard will display the first step of the setup process, as shown in Figure 2-14. This step prompts you to select a directory in which to install the add-in.

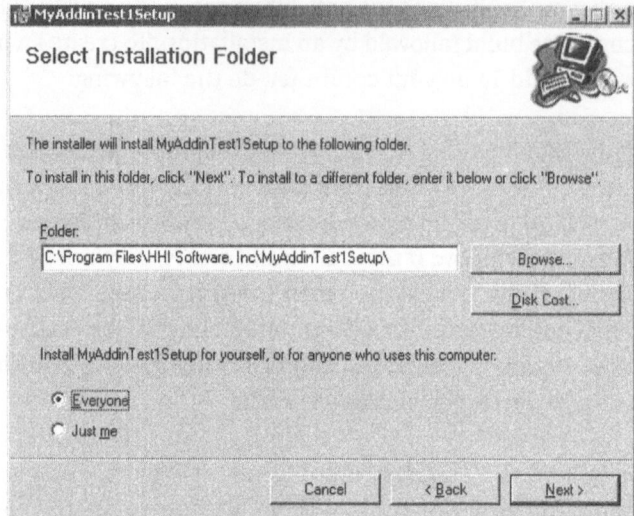

Figure 2-14. Selecting the setup directory

4. You may enter the folder in which you want the add-in installed. I have entered a path different from the one the wizard suggested. Again, you have the option to choose who will be able to use your add-in on the computer on which you are installing it. Let's let everyone use it. When you click the Next button to proceed, the wizard displays a window in which you can confirm the installation directory, or you can click the Back button and change the directory. That window is shown in Figure 2-15.

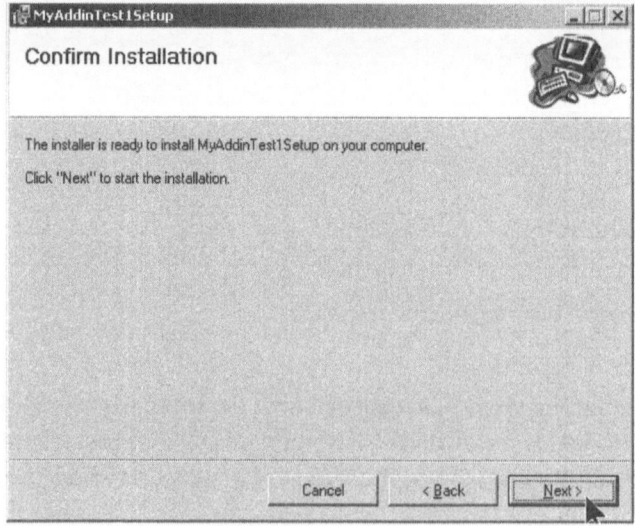

Figure 2-15. Confirming the installation path

5. Click the Next button to proceed. While the Setup Wizard is creating and executing the installation, a progress box is displayed. When the setup and installation process is complete, the completion window shown in Figure 2-16 is displayed.

Figure 2-16. The setup is complete.

Exploring the Connect Class Methods

The Add-in Wizard created the Connect class for you, as you have already seen. Also, you have done some work in several of the methods of the class. At this point, you need to determine the purpose of all of the methods of the class, as the Connect class is the start-up point for any add-in.

OnConnection Method

As you have seen, OnConnection is the method that is called first by the IDE when it starts the add-in. Three parameters are passed to the method. The first is the pointer to the DTE, which is passed as the parameter application. This parameter has already been discussed in detail. The second parameter is ConnectMode. This parameter has the following values, which you can examine in the method to determine how or when the add-in was loaded:

- ext_cm_AfterStartup – 0: The add-in was loaded after the application started or by setting the Connect property of the corresponding add-in to True.

- ext_cm_Startup – 1: The add-in was loaded at IDE start-up.

- ext_cm_External – 2: The add-in was loaded externally by another program or component.

- ext_cm_CommandLine – 3: The add-in was loaded through the Visual Studio devenv command line.

- ext_cm_Solution – 4: The add-in was loaded when a user loaded a solution that required the add-in.

- ext_cm_UISetup – 5: The add-in was started for the first time since being installed.

You can see that the wizard creates code to test the ConnectMode parameter. It initially checks for ext_cm_UISetup, and if this is the setting, it places the UI menu option on the Tools menu. I changed it to check for ext_cm_Startup. The reason for this is that I always place and remove the UI from the IDE in the OnConnection and OnDisconnection procedures. In this case, you can actually remove the code for testing the ConnectMode parameter. It is really academic because of the way that I recommend that you place and remove the UI. The third parameter, addInInst, is an object representing the instance of the add-in. It is passed to the AddNamedCommand method of the Commands object when adding a menu to the IDE. It provides a pointer to the add-in connecting to the new command being created. The OnConnection method is the obvious point to place your UI (menus, toolbars, tool buttons) through which the user will communicate to the add-in. This method is also the place to put your validation code if you are licensing the add-in. You would normally do this before putting up the UI. If the user is not a valid user, you would not want to put the UI into the IDE.

OnDisconnection Method

This event occurs when the add-in is unloaded. Two parameters are passed, but Visual Studio .NET does not use the second parameter. The one parameter that is used is RemoveMode. It has four possible different values, which you can look up in the help file. Because I always remove the UI on add-in shutdown, I see no value in testing the RemoveMode parameter. This is also a good place to unload any forms that you may have loaded in the add-in. Because you never know when the IDE will shut down your add-in, either because the IDE is shutting down or because the user has unloaded the add-in from the Add-in Manager, you should unload any forms here. Forms can be left standing alone if you do not proactively remove them. Do not assume that your user has closed all of the forms before unloading the add-in or the IDE.

QueryStatus Event

When the user clicks a command (menu or tool button), the QueryStatus event is fired. The QueryStatus event returns the current status of the specified named command, whether it is enabled, disabled, or hidden in the vsCommandStatus parameter, which is passed to the event by reference. The event has the following parameters:

- *CmdName:* The name of the command to check.

- *NeededText:* A vsCommandStatusTextWanted constant specifying whether information is returned from the check, and if so, what type of information is returned.

- *StatusOption:* A vsCommandStatus specifying the current status of the command. This parameter determines if the Exec event will be fired.

- *CommandText:* The text to return if vsCommandStatusTextWantedStatus is specified.

The Add-in Wizard created the code for this event, and you have not modified it. If you use this event and have multiple commands, you will have to add more tests for the bold line of code in the event shown in Listing 2-6. If you have multiple commands, you would want to replace the "If neededText" with a Select Case construct. I discuss the use of multiple commands in Chapter 7. In that chapter, I also show you how to create a variety of types of user interfaces.

Listing 2-6. QueryStatus Event

```
Private Sub QueryStatus(ByVal cmdName As String, _
            ByVal neededText As vsCommandStatusTextWanted, _
            ByRef statusOption As vsCommandStatus, _
            ByRef commandText As Object) _
            Implements IDTCommandTarget.QueryStatus
    If neededText = _
    EnvDTE.vsCommandStatusTextWanted.vsCommandStatusTextWantedNone _
    Then
    If cmdName = "MyAddinTest1.Connect.MyCommand1" Then
        statusOption = _
        CType(vsCommandStatus.vsCommandStatusEnabled + _
        vsCommandStatus.vsCommandStatusSupported, _
        vsCommandStatus)
    Else
        statusOption = vsCommandStatus.vsCommandStatusUnsupported
    End If
    End If
End Sub
```

Exec Event

The Exec event is fired after the QueryStatus event is fired, assuming that the return to the statusOption parameter of QueryStatus is supported and enabled. This is the event where you place the actual code for handling the response to the user click on the command. Again, if you have multiple commands, you will need to replace the bold text in Listing 2-7 with a Select Case construct.

Listing 2-7. Exec Event

```
Public Sub Exec(ByVal cmdName As String, _
            ByVal executeOption As vsCommandExecOption, _
            ByRef varIn As Object, _
            ByRef varOut As Object, _
            ByRef handled As Boolean) _
            Implements IDTCommandTarget.Exec
    Dim oFrm As New frmTreeView()
```

```
         handled = False
         If (executeOption = _
             vsCommandExecOption.vsCommandExecOptionDoDefault) _
             Then
             If cmdName = "MyAddinTest1.Connect.MyCommand1" Then
                 handled = True
                 'MsgBox("You Rang?", MsgBoxStyle.Question, "MyAddinTest1")
                 Try
                     oFrm.Show()
                 Catch
                     MsgBox("Can't load frmTreeview", MsgBoxStyle.Critical)
                 End Try
                 Exit Sub
             End If
         End If
     End Sub
```

Summary

In this chapter, you saw that you do not have to start from scratch to create the base and most important class of an add-in—namely, the Connect class. Rather, you can use the Add-in Wizard to do it for you, and very quickly, by the way.

Next, you learned that the add-in has to be registered in the registry, not only as a COM component, but so that the Add-in Manager will know to add it to its list of add-ins.

You learned how to make simple modifications to the generated Connect class, so that your first add-in will actually do something, such as place a command button and respond to its Click event.

You reviewed the structure of the registry entry for the add-in and learned how to manually register the add-in, should the occasion ever arise.

You ran through an installation of the add-in using the Setup Wizard. This deployment wizard is only one of the many nice, new features in Visual Studio .NET.

Finally, although you used a very simple example, you learned that add-ins aren't "black boxes" developed only by "gurus" locked in an ivory tower. Your first add-in may not do much, but you've succeeded in creating a real, live, working add-in that automatically connects, responds to user action, and disconnects. All you have to do now is add a little bit more code, and you've got it licked. And if you believe that, I have some "oceanfront property in Arizona" (to borrow a line from George Strait) that I'd like to sell you. Seriously, you'll do some amazing things in no time at all.

In Chapter 3, you'll add a more sophisticated UI and several very useful functions to the add-in. There, you'll begin to build a real add-in.

CHAPTER 3

The Smart Desktop Add-in

"The value of most critics cannot be measured."
—Don Howard

In Chapter 2, you learned how to use the Add-in Wizard to create a simple add-in. You made some minor modifications to the wizard-generated code in order to trace the flow of the add-in operation and to make the add-in actually respond to communication to and from the user.

In this chapter, you are going to build on the base add-in code that you already have and take the add-in a few steps further to make it do some useful work for you. About 90 percent of the features that I have built into my add-ins have been the result of running into two situations in application development. First, I was faced with doing some mundane task associated with application code over and over. Second, I found that mass find and replace and a series of "cut and paste" was going to be a very long and error-prone process.

For these and other reasons, I constantly keep in mind that adding a feature to an existing add-in is usually a task that will take from a few minutes to a few hours at the most. Next, I try to think ahead and see if the current problem will present itself to me again in the near future. If so, I determine whether or not it will be a constantly recurring problem. Finally, I consider if a new add-in feature can be added relatively quickly and easily. If so, I usually stop what I am doing, bite the bullet for a short time, and develop the new add-in feature. Usually, the time that I spend creating the new functionality will be paid for the first time that I use it. In other words, it usually does not take any more time to create the new add-in feature than it would to have performed the mundane, repetitive, error-prone manual process, and now I have a tool built that will save me hours the next time that I encounter the problem.

Deciding When to Add a Feature to an Add-in

Keep in mind that every time you run into a tough editing problem, it doesn't necessarily mean that you need to add a new feature to your existing add-in. Determining whether to build an add-in is kind of like doing a quick marketing survey to determine if there's a market for a new product. Make sure you don't spend a lot of time creating a new feature that you'll only use once. In such cases, it's probably not worth the time and effort to create the new feature.

However, as I look at Visual Studio .NET, I constantly see places with room for new features or improvements on existing features. Obviously, Microsoft developers can't think of everything. They've made strides of geometric proportions since the early days of Visual Basic, but many times application developers like you and me are constantly running into new challenges that the tool developers will never encounter. If I didn't make my living as an application developer, I probably would never have written an add-in.

As I work with Visual Studio .NET, I see a world of new functionality, but again, there are obvious holes. As an add-in developer, I can capitalize on these holes. As an enterprise developer, you can use the functionality if you take the time to be creative and develop your own add-in functionality. I'm not going to take the time here to try to think of and list every place you could improve the IDE. However, I do suggest just two or three new features right now and others at a later time. I suggest them because you'll use them in the enhancement of your add-in.

For example, Visual Studio .NET has a good commenting and uncommenting feature. However, most programmers would like to have the comments "blocked" with a header and footer denoting the name of the developer that changed the code, the date of the change, and possibly a reason for the change.

In previous versions of the Visual Basic IDE, there was no way to easily indent your code to keep it readable. This was a place for the add-in developer to shine. Now in .NET indentation is automatic. However, the indent feature does not take continuation lines into consideration. Consequently, the first and subsequent continued lines are lined up at the same place. This does not make for good readability. A smart indenting feature will not only indent the second and subsequent lines, but it will also give you an option for how many spaces to indent the continued lines.

I offer one more possibility that you might want to consider if you really want to get into heavy features in an add-in. In Visual Studio .NET, the IDE has some powerful features for aligning, sizing, and spacing controls on a form. But if the form is locked, which is normally the case, to prevent the accidental movement of controls with a mouse click, the formatting buttons are disabled and therefore of no value. Why that was done is beyond my comprehension. In VB 6.0, at least you could "nudge" the controls for sizing and spacing through the use of the Shift, Ctrl, and arrow keys. But in .NET if the form is locked, it is really locked, and you cannot even nudge the controls. In my opinion, this is not a step in the right direction. It is obvious that some work can be done in an add-in to improve on the ability to manipulate controls on a form.

Enhancing the Add-in

In Chapter 2, you placed some code in several places in the Connect class to trace the flow of the add-in connect and disconnect processes and to cause the add-in to make a simple response to clicking the user interface menu option. To enhance the add-in, you will remove all of the temporary demonstration code and replace it with the code that will allow you to communicate with the new functionality that you will be adding.

Modifying the Connect Class

The first thing I have done in Listing 3-1 is removed the message boxes to clean up the interface. Here is the OnConnection method from your add-in, as I left it in Chapter 2. You will note that I have changed the object variable applicationObject to oVB. This was done simply to shorten the length of the variable, which will make the code more readable because it is used constantly. Next, I have changed the text of the add-in's menu from "MyAddinTest1" to "Smart Desktop." This will make my add-in look a little more professional. Finally, I have added a variable for the specification of the Office icon button. I have done this so that the variable can be changed at runtime without recompiling, thus allowing me to try different icons in the menu. There are numerous icons in Office.DLL, and you can experiment with the one that you want to use. All of these changes appear in boldface.

Listing 3-1. Modifying the OnConnection Method

```
Public Sub OnConnection(ByVal application As Object, _
            ByVal connectMode As ext_ConnectMode, _
            ByVal addInInst As Object, _
            ByRef custom() As Object) _
            Implements IDTExtensibility2.OnConnection
    Dim iBitMap As Integer

    oVB = CType(application, EnvDTE.DTE)
    addInInstance = CType(addInInst, EnvDTE.AddIn)

    ' changed test of connectmode from
    ' ext_ConnectMode.ext_cm_UISetup
```

```
            If connectMode = ext_ConnectMode.ext_cm_Startup Then
                Dim objAddIn As AddIn = CType(addInInst, AddIn)
                ' moved to module level so OnDisconnect can see it
                ' Dim CommandObj As Command

                'IMPORTANT!
                'If your command no longer appears on the appropriate
                ' command bar, you add a new or modify an existing
                ' command, or if you would like
                ' to re-create the command, close all instances of Visual
                ' Studio .NET and double-click the file
                ' ReCreateCommands.reg'
                ' in the folder holding the source code to your add-in.
                ' IMPORTANT!
                ' Remove the MsgBox at Connect Time
                ' MsgBox("On Connection")
                Try
                    IBitMap = 59
                    CommandObj = _
                        oVB.Commands.AddNamedCommand(objAddIn, _
                        "MyCommand1", _
                        "Smart Desktop", _
                        "Executes the command for MyAddinTest1", _
                        True, iBitMap, Nothing, 1 + 2) _
                        '1+2 == vsCommandStatusSupported+vsCommandStatusEnabled
                    CommandObj.AddControl( _
                            oVB.CommandBars.Item("Tools"))
                Catch e As System.Exception
                    MsgBox("Can't place toolbutton, error: " & _
                            e.Message, MsgBoxStyle.Critical, _
                            "MyAddinTest1")
                End Try
            End If
    End Sub
```

Now I need to make a minor change to the OnDisconnection method. I remove the MsgBox that tells you that you are in the OnDisconnection method, as shown in Listing 3-2. Because you have already seen how and when the OnDisconnection method is called, you no longer need this MsgBox. The code that I removed appears in boldface.

Listing 3-2. Modifying the OnDisconnection Method

```
Public Sub OnDisconnection( _
                ByVal RemoveMode As ext_DisconnectMode, _
                ByRef custom() As Object) _
                Implements IDTExtensibility2.OnDisconnection
        Try
            ' display a message to tell what we are about to do
            ' MsgBox("Disconnect, remove Tool Button", _
                    MsgBoxStyle.Information, "MyAddinTest1")
            ' remove the add-in command button
            CommandObj.Delete()
        Catch e As System.Exception
            ' if we should fail to remove the button, display the error
            MsgBox("Error in Disconnect: " & _
                    e.Message, _
                    MsgBoxStyle.Critical, _
                    "MyAddinTest1")
        End Try
End Sub
```

Next, I make a change to the event handler for the Add-in menu Click event. Instead of putting up a MsgBox, which is not really impressive, I display the UI for the new functionality that the add-in is now going to have. Although I have not designed the UI (form) yet, I name it frmTreeView so that I can go ahead and change the event handler to load it. The code for the event handler has been modified, as shown in Listing 3-3.

Listing 3-3. Modifying the Event Handler

```
Public Sub Exec(ByVal cmdName As String, _
                ByVal executeOption As vsCommandExecOption, _
                ByRef varIn As Object, _
                ByRef varOut As Object, _
                ByRef handled As Boolean) _
                Implements IDTCommandTarget.Exec
        Dim oFrm As New frmTreeView ()

        handled = False
        If (executeOption = _
            vsCommandExecOption.vsCommandExecOptionDoDefault) _
            Then
            If cmdName = "MyAddinTest1.Connect.MyCommand1" Then
```

```
            handled = True
            'MsgBox("You Rang?", MsgBoxStyle.Question, "MyAddinTest1")
            oFrm.Show()
            Exit Sub
        End If
    End If
End Sub
```

I have done several things to the event handler. First, I commented out the MsgBox, which was the original response to the user clicking the menu item. Second, I added a dimension of the form to be loaded. In VB 6.0, I could have simply written the following instruction to load the form:

```
frmTreeView.Show
```

In Visual Basic .NET, you first have to dimension the object and then show the form, as shown in the following code and in the previous code:

```
Dim oFrm As New frmTreeView()
oFrm.Show()
```

Once the UI (frmTreeView) is loaded, it will act as the vehicle of communication with the features of your add-in.

Designing the UI Form (frmTreeView)

First, open up the MyAddinTest1 project in .NET. Next, add a form to the project. You can do this by clicking the down arrow next to the Add New Item tool button (the second button from the left on the main toolbar). A drop-down list will appear, as shown in Figure 3-1.

Select Add Windows Form. A form appears in the Forms Designer, as shown in Figure 3-2.

Size the form as shown in Figure 3-2. Press F4 to bring up the property page for the form. The property page should appear as shown in Figure 3-3, after you make the following changes. In the property page, change the Text property (formerly the Caption in previous versions of VB) to **MyAddinTest1**. Also, change the Name property to **frmTreeView**. Next, change the TopMost property to **True**. This will cause the form, which will be the UI for the add-in, to remain on top of the IDE, even if you click somewhere else on the IDE. I do not want the UI of the add-in to go behind the IDE, leaving you to wonder what happened to it. The TopMost property is a neat new property in VB .NET. In earlier versions of Visual Basic, I would have had to use the API SetWindowPos to cause the form to stay on top.

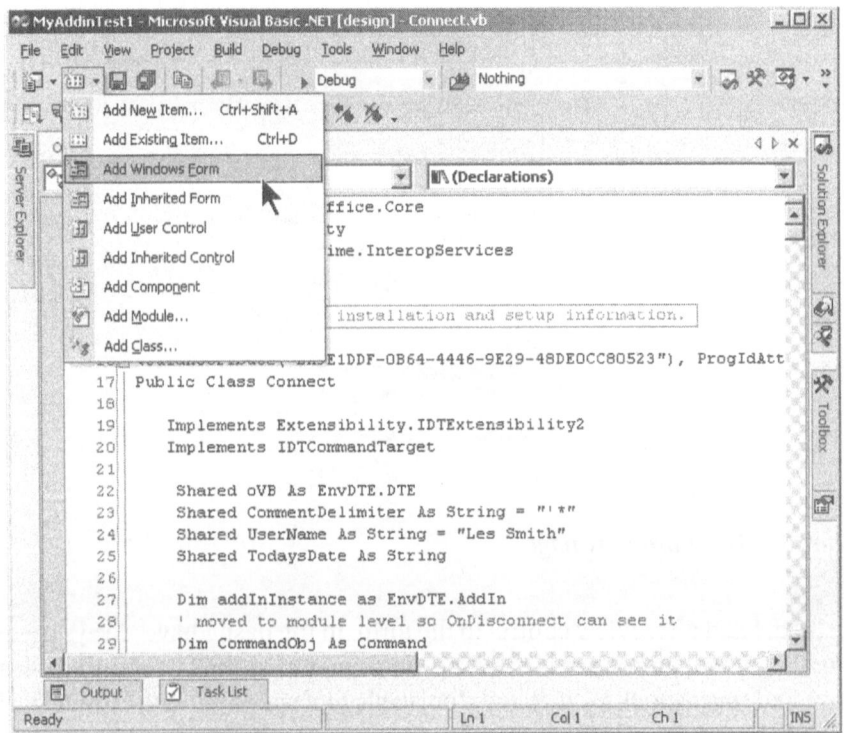

Figure 3-1. Adding a Windows Form

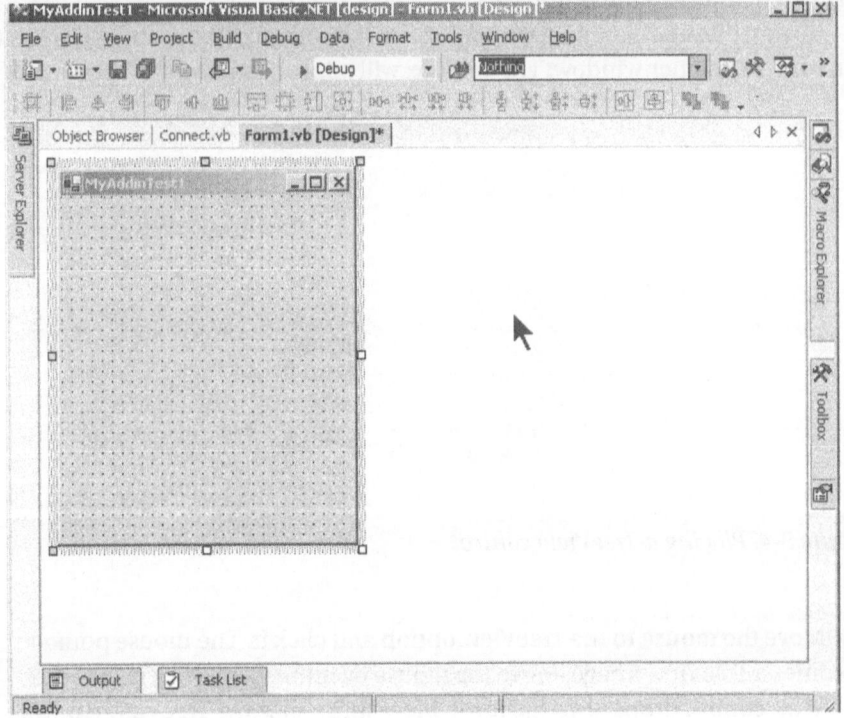

Figure 3-2. Configuring the Windows Form

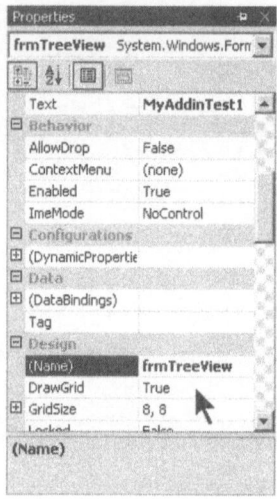

Figure 3-3. Form property page

Next, I add a TreeView control to the form. In the past, I have always used a number of tool buttons that had drop-down menus as the UI for my add-ins. I have had suggestions for making a "dockable tool window," with a TreeView for the hierarchical menu. This saves a lot of space in the IDE, especially when the add-in is not currently in use. Although I will not take the time here to create a dockable window, I am implementing the same concept here, just in a simpler form for demonstration purposes.

To add the TreeView control to the form, click the Toolbox tab on the right of the Forms Designer window. The Toolbox will appear, as shown in Figure 3-4.

Figure 3-4. Placing a TreeView control

Move the mouse to the TreeView option and click it. The mouse pointer becomes a TreeView image. Move the mouse over the form, click it, and the TreeView control drops onto the form. Move and resize the TreeView control to cover the form, as shown in Figure 3-5.

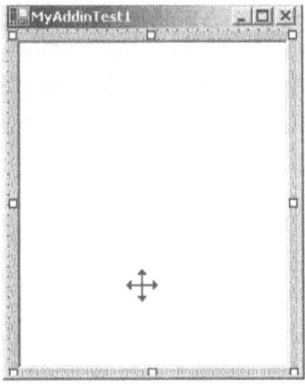

Figure 3-5. The resized TreeView control

Press F4 to bring up the property page for the TreeView control. Change the name of the TreeView control to **tvMenu**. In the property page, scroll down to the Nodes property. You will see that it is a Collection property. Click in the right-hand box marked Collection, and an ellipsis will appear. Click the ellipsis and the TreeNode Editor dialog box (see Figure 3-6) displays.

To begin building the TreeView menu, click the Add Root button. Enter **Smart Desktop** into the Label box. Next, click the Add Child button and enter **Block Comment** into the Label box. Then click the top node (Smart Desktop), so you can add another child node to it. Next, click Add Child and enter **Uncomment** into the Label box. After you've made these changes, the dialog box shown in Figure 3-6 should appear.

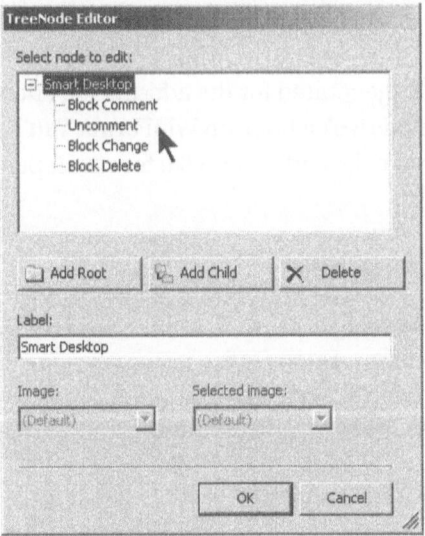

Figure 3-6. Configuring the TreeView

To finish configuring the TreeView control, click the OK button on the TreeNode Editor dialog box. This causes the TreeView to be configured. In the TreeView, click the + box, and the TreeView opens, as shown in Figure 3-7.

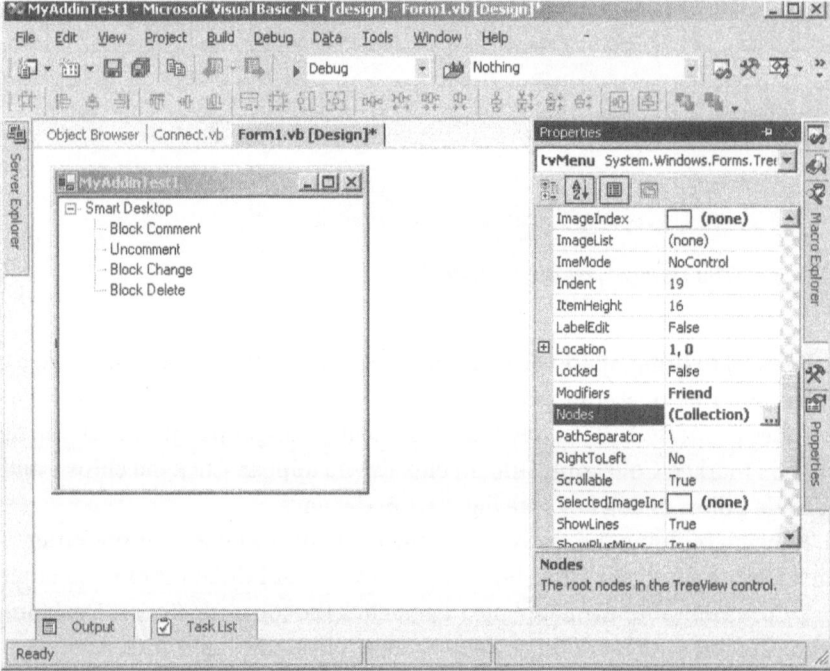

Figure 3-7. The completed TreeView

Code Generated by the Forms Generator

Listing 3-4 is the code I generated for the add-in's UI. I don't explain all of the code in the listing, as this isn't a book on WinForms. You'll see that the code for this form is totally unlike the code for VB 6.0 forms. Hopefully, this isn't the first time you've noted this.

Listing 3-4. Code for frmTreeView

```
Public Class frmTreeView
    Inherits System.Windows.Forms.Form

#Region " Windows Form Designer generated code "

    Public Sub New()
        MyBase.New()
```

```
        'This call is required by the Windows Form Designer.
        InitializeComponent()


        'Add any initialization after the InitializeComponent() call

    End Sub


    'Form overrides dispose to clean up the component list.
    Protected Overloads Overrides Sub Dispose(ByVal disposing As Boolean)
        If disposing Then
            If Not (components Is Nothing) Then
                components.Dispose()
            End If
        End If
        MyBase.Dispose(disposing)
    End Sub
    Friend WithEvents tvMenu As System.Windows.Forms.TreeView


    'Required by the Windows Form Designer
    Private components As System.ComponentModel.IContainer


    'NOTE: The following procedure is required by the Windows Form Designer
    'It can be modified using the Windows Form Designer.
    'Do not modify it using the code editor.
    <System.Diagnostics.DebuggerStepThrough()> Private Sub InitializeComponent()
        Me.tvMenu = New System.Windows.Forms.TreeView()
        Me.SuspendLayout()
        '
        'tvMenu
        '
        Me.tvMenu.ImageIndex = -1
        Me.tvMenu.Name = "tvMenu"
        Me.tvMenu.Nodes.AddRange(New System.Windows.Forms.TreeNode() _
        {New System.Windows.Forms.TreeNode("Smart Desktop", _
        New System.Windows.Forms.TreeNode() _
        {New System.Windows.Forms.TreeNode("Block Comment"), _
                New System.Windows.Forms.TreeNode("Uncomment"), _
                New System.Windows.Forms.TreeNode("Block Change"), _
                New System.Windows.Forms.TreeNode("Block Delete")})})
        Me.tvMenu.SelectedImageIndex = -1
        Me.tvMenu.Size = New System.Drawing.Size(248, 232)
        Me.tvMenu.TabIndex = 0
        '
        'frmTreeView
        '
```

```
                    Me.AutoScaleBaseSize = New System.Drawing.Size(5, 13)
                    Me.ClientSize = New System.Drawing.Size(232, 213)
                    Me.Controls.AddRange(New System.Windows.Forms.Control() _
                        {Me.tvMenu})
                    Me.Name = "frmTreeView"
                    Me.Text = "MyAddinTest1"
                    Me.TopMost = True
                    Me.ResumeLayout(False)


            End Sub


        #End Region

        End Class
```

Adding Code to Handle TreeView Click Events

When the user clicks the TreeView, which is your menu for the add-in, you must have code to handle the Click event. Actually, you will key off of the AfterSelect event. The code for the AfterSelect event is shown in Listing 3-5.

Listing 3-5. TreeView AfterSelect Event

```
        Private Sub tvMenu_AfterSelect(ByVal sender As Object, _
            ByVal e As System.Windows.Forms.TreeViewEventArgs) _
            Handles tvMenu.AfterSelect
            Select Case UCase$(e.Node.Text)
                Case "SMART DESKTOP" 'ignore root clicks
                Case "BLOCK COMMENT"
                    Call Connect.BlockComment()
                Case "UNCOMMENT"
                    Call Connect.BlockUnComment()
                Case "BLOCK CHANGE"
                    Call Connect.BlockChange()
                Case "BLOCK DELETE"
                    Call Connect.BlockDelete()
                Case Else
                    MsgBox("Please click on a Child Node.", _
                        MsgBoxStyle.Information, "Unknown Request")
            End Select


        End Sub
```

Because it is never good practice to place non–event handler code in the form, I have placed it in the Connect class for simplicity. Obviously, as you create a large add-in, you would probably want to create different classes for ease of maintainability. Note that the event handler calls Connect.BlockComment. Because the form itself does not have a pointer to an instance of the Connect class, you will use a Shared method, which is a new feature of VB .NET.

BlockComment Method

In VB 6.0, you would have to create an instance of a class to reference a method of that class from outside the class. Even a Friend method could not be referenced without instantiating an object of the class.

In VB .NET, Shared methods are introduced. They are somewhat analogous to a Public or Global method in a .BAS module in VB 6.0. The BlockComment function shown in Listing 3-6 is an example of such a method. This feature allows you to place a Shared method in a class, and then reference it from anywhere within the project without having to create an instance of the class in which the Shared method resides.

Listing 3-6. The BlockComment Method

```
Shared Sub BlockComment()
      Dim selCodeBlock As TextSelection '= oVB.ActiveDocument.Selection()
      Dim sp As EditPoint '= selCodeBlock.TopPoint.CreateEditPoint()
      Dim ep As TextPoint '= selCodeBlock.BottomPoint
      Dim comntChr As String = "'"

      ' Option Strict does not allow implied conversion of an object
      Try
         oVB.UndoContext.Open("Block Comment")
         selCodeBlock = CType(oVB.ActiveDocument.Selection(), _
               EnvDTE.TextSelection)
         sp = CType(selCodeBlock.TopPoint.CreateEditPoint(), envdte.EditPoint)
         ep = CType(selCodeBlock.BottomPoint, EnvDTE.TextPoint)
         'ep = selCodeBlock.BottomPoint
      Catch
         MsgBox("Failed to set up text objects.", MsgBoxStyle.Critical)
         'set up an undo context for the whole commented block
      End Try

      Try
         sp.Insert("'* Block Commented by Les Smith on " & _
```

```
                          Format(DateValue(CType(Today,
                              String)), "mm/dd/yyyy") & vbCrLf)
        Do While (sp.Line < ep.Line)
            sp.Insert(comntChr)
            sp.LineDown()
            sp.StartOfLine()
        Loop
        sp.Insert("'* End of Block Commented by Les Smith " & vbCrLf)
    Catch
        ' if error, clean up the undo context
        ' otherwise the editor can be left in perpetual undo context
        oVB.UndoContext.Close()
    End Try
End Sub
```

Making BlockComment Simpler

At this point, I need to digress for just a bit. Compared to .NET, the VB 6.0 extensibility model was simpler, much smaller, and relatively easier to use. In my humble opinion, the .NET developers went off the deep end with complexity—too many objects, methods, properties, and so forth. This is not to say that you could never find a use for all of the new objects. However, if you examine the BlockComment method in Listing 3-6, you will quickly see that most of the code is taken up with manipulating the TextSelection object and with creating and using such objects as EditPoint, TextPoint, and their associated methods. This is only one of many processing methods that you would normally create to get the work of my add-ins done. Consequently, in the method shown in Listing 3-6, I spend more time trying to figure out which objects and methods to use than I do in doing the actual work that I want the BlockComment method to perform.

Now, don't get me wrong, there will come a time when I will want to use some of the objects illustrated previously. My point here is that I would like to retrieve the block of text that the user selected, perform the operation of commenting the block, and put it back in the code window. And I would like to do that without spending my life analyzing the numerous objects, methods, and properties available to me in the extensibility model.

What I'm saying is that you can use all of the new objects, spending many, many hours trying to debug their use in a debugger, which doesn't allow you to make changes and execute the changed code without rebuilding your application.

Optionally, you can use a few methods I'm going to give you that will allow you to use the following methodology. You'll use these methods over and over again as you build new functionality in your add-ins.

- GetCodeFromWindow

- Perform the desired work on the code block

- PutCodeBack

I compare the VB 6.0 objects to the .NET objects in later chapters, but for now, I am going to use some simple shortcut methods, a few of which I provide to you in the code supplied with this book.

Compare the code in Listing 3-6 with the code in the alternate BlockComment in Listing 3-7. Don't be concerned with the functions that it calls. They are supplied with the code in this book also, and you will find that they simply do the grunt work for you, leaving you to work out the processing logic without having to worry about what I call "housekeeping."

Listing 3-7. Alternate BlockComment Method

```
Shared Sub BlockComment()
      Dim iNL As Integer ' number of lines in block
      Dim sIN As String ' input selection
      Dim sOUT As String ' commented output
      Dim i As Integer
      ' Nbr chars before first non blank in first line
      Dim n As Short         ' Nbr chars before first nb char subsequent lines
      Dim s As String

      Try
          ' Get selected text from active window
          sIN = GetCodeFromWindow()

          ' ensure the user selected something
          If sIN.Length < 1 Then
            MsgBox("Please select block to be commented.", _
                vbExclamation, "BlockComment")
            Exit Sub
          End If

          ' Get the number of lines in the selected text
          iNL = MLCount(sIN, 0)

          ' Comment the block by looping thru the text
          For i = 1 To iNL
             ' get the next line from the block
```

```
              s = MemoLine(sIN, 0, i)
' Put a block comment line in front of the block
              If i = 1 Then
      sOUT = "'* Block Commented by Les Smith on " & _
                    Format(DateValue(CType(DateTime.Today, String)), _
                    "mm/dd/yyyy") & vbCrLf
          End If
  sOUT = sOUT & "'* " & s & vbcrlf
      Next i

      ' The block is commented, now end the block with
      ' a block delimiter
      sOUT = sOUT  & "'* End of Block Commented by Les Smith" &      vbCrLf

      ' Now put the code back in the window
      PutCodeBack(sOUT)
  Catch e As System.Exception
      MsgBox("Error: " & e.Message, vbCritical, "BlockComment")
  End Try
End Sub
```

Although I have a few more lines of code, and I will have to add several more methods to the class to support this new BlockComment method, the code is more straightforward and easier to follow than the code in Listing 3-6. You have no extensibility objects to worry about. You establish a set of common methods, which you can use every time you want to retrieve and put back a selected code block, without having to concern yourself with the extensibility objects. Using a few standard methods I have coded for you, you are only left to deal with the task of putting the comment headers and footers and the comment characters around the selected code. Later in this chapter, I show you the library methods provided with the book's code.

Making BlockComment Smarter

As I discussed earlier in this chapter, the block comment feature of the IDE is great, considering that VB 3.0 had no such feature. However, it sure would be better if the commenting characters just preceded the block being commented. You can do this by counting the number of spaces that precede the first nonblank character of the first line of the selection. In the improved BlockComment method shown in Listing 3-8, you call a method that will help you put the comments immediately in front of the selected code, where they should be.

Listing 3-8. Improved BlockComment Method

```
Shared Sub BlockComment()
    Dim iNL As Integer ' number of lines in block
    Dim sIN As String ' input selection
    Dim sOUT As String ' commented output
    Dim i As Integer
    Dim n As Short ' number of chars before first non blank in first line
    Dim s As String

    Try
        ' Get selected text from active window
        sIN = GetCodeFromWindow()

        ' ensure the user selected something
        If sIN.Length < 1 Then
            MsgBox("Please select block to be commented.", _
                vbExclamation, "BlockComment")
            Exit Sub
        End If
        ' get the number of lines in the text
        iNL = MLCount(sIN, 0)

        ' comment the block
        For i = 1 To iNL
            s = MemoLine(sIN, 0, i)
            If i = 1 Then
                n = CountSpacesBeforeFirstChar(s)
                sOUT = CType(IIf(n = 0, "", Space(n)), String) & _
                    "'* Block Commented by Les Smith on " & _
                    Format(DateValue(CType(DateTime.Today, String)), _
                    "mm/dd/yyyy") & vbCrLf
            End If
            sOut =sOut & Space(n) & CommentDelimiter & s & vbCrlf
        Next i

        ' now end the block
        sOUT = sOUT & CType(IIf(n = 0, "", Space(n)), String) & _
            "'* End of Block Commented by Les Smith" & vbCrLf

        ' now put the code back
        PutCodeBack(sOUT)
    Catch e As System.Exception
```

```
            MsgBox("Error: " & e.Message, vbCritical, "BlockComment")
        End Try
    End Sub
```

You will notice that I have added a call to a method called CountSpacesBeforeFirstChar. Also, you will see where I use the return values from the method. I have highlighted this new functionality in bold. By determining the number of blank characters before the first selected line and each subsequent line, I can position the comment characters immediately preceding the commented text lines without a lot of white space between the comment character and the text. I call this "smart commenting." Figure 3-8 shows the selected code prior to commenting it.

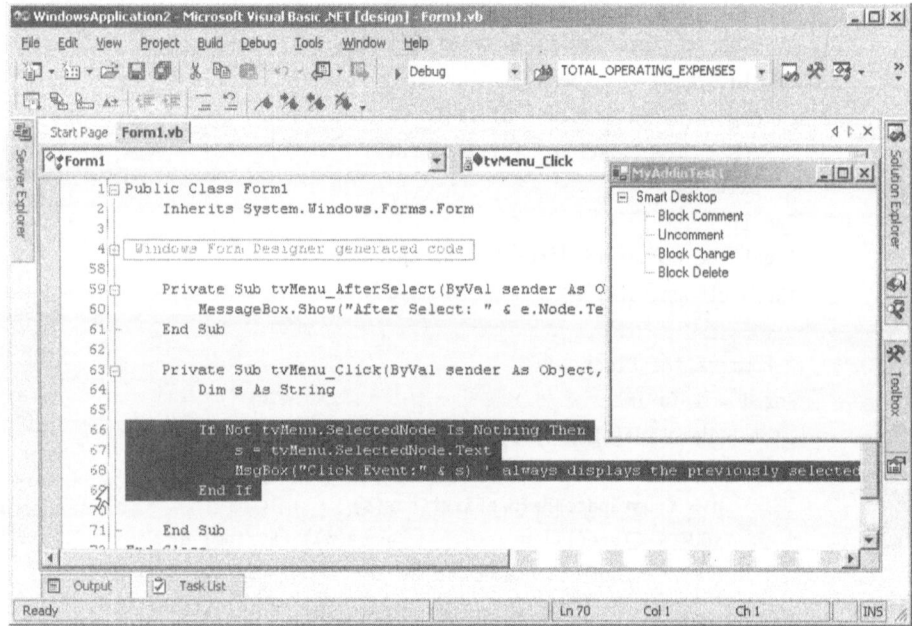

Figure 3-8. Select the code for commenting.

Once you have selected the code, if you have not already loaded the UI for the add-in, click the Smart Desktop menu option on the Tools menu. That will cause the UI form to be loaded as shown in Figure 3-8. Next, open the TreeView by clicking the plus sign (+) to the left of the Smart Desktop root node. Now, click the Block Comment node in the TreeView. Figure 3-9 shows the commented code.

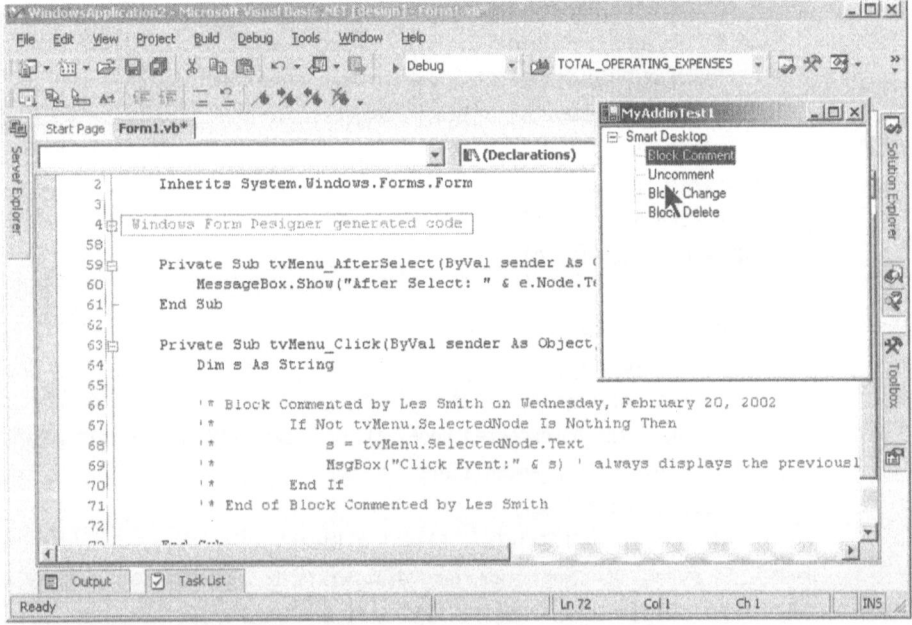

Figure 3-9. The commented code

BlockUnComment Method

The function shown in Listing 3-9 is activated by a click on the Uncomment node of the TreeView. Its purpose is to uncomment a selected block of code that was previously commented by the BlockComment function.

Listing 3-9. The BlockUnComment Method

```
Shared Sub BlockUnComment()
    Dim iNL As Integer ' number of lines in block
    Dim sIN As String ' input selection
    Dim sOUT As String ' commented output
    Dim i As Integer
    Dim n As Short ' number of chars before first non blank in first line
    Dim s As String
    Dim lsCD As String = "'* "

    Try
        ' Get selected text from active window
        sIN = GetCodeFromWindow()
```

```
        ' ensure the user selected something
        If sIN.Length < 1 Then
            MsgBox("Please select block to be commented.", _
                vbExclamation, "BlockComment")
            Exit Sub
        End If
        ' get the number of lines in the text
        iNL = MLCount(sIN, 0)

        ' comment the block
        For i = 1 To iNL
            s = MemoLine(sIN, 0, i)
            ' check the uncommented code, it is leaving it to the left margin
            ' look for commented lines
            Select Case True
                Case Left(Trim(s), 8) = "'* Block"
                    ' comment header, dont write to output
                Case Left(Trim(s), 15) = "'* End of Block"
                    ' comment footer, dont write to output
                Case Left(Trim(s), 3) = lsCD
                    sOUT = sOUT & Replace(s, lsCD, "", , 1) & vbCrLf
                Case Left(Trim(s), 1) = "'"
                    sOUT = sOUT & Replace(s, lsCD, "", , 1) & vbCrLf
            End Select
        Next i

        ' now put the code back
        PutCodeBack(sOUT)

    Catch e As System.Exception
        MsgBox("Error: " & e.Message, vbCritical, "BlockUnComment")
    End Try
End Sub
```

BlockChange Method

Sometimes you will want to mark a block of code with a special header that denotes the code has been changed. The BlockChange method shown in Listing 3-10 performs that functionality. This code is called by clicking the Block Change node of the TreeView control.

Listing 3-10. The BlockChange Method

```
Shared Sub BlockChange()
    Dim sText As String
    Dim sCC As String
    Dim liCnt As Integer
    Dim lsLine As String

    Try
        sText = GetCodeFromWindow()

        If Trim$(sText) = "" Then
            MsgBox("No change text selected!")
            Exit Sub
        End If
        liCnt = MLCount(sText, 0)
        If liCnt > 0 Then
            lsLine = MemoLine(sText, 0, 1)
            liCnt = CountSpacesBeforeFirstChar(lsLine)
        Else
            liCnt = 0
        End If

        sCC = vbCrLf & IIf(liCnt > 0, Space(liCnt), "") & CommentDelimiter & _
            " Block Changed by " & UserName & " on " & TodaysDate & vbCrLf
        sCC = sCC & sText & vbCrLf
        sCC = sCC & IIf(liCnt > 0, Space(liCnt), "") & CommentDelimiter & _
            " End of Block Changed by " & UserName & " on " & _
            TodaysDate & vbCrLf & vbCrLf

        PutCodeBack(sCC)
        Exit Sub
    Catch e As System.Exception
        MsgBox("Error in Block Change: " & e.Message)
    End Try
End Sub
```

NOTE *In the BlockChange method shown in Listing 3-10 and the BlockDelete method shown in Listing 3-11, you begin to see the logic of using the common methods GetCodeFromWindow, PutCodeBack, and so forth. You can now implement many new "business functionalities" without having to be concerned with the extensibility objects.*

Figure 3-10 shows the selected block of code after it has been marked with the Block Change option.

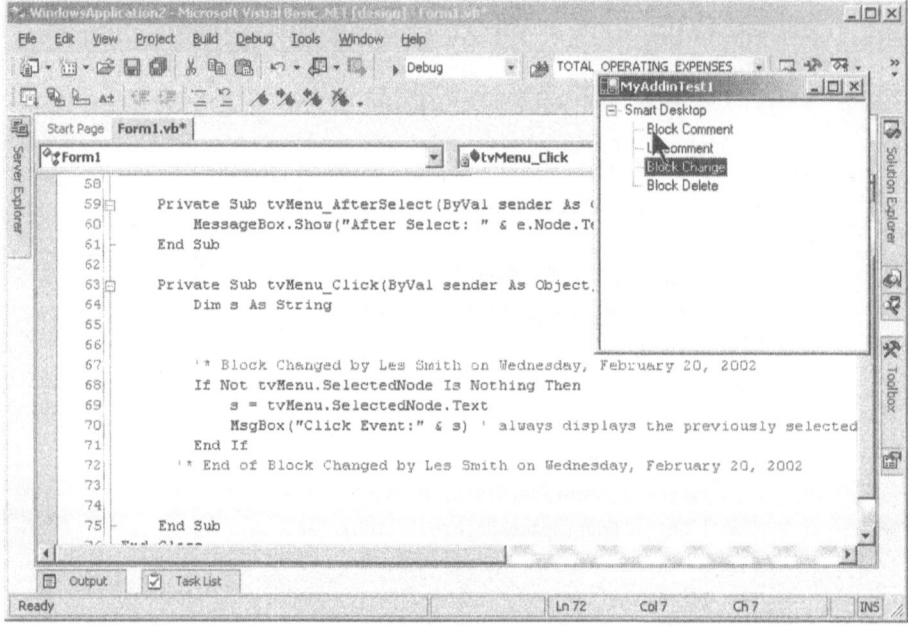

Figure 3-10. Code block marked as changed

BlockDelete Method

I add one final feature to the add-in in this chapter: the BlockDelete method. This method will mark a block of code as deleted. You might ask, "Why so many ways of marking blocks of code?" The obvious answer is that later I could implement a search functionality that could find code that has been deleted, added, or changed by programmer and date (range). To facilitate this, I should mark the code respectively so that I can find categories of code that was commented in a specific way. In other words, show me all of the code that was deleted by Les Smith in the last two months, for example. Listing 3-11 shows the code for the BlockDelete method. You can invoke it by clicking the Block Delete node of the TreeView.

Listing 3-11. The BlockDelete Method

```
Shared Sub BlockDelete()
    ' Insert a deletion comment block around a block
    ' that is about to be deleted
    Dim sCC As String
    Dim sText As String
```

```vb
        Dim sLine As String
        Dim i As Long
        Dim nL As Integer
        Dim sTmpText As String
        Dim liCnt As Integer
        ' get the selected code from the code window
        Try

            sText = GetCodeFromWindow()

            If Trim$(sText) = "" Then
                MsgBox("No deletion text selected!")
                Exit Sub
            End If


            ' we have the text that is to be deleted
            ' comment it to delete it
            sTmpText = ""
            nL = MLCount(sText, 0)

            For i = 1 To nL
                sLine = MemoLine(sText, 0, i)
                If i = 1 Then
                    liCnt = CountSpacesBeforeFirstChar(sLine)
                End If
                sTmpText = sTmpText & IIf(liCnt > 0, Space(liCnt), "") _
                        & "'* " & sLine & vbCrLf
            Next i

            sCC = IIf(liCnt > 0, Space(liCnt), "") & CommentDelimiter & _
                    " Block Deleted by " & UserName & " on " & _
                    TodaysDate & vbCrLf
            sCC = sCC & sTmpText
            sCC = sCC & IIf(liCnt > 0, Space(liCnt), "") & CommentDelimiter & _
                    " End of Block Deleted by " & UserName & " on " & _
                    TodaysDate & vbCrLf


            PutCodeBack(sCC)
        Catch e As System.Exception
            MsgBox("Error in Block Delete: " & e.Message)
        End Try
        Exit Sub
    End Sub
```

Figure 3-11 shows the selected code block after being marked by the Block Delete option.

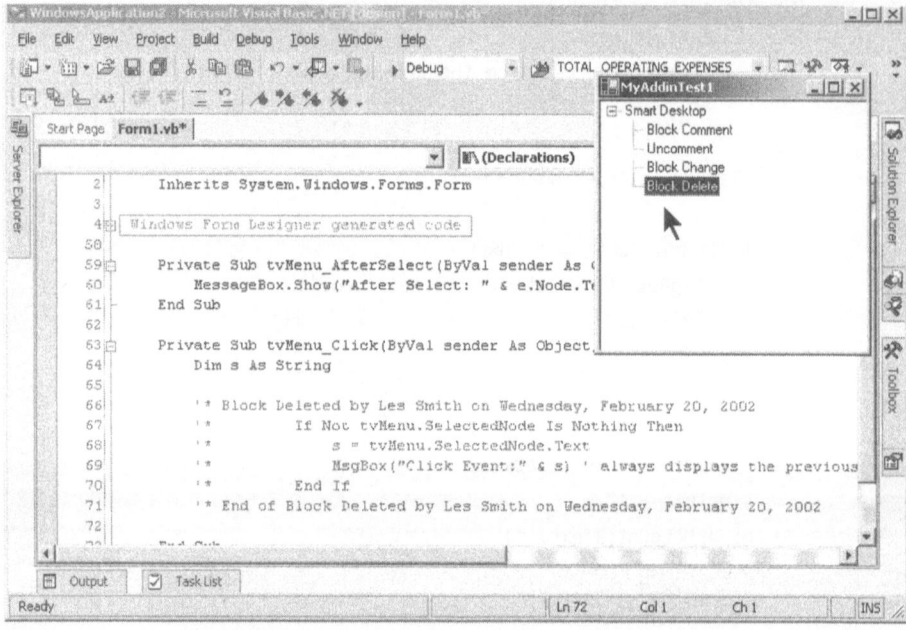

Figure 3-11. Code block marked by Block Delete

Library Functions

Here I list the several functions that I have previously called from the BlockComment method. This is only a sampling of code that is provided in the Utility class of this book's code.

GetCodeFromWindow

You will want to use this simple function anytime you need to retrieve the selected block of code from the active code window. It uses the TextSelection object to retrieve the whole selected block of code, so you may perform any operation on it without having to be concerned with extensibility. This is one of the functions that separates the housekeeping complexity of extensibility from your add-in business processing.

Listing 3-12. GetCodeFromWindow

```
Shared Function GetCodeFromWindow() As String
    Dim s As String
    Dim selCodeBlock As TextSelection '= oVB.ActiveDocument.Selection()

    Try
        selCodeBlock = CType(oVB.ActiveDocument.Selection(), _
            EnvDTE.TextSelection)
        GetCodeFromWindow = selCodeBlock.Text
    Catch e As System.Exception
        MsgBox("Error: " & e.Message, MsgBoxStyle.Critical, _
            "GetCodeFromWindow")
    End Try
End Function
```

NOTE *Option Strict does not allow the direct use of ActiveDocument.Selection. You must cast it to Type TextSelection by the use of the Ctype function.*

PutCodeBack

This simple function, shown in Listing 3-13, will place the code on which you have completed your work in the active code window. Again, this function separates the extensibility objects from the business rules.

Listing 3-13. PutCodeBack

```
Shared Sub PutCodeBack(ByVal s As String)
    Dim selCodeBlock As TextSelection
    Dim datobj As New System.Windows.Forms.DataObject()

    Try
        ' set an object = to the selected text in the client window
        selCodeBlock = CType(oVB.ActiveDocument.Selection(), _
            EnvDTE.TextSelection)

        ' put the formatted text on the clipboard
        datobj.SetData(System.Windows.Forms.DataFormats.Text, s)
        System.Windows.Forms.Clipboard.SetDataObject(datobj)
```

```
        ' paste the code back into the window
        selCodeBlock.Paste()


    Catch e As System.Exception
        MsgBox("Could not put code back in window.", _
            MsgBoxStyle.Critical, _
            "PutCodeBackInWindow")
    End Try
End Sub
```

NOTE   *The use of the clipboard has changed in .NET. The Clipboard object is part of the System.Windows.Forms namespace, and it has two methods: GetDataObject() and SetDataObject().*

CountSpacesBeforeFirstChar

This function, shown in Listing 3-14, simply returns the number of space characters before the first nonblank character in the passed line.

Listing 3-14. CountSpacesBeforeFirstChar

```
Shared Function CountSpacesBeforeFirstChar(ByVal sIN As String) As Short
    ' Return the number of spaces before the first non blank character
    Dim iSpCnt As Short = 0
    Try
        For iSpCnt = 0 To CType(sIN.Length - 1, Short)
            If Mid$(sIN, iSpCnt + 1, 1) <> " " Then
                Return iSpCnt
            End If
        Next iSpCnt
    Catch
        CountSpacesBeforeFirstChar = iSpCnt
    End Try
End Function
```

NOTE   *Notice the use of the Return keyword. This is new to VB .NET and is used to exit a function early while returning the function return value in one line.*

Reading Through the Selected Code Block

In Clipper, there were a couple of powerful functions that when used together provided the functionality of reading one line at a time from the selected code block. I have rewritten these functions in VB and provided them for your use. As you work with blocks of code or memo fields, two of the most useful functions in the library of functions are MLCount and MemoLine. MLCount scans through the selected code, counting the number of lines delimited by carriage return and line feed combinations. It returns the number of lines in the block. MemoLine will return the requested line from the string. You use MLCount to determine the number of lines. You subsequently use MemoLine to retrieve the individual lines, usually in sequence.

MLCount

MLCount requires two parameters. The first is the code block as String. The second is either zero (0) or n, where n is the number of characters to terminate the scan for an end of line (EOL). Both MLCount and MemoLine (described in the next section) can handle word wrap. If you pass 0 as the second parameter, MLCount will look for CrLf to terminate a line. If you pass a positive number, MLCount will terminate a line at the end of the last word that will fit under the length (n), thus providing for word wrap to any length desired.

You call MLCount first to get the number of lines within the block that the user has selected. Listing 3-15 contains the code for MLCount.

MemoLine

Having retrieved the number of lines in the selected block by calling MLCount, you can set up a loop, shown in the BlockComment method, to call Memo Line for next line in the selected block. Listing 3-15 contains the code for MemoLine.

Complete Connect Class

Throughout this chapter, I have been adding new methods to the Connect class. I've added several new methods that are used to perform the new functionalities that have been added. Table 3-1 lists these methods.

Table 3-1. New Methods

METHOD	DESCRIPTION
BlockComment	Encapsulates selected code in Block Comments denoting the programmer name and date commented
BlockUncomment	Strips comment blocking from selected code
BlockChange	Encapsulates selected code in Block Comments and marks as "Changed"
BlockDelete	Encapsulates selected code in Block Comments and marks as "Deleted"
GetCodeFromWindow	Retrieves selected code form text window and returns it in a String variable
PutCodeBack	Returns processed code to the Text Editor window
CountSpacesBeforeFirstChar	Helper function for commenting methods
MLCount	Returns a count of lines in a memo string delimited by CrLfs
MemoLine	Returns a specified line from a memo string

Because I have added so many new methods to the Connect class, I list the complete code for the class in Listing 3-15. For purposes of simplicity, I placed all of the new code into the one class. In Chapter 10, I show you how to reorganize the code into several classes according to specific functionalities, such as code manipulation, utilities, and so forth.

Listing 3-15. Complete Connect Class

```
Imports Microsoft.Office.Core
imports Extensibility
imports System.Runtime.InteropServices
Imports EnvDTE

#Region " Read me for Add-in installation and setup information. "
' When run, the Add-in wizard prepared the registry for the Add-in.
' At a later time, if the Add-in becomes unavailable for reasons such as:
'    1) You moved this project to a computer other than the one
'         it was originally created on.
'    2) You chose 'Yes' when presented with a message asking if you
'         wish to remove the Add-in.
'    3) Registry corruption.
' you will need to re-register the Add-in by building the MyAddin
```

```vb
' Test1Setup project
' by right-clicking the project in the Solution Explorer, then choosing install.
#End Region


<GuidAttribute("EA9E1DDF-0B64-4446-9E29-48DE0CC80523"),
ProgIdAttribute("MyAddinTest1.Connect")> _
Public Class Connect


    Implements Extensibility.IDTExtensibility2
    Implements IDTCommandTarget


  Shared oVB As EnvDTE.DTE
  Shared CommentDelimiter As String = "'*"
  Shared UserName As String = "Les Smith"
  Shared TodaysDate As String


  Dim addInInstance as EnvDTE.AddIn
  ' moved to module level so OnDisconnect can see it
  Dim CommandObj As Command


  Public Sub OnBeginShutdown(ByRef custom As System.Array) ⤶
      Implements Extensibility.IDTExtensibility2.OnBeginShutdown
  End Sub


  Public Sub OnAddInsUpdate(ByRef custom As System.Array) ⤶
      Implements Extensibility.IDTExtensibility2.OnAddInsUpdate
  End Sub


  Public Sub OnStartupComplete(ByRef custom As System.Array) ⤶
      Implements Extensibility.IDTExtensibility2.OnStartupComplete
  End Sub


  Public Sub OnDisconnection(ByVal RemoveMode As _
            Extensibility.ext_DisconnectMode, _
            ByRef custom As System.Array) _
            Implements _
            Extensibility.IDTExtensibility2.OnDisconnection
      Try
          CommandObj.Delete()
          ' MsgBox("Disconnect, remove Tool Button", _
          '       MsgBoxStyle.Information, "MyAddinTest1")
```

```vb
            Catch e As System.Exception
                MsgBox("Error in Disconnect: " & _
                        e.Message, _
                        MsgBoxStyle.Critical, _
                        "MyAddinTest1")
        End Try
    End Sub


    Public Sub OnConnection(ByVal application As Object, _
        ByVal connectMode As Extensibility.ext_ConnectMode, _
        ByVal addInInst As Object, ByRef custom As System.Array) _
        Implements Extensibility.IDTExtensibility2.OnConnection
        Dim iBitMap As Integer

        ' set up today's date for use in all methods
        TodaysDate = Format(Now(), "Long Date")

        oVB = CType(application, EnvDTE.DTE)
        addInInstance = CType(addInInst, EnvDTE.AddIn)
        If connectMode = Extensibility.ext_ConnectMode.ext_cm_AfterStartup Or _
            connectMode = Extensibility.ext_ConnectMode.ext_cm_Startup _
            Then
            Dim objAddIn As AddIn = CType(addInInst, AddIn)

            ' When run, the Add-in wizard prepared the registry for the Add-in.
            ' At a later time, the Add-in or its commands may become unavailable
            ' for  reasons such as:
            '   1) You moved this project to a computer other than the one it was
            ' originally created on.
            '   2) You chose 'Yes' when presented with a message asking if you
            ' wish   to remove the Add-in.
            '   3) You add new commands or modify commands already defined.
            ' You will need to re-register the Add-in by building the MyAddin
            ' Test1Setup project,
            ' right-clicking the project in the Solution Explorer, and then
            ' choosing install. Alternatively, you could execute the
            ' ReCreateCommands.reg file the
            ' Add-in Wizard generated in
            ' the project directory, or run 'devenv /setup' from a command prompt.
            Try
                iBitMap = 59
                CommandObj = oVB.Commands.AddNamedCommand(objAddIn, _
                            "MyAddinTest1", "Smart Desktop", _
```

```vbnet
                          "Executes the command for MyAddinTest1", _
                          True, iBitMap, Nothing, 1 + 2) _
                          '1+2=vsCommandStatusSupported+vsCommandStatusEnabled
                CommandObj.AddControl(oVB.CommandBars.Item("Tools"))
        Catch e As System.Exception
            MsgBox("Error in placing control: " & e.Message)
        End Try
    End If
End Sub


Public Sub Exec(ByVal cmdName As String, _
                ByVal executeOption As vsCommandExecOption, _
                ByRef varIn As Object, _
                ByRef varOut As Object, _
                ByRef handled As Boolean) _
                Implements IDTCommandTarget.Exec
    Dim oFrm As New frmTreeView()

    handled = False
    If (executeOption = vsCommandExecOption.vsCommandExecOptionDoDefault) _
        Then
        If cmdName = "MyAddinTest1.Connect.MyAddinTest1" Then
            handled = True
            ' MsgBox("You rang?")
            oFrm.Show()
            Exit Sub
        End If
    End If
End Sub


Public Sub QueryStatus(ByVal cmdName As String, _
            ByVal neededText As vsCommandStatusTextWanted, _
            ByRef statusOption As vsCommandStatus, _
            ByRef commandText As Object) _
            Implements IDTCommandTarget.QueryStatus
    If neededText = EnvDTE.vsCommandStatusTextWanted.↵
        vsCommandStatusTextWantedNone _
        Then
        If cmdName = "MyAddinTest1.Connect.MyAddinTest1" Then
            statusOption = CType(vsCommandStatus.vsCommandStatusEnabled + _
                        vsCommandStatus.vsCommandStatusSupported, _
                        vsCommandStatus)
```

```
            Else
                statusOption = vsCommandStatus.vsCommandStatusUnsupported
            End If
        End If
End Sub


Shared Sub BlockComment()
    Dim iNL As Integer ' number of lines in block
    Dim sIN As String ' input selection
    Dim sOUT As String ' commented output
    Dim i As Integer
    Dim n As Short ' number of chars before first non blank in first line
    Dim s As String


    Try
        ' Get selected text from active window
        sIN = GetCodeFromWindow()

        ' ensure the user selected something
        If sIN.Length < 1 Then
            MsgBox("Please select block to be commented.", _
                vbExclamation, "BlockComment")
            Exit Sub
        End If
        ' get the number of lines in the text
        iNL = MLCount(sIN, 0)

        ' comment the block
        For i = 1 To iNL
            s = MemoLine(sIN, 0, i)
            If i = 1 Then
                n = CountSpacesBeforeFirstChar(s)
                sOUT = CType(IIf(n = 0, "", Space(n)), String) & _
                    "'* Block Commented by " & UserName & " on " & _
                    TodaysDate & vbCrLf
            End If
            sOut =sOut & Space(n) & CommentDelimiter & s & vbCrlf
        Next i

        ' now end the block
        sOUT = sOUT & CType(IIf(n = 0, "", Space(n)), String) & _
            "'* End of Block Commented by " & UserName & vbCrLf

        ' now put the code back
```

```
            PutCodeBack(sOUT)
        Catch e As System.Exception
            MsgBox("Error: " & e.Message, vbCritical, "BlockComment")
        End Try
    End Sub


    Shared Sub BlockDelete()
        ' Insert a deletion comment block around a block
        ' that is about to be deleted
        Dim sCC As String
        Dim sText As String
        Dim sLine As String
        Dim i As Long
        Dim nL As Integer
        Dim sTmpText As String
        Dim liCnt As Integer
        ' get the selected code from the code window

        Try

            sText = GetCodeFromWindow()

            If Trim$(sText) = "" Then
                MsgBox("No deletion text selected!")
                Exit Sub
            End If

            ' we have the text that is to be deleted
            ' comment it to delete it
            sTmpText = ""
            nL = MLCount(sText, 0)

            For i = 1 To nL
                sLine = MemoLine(sText, 0, i)
                If i = 1 Then
                    liCnt = CountSpacesBeforeFirstChar(sLine)
                End If
                sTmpText = sTmpText & IIf(liCnt > 0, Space(liCnt), "") _
                        & "'* " & sLine & vbCrLf
            Next i
            sCC = IIf(liCnt > 0, Space(liCnt), "") & CommentDelimiter & _
                    " Block Deleted by " & UserName & " on " & _
                    TodaysDate & vbCrLf
            sCC = sCC & sTmpText
            sCC = sCC & IIf(liCnt > 0, Space(liCnt), "") & CommentDelimiter & _
```

```
                          " End of Block Deleted by " & UserName & " on " & _
                          TodaysDate & vbCrLf


                 PutCodeBack(sCC)
            Catch e As System.Exception
                 MsgBox("Error in Block Delete: " & e.Message)
            End Try
            Exit Sub
      End Sub


      Shared Sub BlockChange()
            Dim sText As String
            Dim sCC As String
            Dim liCnt As Integer
            Dim lsLine As String


            Try
                 sText = GetCodeFromWindow()


                 If Trim$(sText) = "" Then
                      MsgBox("No change text selected!")
                      Exit Sub
                 End If
                 liCnt = MLCount(sText, 0)
                 If liCnt > 0 Then
                      lsLine = MemoLine(sText, 0, 1)
                      liCnt = CountSpacesBeforeFirstChar(lsLine)
                 Else
                      liCnt = 0
                 End If


                 sCC = vbCrLf & IIf(liCnt > 0, Space(liCnt), "") & CommentDelimiter & _
                      " Block Changed by " & UserName & " on " & TodaysDate & vbCrLf
                 sCC = sCC & sText & vbCrLf
                 sCC = sCC & IIf(liCnt > 0, Space(liCnt), "") & CommentDelimiter & _
                      " End of Block Changed by " & UserName & " on " & _
                      TodaysDate & vbCrLf & vbCrLf


                 PutCodeBack(sCC)

                 Exit Sub
            Catch e As System.Exception
                 MsgBox("Error in Block Change: " & e.Message)
```

```
        End Try
    End Sub


    Shared Sub BlockUnComment()
        Dim iNL As Integer ' number of lines in block
        Dim sIN As String ' input selection
        Dim sOUT As String ' commented output
        Dim i As Integer
        Dim n As Short ' number of chars before first non blank in first line
        Dim n2 As Short ' nbr chars before first nb char subsequent lines
        Dim s As String
        Dim lsCD As String = "'* "


        Try
            ' Get selected text from active window
            sIN = GetCodeFromWindow()

            ' ensure the user selected something
            If sIN.Length < 1 Then
                MsgBox("Please select block to be commented.", _
                        vbExclamation, "BlockComment")
                Exit Sub
            End If
            ' get the number of lines in the text
            iNL = MLCount(sIN, 0)


            ' comment the block
            For i = 1 To iNL
                s = MemoLine(sIN, 0, i)
                ' check the uncommented code, it is leaving it to the left margin
                ' look for commented lines
                Select Case True
                    Case Left(Trim(s), 8) = "'* Block"
                        ' comment header, dont write to output
                    Case Left(Trim(s), 15) = "'* End of Block"
                        ' comment footer, dont write to output
                    Case Left(Trim(s), 3) = lsCD
                        sOUT = sOUT & Replace(s, lsCD, "", , 1) & vbCrLf
                    Case Left(Trim(s), 1) = "'"
                        sOUT = sOUT & Replace(s, lsCD, "", , 1) & vbCrLf
                End Select
            Next i
```

```
                            ' now put the code back
                            PutCodeBack(sOUT)


                    Catch e As System.Exception
                        MsgBox("Error: " & e.Message, vbCritical, "BlockUnComment")
                    End Try
            End Sub


            Shared Function GetCodeFromWindow() As String
                Dim s As String
                Dim selCodeBlock As TextSelection '= oVB.ActiveDocument.Selection()

                Try
                    selCodeBlock = CType(oVB.ActiveDocument.Selection(), _
                        EnvDTE.TextSelection)
                    GetCodeFromWindow = selCodeBlock.Text
                Catch e As System.Exception
                    MsgBox("Error: " & e.Message, MsgBoxStyle.Critical, _
                        "GetCodeFromWindow")
                End Try
            End Function


            Shared Sub PutCodeBack(ByVal s As String)
                Dim selCodeBlock As TextSelection
                Dim datobj As New System.Windows.Forms.DataObject()

                Try
                    selCodeBlock = CType(oVB.ActiveDocument.Selection(), _
                        EnvDTE.TextSelection)
                    datobj.SetData(System.Windows.Forms.DataFormats.Text, s)
                    System.Windows.Forms.Clipboard.SetDataObject(datobj)

                    selCodeBlock.Paste()

                Catch e As System.Exception
                    MsgBox("Could not put code back in window.", _
                        MsgBoxStyle.Critical, _
                        "PutCodeBackInWindow")
                End Try
            End Sub


            Shared Function CountSpacesBeforeFirstChar(ByVal sIN As String) As Short
                ' Return the number of spaces before the first non blank character
                Dim iSpCnt As Short = 0
```

```
    Try
        For iSpCnt = 0 To CType(sIN.Length - 1, Short)
            If Mid$(sIN, iSpCnt + 1, 1) <> " " Then
                Return iSpCnt
            End If
        Next iSpCnt
    Catch
        CountSpacesBeforeFirstChar = iSpCnt
    End Try
End Function


Shared Function MLCount(ByVal cStrng As String, _
                                        ByVal nL As Integer) _
                                        As Integer
    ' VB Replacement for Clipper MLCount Function
    ' It does handle word wrap, nL is the max char
    ' count per line.
    Dim nStptr As Integer, nLenStr As Integer, nLineCtr As Integer
    Dim sTemp As String
    Dim i As Integer

    ' nStPtr is the pointer to position in cStrng
    Try
        nStptr = 1
        nLenStr = Len(cStrng)
        nLineCtr = 0

        While True
            ' If the pointer to the beginning of the next line
            ' is >= the length of the string, we are outta here!
            If nStptr >= nLenStr Then
                Return nLineCtr
                Exit Function
            End If

            ' Get the next line, not to exceed the length of nL
            ' if nL was greater than 0
            If nL > 0 Then
                sTemp = Mid$(cStrng, nStptr, nL)
                If InStr(sTemp, vbCrLf) > 0 Then
                    ' there is a CRLF in the string
                    sTemp = Left$(sTemp, InStr(sTemp, vbCrLf) - 1)
                    nStptr = nStptr + Len(sTemp) + 2
```

```
                    Else
                        ' new code to handle lines with no crlf
                        If Len(sTemp) = nL Then
                            ' we have a full line left (at least)
                            i = InStrRev(" ", sTemp)
                            ' truncate the partial word from the end
                            sTemp = Left$(sTemp, i - 1)
                            'set the pointer to start the next line at
                            'current start point + len(stemp)
                            nStptr = nStptr + Len(sTemp)
                        Else
                            ' this is the last line, because the string is
                            ' shorter than the nL length
                            Return nLineCtr + 1
                            Exit Function
                        End If
                    End If
                Else
                    ' nL was supplied as 0 meaning we just look for CRLf
                    nStptr = InStr(nStptr, cStrng, vbCrLf) + 2
                End If

                ' if the ptr = 2 then there was no crlf in the line
                If nStptr = 2 Then
                    Return nLineCtr + 1
                End If

                nLineCtr = nLineCtr + 1
                If nStptr + 1 > nLenStr Then
                    Return nLineCtr
                End If
            End While
            Exit Function
        Catch e As System.Exception
            MsgBox("Error: " & e.Message, vbCritical, "MLCount")
        End Try
    End Function
    Shared Function MemoLine(ByVal cStrng As String, _
            ByVal nLL As Integer, ByVal nL As Integer) As String
        ' VB Replacement for Clipper MemoLine() Function.
        ' Handles Word Wrap.  nLL is the max char/line.
        ' Note that if the user asks for a line that is beyond the
        ' end of the string, i.e. more lines than are in the string
```

```
' unpredictable results will be returned, assuming we
' return at all.  Therefore, MLCount() must be called
' before calling MemoLine() and MemoLine must not be called
' to return a line numbered higher than MLCount() returned.
Static nStptr As Integer
Dim i As Integer
Dim nTmpPtr As Integer
Dim sTemp As String
Dim nPrevStPtr As Integer
Dim lFoundSpace As Integer
Static j As Integer
Dim iST As Integer

Try
    ' if NL is 1 > than J then
    ' this is a subsequent call to get the next
    ' line
    If nL = 1 Then
        nStptr = 1
        iST = 1
    ElseIf (nL - (j - 1) = 1) And (j <> 0) Then
        iST = nL
    Else
        nStptr = 1
        iST = 1
    End If

    ' Loop through the string until we find the requested line.
    For j = iST To nL
        ' Remembering where the previous line started will allow
        ' us to know where the requested line began when we have gone
        ' just past it with the following loop
        nPrevStPtr = nStptr
        ' Get the next line, not to exceed the length of nLL
        ' if nL was greater than 0
        If nLL = 0 Then
            ' nL was supplied as 0 meaning we just look for CRLf
            nStptr = InStr(nStptr, cStrng, Chr(13) & Chr(10)) + 2
        Else
            sTemp = Mid$(cStrng, nStptr, nLL)
            If InStr(sTemp, Chr(13) & Chr(10)) > 0 Then
                ' there is a CRLF in the string
                sTemp = Left$(sTemp, InStr(sTemp, Chr(13) & Chr(10)) - 1)
```

```
                        nStptr = nStptr + Len(sTemp) + 2
                Else
                    ' new code to handle lines with no crlf
                    If Len(sTemp) = nLL Then
                        ' we have a full line left with no crlf
                        ' find last space
                        i = InStrRev(" ", sTemp)

                        ' truncate the partial word from the end
                        sTemp = Left$(sTemp, i - 1)
                        ' set the pointer to start the next line  at current
                        ' start point + len(stemp)
                        nStptr = nStptr + Len(sTemp)
                    End If
                End If
            End If
        Next j


        ' nStPtr is now positioned to the end of the requested line
        ' Now find the end of the current (requested) line.
        If nLL = 0 Then
            If nStptr = 2 Then
                Return Mid$(cStrng, nPrevStPtr)
            Else
                Return Mid(cStrng, nPrevStPtr, nStptr - (nPrevStPtr + 2))
            End If
        Else
            Return Trim$(sTemp)
        End If
        Exit Function
    Catch e As System.Exception
        MsgBox("Error: " & e.Message, vbCritical, "MemoLine")
    End Try
End Function
End Class
```

Summary

This has been a long chapter, and I have covered a lot of ground. However, I thought it necessary to get you into an add-in that is not really complex, but does something really useful. This allows you to get your feet wet developing a real add-in with some substance, without overwhelming you with the enormity of the extensibility object.

You learned that through the use of some common library methods, you can introduce new code manipulation functionality without having to concern yourself with the intricacies of the extensibility object every time you want to get code from a text editor, operate on it, and put it back. In several future chapters, you'll consider some of the many things that can be done with this framework of library methods.

In Chapter 4, I discuss the challenges presented to you when you have to debug an add-in. Debugging in Visual Studio .NET has some negatives, but I think you'll see that the plusses of the new debugging features outweigh the minuses.

CHAPTER 4

Debugging an Add-in

*"If builders built buildings the way most programmers write programs, the
first woodpecker that came along would destroy civilization."*
—Weinberg's Second Law

THERE ARE TWO WAYS to view people who are good at debugging. You might assume
that they are good at debugging because they have had a lot of practice at it.
I personally don't believe that's the way most good debuggers should be viewed.
Good debuggers don't necessarily spend a lot of time debugging. In fact, if good
programmers design correctly, code carefully, and spend the right amount of
time initially debugging a program before it goes live, they won't have to come
back and fix a lot of problems, assuming the requirements were defined properly
at the outset of the project.

I'm a firm believer in debugging up front, rather than telling the user to "try it
and let me know if you have any problems." I believe in debugging code incre-
mentally, as I develop it, rather than waiting until the whole program is
developed and then tackling it all at once. I believe in stepping through a complex program or routine the first time it is run, rather than just running it to see
what it will do. In other words, I'm always going to use F8 before I use F5. I rarely,
if ever, use F5 to test a complex algorithm, no matter how confident I am about
how well I wrote it.

As a lead programmer, I've always encouraged developers to step through
complex programs before they ever try letting them run. I've encountered dis-
agreement with this rule, and I've also watched the naysayers spend countless
days trying to get the bugs out of programs that have been released to users. Far
too many programmers, when a program compiles with no errors, effectively say,
"Let's throw it up on the wall and see if it sticks!" If you would like further excellent reading on this subject, get a copy of Steve McConnell's *Code Complete*
(Microsoft Press, 1995) or Steve McGuire's *Debugging the Development
Process* (Microsoft Press, 1994).

Bug-free code should be a design goal of every programmer. Too many programmers believe that bugs are inevitable and they take for granted that they will
have to go back and fix bugs. This attitude should be fought constantly by the
good lead programmer, as it results in too little effort being spent looking for
every bug and testing every path that's feasible.

While I'm on the subject, crash-free code should be a design goal also. Never allow a program to "go down hard," if at all possible. No one wants to see the "blue screen of death, where you are all alone, and no one hears your screams." To avoid that, you must discipline yourself to put error handling anywhere and everywhere that you can possibly get a failure. That's why one of my commercial add-ins has features to automatically create error-handling code in a selected procedure, as well as create the module level handler, which displays all the available information about the error.

In this chapter, I go into detail regarding the debugging of add-ins. Although add-ins are DLLs, they are a special type of DLL and require special procedures that pertain only to add-ins. Normal DLLs can be debugged in one instance of the Visual Studio IDE. However, in order to debug an add-in, the add-in must run in its own instance of the IDE and the application using the add-in must run in another instance of the IDE. I show you how to do this at the same time I give you tips I have learned while debugging add-ins. Finally, I present what I believe to be good practices for the debugging process.

Setting Debug Options

Before you begin debugging, you should set the debug options that you prefer in the .NET Options dialog box. To do this, select Tools ➤ Options. The Options dialog box will display. Click the Debug folder icon to get to the debugging options. The Debugging General Options dialog box will appear as shown in Figure 4-1.

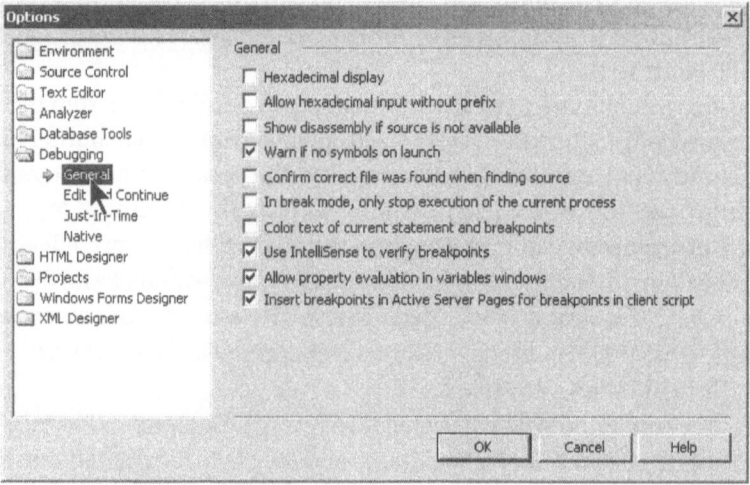

Figure 4-1. The Debugging General Options dialog box

There appear to be no options on the General tab that are of interest to us at this point. Click the Edit and Continue option. The Edit and Continue Options dialog box will appear as shown in Figure 4-2.

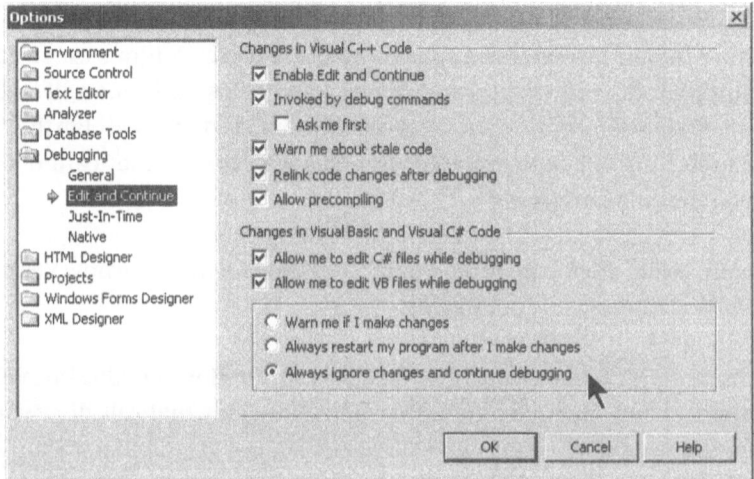

Figure 4-2. The Edit and Continue Options dialog box

Edit and Continue, in the strictest sense, is limited to C/C++ programs. As previously described, the ability to change code and execute the changed code available in previous versions of Visual Basic does not exist in VB .NET or Visual C#. The traditional Edit and Continue feature isn't supported in Visual Studio .NET for Visual Basic or Visual C#. That isn't to say you can't change code while you're debugging either of these two languages. You simply cannot execute the changed code without stopping the debugging session and recompiling.

You need to select the action you want Visual Studio to take when you change code in a Visual Basic or Visual C# debugging session. You do this in the view shown in Figure 4-2.

First, check the Enable Edit and Continue check box. This will allow you to make changes and continue. Next are the two check boxes for allowing Visual Basic and Visual C# changes in the debugger:

> *Allow me to edit C# files while debugging:* If you select this option, you will be allowed to edit files while debugging; however, Visual Studio cannot apply the code changes until you stop debugging, build a fresh version of the code, and restart the application. If you try to continue execution after editing code while debugging, the action that Visual Studio will take depends on the option that you select, which is discussed shortly.

Deselecting this option makes your files read-only so they cannot be edited while debugging.

Allow me to edit VB files while debugging: If you select this option, you will be allowed to edit files while debugging; however, Visual Studio cannot apply the code changes until you stop debugging, build a fresh version of the code, and restart the application. If you try to continue execution after editing code while debugging, the action that Visual Studio will take depends on the option that you select, which is discussed shortly. Deselecting this option makes your files read-only so they cannot be edited while debugging.

Finally, select one of the three option buttons to determine how Visual Studio will react to changes while debugging:

Warn me if I make changes: If you select this option, a dialog box will appear when you make changes when debugging that will allow you to continue or stop.

Always restart my program after I make changes: If you select this option, the debugger terminates execution of your program, builds a fresh version of the code, and restarts the program.

Always ignore changes and continue debugging: If you select this option, the debugger allows you to edit the code, but when you continue debugging, the debugger steps or continues execution in the old code (without the code changes).

My personal preference is to select the "Always ignore changes and continue debugging" option. This allows me to make the necessary changes while in the debugger and not lose my train of thought. I can still use the Immediate window to evaluate expressions or function calls, even though I can't execute the edited code. The "Always restart my program after I make changes" option is a little too drastic for me, because as soon as you make a change to a line of code, the debugger stops without warning and you lose any state that you may have achieved through a possibly lengthy process to get to where you are in the debugging session.

Before Beginning a Debugging Session...

The Visual Studio .NET IDE is much smarter than previous versions of the VB IDE. One of the great improvements is that Visual Studio .NET automatically

underlines any error, with respect to objects, type casting, and so forth, that it
knows will fail at runtime. For example, Figure 4-3 shows an IDE error notification.

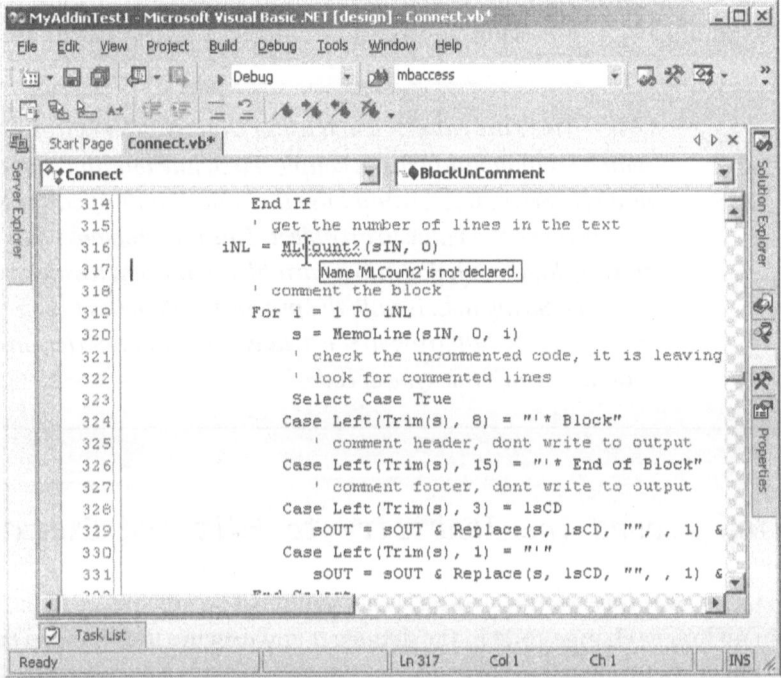

Figure 4-3. IDE error notification

You should always look for this indication of an error, especially in new code.
It will save you from having to wait while the compiler compiles your program,
only to respond that you have a failure to compile successfully. Perusing all new
code for underlined code will save you much wasted compile time. When you
place your mouse cursor over the underlined code, Visual Studio displays a tool
tip denoting the cause of the error.

An even more helpful tool for finding error information is the Task List window. This is new in Visual Studio .NET, at least for VB users. The Task List window
normally appears at the bottom of the IDE, and its caption bar always contains
the number of errors that the IDE knows about in your code displayed in the
form "0 Build Error tasks shown (filtered)". If the number is something other than
"0," you have an error somewhere in the code. If this is the case, the error will be
listed in the body of the Task List, and you can go directly to the error by double-
clicking it. So to keep from wasting time compiling when the IDE already knows
that you have errors, always ensure that the number of Build Errors shown is 0.

Using Option Strict

Visual Studio by default creates new modules or classes with Option Strict On. This means that the IDE will automatically underline a line of code that will either compile or fail at runtime. This is a great improvement over earlier versions of Visual Studio. I strongly recommend that Option Strict always be left on.

NOTE *There are caveats when using Option Strict On, of which I will mention just a couple. First, late binding is not allowed. Second, you cannot use the concatenate operator (&) to concatenate a value to an object. This is a problem when storing database fields into a variable. To prevent raising an error if a String field is null, the practice in VB 6.0 is to concatenate a vbNullString to the field value. Option Strict On will not permit this type of code.*

Working Around the Inability to Edit and Execute

What I mean by this section's heading is that you must be constantly aware that you can no longer change code in the debugger and execute the changed code. I know I have mentioned this several times already, but it is a real disadvantage, and you must look for ways to work around it when you can. Fortunately, there are a couple of ways to work around this reduced functionality in the debugger. First, you can change the code, assuming you set the correct options as previously discussed. Once you have changed a line of code, it will still execute, but stepping through the line will execute it as it was coded originally. However, you can execute the changed line by copying it to the Immediate window and executing it there. Then, right-click the next line of code and click the Set Next Statement option to execute the line following the changed line.

NOTE *This method will not always work, especially when system objects are involved. It will work on simple instructions that are storing into a string or scalar variable, for example.*

Second, use variables to contain values rather than including a string or number value in a line of code. If you are going to have strings or other values that could require changing at runtime, always Dim and set a variable instead of coding the string or other value into a line of code.

How will that help you? Here is an example:

```
Dim iBitMap As Integer
iBitMap = 59
CommandObj = oVB.Commands.AddNamedCommand(objAddIn, _
            "MyAddinTest1", "Smart Desktop", _
            "Executes the command for MyAddinTest1", _
            True, iBitMap, Nothing, 1 + 2) _
            '1+2 == vsCommandStatusSupported+ _
            ' vsCommandStatusEnabled
CommandObj.AddControl(oVB.CommandBars.Item("Tools"))
```

In this code snippet, iBitMap is an integer that indexes to an icon in Office.DLL. After seeing the icon on your menu, you may decide that you want a different icon. Without recompiling the add-in, you can simply disconnect the add-in and set a breakpoint on the line following the highlighted line of code. When you reconnect the add-in, it will stop on the breakpointed line. Then you can go to the Immediate window and execute the following line of code:

```
IBitMap = 110
```

Now the value of iBitMap has been changed to point to a different icon and you effectively have changed the code in debug mode without having to rebuild your add-in. This is a very simple example, but if you apply it across the application, you will be able to test different options, strings, and so forth without having to rebuild your application.

Stepping Through Complex Code

I have already discussed this at length, but add-in debugging can be hard enough without letting code run rampant and then viewing the results, only to discover that your add-in has made a mess and you have no idea why! If you are not in the habit of stepping through complex code, trust me, trying my approach to debugging will save you untold hours of headaches.

Using Breakpoints Generously

In addition to stepping through complex code, I use breakpoints generously. I like to know where the code is going at all times. Setting breakpoints at the beginning of complex code segments before you begin debugging is a great way to progress through a debugging session in an organized manner.

 **NOTE** *Another nice new feature of .NET is that breakpoints are saved when you exit .NET and restored in the code the next time you open the project for debugging. This is a much-needed addition to the debugger.*

Debugging an Add-in

Debugging an add-in is very similar to debugging a COM object (DLL) in earlier versions of VB. This is because an add-in is a COM DLL. To debug a COM object, you have to have two sessions of Visual Studio running. One will contain the COM object, in your case the add-in, and the second will be a client application that calls or uses the COM object. Again, one of the nicer improvements in debugging an add-in in .NET is that when you press F5 or click the Debug arrow on the toolbar, Visual Studio compiles your add-in, and if there are no compile errors, it automatically starts a new session of Visual Studio from which you invoke the add-in and its associated functionality.

Disconnecting Between Debugging Sessions

When you start to debug your add-in, Visual Studio .NET may automatically set the flags in the registry, which will cause your add-in to be connected, or loaded, when the second instance of Visual Studio .NET is started. This is all right, and it is not necessary to follow my suggestion here. But what can happen upon occasion is that you will get a diagnostic, or error, denoting that your project files cannot be copied to their destination directory. This happens, apparently, when some part of your debugging session does not shut down properly or clean up itself properly. The only way to recover from it is to first go to the Add-in Manager dialog box and disconnect the add-in. Then you will also probably have to get completely out of .NET and reload your add-in solution.

The best way to prevent this from occurring is to disconnect the add-in in the Add-in Manager in the client (second copy of .NET) that is using the add-in. I call the second copy of .NET the "client," because your add-in is a COM server.

Sometimes, you will not be able to do this, due to the fact that you reach a point in your add-in's code at which you cannot continue. If you have to stop the debugging session in the add-in, the client session of .NET will be automatically terminated because it was automatically started by .NET. At that point, you may be able to prevent any copying problems by going to the Add-in Manager and deselecting the check boxes related to your add-in in the add-in session of .NET.

Again, this whole discussion can be overkill, because if everything goes according to plan and the debugging session is shut down normally, you may never encounter the problem. However, I have come across the problem on numerous occasions, and I wanted you to know what was causing it and how to recover from it or possibly avoid it.

Running with an Error

I am going to intentionally try to debug with a known error in the code to show you what will happen. After I press F5 or click the Run button, the compiler, upon finding the error, displays an error dialog box as shown in Figure 4-4.

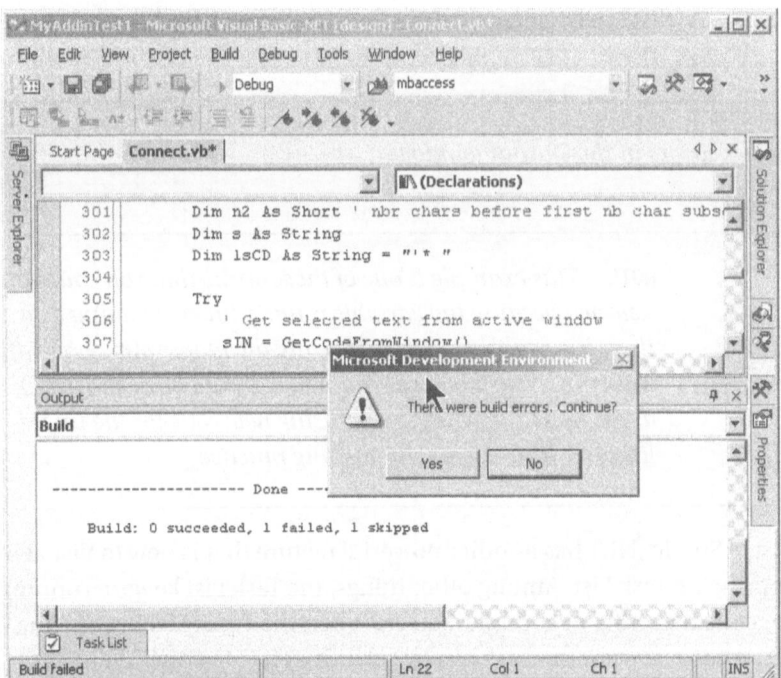

Figure 4-4. Compiler-detected error

If I click No in the message box asking me if I want to continue with the error, the error(s) will be displayed in the Output window, as shown in Figure 4-5.

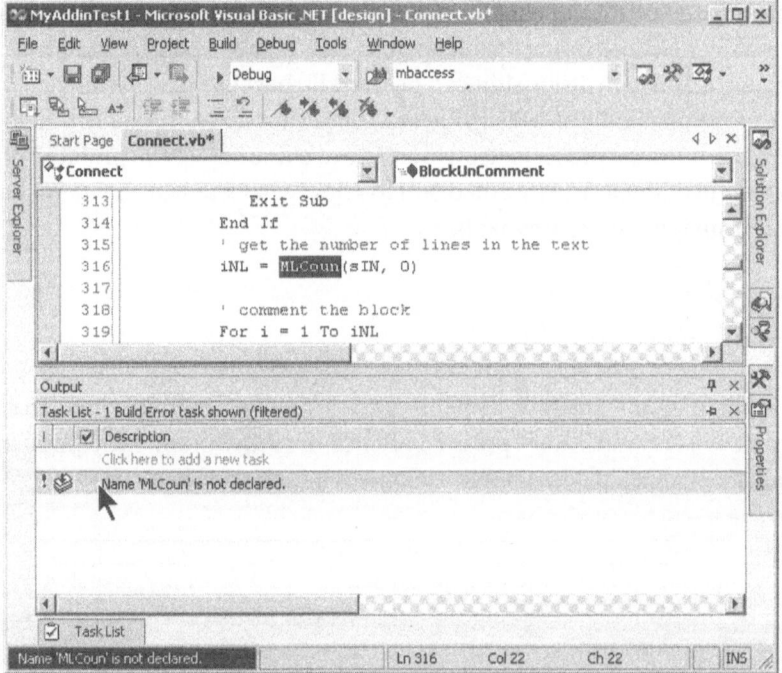

Figure 4-5. Errors in the Output window

 **NOTE** *This example is one of those errors that you could have detected because the variable is underlined, denoting that there is a problem with it. Holding the mouse cursor over the underlined variable will cause the error to be displayed in a tool tip window. Again, perusing new code for the underlined errors is a good, timesaving practice.*

Visual Studio .NET has another powerful feature that is new to Visual Basic developers: the Task List. Among other things, the Task List keeps a running list of lines of code that will not compile. You can open the Tasks List by pressing Ctrl-Alt-K. You can also view the Task List by selecting View ➤ Other Windows ➤ Task List. The Task List can hold a maximum of 102 uncompilable lines of code. Therefore, you should always look at the Task List before attempting to compile your application. If you double-click any item in the Task List, you will be taken to the bad line of code and it will be highlighted in the code window, as shown in Figure 4-6.

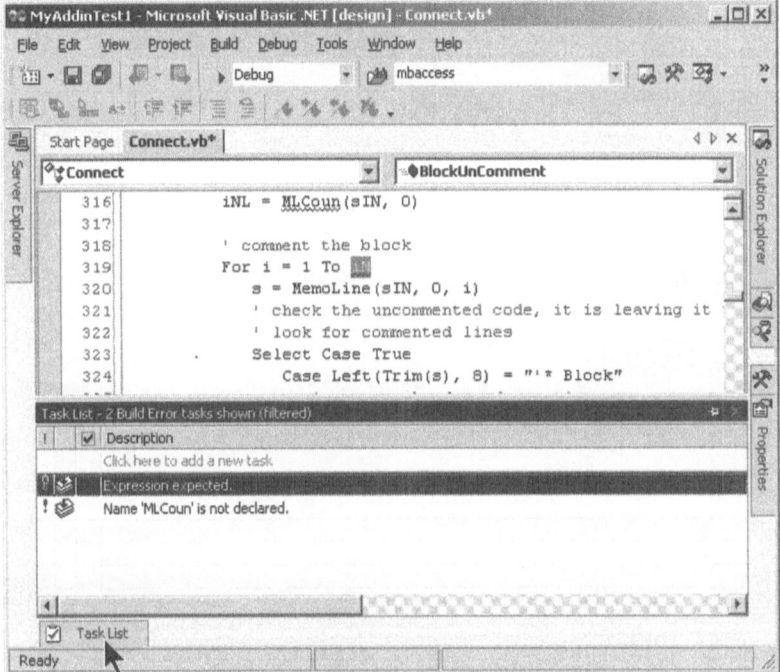

Figure 4-6. Error automatically highlighted in the code window

If you decide to ignore an error, you can click Yes in the dialog box about continuing to debug. When you do that, a second copy of Visual Studio .NET opens
automatically.

Now if you go to the Add-in Manager and check both boxes for your add-in,
you will get an error and you will not be able to continue debugging the
add-in. Visual Studio will ask if you want to remove the add-in from the registry. It
does this because it cannot connect to an add-in that will not compile without
errors.

At this point, you should answer No to the question regarding removal of the
add-in from the registry. In earlier versions of Visual Basic, you had the "Compile
on Demand" option, which allowed you to debug parts of a program while there
were still compile errors in other parts of the program. Although there doesn't
appear to be such an option in .NET, you can ignore the errors in a standard
Windows application. You just can't ignore errors in an add-in and expect to get it
connected to a client. However, you should note that if you try to ignore errors,
even in a standard Windows application, the code beyond the error does not
compile, and you won't be able to get to it. Figure 4-7 contains code with an
error in it. Note that I have placed a breakpoint on every line following the error.

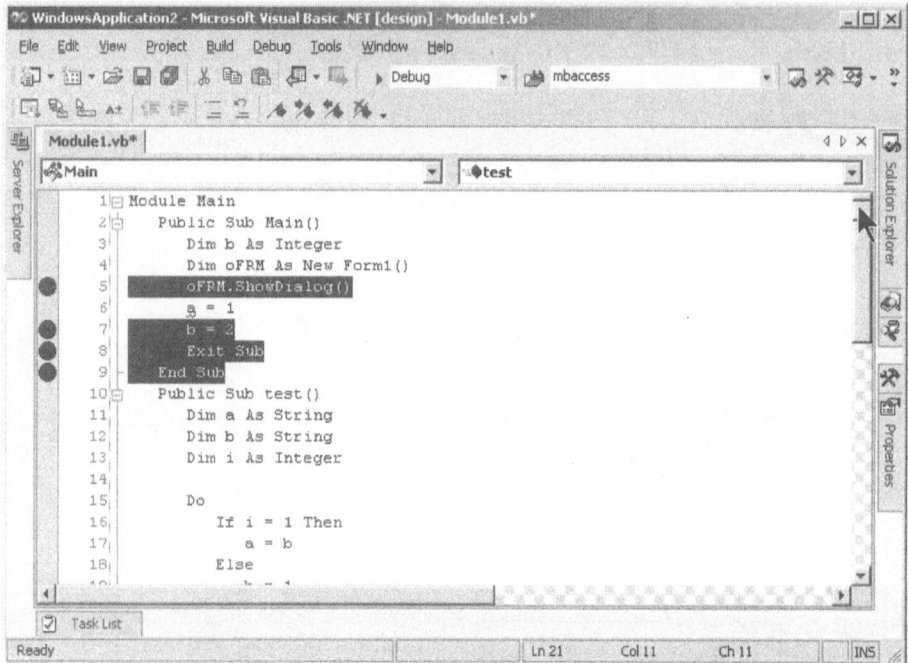

Figure 4-7. Breakpoints beyond an error line

Next, I run the application, ignoring the errors. Sub Main runs and loads the instance of Form1 (oFrm.ShowDialog), but control never reaches the lines after the line with the error in it. In fact, all breakpoints are ignored, as shown in Figure 4-8, and execution does not even stop on the line that displays the form. I think the lesson to be learned here is that in .NET, you must correct your compile errors before attempting to debug your code. In VB 6.0, the ability to compile on demand was a very useful feature at times, but that type of functionality seems to be gone in .NET.

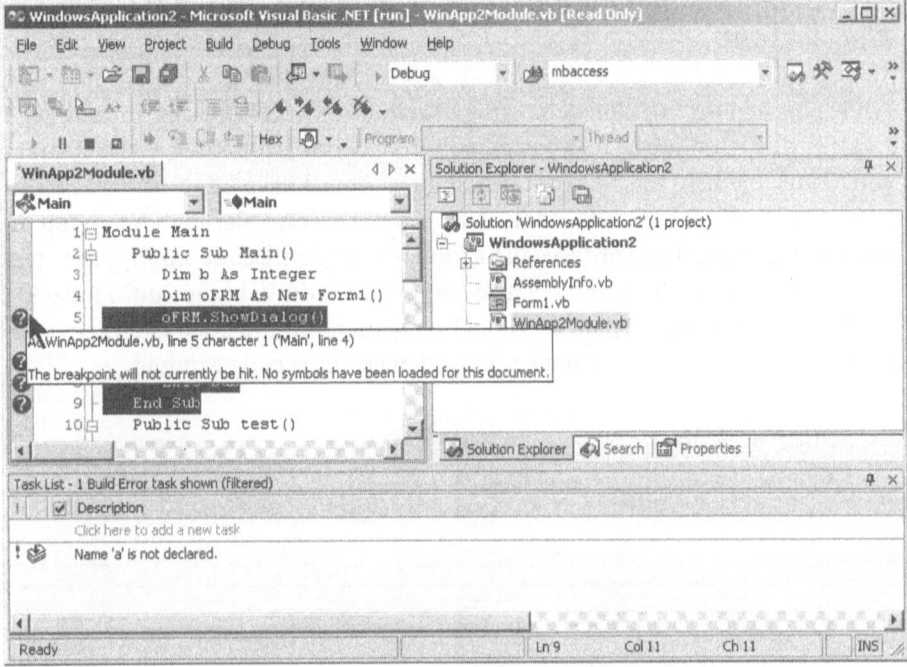

Figure 4-8. Breakpoints ignored in bad code

Stopping the Debugging Session

To bring the debugging session to an orderly halt, select Debug ➤ Stop Debugging or click the Stop Debugging button. This is done in the add-in (server) session of .NET. When you click the Stop Debugging option, the second session (client) of .NET shuts down automatically.

> **NOTE** *You should always select the Stop Debugging menu option or click the Stop Debugging button in the add-in (server) instance of .NET, rather than closing the second (client) instance manually. Remember that the server instance automatically started the second instance, and it expects it to be there when you finally stop debugging the add-in. If the server instance of .NET does not find the second instance, it prints all kinds of extraneous error messages in the Output window.*

Stepping Through Code and Watching the Results in the Client

While you step through the debugging of an add-in, you can position your .NET sessions and windows so that you can observe what's happening in the client as you execute code in the add-in server. For example, I have a debugging session going in Figure 4-9. I've reduced the size of the IDEs and placed them on top of each other, so that I can observe the action in the client's code window as I step through the add-in. In Figure 4-9, I've stopped the add-in in the PutCodeBack method, which was called by the BlockDelete method. You'll see that execution has stopped just before the block is pasted back to the code window.

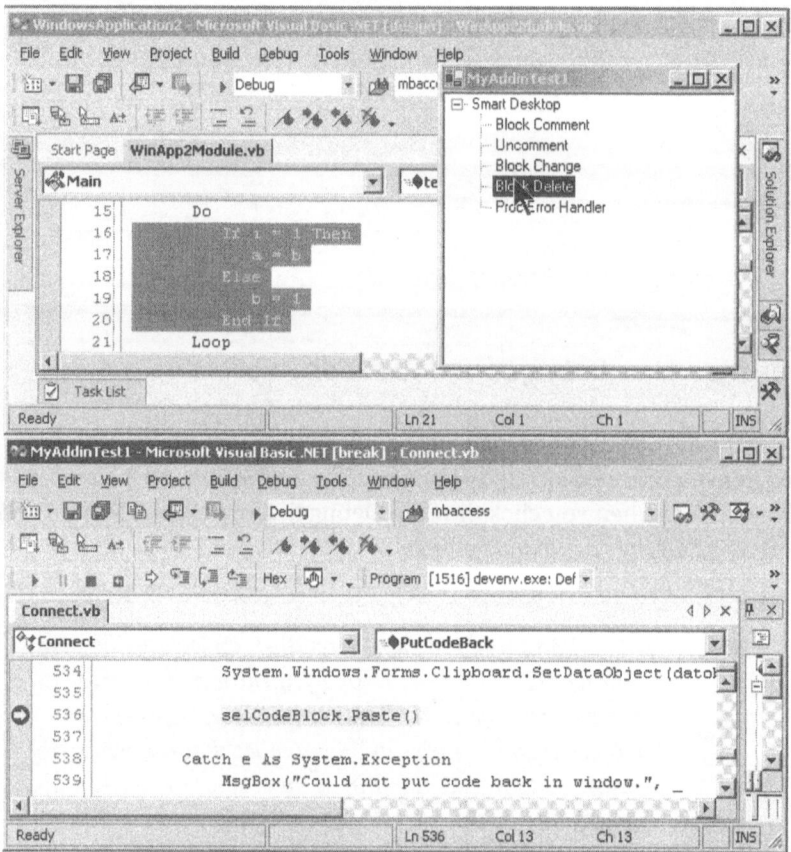

Figure 4-9. Just before pasting the deleted block

Next, I've stepped through the selCodeBlock.Paste instruction, and in Figure 4-10, you can see that the paste of the code has taken place and the window has been repainted immediately. Thus, you can see immediately the action that the add-in has effected, as it completes it.

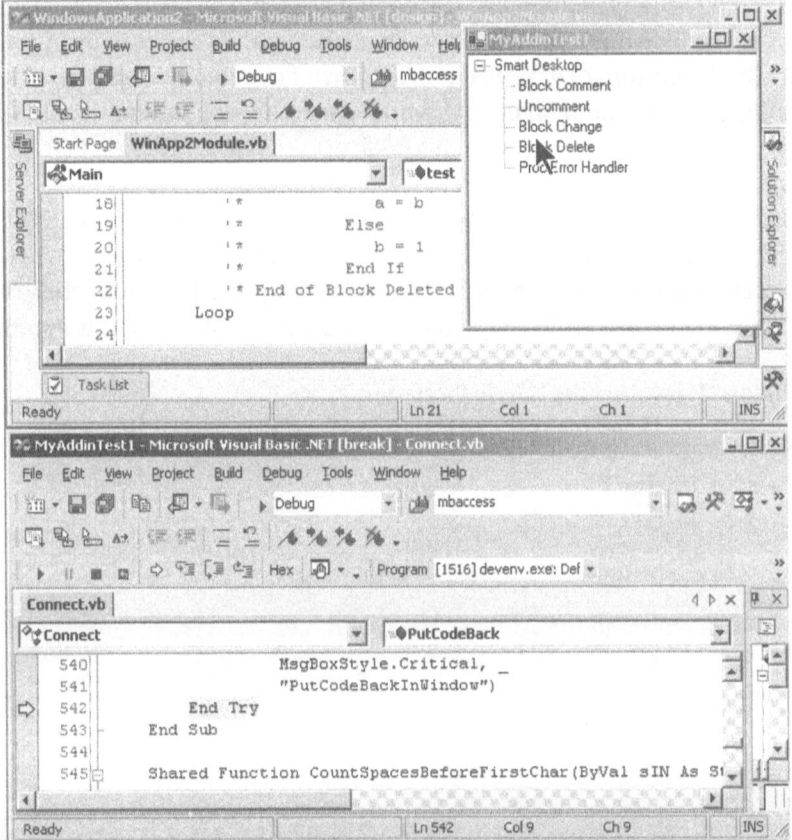

Figure 4-10. Deleted block pasted back to the code window

Error Handling in the Add-in

There appears to be no better place to discuss error handling than in this chapter on debugging. I have already stressed the point of placing error handlers in every method that could possibly encounter an error.

Visual Studio .NET introduces true structured error handling. The error-handling methodology that was used in previous versions of Visual Basic will still work in VB .NET—you just can't mix the new Try/Catch structured handling with the old On Error GoTo ErrHandler construct in the same procedure. Most of my peers decry the evils of the GoTo statement. I certainly understand the shortcomings of GoTo, but I've never shared their total disdain for it. I, along with others, believe there are places for GoTo, albeit not many. VB is missing a "basic" statement, Continue, which allows you to go to the bottom of a For/Next, Do/Loop, and While/Wend loop. Without this statement, which C/C++ and other languages such as Clipper (dBase Compiler) have, GoTo provides the only easy way to get to the bottom of a loop. Sometimes, a loop that is already nested to several levels can only be made more complex by trying to maintain a structured approach for getting to the bottom of it. Well, enough of that! I'm beating a dead horse here. Regardless of your stand on the old syntax, assuming you programmed in earlier versions of VB, the code in this book uses the new structured error-handling code.

Because this book is not meant to explain all of the new things in .NET, I won't go into a lot of detail about the Try/Catch coding construct. There are two ways that I normally use error-handling code. First, I might include the whole procedure's code in a Try/Catch sequence. Listing 4-1 illustrates this approach.

Listing 4-1. Protecting the Whole Procedure

```
Public Sub CatchAnyProcedureError()
    Dim s As String
    Dim I As Integer

    Try
        For i = 1 to 10
            S = s & "a"
        Next i

        ' add as many lines as needed

    Catch e As System.Exception
        MsgBox("We encountered an error: " & e.Message)
    End Try
End Sub
```

Obviously, the method in Listing 4-1 does nothing but illustrate how to protect the whole subroutine in case of an error. The second way that I normally use error-handling code is to specifically catch errors in a small section of a method where I might try opening a file and want to take action within the context of that small section of code. The section of code shown in Listing 4-2 illustrates a sequence of code in which an error will be raised if the file name being erased does not exist. Likewise, if the new file cannot be created or written to, an error will be raised. You must always protect code that does file handling.

Listing 4-2. Selective Error Handling

```
    Private Sub Test2()
        Dim count As Integer
        Dim fileHandle As Integer
```

```
' might have a code sequence here
'....
'....


For count = 1 To 5
    fileHandle = FreeFile()

    ' if the file being killed does not exist, an error
    ' will be raised.
    ' also, if a file can't be opened, ignore and try the next
    Try
        Kill("TEST" & count & ".TXT")
        FileOpen(fileHandle, "TEST" & count & ".TXT", OpenMode.Output)
        PrintLine(fileHandle, "This is a sample.")
        FileClose(fileHandle)
    Catch e As System.Exception
        ' ignore the error
    End Try
Next

' more code...
'...
End Sub
```

Again, the code does not really do anything or make a lot of sense, but it does illustrate the protection of a small block of code within a larger procedure.

Automating Production of Error-Handling Code

Because this book's topic is writing add-ins, let's add more functionality to the test add-in you created and enhanced in Chapters 2 and 3 to automate insertion of error-handling code.

First, you will add a new method to the Connect class named GenLocalErrorTrap, which is shown in Listing 4-3. This new method will retrieve the selected procedure and insert a Try/Catch error-handling construct around all of the executable code in the procedure. It does this by looking for the first line of executable code in the procedure and then inserting the Try statement. It then looks for the End Sub or End Function. Upon finding it, it will insert the Catch statement prior to writing the End statement to the output string. It will then put the code back into the active code window.

Listing 4-3. GenLocalErrorTrap Method

```
Shared Sub GenLocalErrorTrap()
    Dim sLine As String
    Dim sTemp As String
    Dim sTemp2 As String
    Dim sWord As String
    Dim i As Long
    Dim nL As Integer
    Dim bFound As Boolean
    Dim sTempLine As String
    Dim sProcType As String
    Dim sProcName As String
    Dim bFoundDefLine As Boolean

    Try
        sTemp = GetCodeFromWindow()

        sTemp2 = ""

        nL = MLCount(sTemp, 0)
        bFound = False

        For i = 1 To nL

            ' look for the first line of code
            sLine = MemoLine(sTemp, 0, i)

            ' get the procname to make the goto label unique
            If Not bFoundDefLine Then
                If InStr(sLine, "Sub ") > 0 Then
                    sProcType = "Sub"
                ElseIf InStr(sLine, "Function ") > 0 Then
                    sProcType = "Function"
                Else
                    sTemp2 = sTemp2 & sLine & vbCrLf
                    GoTo JustOutPutThisLine
                End If
                bFoundDefLine = True
                sTempLine = sLine
                Do While Trim$(sTempLine) <> ""
                    sWord = GetToken(sTempLine, "_")
                    ' when we find the Proc type, term the loop
```

```
                    ' and retrieve the name next below
                    If sWord = "Sub" Or sWord = "Function" Then Exit Do
                    If Trim$(sWord) = "" Then Exit Do
                    sProcName = sWord
            Loop
            sProcName = GetToken(sTempLine, "_")
    End If


    If Not bFound Then
        If InStr(sLine, "Sub ") > 0 Or _
            InStr(sLine, "Function ") > 0 Or _
            InStr(sLine, "Global ") > 0 Or _
            InStr(sLine, "Const ") > 0 Or _
            InStr(sLine, "Dim ") > 0 Then
                sTemp2 = sTemp2 & sLine & vbCrLf
        ElseIf Left$(Trim$(sLine), 1) = "'" Then
                sTemp2 = sTemp2 & sLine & vbCrLf
        ElseIf Trim$(sLine) = "" Then
                sTemp2 = sTemp2 & sLine & vbCrLf
        Else
            bFound = True
            sTemp2 = sTemp2 & vbCrLf & "        Try" & vbCrLf
            If Trim$(sLine) <> "End " & sProcType Then
                    sTemp2 = sTemp2 & sLine & vbCrLf
            Else
                sTemp2 = sTemp2 & _
                    "        Catch e as System.Exception" & vbCrLf
                sTemp2 = sTemp2 &_
                    "            MsgBox(" & Chr(34) & "Error in " &

                    sProcName & ": " & Chr(34) & " & _
                    e.Message)" & vbCrLf
                sTemp2 = sTemp2 & "        End Try" & vbCrLf
                sTemp2 = sTemp2 & sLine & vbCrLf
            End If
        End If
    Else

        If InStr(sLine, "End " & sProcType) > 0 Then
            sTemp2 = sTemp2 & _
                "        Catch e as System.Exception" & vbCrLf
            sTemp2 = sTemp2 & _
                "            MsgBox(" & Chr(34) & "Error in " & _
```

```
                                    sProcName & ": " & Chr(34) & " & _
                                    e.Message)" & vbCrLf
                            sTemp2 = sTemp2 & "        End Try" & vbCrLf
                            sTemp2 = sTemp2 & sLine & vbCrLf
                            Exit For
                    Else
                            sTemp2 = sTemp2 & sLine & vbCrLf
                    End If
            End If
JustOutPutThisLine:
        Next

        ' now the proc with err code added is ready to paste
        PutCodeBack(sTemp2)
        Exit Sub
    Catch e As System.Exception
        MsgBox("Error in GenLocalErrorTrap: " & e.Message)
    End Try
End Sub
```

Next, you will insert another supporting method named GetToken, which is shown in Listing 4-4. This is a parsing function that retrieves the next token from a source line. The comments in the code describe how this function is called. You can pass it a delimiter or a set of characters that are not delimiters. This function is another of the library procedures provided with this book's code.

NOTE *GetToken consumes the source string, which is passed by reference. This means that as token is returned, the token is removed from the front of the string. Therefore, if you want to maintain the original string, you must save a copy of it before your first call to GetToken.*

Listing 4-4. GetToken

```
Shared Function GetToken(ByRef srcline As String, _
                    ByVal rsNonDelimiters As String, _
                    Optional ByVal rsDel As String = "N") _
                    As String
    '-----
    ' If rsDel = "N" then the rsNondelimiters is a list of non delimiters
    ' which is added to a list of AN Chars (a-z, A-Z, 0-9), which are
    ' always assumed to be non delimiters.
```

```
' If rsDel="D" then rsNonDelimiters is the list of delimiters, anything
' else in the string is assumed to be non delimiter.
' Get Next word from srcLine.  An alphanumeric and any character
' found in strDelimtrs is a valid char for the word.  i.e. a char
' which is not alphanumeric and not found in the delimiter string
' will terminate the word.  If space is not a delimiter it must be
' included in the strNonDelimitrs.
' Typical call is:
'       srcLine = GetToken(srcLine, " ().!" or
'       srcLine = GetToken(srcLine, " ,")
' where space and are the delimiters
' Any non alphanumeric and not in the " ().!" would terminate the string
' To include " in the set of allowable chars, concatenate
'  chr(34) with the' other non delimiters.
' If non delimiters are not supplied, don't compare for them
' and performance is increased...
'-----
Dim n_w As String ' staging area for return string
Dim FC As String ' first char of string
Dim lsTemp As String
Dim lsTemp2 As String
Const AN_DIGITS = "abcdefghijklmnopqrstuvwxyz" & _
                  "ABCDEFGHIJKLMNOPQRSTUVWXYZ1234567890"
Try
    n_w = ""
    If rsDel = "N" Then
        lsTemp2 = AN_DIGITS & rsNonDelimiters
    Else
        lsTemp2 = rsNonDelimiters
    End If

    Do While Trim$(srcline) <> ""
        FC = Left$(srcline, 1)
        lsTemp = "*" & FC & "*"
        If rsDel = "N" Then
            If Not (lsTemp2 Like lsTemp) Then
                ' save all but first char for next call
                srcline = Mid(srcline, 2)
                If Trim$(n_w) <> "" Then
                    GetToken = n_w
                    Exit Function
                End If
```

```
                    Else
                        n_w = n_w & FC
                        srcline = Mid(srcline, 2)
                    End If
                Else
                    If (lsTemp2 Like lsTemp) Then
                        ' save all but first char for next call
                        srcline = Mid(srcline, 2)
                        If Trim$(n_w) <> "" Then
                            GetToken = n_w
                            Exit Function
                        End If
                    Else
                        n_w = n_w & FC
                        srcline = Mid(srcline, 2)
                    End If
                End If
            Loop

            GetToken = n_w
            Exit Function
        Catch e As System.Exception
            MsgBox("Error in GetToken: " & e.Message)
            GetToken = n_w
        End Try
    End Function
```

Next, you add another node to the TreeView named Proc Error Handler, as shown in Figure 4-11. Follow the same procedure for adding a child node to the TreeView that you learned in Chapter 3.

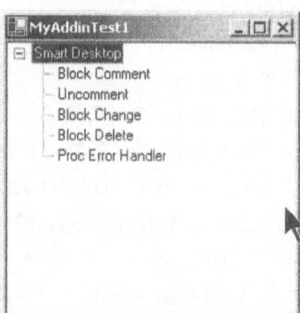

Figure 4-11. Adding the Proc Error Handler node to the TreeView

Finally, add a new Case statement to the AfterSelect event in the frmTreeView. This new code is shown in bold in Listing 4-5.

Listing 4-5. Error Handling in the AfterSelect Event

```
Private Sub tvMenu_AfterSelect(ByVal sender As Object, _
         ByVal e As  System.Windows.Forms.TreeViewEventArgs) _
         Handles tvMenu.AfterSelect
    Dim i As Integer

    Select Case UCase$(e.Node.Text)
        Case "SMART DESKTOP" 'ignore root clicks
        Case "BLOCK COMMENT"
            Call Connect.BlockComment()
        Case "UNCOMMENT"
            Call Connect.BlockUnComment()
        Case "BLOCK CHANGE"
            Call Connect.BlockChange()
        Case "BLOCK DELETE"
            Call Connect.BlockDelete()
        Case "PROC ERROR HANDLER"
            Call Connect.GenLocalErrorTrap()
        Case Else
            MsgBox("Please click on a Child Node.", _
                    MsgBoxStyle.Information, "Unknown Request")
    End Select
End Sub
```

Testing the Error Handler Generator

After all of the code has been successfully added to the add-in, press F5 to test the new code. A second version of Visual Studio .NET will start. I have created a standard Windows application (WindowsApplication2) to use in testing the add-in. It has several procedures of dummy code, which you will find in the code for this chapter. Once you have selected the test project, go to the Add-in Manager and connect the add-in. Next, select Tools ➤ Smart Desktop. This will cause the add-in menu TreeView form to be loaded. Open the nodes of the TreeView. Finally, select the whole Sub Test, as shown in Figure 4-12, and click the Proc Error Handler TreeView node.

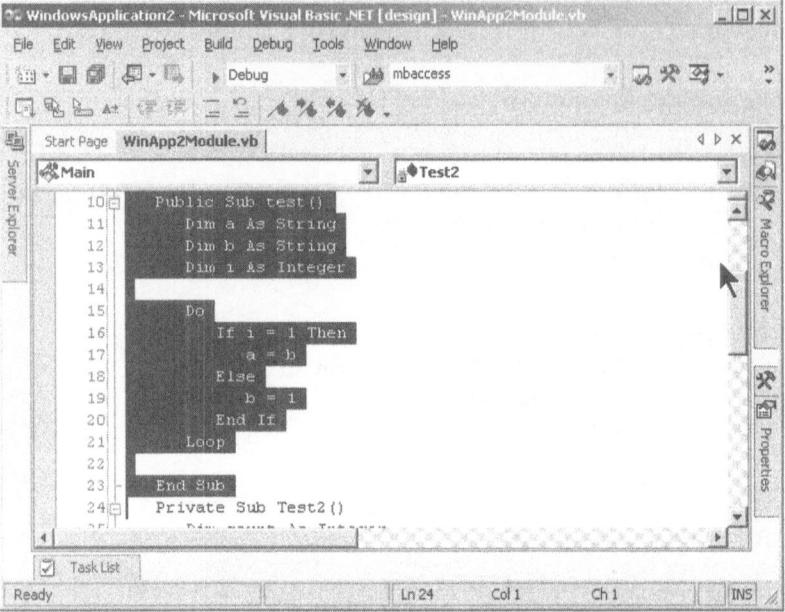

Figure 4-12. Select the procedure to receive an error handler.

The error handler will be automatically added to the procedure, as shown in Figure 4-13. A simple exercise that you can try on your own would be to clone the GenLocalErrorTrap method, rename the cloned method, and modify it to block only a selected block of code. You would then add another node to the TreeView menu and add a call to the newly cloned method in the AfterSelect event of the TreeView.

Again, in this enhancement to the add-in, you have been able to add new functionality, or business logic, without having to have any interface to the .NET extensibility model. By building and reusing the same basic library methods (GetCodeFromWindow and PutCodeBack), you are able to concentrate on the creative part of building add-in functionality, which manipulates blocks of code in the text editor of Visual Studio .NET. Believe me, there are unlimited things you can do with the selected code block once you have it extracted into a string. All you have to do is put your thinking cap on (or keep it on). In VBCommander, I have added well over 100 new features to the VB 6.0 IDE. Almost every one of them was created as a result of encountering something repetitive that I needed to automate when operating with blocks of code. Necessity really is the mother of invention.

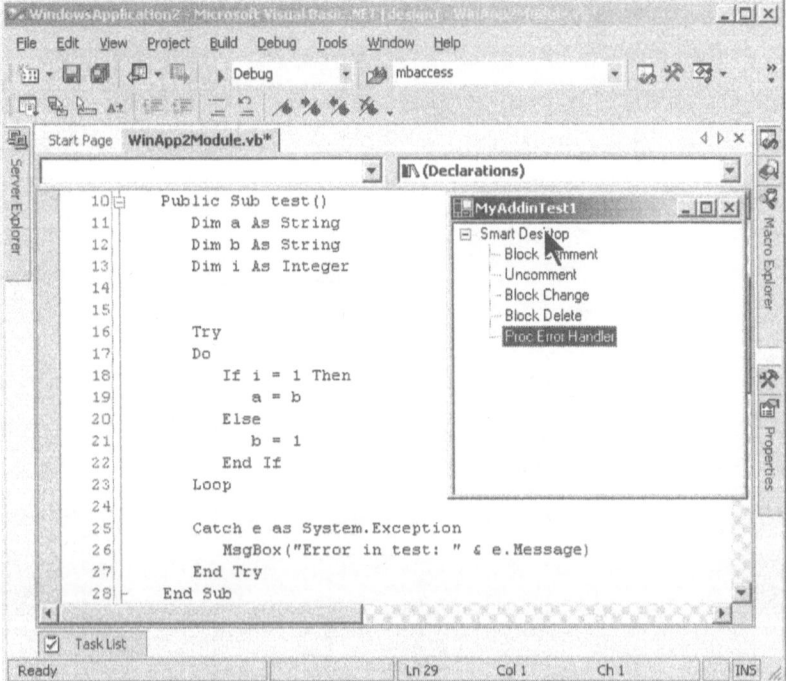

Figure 4-13. Error handler placed in Sub Test()

Summary

In this chapter, you saw how to set up the debugging environment in the Options dialog box. You learned that there are both positives and negatives in the debugger, and you explored ways to work around some of the negatives. You saw how to step through the debugging of an add-in, observing the results that the add-in is effecting on the client IDE as it progresses through the add-in's code. There is no great mystery to debugging an add-in; it just requires that you coordinate the operation of two instances of .NET. But you learned that enhancements have been made to facilitate this process.

Finally, you explored .NET's structured error handling and enhanced your add-in to automatically add error handling to a selected procedure.

In Chapter 5, you will move up a level in complexity, as you learn how to manipulate code in code windows. Chapter 5 is one of the most useful chapters in the book because you will probably build more features to do code manipulation than any other single type of functionality.

Manipulating Code in Windows

"What matters most in life is not so much how much time we have, but what we do with the time we are given."
—*Author Unknown*

THUS FAR, IN WORKING WITH CODE in the IDE's Text Editor windows, I've made very few references to the extensibility object of Visual Studio .NET. I've done this for two reasons. First, I wanted to get quickly and simply into building some usable functionality in an add-in. Second, I wanted to demonstrate the use of some common methods that you can reuse most of the time for retrieving code from a code window, performing some operation on the code, and subsequently putting it back into the code window without having to constantly be concerned with the complex syntax of the extensibility object. I suspect that the library routines I've provided for retrieval and replacement of code in a window will work for you 90 percent of the time you want to work on code.

In this chapter, I concentrate on the text-handling objects in the extensibility model. There will obviously be times when you will need to do something to or with code windows that goes beyond simply retrieving and putting back code. Therefore, you must explore some of the extensive details of the text-handling objects. In this chapter, I introduce you to the Documents collection and the Document object as a lead-in to learning how to control the Visual Studio .NET Code Editor.

TIP   *I don't want to jump ahead into the subject of macros (which is reserved for Chapter 8). However, if you're already familiar with the use of macros in Visual Studio .NET, you can take the code from the short example snippets in the next few topics, enclose it with Sub/End Sub, and actually execute these examples in the Macros IDE. Because I'm illustrating code snippets in the context of an add-in, if you choose to execute the code in the Macro Explorer, substitute DTE for oVB wherever you find it in the code samples.*

The Documents Collection

The Documents collection contains all of the Document objects in the IDE. Each object represents an open document. You can reference all of the open documents by looping through the Documents collection. Executing the code sample in Listing 5-1 in an add-in closes all open documents that have been previously saved.

> **NOTE** *When DTE is the parent object in sample code, and I am discussing code within an add-in, I will always use the application object and substitute the variable name oVB for DTE. You will remember from Chapter 3 that I used oVB as a short name for the application object. DTE will be used as the real object when I discuss code examples in Chapter 8.*

Listing 5-1. Closing Saved Documents

```
' Close all saved documents.
Dim i As Integer

With oVB
    Try
        For i = 1 To .Documents.Count
            If .Documents.Item(i).Saved Then
                .Documents.Item(i).Close()
            End If
        Next I
    Catch
    ' Ignore any error we raise attempting to close
    End Try
End With
```

The Document Object

The Document object refers to an open document or designer in the IDE. This basically means the code windows, form designers, and other windows that are not tool windows. Additionally, these windows have an area in which text can be edited. The Document object has properties, methods, and events, all of which can be called members, with which you can manipulate the active document or the document that you make the active document. If you are editing a text file in the Visual Studio editor, a TextDocument object is associated with it. The default property for a Document object is the Name property. You can reference the object by using oVB.Documents.Item(...) or oVB.ActiveDocument.

A simple example of referencing the active document in the IDE is shown in Listing 5-2. If you execute this code in an add-in, a message box will display the name of the active document or code window, including its full path, and a text message denoting whether the document is read-only or writable.

Listing 5-2. Document Object Example

```
Dim doc As Document
Dim s As String

Set doc = oVB.ActiveDocument
s = "Active Document: "
s = s & doc.Path & doc.Name & " is " & Iif(doc.ReadOnly, "Read-Only", _
    "Writable")
MsgBox(s)
```

Manipulating the Code Editor

The Visual Studio .NET Code Editor is a sophisticated text editor that handles the text editing for the .NET languages, such VB .NET, Visual C++ .NET, and Visual C# .NET. Text is written to a buffer that displays in a text document. You can use the automation objects of the Visual Studio .NET Code Editor to control the operation of the text behind the scenes in the text buffer as well as the view.

NOTE *Two entities are being controlled by the Visual Studio .NET Code Editor. First, there is the text displayed in the Code Editor that you are viewing. Second, there is a text buffer that is being manipulated behind the scenes. Two different automation objects control these two distinct objects, TextPoint and EditPoint, which I discuss in the following sections. TextSelection refers to the visible text selection. You can assign multiple TextSelection objects, but they always refer to the same selected text. You can have multiple EditPoint objects, and they can all have different positions in the text buffer.*

You can use four major objects in the Code Editor to control the operation of the editor:

- *TextSelection object:* Use this object to manipulate text in the visible document. The TextSelection object represents the insertion point where the caret is currently positioned or the selected text in the visible document.

- *TextPoint object:* This object allows you to find locations in a document. You can use the TextPoint object to find line numbers, characters in a line, absolute character locations from the beginning of a document, and display columns. TextPoint objects operate on text displayed in a code editor, which is different from the EditPoint object (described next). When you edit a document, TextPoint objects do not move relative to their surrounding text. This means that if text is inserted before a TextPoint, the value of its AbsoluteCharOffset property is incremented to reflect its new location because the TextPoint has moved further down in the document.

- *EditPoint object:* This object is similar to the TextPoint object, but it can be moved around and can modify text in the text buffer.

- *VirtualPoint object:* This object is similar to the TextPoint object except that it has an added capability to query virtual space locations in a document. TextSelection.StartPoint and TextSelection.EndPoint return VirtualPoint objects. *Virtual space* is the empty space to the right of existing lines of text, and virtual points exist in this area.

The TextSelection and EditPoint objects are the two main objects with which you can manipulate code in the Visual Studio .NET Code Editor. You can use these objects to

- Select, delete, add, and move text around in the text buffer or the visible code window.

- Move the caret, or insertion point, around in the text buffer or the visible code window.

- Indent text in the text buffer or the visible code window.

- Add, remove, and navigate to bookmarks in the Code Editor.

- Find and replace text based on a specified pattern.

- Create an outline section in the text buffer and visible code window. To create an outline means to create a Region, which can be collapsed (hidden) or expanded.

- Retrieve information about the text, such as the top and bottom of the document, text position, and so forth.

TextSelection Object

The properties and methods of the TextSelection object are analogous to editor commands in the Visual Studio IDE. Like the IDE, text selection operations are affected by the Code Editor's global state. Any operation attempting to modify a text document will fail if it affects any characters contained in a read-only block or if the text document itself is read-only.

If you place the code snippet in Listing 5-3 in an add-in, it will comment a selected block of Visual Basic code using the TextSelection object. This snippet is designed to be used in an add-in, but you could also use it in a macro by changing oVB to DTE.

Listing 5-3. Using the TextSelection Object

```
Dim sel As TextSelection = DTE.ActiveDocument.Selection()
Dim stpt As EditPoint = sel.TopPoint.CreateEditPoint()
Dim endpt As TextPoint = sel.BottomPoint

Try
    Do While (stpt.LessThan(endpt))
        stpt.Insert("'")
        stpt.LineDown()
        stpt.StartOfLine()
    Loop
Catch
End Try
```

Listing 5-3 illustrates the use of several properties and methods of the TextSelection object:

- *Insert:* Moves the selection object to the end of the current line.

- *LineDown:* Moves the pointer to the selected line down the number of lines indicated by the parameter passed to the method. The default parameter is 1. Although it is not illustrated in this example, the LineUp method moves the line pointer up a number of lines.

- *StartOfLine:* Moves the object to the beginning of the current line.

Listing 5-3 also illustrates the use of the EditPoint and TextPoint objects. The lines of code extracted from the larger snippet set a pointer to the beginning of the selection by creating an EditPoint object:

```
Dim stpt As EditPoint = sel.TopPoint.CreateEditPoint()
```

The next line creates a TextPoint object that points to the bottom of the selected text block:

```
Dim endpt As TextPoint = sel.BottomPoint
```

VirtualPoint Object

You can use the VirtualPoint object to manipulate text beyond the right margin (the left margin in bidirectional windows) of the text document. The code snippet in Listing 5-4 inserts a comment at the end of the line when the cursor is positioned anywhere in a line of code.

Listing 5-4. Insert Method of the TextSelection Object

```
Dim objSel As TextSelection = oVB.ActiveDocument.Selection
objSel.EndOfLine()
objSel.Insert(" ' End of line comment")
```

For example, you can position the cursor anywhere in the following line:

```
intNum = 1
```

Now if you execute the code snippet using the VirtualPoint object shown in the previous line of code, the line of code will look like this:

```
intNum = 1 ' End of line comment
```

With the VirtualPoint object, you can find and display (for illustrative purposes) several points within a selected line of code. For example, the block of code in Listing 5-5 will display three different values.

Listing 5-5. Using the VirtualPoint Object

```
' VirtualPoint Example
' Before running this example, open a text document.
Dim objSel As TextSelection = DTE.ActiveDocument.Selection
Dim objActive As VirtualPoint = objSel.ActivePoint

' Collapse the selection to the beginning of the line.
objSel.StartOfLine()

' objActive is "live", tied to the position of the actual selection,
' so it will reflect the new position.
Dim iCol As Long = objActive.DisplayColumn

' Move the selection to the end of the line.
objSel.EndOfLine()

' Display the DisplayColumn
MsgBox("DisplayColumn: " & iCol & Chr(10) & _
        "Line length: " & (objActive.DisplayColumn - iCol) & _
        " display characters." & Chr(10) & _
        "VirtualCharOffset value: " & objActive.VirtualCharOffset &_
            vbCr &"VirtualDisplayColumn value: " & _
        objActive.VirtualDisplayColumn)
```

In Figure 5-1, you will note a block of code with the cursor positioned at the beginning of line 88 in the code editor.

 **NOTE** *To illustrate the VirtualPoint object, I am using the macro facility to run the code example. It is easier to do that for this simple example than to use an add-in. The code will execute in an add-in in exactly the same way that it will execute in the Macro Explorer. The only modification required in the code is changing DTE to oVB. Chapter 8 explores the macro facility in depth.*

If you run the VirtualPoint example code snippet in Listing 5-5, you will see the MessageBox shown in Figure 5-2.

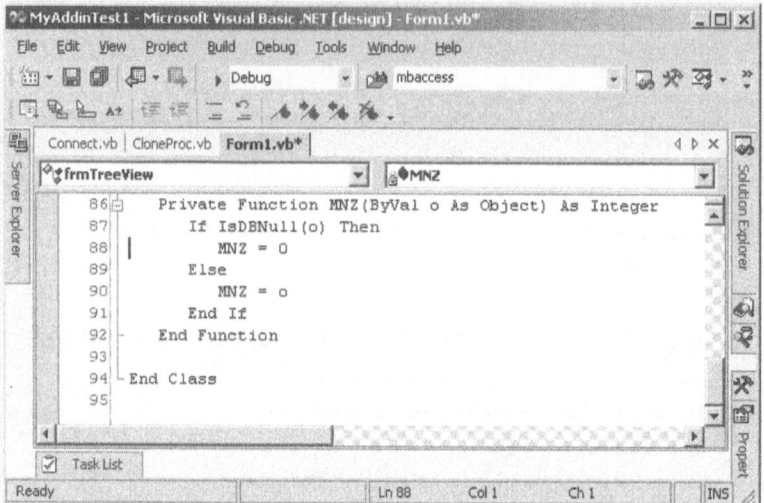

Figure 5-1. Code sample to use the VirtualPoint example

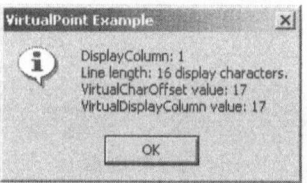

Figure 5-2. VirtualPoint code example message

Now what has this example shown you? The first line of the MessageBox shows the original DisplayColumn. You can see in the VirtualPoint code snippet that the DisplayColumn is set to column 1 by this line of code:

```
' Collapse the selection to the beginning of the line.
objSel.StartOfLine()
```

After capturing "iCol", the code shown next moves to the end of the line of code.

Next, the second line of the MessageBox indicates that there are 16 DisplayColumns, including the white space at the beginning of the line. The third line conveys the value of the VirtualCharOffset, which in this case is the same as the new DisplayColumn value. The VirtualCharOffset returns the number of characters the VirtualPoint is from the left side of a line in the document. The fourth line of the MessageBox conveys the value of the VirtualDisplayColumn. This is the display column of the current position.

Practical Uses for Editor Automation Objects

At this point, you have only scratched the surface with respect to the large number of properties and methods you can use to manipulate code in editor windows. It is beyond the scope of this chapter to investigate each and every one of those properties and methods. You can do that on your own as you find that you have a specific need I have not covered. MSDN for Visual Studio .NET contains a hierarchical chart of all of the objects within the automation model.

Now I want to illustrate how to use some of the objects, methods, and properties that I believe you'll find most useful. Again, you'll place them into reusable code methods so that you can continue to use them in your development of add-in functionality. As I've stated more than once, this will allow you to quickly implement new functionality without concerning yourself with the details of the extensibility model.

Retrieving Code from a Document

The Selection property of the TextSelection object returns an object representing the current selection on the object. For example, if a user selects a block of text in a document or code window, the code snippet in Listing 5-6 will retrieve the selected block and place it into a string object named selCodeBlock.

Listing 5-6. Retrieving Code from the Text Editor

```
Dim selCodeBlock As TextSelection  = oVB.ActiveDocument.Selection()
Dim S As String
S = selCodeBlock.Text
```

The variable (object) S will now contain the text the user selected in the active document or code window. I illustrated the use of the Selection property in Chapter 3, when I demonstrated the GetCodeFromWindow method shown in Listing 5-7.

Listing 5-7. Retrieving Code from a Document

```
Shared Function GetCodeFromWindow() As String
    Dim s As String
    Dim selCodeBlock As TextSelection = oVB.ActiveDocument.Selection()

    Try
        GetCodeFromWindow = selCodeBlock.Text
```

```
        Catch e As System.Exception
            MsgBox("Error: " & e.Message, MsgBoxStyle.Critical, _
                "GetCodeFromWindow")
        End Try
    End Function
```

Calling GetCodeFromWindow, as shown in the following code snippet, will
return in the variable S the block of code the user selected in the Text Editor
window.

```
Dim S As String
S = GetCodeFromWindow()
```

Putting Code Back into the Window

The second method in the pair that retrieves and replaces code in the Code
Editor is the PutCodeBack method shown in Listing 5-8.

Listing 5-8. Replacing Code in the Text Editor Window

```
    Shared Sub PutCodeBack(ByVal s As String)
        Dim selCodeBlock As TextSelection
        Dim datobj As New System.Windows.Forms.DataObject()

        Try
            selCodeBlock = CType(oVB.ActiveDocument.Selection(), _
                EnvDTE.TextSelection)
            datobj.SetData(System.Windows.Forms.DataFormats.Text, s)
            System.Windows.Forms.Clipboard.SetDataObject(datobj)

            selCodeBlock.Paste ()

        Catch e As System.Exception
            MsgBox("Could not put code back in window.", _
                MsgBoxStyle.Critical, _
                "PutCodeBackInWindow")
        End Try
    End Sub
```

This method not only illustrates the use of the TextSelection object, but it
also shows how to put text onto the Clipboard. In VB 6.0, you could place code on
the Clipboard with this one line of code:

```
Clipboard.SetText S
```

In VB .NET, placing code on the Clipboard is a little more involved, as shown by this snippet from the PutCodeBack method, which I demonstrated in Chapter 3:

```
Dim datobj As New System.Windows.Forms.DataObject()
datobj.SetData(System.Windows.Forms.DataFormats.Text, s)
```

Once the code has been placed on the Clipboard, you can use the Paste method of the TextSelection object to replace the code in the ActiveSelection.

Inserting Code at the Top of a Module

In the process of building add-in functionality, you will probably encounter the need to build and insert module-level variables into a code module. This is a fairly common requirement for more advanced add-ins. The code in Listing 5-9 illustrates how to do this.

Listing 5-9. Inserting Module-Level Variables

```
01      Dim objTextDoc As TextDocument
02      Dim objMovePt As EditPoint
03      Dim objEditPt As EditPoint, iCtr As Integer
04
05      ' Get a handle to the current document and create an EditPoint.
07      objTextDoc = DTE.ActiveDocument.Object
08      objEditPt = objTextDoc.StartPoint.CreateEditPoint
09      objEditPt.LineDown(1)
10
11      ' Insert a new variable line
12      objEditPt.Insert("   Public s As String" & vbCr)
```

Line 07 sets a TextDocument object (pointer) to the current document in the text editor. Line 08 moves the insertion point to the top of the document by creating an EditPoint object. Because you want to insert the new variable within the module (in other words, after the module definition line), line 09 moves the insertion point down one line. Line 12 simply uses the EditPoint object's Insert method to insert the new module-level variable. Figure 5-3 shows the sample module before the code to insert the variable is executed.

Once the code to insert the variable is executed, the code window will appear as shown in Figure 5-4. The inserted line is highlighted. Obviously, this is a very simple example that includes no Imports or Inherits statements. If either of these statements were included, you would need to move down past them before inserting the variable.

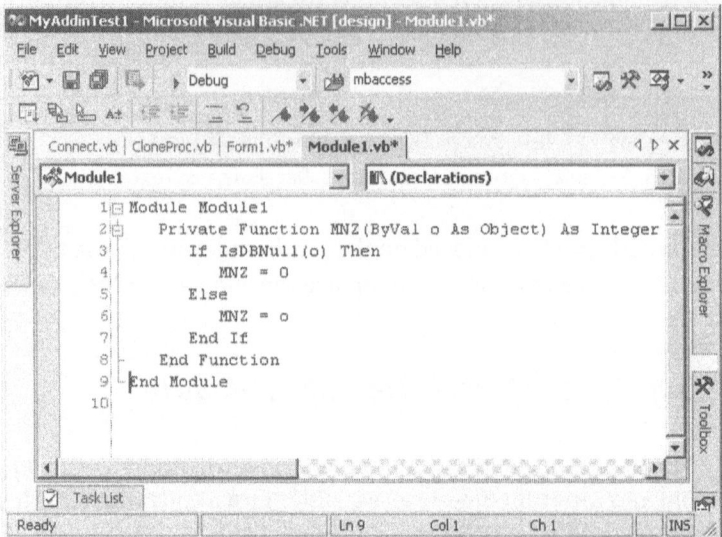

Figure 5-3. Module before the insertion of a module-level variable

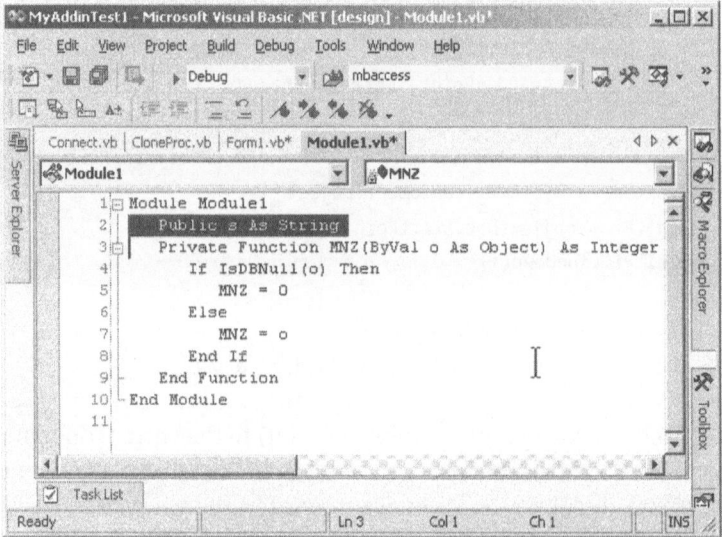

Figure 5-4. Module after the variable is inserted

Adding a Procedure to the Bottom of the Document

There are many times when you will need to add a new procedure to a class or module. First I illustrate how to do so, and then you will enhance your add-in with some more useful functionality. To add a new procedure to the active code window, use the code in Listing 5-10.

Listing 5-10. Adding a Procedure to the Bottom of a Document

```
Dim objTD As TextDocument = oVB.ActiveDocument.Object
Dim objEP As EditPoint = objTD.EndPoint.CreateEditPoint

' We are past the end of the last line of the document
' move back in front of the End Module/Class
objEP.LineUp(1)
objEP.Insert("Public Function Test()" & vbCr & _
                "     ' test comment" & vbCr & _
                "End Function" & vbCr)
```

After you execute the code in Listing 5-10, the new method will be added to the end of the current code window. The new method is highlighted, as shown in Figure 5-5.

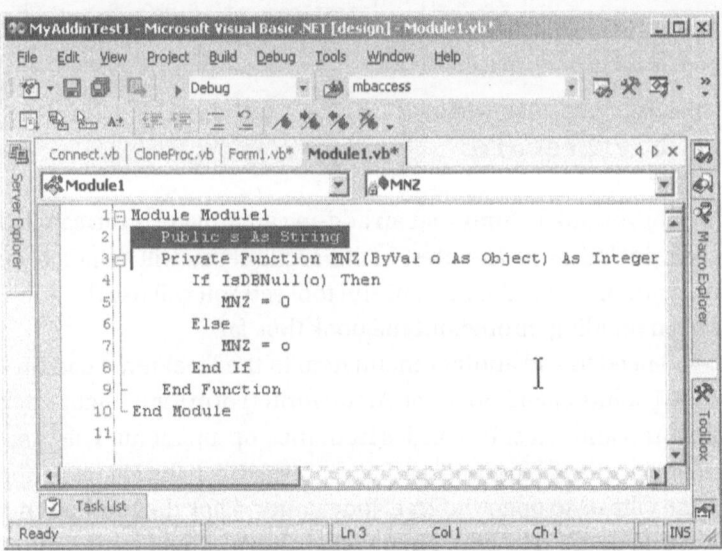

Figure 5-5. New method added to the end of a module

Now you will create a new method for your library of reusable methods. Again, you will be able to use this one in the future. To create the reusable method, simply remove the hard code that adds Function Test and add a parameter to the procedure definition in which you will encapsulate the code (see Listing 5-11). Obviously, you will make this a Shared procedure so that it can be called from anywhere in the project.

Listing 5-11. AddMethodToEndOfDocument

```
Shared Sub AddMethodToEndOfDocument(ByVal NewMethod As String)
    Dim objTD As TextDocument = oVB.ActiveDocument.Object
    Dim objEP As EditPoint = objTD.EndPoint.CreateEditPoint

    ' We are past the end of the last line of the document
    ' move back in front of the End Module/Class
    objEP.LineUp(1)
    objEP.Insert(NewMethod)
End Sub
```

Finally, a typical call to create a new method is shown in the following code. Although this is no more creative than the original example, you will go on to add real, usable functionality to your add-in.

```
AddMethodToEndOfDocument("    Public Function Test()" & vbCr & _
                         "        ' test comment" & vbCr & _
                         "    End Function" & vbCr)
```

Cloning a Procedure

One of the most useful features that an add-in can provide is the capability to clone objects, including procedures. In this section, you will enhance your add-in once again, with probably the most useful tool yet! You will use the add-in that you have been building throughout the book thus far.

First, you need to add another menu item to the TreeView. Load up the MyAddinTest1 solution and open the menu form (Form1.vb). Right-click the TreeView control and select Properties from the pop-up menu. The property window should be displayed for the TreeView control. Click the Nodes property and then click the ellipsis to open the TreeNode Editor. Click the top-level node (Smart Desktop) of the TreeView. Finally, click the AddChild button and type **Clone Procedure** into the Label box. Click the OK button to close the designer. If you open the TreeView by clicking the plus sign (+) on the top-level node, you will see that you have added your new menu item.

Next, you need to add a handler for the new menu option. To do so, go to the code for Form1.vb and add the code in Listing 5-12 to the tvMenu_AfterSelect event handler. Add the two boldface lines just before the Case Else statement in the event handler.

Listing 5-12. Adding to the AfterSelect Event

```
Private Sub tvMenu_AfterSelect(ByVal sender As Object, ByVal e As _
            System.Windows.Forms.TreeViewEventArgs) Handles↵
            tvMenu.AfterSelect
    Dim i As Integer

    Select Case UCase$(e.Node.Text)
        Case "SMART DESKTOP" 'ignore root clicks
        Case "BLOCK COMMENT"
            Call Connect.BlockComment()
        Case "UNCOMMENT"
            Call Connect.BlockUnComment()
        Case "BLOCK CHANGE"
            Call Connect.BlockChange()
        Case "BLOCK DELETE"
            Call Connect.BlockDelete()
        Case "PROC ERROR HANDLER"
            Call Connect.GenLocalErrorTrap()
        Case "CLONE PROCEDURE"
            Call Connect.CloneProcedure()
        Case Else
            MsgBox("Please click on a Child Node.", _
                        MsgBoxStyle.Information, "Unknown Request")
    End Select
End Sub
```

You now need to add two new methods to the Connect class (Connect.vb). The first is named CloneProcedure, which is shown in Listing 5-13. When the add-in user selects a procedure to clone, the CloneProcedure method will retrieve the selected procedure from the active document. CloneProcedure will call GetCodeFromWindow to get the selected block from the active window. After performing a cursory test to ensure that the user has selected a procedure, it calls a public Display function of a new form that you have yet to build. This form will display the selected procedure, and allow the user to change the name of the procedure and elect to either paste the new procedure to the current window or copy the new procedure to the Clipboard.

You can actually call a function in a form, pass it some data, have it manipulate the data, and have it return the resulting data to the calling code. What this amounts to is logically calling a form! This is accomplished by the code that appears in bold in Listing 5-13. If the Display Function of the CloneProc form returns an empty string, it means that the user elected to copy the new procedure to the Clipboard. If there is something in the string, the user has elected to paste the new procedure to the end of the current document. This is accomplished by a call to AddMethodToEndOfDocument, passing the new procedure that has been returned in the string rs.

Listing 5-13. CloneProcedure

```
Shared Sub CloneProcedure()
    Dim s As String
    Dim i As Integer
    Dim rs As String

    Try
        ' get selected proc from active window
        s = GetCodeFromWindow()

        If InStr(1, s, " Sub ", 0) = 0 And _
            InStr(1, s, " Function ", CompareMethod.Binary) = 0 Then
            MsgBox("Please select a whole Procedure to be cloned.", _
                        MsgBoxStyle.Exclamation)
            Exit Sub
        End If
        Dim oFrm As New CloneProc()
        rs = oFrm.Display(s)
        oFrm.Dispose()
        If rs <> "" Then
            AddMethodToEndOfDocument(rs)
        End If
    Catch e As System.Exception
        MsgBox("Error: " & e.Message, MsgBoxStyle.Critical, "Clone Procedure")
        Exit Sub
    End Try
End Sub
```

Next, you add the AddMethodToEndOfDocument method to the Connect class. This method was developed earlier and shown in Listing 5-11. The purpose of this method is to paste the new procedure at the end of current document (module).

Finally, you add a new form to the add-in project. You create the form, create a scrolling TextBox, and place two command buttons on the TextBox. Listing 5-14 contains the complete code for the form.

Listing 5-14. CloneProc Form Code

```
Option Strict On
Public Class CloneProc

    Inherits System.Windows.Forms.Form

#Region " Windows Form Designer generated code "

    Public Sub New()
        MyBase.New()

        'This call is required by the Windows Form Designer.
        InitializeComponent()

        'Add any initialization after the InitializeComponent() call

    End Sub


    'Form overrides dispose to clean up the component list.
    Protected Overloads Overrides Sub Dispose(ByVal disposing As Boolean)
        If disposing Then
            If Not (components Is Nothing) Then
                components.Dispose()
            End If
        End If
        MyBase.Dispose(disposing)
    End Sub


    'Required by the Windows Form Designer
    Private components As System.ComponentModel.IContainer

    'NOTE: The following procedure is required by the Windows Form Designer
    'It can be modified using the Windows Form Designer.
    'Do not modify it using the code editor.
    Friend WithEvents txtProcToClone As System.Windows.Forms.TextBox
    Friend WithEvents btnPasteToModule As System.Windows.Forms.Button
    Friend WithEvents btnCopyToClipboard As System.Windows.Forms.Button
    <System.Diagnostics.DebuggerStepThrough()> _
```

```
Private Sub InitializeComponent()
    Me.txtProcToClone = New System.Windows.Forms.TextBox()
    Me.btnPasteToModule = New System.Windows.Forms.Button()
    Me.btnCopyToClipboard = New System.Windows.Forms.Button()
    Me.SuspendLayout()
    '
    'txtProcToClone
    '
    Me.txtProcToClone.Multiline = True
    Me.txtProcToClone.Name = "txtProcToClone"
    Me.txtProcToClone.ScrollBars = System.Windows.Forms.ScrollBars.Both
    Me.txtProcToClone.Size = New System.Drawing.Size(512, 229)
    Me.txtProcToClone.TabIndex = 0
    Me.txtProcToClone.Text = ""
    '
    'btnPasteToModule
    '
    Me.btnPasteToModule.Location = New System.Drawing.Point(389, 240)
    Me.btnPasteToModule.Name = "btnPasteToModule"
    Me.btnPasteToModule.Size = New System.Drawing.Size(115, 32)
    Me.btnPasteToModule.TabIndex = 1
    Me.btnPasteToModule.Text = "&Paste To Module"
    '
    'btnCopyToClipboard
    '
    Me.btnCopyToClipboard.Location = New System.Drawing.Point(263, 240)
    Me.btnCopyToClipboard.Name = "btnCopyToClipboard"
    Me.btnCopyToClipboard.Size = New System.Drawing.Size(115, 32)
    Me.btnCopyToClipboard.TabIndex = 2
    Me.btnCopyToClipboard.Text = "&Copy To Clipboard"
    'Label1
    '
    Me.Label1.Location = New System.Drawing.Point(16, 240)
    Me.Label1.Name = "Label1"
    Me.Label1.Size = New System.Drawing.Size(192, 24)
    Me.Label1.TabIndex = 3
    Me.Label1.Text = _
        "Change the name of the Method and click the desired button."
    '
    'CloneProc
    '
    Me.AutoScaleBaseSize = New System.Drawing.Size(5, 13)
    Me.ClientSize = New System.Drawing.Size(514, 277)
```

```
        Me.Controls.AddRange(New System.Windows.Forms.Control() _
        {Me.btnCopyToClipboard, Me.btnPasteToModule, Me.txtProcToClone})
        Me.Name = "CloneProc"
        Me.Text = "CloneProc"
        Me.TopMost = True
        Me.ResumeLayout(False)

    End Sub


#End Region
    Dim sTextSave As String
    Dim sOrigType As String
    Dim sOrigName As String
    Dim bFormLoading As Boolean
    Dim mbWait As Boolean

    Public Function Display(ByVal sText As String) As String
        Dim sTemp As String
        Dim sWord As String
        Dim i As Integer

        sTextSave = sText

        ' get the "Sub Name("
        sTemp = Microsoft.VisualBasic.Left(sText, InStr(sText, "(") - 1)

        If InStr(sTemp, "Sub") > 0 Then
            sOrigType = "Sub"
        Else
            sOrigType = "Function"
        End If

        ' loop to get proc orig name
        ' when loop terminates, sOrigName is the name

        Do While Len(Trim$(sTemp)) > 0
            sWord = Connect.GetToken(sTemp, "_")
            If Trim$(sWord) <> "" Then
                sOrigName = sWord
            Else
                Exit Do
            End If
        Loop
```

```
            Me.Show()
            mbWait = True
            Do While mbWait
                System.Windows.Forms.Application.DoEvents()
            Loop

            sTemp = sTextSave
            Return sTemp
            Return sTextSave
    End Function


    Private Sub UpdateFunctionReturns()
        ' If the procedure is a function, get the
        ' name and propagate it through the function
        ' also propagate any changes from the sub to a
        ' function and vice versa through the proc.
        Dim sWord As String
        Dim NextWord As String
        Dim sTemp As String
        Dim nL As Integer
        Dim sTemp2 As String
        Dim i As Integer
        Dim sNewName As String
        Dim sNewType As String
        Dim sLine As String
        Dim sTempLine As String
        Dim bFoundProcType As Boolean

        sTemp = Me.txtProcToClone.Text
        sTemp2 = ""

        nL = Connect.MLCount(sTemp, 0)
        For i = 1 To nL
            sLine = Connect.MemoLine(sTemp, 0, i)

            ' if Proc Def Line get new name, assumming it was changed

            If Not bFoundProcType And _
                (InStr(sLine, "Sub ") > 0 Or _
                InStr(sLine, "Function ") > 0) _
                Then
                ' loop to get proc new name and new type
```

```
                        ' when loop terminates, sNewName is the name
                        bFoundProcType = True

                        sTempLine = sLine
                        Do While Trim$(sTempLine) <> ""
                            sWord = Connect.GetToken(sTempLine, "")
                            If sWord = "Sub" Then
                                sNewType = "Sub"
                                Exit Do
                            ElseIf sWord = "Function" Then
                                sNewType = "Function"
                                Exit Do
                            End If
                        Loop
                        sNewName = Connect.GetToken(sTempLine, "_")
                    ElseIf bFoundProcType Then
                        ' if the type changed, we must substitute the new type
                        ' for the old type and change any functions name returns
                        ' if new type is a function
                        sLine = Replace(sLine, sOrigType, sNewType)
                        sLine = Replace(sLine, sOrigName, sNewName)
                    End If
GetNextLine:
                    ' write the output string
                    sTemp2 = sTemp2 & sLine & vbCrLf

        Next

        Me.txtProcToClone.Text = sTemp2
    End Sub

    Private Sub CloneProc_Load(ByVal sender As System.Object, ByVal e As _
            System.EventArgs) Handles MyBase.Load
        Me.txtProcToClone.Text = sTextSave
    End Sub

    Private Sub btnCopyToClipboard_Click(ByVal sender As System.Object, _
        ByVal e As _
        System.EventArgs) _
        Handles btnCopyToClipboard.Click
        Dim datobj As New System.Windows.Forms.DataObject()
        UpdateFunctionReturns()
        datobj.SetData(System.Windows.Forms.DataFormats.Text, txtProcToClone.Text)
```

```
            mbWait = False
      End Sub

      Private Sub btnPasteToModule_Click(ByVal sender As System.Object, ByVal e As _
            System.EventArgs) Handles btnPasteToModule.Click
         UpdateFunctionReturns()
         sTextSave = Me.txtProcToClone.Text
         mbWait = False
      End Sub
      Protected Overrides Sub Finalize()
         MyBase.Finalize()
      End Sub

      Private Sub CloneProc_Closed(ByVal sender As Object, _
            ByVal e As System.EventArgs) Handles MyBase.Closed
         sTextSave = ""
         mbWait = False
      End Sub
   End Class
```

Two major methods of interest are in the form in Listing 5-14. The first is the Display function. This function facilitates the "calling" of the form from the CloneProcedure method of the Connect class. This function puts the passed parameter, in this case a procedure to be cloned, into the module-level variable sTextSave. The contents of sTextSave then gets placed into the TextBox of the form in the CloneProc_Load event. It then sets a Boolean, mbWait, to True. Finally, the method shows the form and loops in a DoEvents loop, waiting on mbWait to be changed to False. This Boolean will be set to false by either of the button handler events.

The second major method of interest is UpdateFunctionReturns. Once the user has changed the name of the procedure in the TextBox and one of the two buttons is clicked, the Display function breaks out of the wait loop. At that point, it calls the UpdateFunctionReturns method. This method loops through each line of code in the cloned procedure, replacing any occurrence of the original name of the procedure with the new name. You can even change the procedure from a Sub to a Function or vice versa.

After you add the new form and all of the new code previously described to the project, you run the add-in, as I have illustrated in previous chapters. In the second, or client, version of Visual Studio, select the WindowsApplication1 project. Next, select the procedure named MNZ in total, as shown in Figure 5-6.

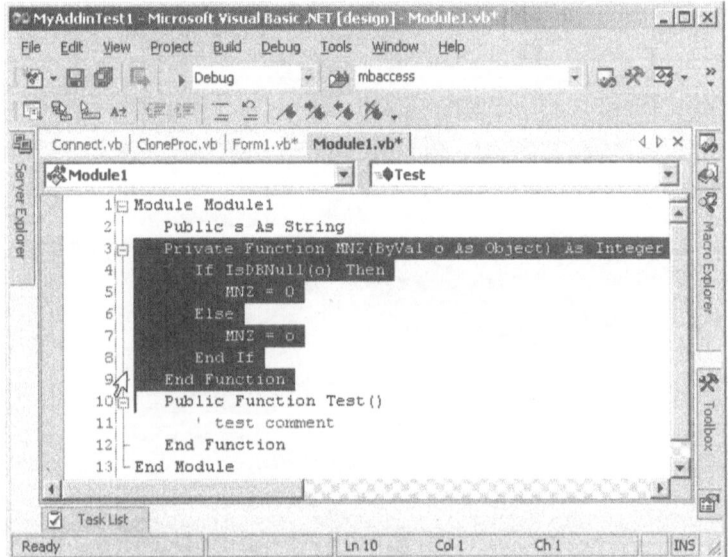

Figure 5-6. Selecting the procedure to be cloned

Now, click the Clone Procedure node of the TreeView in the add-in's menu form. This will cause the CloneProc form to be loaded with the selected procedure displayed in its text box, as shown in Figure 5-7.

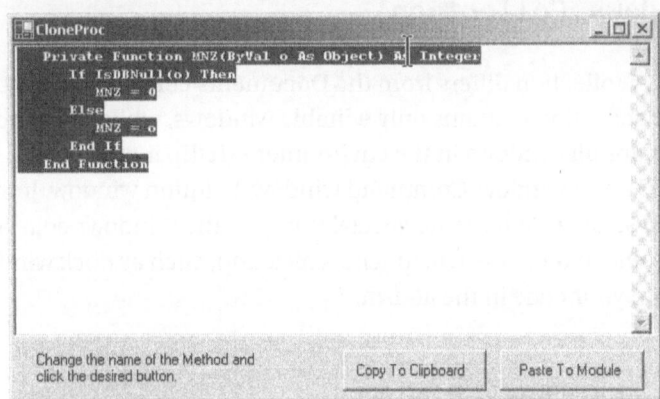

Figure 5-7. CloneProc form

Then change the name of the procedure from MNZ to MakeNullZero. Finally, click the Paste to Module button. The new procedure will be added to the end of the module as shown in Figure 5-8.

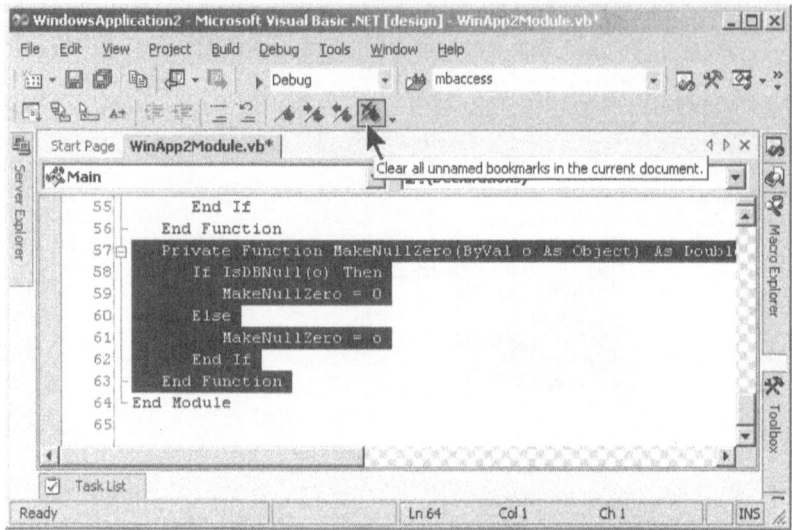

Figure 5-8. Cloned procedure

The new functionality enhances your add-in with a very useful feature. Of course, you can use your imagination and add to the functionality of the UpdateFunctionReturns method so that it will make adjustments to the return value in case the user changes from a Function to Sub, for example.

The Windows Collection

The Windows collection differs from the Documents collection in that the Documents collection contains only editable windows, while the Windows collection contains all windows in the environment (IDE), including tool windows, such as the Output window, Command window, Solution window, Immediate window, and so forth. You can do special things in the Windows collection that you are not able to do in the Documents collection, such as dock windows together from your code in the add-in.

Manipulating Docked Windows

It might not be likely that you'll use the facility described in this section. However, I'll demonstrate docking some of the tool windows in the IDE, just to illustrate that you can control just about everything in the IDE from your add-in. The code sample in Listing 5-15 will frame and dock three dockable tool windows together, change the size of one of the windows, and finally undock a window from the frame. Because it's fairly unlikely that you would use this particular code in an add-in, I'm going to use a feature of the IDE that I haven't yet introduced: the Macro Explorer. You'll investigate the Macro Explorer in Chapter 8, but for now, if you have never used it, this will be a simple exercise.

First, open any project in Visual Studio. The type of project does not matter, as this demo will not alter the project. This demo will only manipulate tool windows, but there must be a project open in order for the tool windows to be visible.

Next, if the Macro Explorer window is not visible, select Tools ➤ Macros ➤ Macro Explorer. You can also open the Macro Explorer by pressing Alt-F8. In the window, you should see a TreeView with a node named My Macros. If there are no modules under My Macros, right-click the My Macros node and click the New Module menu option. If there is a module (child node) there already, you can open the Macros IDE by right-clicking the module and clicking the Edit menu option.

When the Macros IDE opens, it will look much like the regular IDE. Copy the code in its entirety from Listing 5-15 and paste it into the macro module that you opened in the Macros IDE.

Next, switch back to the regular IDE, and in the Macro Explorer window right-click the DockingExample TreeView node. When the pop-up menu appears, click Run and watch the tool windows as they are manipulated. Message boxes will describe what's happening. That's all there is to it!

 **NOTE** *Because this code is being executed in the Macros IDE rather than in an add-in, I have changed the normal application object name oVB to DTE. You must always reference the development environment in the Macros IDE by using the DTE object.*

Listing 5-15. Docking Tool Windows Example

```
Sub DockingExample()
    Dim WinFrame As Window
    Dim Win1 As Window
    Dim Win2 As Window
    Dim Win3 As Window

    ' Create three tool windows in the IDE
    Win1 = DTE.Windows.Item(Constants.vsWindowKindSolutionExplorer)
    Win2 = DTE.Windows.Item(Constants.vsWindowKindToolbox)
    Win3 = DTE.Windows.Item(Constants.vsWindowKindCommandWindow)
```

```
'Create a linked window frame and dock the Solution Explorer
' and Toolbox windows together inside it.
WinFrame = DTE.Windows.CreateLinkedWindowFrame(Win1, Win2, _
                      vsLinkedWindowType.vsLinkedWindowTypeDocked)
MsgBox("Total number of windows in the linked window frame: " & _
             WinFrame.LinkedWindows.Count)


' Add the Command window
' to the frame with  the other two.
WinFrame.LinkedWindows.Add(Win3)
MsgBox("Total number of windows in the linked window frame: " & _
             WinFrame.LinkedWindows.Count)


'Resize the entire linked window frame.
WinFrame.Width = 400
WinFrame.Height = 700
MsgBox("Frame height and width changed. Now " & _
       "changing Command window height.")


'Resize the Command window.
WinFrame.LinkedWindows.Item(3).Height = 600


MsgBox("Now undocking the Command window from the frame.")


' Undock the Command window from the frame.
WinFrame.LinkedWindows.Remove(Win3)
End Sub
```

Clearing the Command Window

Let's take time for one more simple exercise related to the tool windows in the IDE. This time you will open a new instance of the Output window, which is where the results of Debug.Writeline messages appear. You will place some text into the window and then display a message box so that you can see the text in the Output window. Finally, the code will clear the Output window, which, by the way, might be a feature that you'll want to add to your add-in. I'm sure that by now you are able to do that without my help if you choose.

Again, you will use the macro facility to demonstrate this functionality. Follow the steps described in the previous section and place the code from Listing 5-16 into the Macros IDE. In the regular IDE, right-click OutputWindowExample and choose the Run option.

Listing 5-16. Output Window Example

```
Sub OutputWindowExample()
    ' Get a reference to the Command window.
    Dim win As Window = _
            DTE.Windows.Item(EnvDTE.Constants.vsWindowKindCommandWindow)
    Dim CW As CommandWindow = win.Object

    ' Insert some information text into the Command window.
    CW.OutputString("This text will be displayed in the output window")

    ' Clear the contents of the Command window.
    MsgBox("Click Ok to clear the Command window...")
    CW.Clear()
End Sub
```

Summary

In this chapter you explored several of the many objects and properties with which you can manipulate code in the text editor. There are others, and you will see some of them in Chapter 6 when I discuss the manipulation of forms and controls.

Once again, you added new functionality to the desktop add-in that you have been developing. At the same time, you added to the library of reusable objects that you will use throughout the development of add-ins. Finally, you looked at ways to manipulate the various tool windows in the IDE.

In Chapter 6 you'll learn how to create a Windows application and add a form with associated controls. You'll also manipulate the various properties of the controls, including resizing and repositioning, programmatically from an add-in.

Manipulating Controls on Forms

"Men are always wanting to do something great. Let them overcome themselves, for that is the greatest conquest."
—Henry Drummond

IN THIS CHAPTER, you'll find that you have graduated from Add-ins 101. There are over 3,400 classes in the .NET Framework. The greatest challenge to you as the developer is to determine which class (and its associated methods and properties) provides the functionality that you need to do the job you need done. In a regular Windows application this task is fairly difficult. However, when it comes to developing more complex add-in functionality, sometimes this task is downright frustrating, to put it lightly.

For the demonstration of the objects in this chapter, you'll create a new add-in rather than add to the complexity of the add-in you've been creating thus far. You'll add more functionality to that add-in in future chapters, but for now, you'll go back to the Add-in Wizard and create a new add-in.

This chapter's add-in will demonstrate Windows Forms automation. In it, you will see the code to perform the tasks in the following list, and you will see it all done through automation:

- Create a Windows application project.

- Add a VB form to the project.

- Add to and manipulate two command buttons on the form.

- Delete one of the two command buttons.

- Add a handler for the Click event for one of the buttons.

- Add a menu and submenus to the form.

Since you've already seen how to create an add-in using the wizard, I won't repeat the step-by-step images that illustrate how to do so. Rather, I'll just list the steps and tell you the values that I've set in each of the wizard steps.

Creating the New Add-in

To create the new add-in, open Visual Studio .NET. Click the New Project button in the Start window. When the New Project dialog box opens, click the Other Projects folder and then click the Extensibility Projects folder to open it. Type **WinFormsAutomation** as the Name of the project. Set the path of the new project, either by typing it into the Location box or by using the Browse button to select the destination path for your new add-in project. Highlight the Visual Studio .NET Add-in icon and click the OK button to start the Add-in Wizard.

In Step 1 of the Add-in Wizard, select the "Create an Add-in using Visual Basic" option and click the Next button. In Step 2, check only the Microsoft Visual Studio .NET check box and click the Next button. In Step 3, enter **WinFormsAutomation** as the name of your add-in. Also, enter a description such as **Demo of the WinForms Automation Object Model**. Click the Next button to move to Step 4.

Step 4 is where you choose options for running the add-in. Check the first box, which will cause the wizard to create a menu item on the Tools menu. Do not check the second box, which would otherwise indicate that your add-in would never put up a modal dialog box. Although this add-in will not display a UI form, it will display multiple message boxes to describe the process that the add-in is performing. Therefore, the add-in cannot be considered "command line safe." Check the third box, which indicates that you want the add-in to be loaded when the host application is started. Check the fourth box to allow anyone to use the add-in. Click the Next button to move to the next step.

Because the Add-in Wizard in the current version of Visual Studio will not create an About box, simply skip Step 5 by clicking the Next button. Step 6 is just a summary of the options you have selected. Click the Finish button to cause the wizard to create the initial code for the new add-in.

The code generated by the wizard will be almost identical to the code generated by your first use of the wizard in Chapter 2. Only the name, description, and menu command caption will be different because you have selected a different name, description, and so forth. The code in Listing 6-1 includes the standard template generated by the Add-in Wizard, with a few minor changes. The changes that you have made thus far are the same ones that you made back in the Chapter 2 wizard-generated code. These include such things as moving the CommandObj variable up to the module level, shortening the reference variable from applicationObject to oVB, deleting the add-in's menu from the IDE on shutdown of the add-in, and so forth. In Listing 6-1, the changes made to the wizard-generated code appear in bold.

Listing 6-1. Add-in Generated Code

```
Imports Microsoft.Office.Core
Imports Extensibility
Imports System.Runtime.InteropServices
Imports EnvDTE
#Region " Read me for Add-in installation and setup information. "
' When run, the Add-in wizard prepared the registry for the Add-in.
' At a later time, if the Add-in becomes unavailable for reasons such as:
'    1) You moved this project to a computer other than the one it was originally
'       created on.
'    2) You chose 'Yes' when presented with a message asking if you wish to
'       remove the Add-in.
'    3) Registry corruption.
' you will need to re-register the Add-in by building the
' WinFormsAutomationSetup project
' by right-clicking the project in the Solution Explorer, then choosing install.
#End Region

<GuidAttribute("B404B902-65A3-4335-8BA3-24CE23DA3E24"),
 ProgIdAttribute("WinFormsAutomation.Connect")> _
Public Class Connect
    Implements Extensibility.IDTExtensibility2
    Implements IDTCommandTarget

    Dim oVB As EnvDTE.DTE
    Dim addInInstance As EnvDTE.AddIn
    Dim CommandObj As Command

    Public Sub OnBeginShutdown(ByRef custom As System.Array) Implements _
        Extensibility.IDTExtensibility2.OnBeginShutdown
    End Sub

    Public Sub OnAddInsUpdate(ByRef custom As System.Array) Implements _
        Extensibility.IDTExtensibility2.OnAddInsUpdate
    End Sub

    Public Sub OnStartupComplete(ByRef custom As System.Array) Implements _
        Extensibility.IDTExtensibility2.OnStartupComplete
    End Sub
```

```vb
Public Sub OnDisconnection(ByVal RemoveMode As _
    Extensibility.ext_DisconnectMode, _
    ByRef custom As System.Array) _
    Implements Extensibility.IDTExtensibility2.OnDisconnection
    Try
        ' remove the addins UI menu
        CommandObj.Delete()
    Catch e As System.Exception
        MsgBox("OnDisconnection: " & e.Message)
    End Try
End Sub


Public Sub OnConnection(ByVal application As Object, ByVal connectMode As _
    Extensibility.ext_ConnectMode, ByVal addInInst As Object, _
    ByRef custom As _
    System.Array) Implements Extensibility.IDTExtensibility2.OnConnection
    oVB = CType(application, EnvDTE.DTE)
    addInInstance = CType(addInInst, EnvDTE.AddIn)
    If connectMode = Extensibility.ext_ConnectMode.ext_cm_AfterStartup Or _
        connectMode = Extensibility.ext_ConnectMode.ext_cm_Startup _
        Then
        Dim objAddIn As AddIn = CType(addInInst, AddIn)

        ' When run, the Add-in wizard prepared the registry for the Add-in.
        ' At a later time, the Add-in or its commands may become unavailable
        ' for reasons such as:
        '    1) You moved this project to a computer other than the one it was
        '        originally created on._
        '    2) You chose 'Yes' when presented with a message asking if you
        '        wish to remove the Add-in.
        '    3) You add new commands or modify commands already defined.
        ' You will need to re-register the Add-in by building the
        ' WinFormsAutomationSetup project,_
        ' right-clicking the project in the Solution Explorer, and then
        ' choosing install.
        ' Alternatively, you could execute the ReCreateCommands.reg file the
        ' Add-in Wizard generated in _
        ' the project directory, or run 'devenv /setup' from a command prompt.
        Try
            CommandObj = oVB.Commands.AddNamedCommand(objAddIn, _
```

```
            "WinFormsAutomation", "WinFormsAutomation", _
            "Executes the command for ⅅ
            WinFormsAutomation", True, 59, Nothing, 1 + 2)    '1+2 == _
              vsCommandStatusSupported+vsCommandStatusEnabled
          CommandObj.AddControl(oVB.CommandBars.Item("Tools"))
      Catch e As System.Exception
          MsgBox("OnConnection, Can't Add Command: " & e.Message)
      End Try
    End If
End Sub


Public Sub Exec(ByVal cmdName As String, _
                ByVal executeOption As vsCommandExecOption, _
                ByRef varIn As Object, _
                ByRef varOut As Object, _
                ByRef handled As Boolean) _
                Implements IDTCommandTarget.Exec
    handled = True
    If (executeOption = vsCommandExecOption.vsCommandExecOptionDoDefault) Then
        If cmdName = "WinFormsAutomation.Connect.WinFormsAutomation" Then
            handled = True
            Exit Sub
        End If
    End If
End Sub
Public Sub QueryStatus(ByVal cmdName As String, ByVal neededText As _
    vsCommandStatusTextWanted, ByRef statusOption As vsCommandStatus, _
    ByRef commandText As Object) Implements IDTCommandTarget.QueryStatus
    If neededText = _
      EnvDTE.vsCommandStatusTextWanted.vsCommandStatusTextWantedNone _
      Then
        If cmdName = "WinFormsAutomation.Connect.WinFormsAutomation" Then
            statusOption = CType(vsCommandStatus.vsCommandStatusEnabled + _
                vsCommandStatus.vsCommandStatusSupported, vsCommandStatus)
        Else
            statusOption = vsCommandStatus.vsCommandStatusUnsupported
        End If
    End If
End Sub
```

Adding the WinForms Automation Code

In Listing 6-2, you will see that I have added a lot of code to the Exec method of the add-in. When the user clicks the WinFormsAutomation menu option, the Exec method will receive control. This method is where the actual demonstration of the Windows Forms automation objects will be executed. Listing 6-2 shows all of the code for the add-in, including the wizard-generated code and the code I have added to demonstrate the use of the many automation objects that I discuss in this chapter. There is a lot of code, so do not be dismayed by the objects and their usage. I discuss each segment of the code as you progress through the remainder of the chapter.

In addition to the code added to the Exec method, I have added some additional namespaces, which are boldfaced under the Imports section.

Listing 6-2. WinForms Automation Code

```
Imports Microsoft.Office.Core
Imports Extensibility
Imports System.Runtime.InteropServices
Imports EnvDTE
Imports System.ComponentModel.Design
Imports System.ComponentModel
Imports System.Drawing
Imports System.Windows.Forms


#Region " Read me for Add-in installation and setup information. "
' When run, the Add-in wizard prepared the registry for the Add-in.
' At a later time, if the Add-in becomes unavailable for reasons such as:
'    1) You moved this project to a computer other than the one it was
'       originally created on.
'    2) You chose 'Yes' when presented with a message asking if you wish
'       to remove the Add-in.
'    3) Registry corruption.
' you will need to re-register the Add-in by building the
' WinFormsAutomationSetup project
' by right-clicking the project in the Solution Explorer, then
' choosing install.
#End Region

<GuidAttribute("B404B902-65A3-4335-8BA3-24CE23DA3E24"),
 ProgIdAttribute("WinFormsAutomation.Connect")> _
Public Class Connect
```

```
Implements Extensibility.IDTExtensibility2
Implements IDTCommandTarget

Dim oVB As EnvDTE.DTE
Dim addInInstance As EnvDTE.AddIn
Dim CommandObj As Command

Public Sub OnBeginShutdown(ByRef custom As System.Array) _
    Implements Extensibility.IDTExtensibility2.OnBeginShutdown
End Sub

Public Sub OnAddInsUpdate(ByRef custom As System.Array) _
    Implements Extensibility.IDTExtensibility2.OnAddInsUpdate
End Sub

Public Sub OnStartupComplete(ByRef custom As System.Array) _
    Implements Extensibility.IDTExtensibility2.OnStartupComplete
End Sub

Public Sub OnDisconnection(ByVal RemoveMode As _
            Extensibility.ext_DisconnectMode, _
            ByRef custom As System.Array) _
            Implements _
            Extensibility.IDTExtensibility2.OnDisconnection
    Try
        ' remove the add-ins UI menu
        CommandObj.Delete()
    Catch e As System.Exception
        MsgBox("OnDisconnection: " & e.Message)
    End Try
End Sub

Public Sub OnConnection(ByVal application As Object, _
    ByVal connectMode As Extensibility.ext_ConnectMode, _
    ByVal addInInst As Object, _
    ByRef custom As System.Array) _
    Implements Extensibility.IDTExtensibility2.OnConnection
    oVB = CType(application, EnvDTE.DTE)
    addInInstance = CType(addInInst, EnvDTE.AddIn)
    If connectMode = Extensibility.ext_ConnectMode.ext_cm_AfterStartup Or _
        connectMode = Extensibility.ext_ConnectMode.ext_cm_Startup _
        Then
        Dim objAddIn As AddIn = CType(addInInst, AddIn)
```

```
          ' When run, the Add-in wizard prepared the registry for the Add-in.
          ' At a later time, the Add-in or its commands may become
          ' unavailable for reasons such as:
          '    1) You moved this project to a computer other than the one it
          '         was originally created on.
          '    2) You chose 'Yes' when presented with a message asking if
          '         you wish to remove the Add-in.
          '    3) You add new commands or modify commands already defined.
          ' You will need to re-register the Add-in by building the
          ' WinFormsAutomationSetup project,
          ' right-clicking the project in the Solution Explorer,
          ' and then choosing install.
          ' Alternatively, you could execute the ReCreateCommands.reg file
          ' the Add-in Wizard generated in
          ' the project directory, or run 'devenv /setup' from a command prompt.
          Try
              CommandObj = oVB.Commands.AddNamedCommand(objAddIn, _
                  "WinFormsAutomation", _
                  "WinFormsAutomation", _
                  "Executes the command for WinFormsAutomation", _
                  True, 59, Nothing, 1 + 2) _
                  '1+2 == vsCommandStatusSupported+vsCommandStatusEnabled
              CommandObj.AddControl(oVB.CommandBars.Item("Tools"))
          Catch e As System.Exception
              MsgBox("OnConnection, Can't Add Command: " & e.Message)
          End Try
      End If
  End Sub


  ''' Exec -- This is the add-in wizard's template function
  '' Here we have placed the WinForms Automation Demo Code
  Public Sub Exec(ByVal cmdName As String, _
                  ByVal executeOption As vsCommandExecOption, _
                  ByRef varIn As Object, _
                  ByRef varOut As Object, _
                  ByRef handled As Boolean) _
                  Implements IDTCommandTarget.Exec
      handled = False

      '' WinForms Automation Demo Code
      Dim s As String
      If (executeOption = ↵
          vsCommandExecOption. ↵
```

```
       vsCommandExecOptionDoDefault) Then
If cmdName = "WinFormsAutomation.Connect.WinFormsAutomation" Then
     ' if the creation of the project fails, it probably
     ' means that you have run this test before and you
     ' merely need to delete the WinFormPrj from wherever
     ' your default projects are stored...

     MsgBox("A windows project with one form is about to be created.")

     Try

          '' Winforms automation sample code starts here...
          '' Create a Windows Forms project and give the
          '' designer focus
          '' uncomment the next line and comment the 2nd line
          '' down to create
          ' a VC# project instead of a VB project
          'Dim templatePath As String = _
          '    oVB.Solution.TemplatePath↵
          ("{FAE04EC0-301F-11D3-BF4B-00C04F79EFBC}") & _
          '       "CSharpEXE.vsz"
          Dim templatePath As String = _
              oVB.Solution.TemplatePath↵
              ("{F184B08F-C81C-45f6-A57F- ↵
            5ABD9991F28F}" ) & _
              "WindowsApplication.vsz"

          Dim targetDir As String = _
              CStr(oVB.Properties("Environment", _
              "ProjectsAndSolution")↵
              .Item("ProjectsLocation").Value) & _
              "\WinFormPrj"

          oVB.Solution.AddFromTemplate(templatePath, _
              targetDir, "WinFormPrj")
     Catch e As System.Exception
          MsgBox("You probably need to delete WinFormPrj")
          Exit Sub
     End Try
     MsgBox("The Windows Application Project " & _
             has been added to the IDE.")

     oVB.Windows.Item("Form1.vb [Design]").Activate()
```

```
'' uncomment the next line and comment
'' the previous line
'' to work with a VC# form instead of vb
'oVB.Windows.Item("Form1.cs [Design]").Activate()

'' Get IDesignerHost, the root of the forms
'' designer object model
Dim fdHost As IDesignerHost
fdHost = CType(oVB.ActiveWindow.Object, IDesignerHost)

'' Add two buttons, enumerate and print components.
Dim btn1 As IComponent

s = fdHost.RootComponent.Site.Name

btn1 = fdHost.CreateComponent(fdHost.GetType ⏎ .
    ("System.Windows.Forms.Button, ⏎
     System.Windows.Forms"))

Dim btn2 As IComponent
btn2 = fdHost.CreateComponent(fdHost.GetType ⏎
    ("System.Windows.Forms.Button, ⏎
     System.Windows.Forms"))

Dim parent As PropertyDescriptor = ⏎
        TypeDescriptor.GetProperties(btn1)("Parent")
        parent.SetValue(btn1, fdHost.RootComponent)
parent.SetValue(btn2, fdHost.RootComponent)
ListComponents("form with two buttons...", _
        fdHost.Container.Components)

'' Get the properties of the remaining component,
''  then print their names
Dim pdc As PropertyDescriptorCollection
pdc = TypeDescriptor.GetProperties(btn1)
ListProperties(pdc)

'' Get and set the value of the size property,
'' showing values
'' before and after.
Dim pd As PropertyDescriptor
pd = pdc("Size")
MsgBox("Default Button size = " & _
        pd.GetValue(btn1).ToString())
```

```vb
' resize the button
Dim sz As System.Drawing.Size
sz = New Size(100, 60)
pd.SetValue(btn1, sz)
MsgBox("custom Button size = " & _
        pd.GetValue(btn1).ToString())


'' reposition the button
Try
    pd = pdc("Location")
    Dim loc As System.Drawing.Point
    loc = New Point(30, 30)
    pd.SetValue(btn1, loc)
    MsgBox("New button location = " & _
            pd.GetValue(btn1).ToString())
Catch e As System.Exception
    MsgBox(e.Message)
End Try


'' add text property
Dim s2 As String
s = "&Test Button"
pd = pdc("Text")
s2 = pd.GetValue(btn1).ToString()
pd.SetValue(btn1, s)
MsgBox("Default Text = " & s2 & Chr(10) & _
        "New Text = " & pd.GetValue(btn1).ToString())


'' change Name property
s = "txtTestButton"
pd = pdc("Name")
s2 = pd.GetValue(btn1).ToString()
pd.SetValue(btn1, s)
MsgBox("Default Name = " & s2 & Chr(10) & _
        "New Name = " & pd.GetValue(btn1).ToString())


'' Then remove one of the components, enumerate
'' and print again.
fdHost.DestroyComponent(btn2)
ListComponents("form after removing one button...", _
    fdHost.Container.Components)
```

```
'' Select a component on a form
MsgBox("Selecting button component...")
Dim sel As ISelectionService
sel = CType(fdHost.GetService(Type.GetType ⤶
    ("System.ComponentModel.Design. ⤶
    ISelectionService,System")), _
    System.ComponentModel.Design.ISelectionService)
sel.SetSelectedComponents(New Object() {btn1})

' get the count of selected components
Dim i As Integer = sel.SelectionCount
MsgBox("Selected Component Count = " & CStr(i))

' loop through the selected component collection
' listing properties
Dim ic As IComponent
Dim c As Component
For Each c In sel.GetSelectedComponents
    ic = CType(c, IComponent)
    pdc = TypeDescriptor.GetProperties(ic)
    pd = pdc("Text")
    s = pd.GetValue(ic).ToString
    pd = pdc("Name")
    s2 = pd.GetValue(ic).ToString
    MsgBox("Component Text = " & s & Chr(10) & _
        "Component Name = " & s2)
Next

Try
    'Access designer properties
    MsgBox("Accessing designer grid size...")
    Dim opt As IDesignerOptionService
    opt = CType(fdHost.GetService(Type.GetType ⤶
        ("System.ComponentModel.Design. ⤶
        IDesignerOptionService,System")), _
        System.ComponentModel.Design. ⤶
        IDesignerOptionService)
    Dim siz As Size = CType(opt.GetOptionValue ⤶
        ("WindowsFormsDesigner\General", "GridSize"), _
        Size)
    MsgBox(siz.ToString())
Catch e As System.Exception
    MsgBox("failed accessing designer props")
```

```vbnet
        MsgBox(e.tostring())
    End Try


    'Assign event handler to btn1 click
    Try
        Dim click As EventDescriptor
        click = TypeDescriptor.GetEvents(btn1)("Click")
        Dim eventSvc As IEventBindingService
        eventSvc = CType(fdHost.GetService _
            (Type.GetType("System.ComponentModel.Design. _
            IEventBindingService,System")), _
            System.ComponentModel.Design. _
            IEventBindingService)
        Dim clickProp As PropertyDescriptor
        clickProp = eventSvc.GetEventProperty(click)
        clickProp.SetValue(btn1, "btnTestButton_OnClick")
    Catch e As System.Exception
        MsgBox("assign event handler")
        MsgBox(e.tostring)
    End Try


    ' Link event to component
    Try
        Dim addSvc As IComponentChangeService
        addSvc = CType(fdHost.GetService(Type.GetType _
    ("System.ComponentModel.Design. _
    IComponentChangeService,System")), _
    System.ComponentModel.Design.IComponentChangeService)
    Catch e As System.Exception
        MsgBox("hooking comp event")
        MsgBox(e.tostring)
    End Try


    'Create a menu on the form
    Try
        Dim mainMenuComp As IComponent = _
            fdHost.CreateComponent(Type.GetType _
            ("System.Windows.Forms.MainMenu, _
            System.Windows.Forms"), _
            "mainMenu1")
        Dim fileMenuItemComp As IComponent = _
        fdHost.CreateComponent(Type.GetType _
            ("System.Windows.Forms.MenuItem, _
```

```vb
                                    System.Windows.Forms"), ⏎
                                "fileMenuItem")
                        Dim menuItem2Comp As IComponent = ⏎
                                fdHost.CreateComponent(Type.GetType ⏎
                                ("System.Windows.Forms.MenuItem,⏎
                                System.Windows.Forms"), ⏎
                                "mainItem2")
                        Dim menuItem3Comp As IComponent = ⏎
                                fdHost.CreateComponent(Type.GetType ⏎
                                ("System.Windows.Forms.MenuItem,⏎
                                System.Windows.Forms"), ⏎
                                "mainItem3")
                        Dim menuItem4Comp As IComponent = ⏎
                            fdHost.CreateComponent(Type.GetType ⏎
                            ("System.Windows.Forms.MenuItem,⏎
                            System.Windows.Forms"), ⏎
                            "mainItem4")

                        Dim mainMenu1 As MainMenu = CType(mainMenuComp, _
                            MainMenu)
                        Dim fileMenuItem As MenuItem = _
                            CType(fileMenuItemComp, MenuItem)
                        Dim menuItem2 As MenuItem = CType(menuItem2Comp, _
                            MenuItem)
                        Dim menuItem3 As MenuItem = CType(menuItem3Comp, _
                            MenuItem)
                        Dim menuItem4 As MenuItem = CType(menuItem4Comp, _
                            MenuItem)

                        fileMenuItem.Text = "&File"
                        menuItem2.Text = "&Edit"
                        menuItem3.Text = "&Open"
                        menuItem4.Text = "&Save"

                        mainMenu1.MenuItems.Add(fileMenuItem)
                        mainMenu1.MenuItems.Add(menuItem2)

                        fileMenuItem.MenuItems.Add(menuItem3)
                        fileMenuItem.MenuItems.Add(menuItem4)

                Catch e As System.Exception
                    MsgBox("adding menu")
                    MsgBox(e.tostring)
                End Try
```

```vb
                handled = True
                Exit Sub
            End If
        End If
End Sub


Public Sub QueryStatus(ByVal cmdName As String, _
                        ByVal neededText As _
                        vsCommandStatusTextWanted, _
                        ByRef statusOption As vsCommandStatus, _
                        ByRef commandText As Object) _
                        Implements IDTCommandTarget.QueryStatus
    If neededText = _
        EnvDTE.vsCommandStatusTextWanted.↵
        vsCommandStatusTextWantedNone _
        Then
        If cmdName = _
          "WinFormsAutomation.Connect.↵
          WinFormsAutomation" _
          Then
            statusOption = CType(vsCommandStatus.↵
                vsCommandStatusEnabled + _
                vsCommandStatus.vsCommandStatusSupported, _
                vsCommandStatus)
        Else
            statusOption = _
                vsCommandStatus.vsCommandStatusUnsupported
        End If
    End If
End Sub
'''
''' The following methods were not constructed by the
''' add-in wizard
''' they provide utility functionality for this winforms
''' automation sample.
'''
Public Sub ListComponents(ByVal title As String, _
                            ByVal Components As _
                            ComponentCollection)
    Dim comp As Component
    Dim message As String
    For Each comp In Components
        message = message & _
```

```
                          Microsoft.VisualBasic.Constants.vbCrLf + _
                          comp.ToString()
            Next
            MsgBox(title & Microsoft.VisualBasic.Constants.vbCrLf & _
                    message)
        End Sub

        Public Sub ListProperties(ByVal Properties As _
                    PropertyDescriptorCollection)
            Dim pd As PropertyDescriptor
            Dim message As String = "First ten properties..." & _
                Microsoft.VisualBasic.Constants.vbCrLf
            Dim i As Integer
            For i = 0 To 9
                Try
                    message = message & _
                        Microsoft.VisualBasic.Constants.vbCrLf & _
                        CType(Properties.Item(i).DisplayName, String) & _
                        " = " & _
                        Properties.Item(i).Attributes.ToString
                Catch e As System.Exception
                    MsgBox(e.Message)
                End Try
            Next
            MsgBox(message)
        End Sub
    End Class
```

Creating the Windows Application Project

The code snippet in Listing 6-3 is responsible for creating the Windows application project. I will walk through each line of code in which what is being done is not obvious and give an explanation of the code. I have numbered the lines of code in this listing so that I can refer to the individual lines that need special explanation.

CAUTION   *If you are going to run this add-in a second or subsequent time, you will have to go to the default directory where Visual Studio stores projects and delete WinFormsPrj. If you do not delete the project, the add-in will not work.*

Listing 6-3. Creating the Project

```
01    '' Winforms automation sample code starts here
02    '' Create a Windows Forms project and give the
03    '' designer focus
04    '' uncomment the next line and comment the 2nd
05    ''line down to create
06    ' a VC# project instead of a VB project
07    'Dim templatePath As String = _
08    '    oVB.Solution.TemplatePath↵
09    '    ("{FAE04EC0-301F-11D3-BF4B-00C04F79EFBC}") & _
10    '     "CSharpEXE.vsz"
11    Dim templatePath As String = _
12        oVB.Solution.TemplatePath↵
13        ("{F184B08F-C81C-45f6-A57F-5ABD9991F28F}") & _
14        "WindowsApplication.vsz"
15
16    Dim targetDir As String = _
17        CStr(oVB.Properties("Environment", _
18        "ProjectsAndSolution").Item↵
19        ("ProjectsLocation").Value) & _
20        "\WinFormPrj"
21
22    oVB.Solution.AddFromTemplate(templatePath, _
23        targetDir, "WinFormPrj")
24 Catch e As System.Exception
25    MsgBox("You probably need to delete WinFormPrj")
26    Exit Sub
27 End Try
28
28 MsgBox("The Windows Application Project " & _
29        "has been added to the IDE.")
```

First, you have to create the project itself. The code in Listing 6-3 does that. There are Dim statements at line 07 and line 11. Line 07 is commented out, but it is shown here in order to demonstrate how to create a Visual C# project. Line 22 actually creates a Visual Basic Windows application project. Line 11 sets the path to the Visual Studio template for a Visual Basic Windows application. You will note that the string will have the GUID of {F184B08F-C81C-45f6-A57F-5ABD9991F28F} concatenated into it. Line 11 will use the templatePath variable to retrieve the path to the template file from the registry. If you open the Regedit program and search for the GUID, you will see the layout of the template pointers in the registry, as shown in Figure 6-1. The actual path to the template is as follows:

```
C:\Program Files\Microsoft Visual Studio.NET\Vb7\VBProjects\ ⏎
    WindowsApplication.vsz
```

When Line 18 is executed, Visual Studio will create a new Windows application project in the IDE.

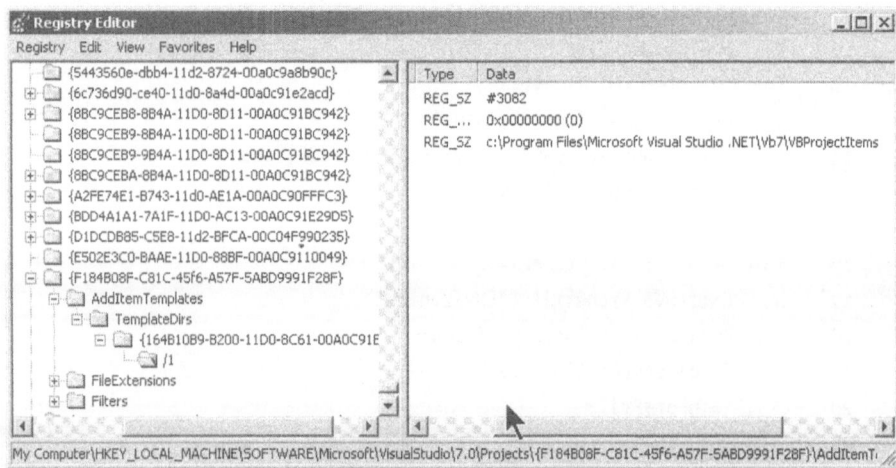

Figure 6-1. Registry pointer to project templates

You will remember that when you start to debug an add-in, a second (client) instance of Visual Studio is started automatically. When the second project opens, you should try to size and position the two copies of the IDE so that they appear side by side, without overlaying each other. This will allow you to see both of them during the automation process. Because all of the work in the second copy (client) will be shown in the upper left corner of the designer, the IDE does not have to be very large.

Once line 22 of the code in Listing 6-3 has been executed, a message box display in the code stops the automation process. This will allow you to view the newly created project. Figure 6-2 shows the newly created project in the second IDE.

You will see that when the Windows application project is created, a Windows Form (Form1.vb) is automatically created.

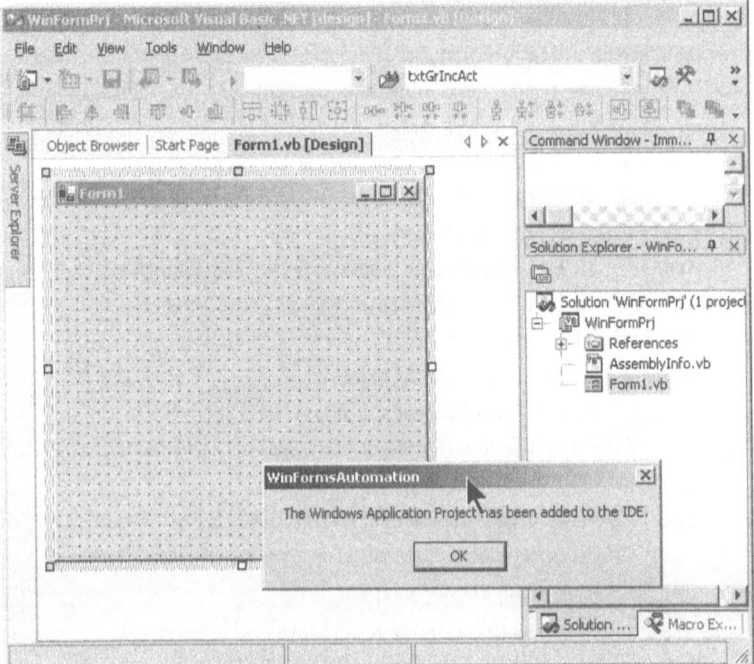

Figure 6-2. Newly created project

Click the OK button on the message box to continue the automation process.

Adding Controls to the Form

Now that the project has been created and Form1 has been added to the project, the add-in proceeds to add two buttons to the form. The code snippet in Listing 6-4 contains the code for adding the two buttons to the form.

NOTE *Owing to the number of topics related to the IDesignerHost and IComponent objects in the MSDN help file, it is beyond the scope of this book to describe all of the numerous objects, methods, properties, and events associated with them. Only the objects and methods being used are described.*

Listing 6-4. Adding Buttons to the Form

```
01          oVB.Windows.Item("Form1.vb [Design]").Activate()
02            '' uncomment the next line and comment the previous line
03            '' to work with a VC# form instead of vb
04            'oVB.Windows.Item("Form1.cs [Design]").Activate()
05            '' Get IDesignerHost, the root of the forms designer object model
06          Dim fdHost As IDesignerHost
07          fdHost = CType(oVB.ActiveWindow.Object, IDesignerHost)
08            '' Add two buttons, enumerate and print components.
09          Dim btn1 As IComponent
10          s = fdHost.RootComponent.Site.Name
11          btn1 = fdHost.CreateComponent(fdHost.GetType ⤴
12              ("System.Windows.Forms.Button,System.Windows.Forms"))
13          Dim btn2 As IComponent
14          btn2 = fdHost.CreateComponent(fdHost.GetType ⤴
15              ("System.Windows.Forms.Button,System.Windows.Forms"))
16          Dim parent As PropertyDescriptor = ⤴
17                  TypeDescriptor.GetProperties(btn1)("Parent")
18          parent.SetValue(btn1, fdHost.RootComponent)
19          parent.SetValue(btn2, fdHost.RootComponent)
20      ListComponents("form with two buttons...", fdHost.Container.Components)
```

Line 01 activates the window containing Form1.vb. Although it would be the active window because it was just added to the project, this line demonstrates how to make any window the active window.

Line 06 creates a pointer object to the WinForms Designer object. This object is an instance of the IDesignerHost interface. IDesignerHost provides an interface for managing designer transactions and components. It is used here for adding components or, in this case, controls to the form.

Lines 09 and 13 dimension two command buttons for placement on the form. They are dimensioned as IComponent objects. IComponent provides functionality required by all components and facilitates the creation of the components that you are placing on the form. Line 10 demonstrates how to display the name of the form currently pointed to by the IDesignerHost object, fdHost. It is not used in the automation process and is provided simply for demonstration purposes.

Lines 11 and 14 actually create the two buttons and place them on the form, using the CreateComponent method of the IDesignerHost object. CreateComponent creates a component of the specified type and adds it to the design document. In this case, calling the fdHost.GetType method specifies the type of Windows Forms button. At this point, the buttons are created but not yet placed on the form. Line 16 creates a parent object as PropertyDescriptor for

placement of the buttons on the form. This line uses the
TypeDescriptor.GetProperties overloaded method. In this case, the method gets
the collection of properties for a specified type of component (Button) using
a specified array of attributes as a filter.

Lines 18 and 19 place the created buttons on the form. Next, the
ListComponents function is called to display the components in a message box.

While the message box is displayed, you can view the buttons on the form, as
shown in Figure 6-3. There is only one problem here: Visual Studio initially loads
all controls at the same place on a form. Therefore, you will see that only one of
the buttons is visible. This is due to the fact that one button is overlaying the
other button.

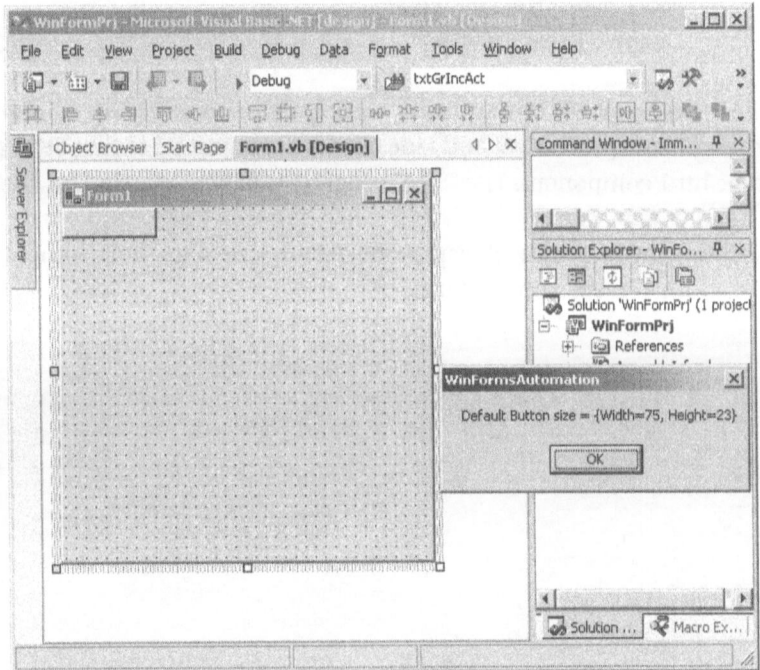

Figure 6-3. Buttons placed on the form

The code snippet in Listing 6-5 simply displays the properties of the components just after they have been placed on the form. Line 03 dimensions pdc as
a PropertyDescriptorCollection. This represents a collection of
PropertyDescriptor objects. A PropertyDescriptor object provides an abstraction
of a property on a class.

You can query the PropertyDescriptorCollection collection about its contents
by using the properties available in the PropertyDescriptorCollection class.
You can use the Count property to determine the number of elements in the

Chapter 6 ⏐

collection. Use the Item property to get a specific property by index number or by name. The Item property is the default property and therefore is assumed in the code in Listing 6-5.

Listing 6-5. Printing the Component Properties

```
01          '' Get the properties of the remaining component,
02          '' then print their names
03          Dim pdc As PropertyDescriptorCollection
04           pdc = TypeDescriptor.GetProperties(btn1)
05             '' Get and set the value of the size property, showing values
06             '' before and after.
07           Dim pd As PropertyDescriptor
08           pd = pdc("Size")
09           MsgBox("Default Button size = " + pd.GetValue(btn1).ToString())
```

Line 04 sets up the PropertyDescriptorCollection for btn1. Line 07 dimensions the PropertyDescriptor object and Line 08 sets the object pd to the "Size" property of the btn1 component. The "Size" property is of type System.Drawing.Size, which denotes (x,y) values.

Executing the MsgBox will display the default size of the btn1 component as it was sized when placed on the form.

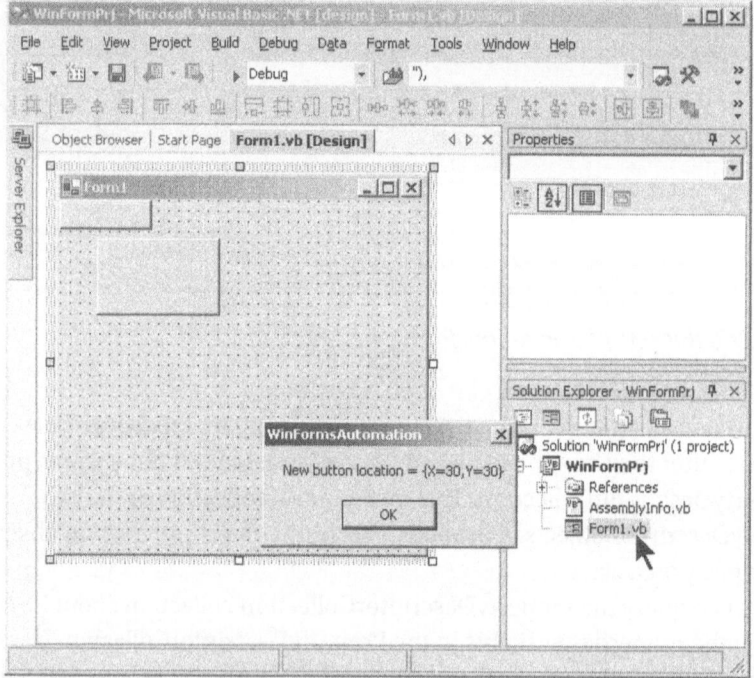

Figure 6-4. Default size of btn1

Now that you've placed two controls on the form, you'll now resize and reposition the controls.

Manipulating Controls on the Form

First, you'll resize one of the buttons. In order to do this, you'll use a couple of the objects that were created in Listing 6-5 but are reproduced here for ease of reference.

Listing 6-6. Resizing a Control

```
01          Dim pdc As PropertyDescriptorCollection
02          pdc = TypeDescriptor.GetProperties(btn1)
03          Dim pd As PropertyDescriptor
04          pd = pdc("Size")
05          Dim sz As System.Drawing.Size
06          sz = New Size(100, 60)
07          pd.SetValue(btn1, sz)
08          MsgBox("custom Button size = " + pd.GetValue(btn1).ToString())
```

Lines 01 through 04 of Listing 6-6 represent the objects that were previously created. A relatively simple object is created in line 05. Here, you create an instance of the System.Drawing.Size object. Line 06 sets the Size object to a new height and width. Line 07 does the actual changing of the size of the button by using the SetValue method of the PropertyDescriptor (pd).

For now, you will not show the execution of the MsgBox(), which would simply display the new size of the button. You will do that after you reposition the button, which is accomplished by the code in Listing 6-7.

Listing 6-7. Repositioning the Button

```
01          pd = pdc("Location")
02          Dim loc As System.Drawing.Point
03          loc = New Point(30, 30)
04          pd.SetValue(btn1, loc)
05          MsgBox("New button location = " & _
06          pd.GetValue(btn1).ToString())
```

Line 01 sets the PropertyDescriptor object (pd) to the Location property. Line 02 dimensions a System.Drawing.Point object named loc. Line 03 sets the Point object to a new top and left, or *x* and *y* in .NET context. Again, line 04 simply sets the new location of the button.

In Figure 6-5, notice that the button (btn2) has been resized and repositioned. You can now see that there was a second button hidden behind the first. Because you are stopping the execution of the add-in while the message boxes are displayed, and because you cannot click the client IDE while the add-in is still executing, you cannot see the values of the property page (shown with blank properties). Once the automation add-in has completed its processing, you will be able to examine all of the properties that have been automatically set by the automation process.

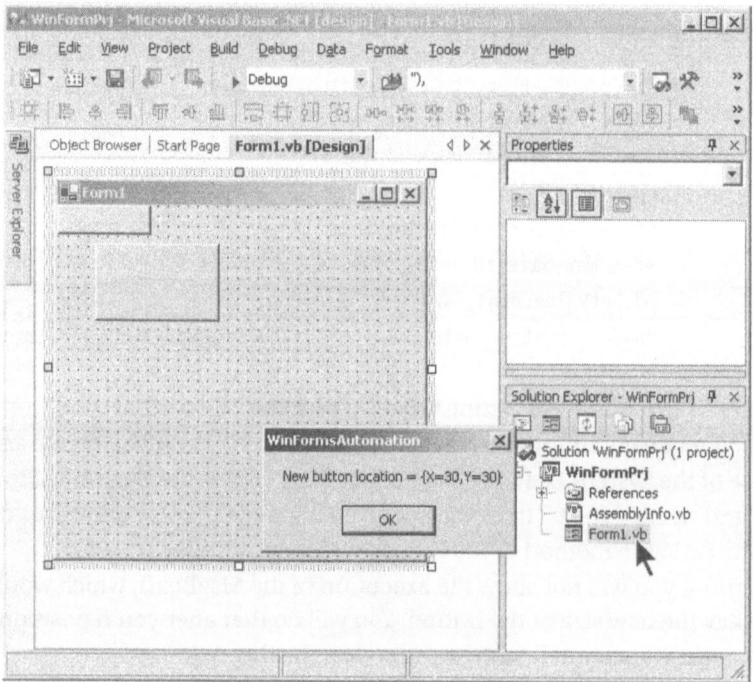

Figure 6-5. Button resized and repositioned

Next, you will change the Name and Text (Caption in VB 6.0) properties of the button. The code for doing this is shown in Listing 6-8.

Listing 6-8. Changing the Button's Name and Text Properties

```
01          '' add text property
02          Dim s2 As String
03          s = "&Test Button"
04          pd = pdc("Text")
05          s2 = pd.GetValue(btn1).ToString()
06          pd.SetValue(btn1, s)
```

```
07                  MsgBox("Default Text = " & s2 & Chr(10) & _
08                       "New Text = " & pd.GetValue(btn1).ToString())
09
10           '' change Name property
11            s = "txtTestButton"
12            pd = pdc("Name")
13            s2 = pd.GetValue(btn1).ToString()
14          pd.SetValue(btn1, s)
15        MsgBox("Default Name = " & s2 & Chr(10) & _
16                  "New Name = " & pd.GetValue(btn1).ToString())
```

Lines 02 and 03 simply set the value to be placed into the Text property in a string variable. Line 04 sets the PropertyDescriptor object to point to the Text property. Line 05 picks up the default Text property, which is always blank, in order to display it along with the new property value. Line 06 sets the new value in the Text property, using the SetValue method of the PropertyDescriptor object.

Line 11 sets a new value for the Name property into a string variable. Line 12 sets the PropertyDescriptor object to the Name property. Line 13 gets the default Name property assigned to the button at the time it was created. In this case it is "button1". Line 14 sets the new value of the Name property in the button.

Figure 6-6 shows the button just after the message box in line 15 is executed.

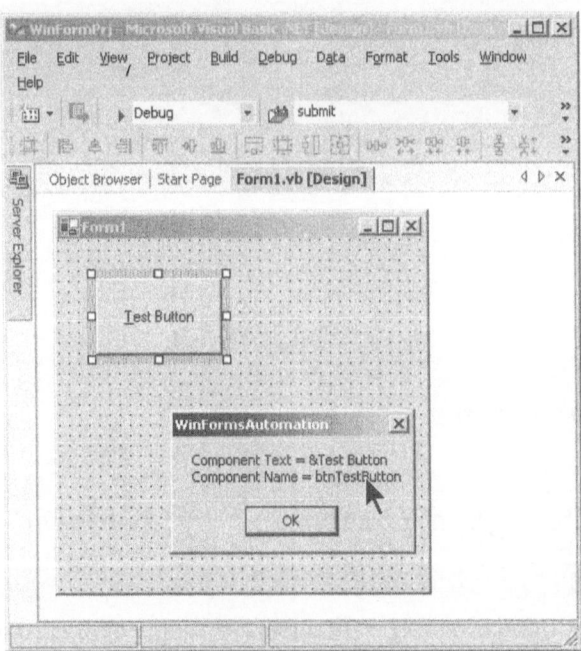

Figure 6-6. Showing the button's new text and name

Now you will remove the second button to show that it is much simpler to destroy a component than it is to create it. (It seems like there is a lesson to be learned about life in that statement!) Actually, it is very simple to remove a component once you have a handle to the Forms Designer. The following snippet removes btn2 from the form:

```
fdHost.DestroyComponent(btn2)
ListComponents("form after removing one button...",
        fdHost.Container.Components)
```

Figure 6-7 shows the form after the second button has been removed from the form. The message box lists the form and its remaining components.

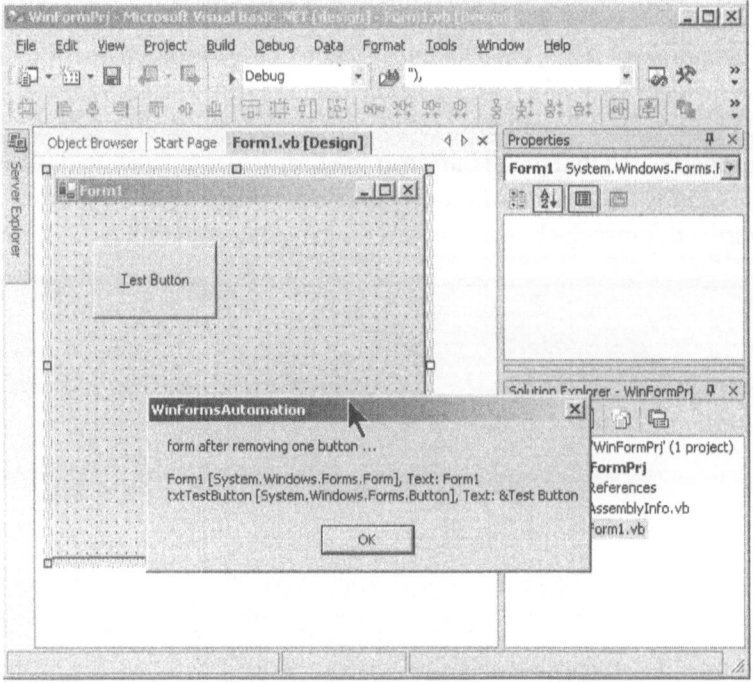

Figure 6-7. Btn2 removed

Looping Through a Collection of Selected Components

In an add-in, you will probably want to perform some operation on one or more selected components on a form. The code in Listing 6-9 shows how to select a component from the add-in. It then shows how to access the properties of each selected component.

Listing 6-9. Selecting a Component

```
01              ' Select a component on a form
02              MsgBox("Selecting button component...")
03              Dim sel As ISelectionService
04              sel = CType(fdHost.GetService(Type.GetType ↵
05                  ("System.ComponentModel.Design.ISelectionService,System")), ↵
06                  System.ComponentModel.Design.ISelectionService)
07              sel.SetSelectedComponents(New Object() {btn1})
08
09              ' get the count of selected components
10              Dim i As Integer = sel.SelectionCount
11              MsgBox("Selected Component Count = " & CStr(i))
```

Line 03 dimensions an object of type ISelectionService. The ISelectionService object provides an interface for a designer to select components. This allows you to select a specific component, such as the code is doing in this code snippet. Lines 04 and 07 select the one remaining button on the form. Line 10 gets the count of selected components. Obviously, there is only one component selected, because you just selected it. Figure 6-8 shows that the button has been selected and displays the count of selected components.

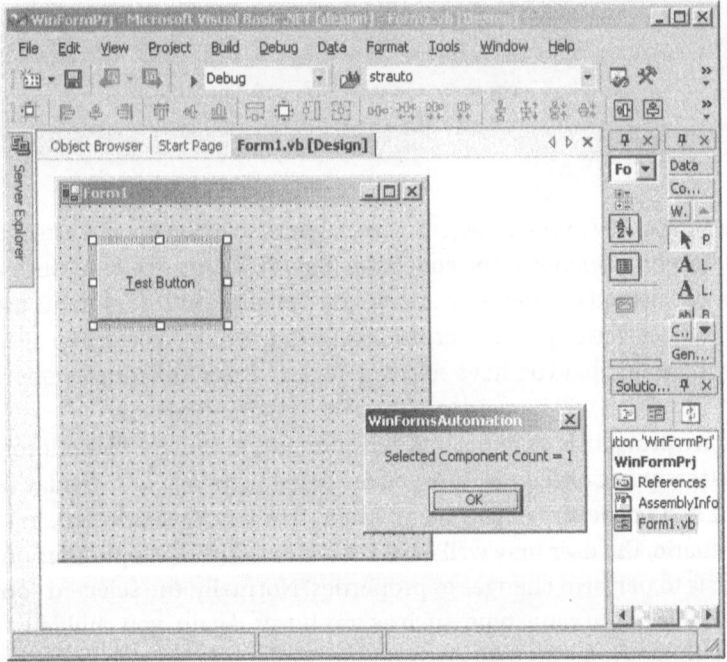

Figure 6-8. Selected component and the count of selected components

Next, you will loop through the collection of selected components. Although there is only one component selected, this code would display the specified properties, regardless of the number of components a user may have selected. It is common practice to select one or more components, usually of the same type, prior to invoking some functionality in an add-in that would perform operations on the properties of all selected components.

Listing 6-10 shows the code for listing two properties of each component in the collection of selected components. Although this code is only displaying the value of the specified properties, Name and Text, you have already seen how to use the SetValue method of the PropertyDescriptor object to change the value of properties.

Listing 6-10. Looping Through the Collection of Selected Components

```
12          ' loop through the selected component collection
13          ' listing properties
14            Dim ic As IComponent
15            Dim c As Component
16            For Each c In sel.GetSelectedComponents
17                ic = CType(c, IComponent)
18                pdc = TypeDescriptor.GetProperties(ic)
19                pd = pdc("Text")
20                s = pd.GetValue(ic).ToString
21                pd = pdc("Name")
22                s2 = pd.GetValue(ic).ToString
23                MsgBox("Component Text = " & s & Chr(10) & _
24                    "Component Name = " & s2)
25            Next
```

Lines 14 and 15 simply dimension two objects, which you will use in the loop to access the components in the collection. Line 16 begins the loop through the collection of selected components. Using the GetSelectedComponents method of the ISelectionService object (sel, created in Listing 6-9), you create a collection of the components that you have selected. Line 17 casts the Component to type IComponent, which will be used to access the specific properties.

You have previously seen the use of IComponent, PropertyDescriptor, and PropertyDescriptorCollection. Here you are using them again to display the Name and Text properties of each component that you have selected. In a real add-in scenario, the user may well have selected multiple components on which the add-in is to perform changes to properties. Normally, the selected components would be of the same type, such as text boxes. Again, you could just as easily be setting properties instead of simply displaying them.

You can let your imagination and creativity run wild thinking of applications for this type of code.

Figure 6-9 shows the display of the properties from the selected component. If there were multiple components in the collection, the message box would be displayed multiple times.

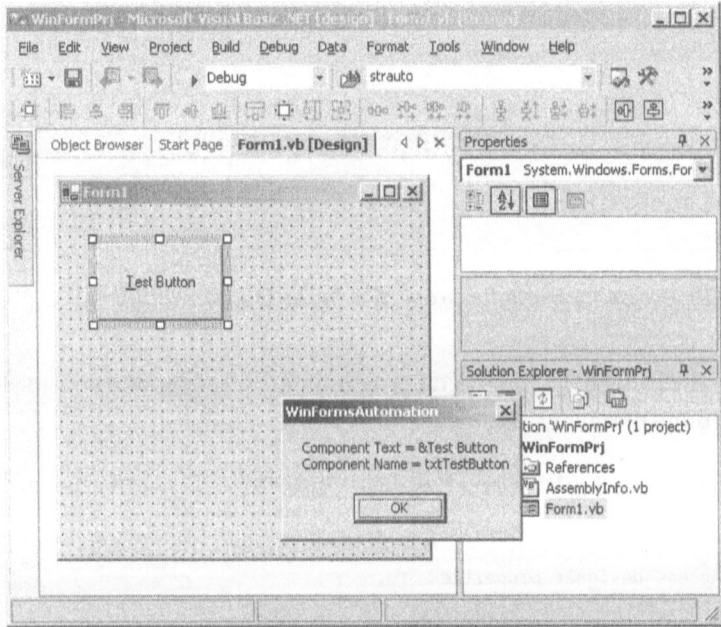

Figure 6-9. Displaying properties of selected component

Accessing Designer Options

Although this topic has nothing to do with the creation of the form, let's take a short side trip in order to show the lengths to which you can go with the objects included in the automation model. The code snippet in Listing 6-11 illustrates how to programmatically access the Window Forms Designer options. These options are exposed to the developer in the IDE by selecting Tools ➤ Options. When the Options dialog box appears, click the Windows Forms Designer folder, and then click the General arrow. Finally, click the plus sign (+) to the left of the GridSize option to expose the separate Height and Width (GridSize) properties. You will see the properties as displayed in Figure 6-10.

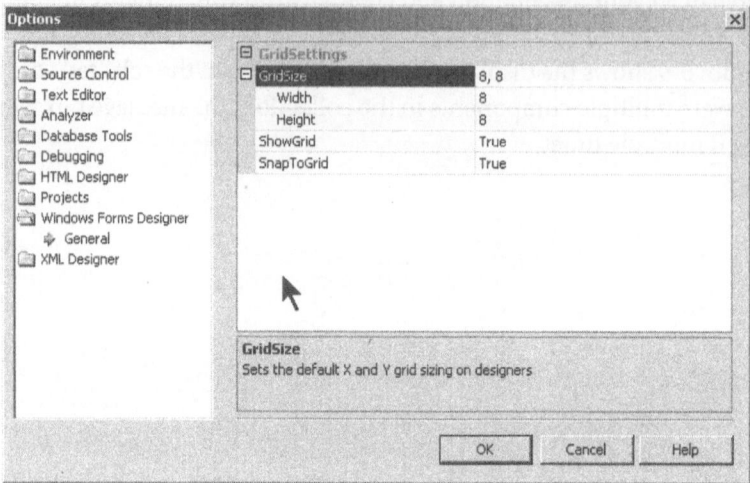

Figure 6-10. Accessing Designer properties in the Options dialog box

Now, in Listing 6-11 you will do programmatically from the add-in what you have just done manually in the IDE.

Listing 6-11. Accessing Windows Designer Properties

```
01   Try
02     'Access designer properties
03     MsgBox("Accessing designer grid size...")
04     Dim opt As IDesignerOptionService
05     opt = CType(fdHost.GetService(Type.GetType⤶
06              ("System.ComponentModel.Design.⤶
07              IDesignerOptionService,System")), _
08              System.ComponentModel.Design.⤶
09              IDesignerOptionService)
10     Dim siz As Size = CType(opt.GetOptionValue⤶
11              ("WindowsFormsDesigner\General", ⤶
12              "GridSize"), Size)
13     MsgBox(siz.ToString())
14     Catch e As System.Exception
15       MsgBox("failed accessing designer props")
16       MsgBox(e.tostring())
17     End Try
```

Line 04 dimensions an object of the IDesignerOptionService type. The IDesignerOptionService class gets the service object of the specified type. Line 04 uses the GetService method to create an object (opt) of the

IDesignerOptionService type. The GetService method returns an object that represents a service provided by the Component or by its Container. Simply stated, opt is an object representing the Options dialog box. It is a Container for system options. Line 10 dimensions a System.Drawing.Size object and points it to the Windows Forms Designer, General folder in the Options dialog box.

Line 13 displays the Size object settings, which are the Height and Width settings for the grid on a form designer. The object, opt, also has a SetOption method, which you could use to change the GridSize settings programmatically.

Admittedly, this is probably not a feature for which you would find a practical use, but it again illustrates the depth of object exposure in the automation model.

Adding an Event Handler

Not only can you add a component (button) to a form programmatically, but you can also add an event handler to a form programmatically. The code in Listing 6-12 adds an event handler to the form for the button component.

Listing 6-12. Adding an Event Handler

```
01        Dim click As EventDescriptor
02        click = TypeDescriptor.GetEvents(btn1)("Click")
03        Dim eventSvc As IEventBindingService
04        eventSvc = CType(fdHost.GetService  ⏎
05            (Type.GetType("System.ComponentModel.Design.  ⏎
06            IEventBindingService,System")),  ⏎
07            System.ComponentModel.Design.IEventBindingService)
08        Dim clickProp As PropertyDescriptor
09        clickProp = eventSvc.GetEventProperty(click)
10        clickProp.SetValue(btn1, "btnTestButton_OnClick")
11        Dim addSvc As IcomponentChangeService  ⏎
12        addSvc = CType(fdHost.GetService(Type.GetType
13            ("System.ComponentModel.Design.  ⏎
14            IComponentChangeService,System")),  ⏎
15            System.ComponentModel.Design.IComponentChangeService)
```

Line 01 dimensions an object as EventDescriptor. An EventDescriptor provides information about an event. Line 02 references the TypeDescriptor class. The TypeDescriptor object is used to get information about the properties and events for a component. The GetEvents method gets information about the "Click" event.

Line 03 dimensions an object of the IEventBindingService type. The event-binding service provides a way to expose events as properties. This service can expose events for a particular component as an array of PropertyDescriptor objects with a data type of string. Line 04 casts the dimensioned object, eventSvc, to System Component Designer. Line 08 simply dimensions a PropertyDescriptor object, which you have used several times before in this chapter.

Line 09 sets the PropertyDescriptor, clickProp, to the object that was created in lines 02 through 04. The PropertyDescriptor object, clickProp, now has the information needed to create the Click event for a button component. Line 10 uses the SetValue method of the PropertyDescriptor object in preparation for setting the event on the form.

Lines 11 and 12 hook the event to the control and place the event on the form. The IComponentChangeService class provides an interface to add and remove the event handlers for events that add, change, remove, or rename components. If you look at the code in the form after the automation process is complete, you will see that the event code appears as follows:

```
Private Sub btnTestButton_OnClick(ByVal sender As System.Object, _
    ByVal e As System.EventArgs) Handles btnTestButton.Click
End Sub
```

Adding a Menu to the Form

The last exercise in the automation code will demonstrate how to place a menu on the form programmatically. Listing 6-13 contains the code to place the menu on the form. Adding a menu to the form programmatically is one of the simpler tasks that you have had to perform in this automation process. If you have not already done so, perhaps you should stop and create a Windows application with one form in it and familiarize yourself with the Menu Designer.

Menus, just like buttons and other controls, are components on the form. In VB 6.0, you could add controls to a form at runtime if you had at least one control of the type that you wanted to add already on the form. However, you could not add a menu from scratch. In .NET, you can add any component (control) to the form at runtime, including a main menu and menu items (submenus).

Listing 6-13. Adding a Menu

```
01    'Create a menu on the form
02    Dim mainMenuComp As IComponent = fdHost.CreateComponent ⏎
03        (Type.GetType("System.Windows.Forms.MainMenu, ⏎
04        System.Windows.Forms"), "mainMenu1")
05    Dim fileMenuItemComp As IComponent = fdHost.CreateComponent ⏎
06        (Type.GetType("System.Windows.Forms.MenuItem, ⏎
07        System.Windows.Forms"), "fileMenuItem")
```

```
08    Dim menuItem2Comp As IComponent = fdHost.CreateComponent ↵
09        (Type.GetType("System.Windows.Forms.MenuItem, ↵
10        System.Windows.Forms"),  "mainItem2")
11    Dim menuItem3Comp As IComponent = fdHost.CreateComponent ↵
12        (Type.GetType("System.Windows.Forms.MenuItem, ↵
13      System.Windows.Forms"),  "mainItem3")
14      Dim menuItem4Comp As IComponent = fdHost.CreateComponent ↵
15        (Type.GetType("System.Windows.Forms.MenuItem, ↵
16      System.Windows.Forms"),  "mainItem4")
17
18      Dim mainMenu1 As MainMenu = CType(mainMenuComp, MainMenu)
19      Dim fileMenuItem As MenuItem = CType(fileMenuItemComp, MenuItem)
20      Dim menuItem2 As MenuItem = CType(menuItem2Comp, MenuItem)
21      Dim menuItem3 As MenuItem = CType(menuItem3Comp, MenuItem)
22    Dim menuItem4 As MenuItem = CType(menuItem4Comp, MenuItem)
23
24      fileMenuItem.Text = "&File"
25      menuItem2.Text = "&Edit"
26      menuItem3.Text = "&Open"
27      menuItem4.Text = "&Save"
28
29      mainMenu1.MenuItems.Add(fileMenuItem)
30      mainMenu1.MenuItems.Add(menuItem2)
31
32      fileMenuItem.MenuItems.Add(menuItem3)
33      fileMenuItem.MenuItems.Add(menuItem4)
```

Line 02 dimensions and creates mainMenuComp as a MainMenu constructor. A MainMenu is an array to which you can add MenuItem objects. Lines 05 through 14 create the MenuItem objects that will be added to the MainMenu array. Note that the menu objects, both the MainMenu array and the individual MenuItem objects, are being named as they are created. If you were manually adding menu items to a menu control in the IDE, you would right-click the item to edit the name. In the automation model, you do that as part of adding the menu item to the array of items. To understand more clearly exactly what is going on with each line of the automation code, you should compare the code in the automation example to the code being generated. The complete code for the whole form is shown in Listing 6-14.

Line 18 dimensions and casts the MainMenu object to type MainMenu, which is the array that will be the container for the MenuItem objects. Lines 19 through 22 dimension and cast the individual MenuItem objects. These are the individual MenuItems, both top-level menus and submenus.

Lines 24 through 27 set the Text property of the MenuItem objects. Finally, lines 29 and 30 add the top-level MenuItem objects to the array. Lines 32 and 33 add the submenus to the File menu.

Now that you have added the menu to the form, the automation demonstration is complete. The completed form displayed in the Designer is shown in Figure 6-11.

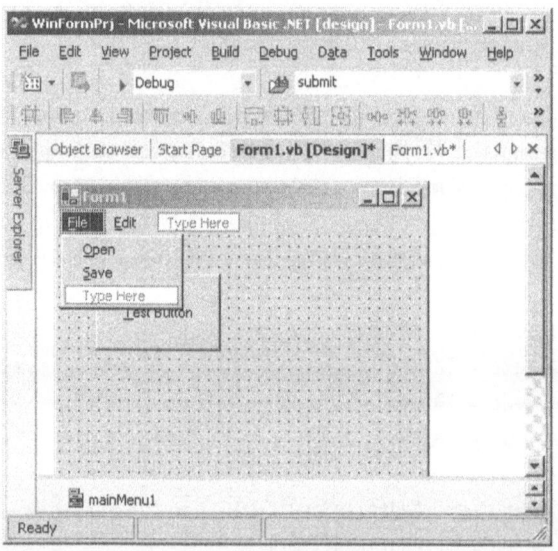

Figure 6-11. Completed form

The complete code for the form as generated by the automation demonstration is shown in Listing 6-14. If you are having trouble understanding any of the processes that you have gone through, it will be most helpful for you to compare the code in the automation code snippets to the generated code in the form.

Listing 6-14. Completed Form Code

```
Public Class Form1
    Inherits System.Windows.Forms.Form

#Region " Windows Form Designer generated code "

    Public Sub New()
        MyBase.New()

        'This call is required by the Windows Form Designer.
        InitializeComponent()
```

```
        'Add any initialization after the InitializeComponent() call

End Sub


'Form overrides dispose to clean up the component list.
Protected Overloads Overrides Sub Dispose(ByVal disposing As Boolean)
    If disposing Then
        If Not (components Is Nothing) Then
            components.Dispose()
        End If
    End If
    MyBase.Dispose(disposing)
End Sub


'Required by the Windows Form Designer
Private components As System.ComponentModel.IContainer

'NOTE: The following procedure is required by the Windows Form Designer
'It can be modified using the Windows Form Designer.
'Do not modify it using the code editor.
Friend WithEvents btnTestButton As System.Windows.Forms.Button
Friend WithEvents mainMenu1 As System.Windows.Forms.MainMenu
Friend WithEvents fileMenuItem As System.Windows.Forms.MenuItem
Friend WithEvents mainItem2 As System.Windows.Forms.MenuItem
Friend WithEvents mainItem3 As System.Windows.Forms.MenuItem
Friend WithEvents mainItem4 As System.Windows.Forms.MenuItem
<System.Diagnostics.DebuggerStepThrough()> Private Sub InitializeComponent()
    Me.btnTestButton = New System.Windows.Forms.Button()
    Me.mainMenu1 = New System.Windows.Forms.MainMenu()
    Me.fileMenuItem = New System.Windows.Forms.MenuItem()
    Me.mainItem2 = New System.Windows.Forms.MenuItem()
    Me.mainItem3 = New System.Windows.Forms.MenuItem()
    Me.mainItem4 = New System.Windows.Forms.MenuItem()
    Me.SuspendLayout()
    '
    'btnTestButton
    '
    Me.btnTestButton.Location = New System.Drawing.Point(30, 30)
    Me.btnTestButton.Name = "btnTestButton"
    Me.btnTestButton.Size = New System.Drawing.Size(100, 60)
    Me.btnTestButton.TabIndex = 0
    Me.btnTestButton.Text = "&Test Button"
    '
```

```
'mainMenu1
'
Me.mainMenu1.MenuItems.AddRange↵
  (New System.Windows.Forms.MenuItem() {Me.fileMenuItem,↵
  Me.mainItem2})
'
'fileMenuItem
'
Me.fileMenuItem.Index = 0
Me.fileMenuItem.MenuItems.AddRange↵
  (New System.Windows.Forms.MenuItem() {Me.mainItem3,↵
  Me.mainItem4})
Me.fileMenuItem.Text = "&File"
'
'mainItem2
'
Me.mainItem2.Index = 1
Me.mainItem2.Text = "&Edit"
'
'mainItem3
'
Me.mainItem3.Index = 0
Me.mainItem3.Text = "&Open"
'
'mainItem4
'
Me.mainItem4.Index = 1
Me.mainItem4.Text = "&Save"
'
'Form1
'
Me.AutoScaleBaseSize = New System.Drawing.Size(5, 13)
Me.ClientSize = New System.Drawing.Size(292, 273)
Me.Controls.AddRange(New System.Windows.Forms.Control() {Me.btnTestButton})
Me.Menu = Me.mainMenu1
Me.Name = "Form1"
Me.Text = "Form1"
Me.ResumeLayout(False)

End Sub

#End Region
```

```
Private Sub btnTestButton_OnClick(ByVal sender As System.Object, _
    ByVal e As System.EventArgs) Handles btnTestButton.Click

    End Sub
End Class
```

Summary

In this chapter, you went through a lot of code, using many of the more complex
objects in the automation model. You created a new Windows application project. You added button components and renamed, resized, and repositioned one
of the components. You learned how to remove components and how to add an
event to a component. You saw how to loop through a collection of selected components, listing properties for the individual selected components, and you
learned how to modify properties of selected components. Finally, you added
a menu with submenus to the form. As you have come to understand with the
objects in this chapter, you can do anything you want to do with the components
on a form programmatically.

In Chapter 7 you will learn a variety of ways to produce a user interface,
including through the use of tool bars, menus, and even the system tray.

The User Interface

"Don't plan with a rainy day in mind."
—*Oswald Chambers*

SOMEONE ONCE APTLY SAID, "You only get one chance to make a good first impression." That being the case, the add-in developer needs to give a lot of thought to his or her add-in's user interface (UI), the means through which users access the functionality of the add-in. If the interface is not intuitive and easy to use, users may give up or simply decide not to bother with the add-in. You cannot count on their reading a manual, or even consulting a help file. With regard to reading a manual, for the most part, manuals are not provided, much less printed. This has been the case with most software products for several years now. And as to consulting a help file, my feeling is that if I have to consult a help file to deduce how to use the basic functionality of a program, the UI is not properly designed, and the program has two strikes against it before I even start to try to use it.

Until now, I have used the same basic UI in all of this book's add-ins. The UI has started with one menu item added to the Tools menu. In the book's first add-in, which was developed in Chapters 2, 3, and 5, I launched a form with a TreeView control. The TreeView provides a great menu, especially when you use parent and child nodes so that the menus can be collapsed, thus providing many menu options in a minimal amount of space. So, you have seen two types of add-in interfaces. In this chapter, I expand on both types and introduce some other possibilities.

A Simple UI: DTE Menu Items

If your add-in does not have many different functions, you may be able to get away with using the simplest type of UI, the DTE menu item. Although you have only used one menu item in this book's add-ins thus far, it is certainly possible to add more than one, as you will see in this section.

NOTE *I call these menu items "DTE menu items" because I am using DTE command methods to create the menus. Later in this chapter I show you how to create menus and toolbars using the Microsoft Office command bar controls.*

To create another new add-in for the creation of multiple menus, go to the Add-in Wizard once again. By now, you should be adept at creating add-ins with the wizard, so I'll simply tell you the options to use, without illustrating the process with figures.

First, open Visual Studio and click the New Project button. Expand the Other Projects node on the TreeView, and then click the Extensibility Projects folder. Single-click the Visual Studio .NET Add-in icon. Enter **UIMenus** into the Name text box, and choose a path where you want this new add-in project saved. I always choose a directory that I've set up for my projects, so I don't have to remember where Visual Studio saves projects by default. Click the OK button to start the wizard.

In Step 1, select the Visual Basic Add-in option. In Step 2, check only the Visual Studio .NET Add-in check box. In Step 3, enter **UIMenus** in the Name box. Enter a description such as **Testing multiple menu items**.

In Step 4, check the first, third, and fourth check boxes. In other words, check all boxes except the one that says your add-in won't display a modal UI. You will be displaying a modal UI, even if only in the form of a message box. Do not check the box in Step 5—just click Next to move to Step 6. If you are satisfied with the options that you have selected, as displayed in Step 6, click the Finish button to create the add-in.

When the wizard creates the add-in, your code should look like Listing 7-1.

NOTE *The code generated by the Add-in Wizard will not be automatically continued. I did that manually so that the code would fit onto the book's pages.*

Listing 7-1. Add-in Code Created by the Add-in Wizard

```
Imports Microsoft.Office.Core
imports Extensibility
imports System.Runtime.InteropServices
Imports EnvDTE


#Region " Read me for Add-in installation and setup information. "
' When run, the Add-in wizard prepared the registry for the Add-in.
' At a later time, if the Add-in becomes unavailable for reasons such as:
'    1) You moved this project to a computer other than
'        the one it was originally created on.
'    2) You chose 'Yes' when presented with a message asking
'        if you wish to remove the Add-in.
'    3) Registry corruption.
```

```
' you will need to re-register the Add-in by building the UIMenusSetup project
' by right-clicking the project in the Solution Explorer, then choosing install.
#End Region

<GuidAttribute("A1DD20DF-FC66-4E5D-B0C3-1831FF589E42"), _
ProgIdAttribute("UIMenus.Connect")> _
Public Class Connect

    Implements Extensibility.IDTExtensibility2
    Implements IDTCommandTarget

    Dim applicationObject As EnvDTE.DTE
    Dim addInInstance As EnvDTE.AddIn

    Public Sub OnBeginShutdown(ByRef custom As System.Array) _
        Implements Extensibility.IDTExtensibility2.OnBeginShutdown
    End Sub

    Public Sub OnAddInsUpdate(ByRef custom As System.Array) _
        Implements Extensibility.IDTExtensibility2.OnAddInsUpdate
    End Sub

    Public Sub OnStartupComplete(ByRef custom As System.Array) _
        Implements Extensibility.IDTExtensibility2.OnStartupComplete
    End Sub

    Public Sub OnDisconnection(ByVal RemoveMode As _
        Extensibility.ext_DisconnectMode, _
        ByRef custom As System.Array) Implements _
        Extensibility.IDTExtensibility2.OnDisconnection
    End Sub

    Public Sub OnConnection(ByVal application As Object, _
        ByVal connectMode As Extensibility.ext_ConnectMode, _
        ByVal addInInst As Object, _
        ByRef custom As System.Array) Implements _
        Extensibility.IDTExtensibility2.OnConnection

        applicationObject = CType(application, EnvDTE.DTE)
        addInInstance = CType(addInInst, EnvDTE.AddIn)
        If connectMode = Extensibility.ext_ConnectMode.ext_cm_UISetup Then
            Dim objAddIn As AddIn = CType(addInInst, AddIn)
            Dim CommandObj As Command
```

```vb
        ' When run, the Add-in wizard prepared the registry for the Add-in.
        ' At a later time, the Add-in or its commands may become
        ' unavailable for reasons such as:
        '    1) You moved this project to a computer other than the
        '         one it was originally created on.
        '    2) You chose 'Yes' when presented with a message asking
        '         if you wish to remove the Add-in.
        '    3) You add new commands or modify commands already defined.
        ' You will need to re-register the Add-in by building the
        ' UIMenusSetup project,
        ' right-clicking the project in the Solution Explorer, and then
        ' choosing install.
        ' Alternatively, you could execute the ReCreateCommands.reg
        ' file the Add-in Wizard generated in
        ' the project directory, or run 'devenv /setup' from a command prompt.
        Try
            CommandObj = applicationObject.Commands. ↵
                AddNamedCommand(objAddIn, _
                "UIMenus", "UIMenus", "Executes the command for UIMenus", _
                True, 59, Nothing, 1 + 2) _
                '1+2 == vsCommandStatusSupported+vsCommandStatusEnabled
            CommandObj.AddControl(applicationObject.CommandBars.Item("Tools"))
        Catch e As System.Exception
        End Try
      End If
    End Sub

    Public Sub Exec(ByVal cmdName As String, _
      ByVal executeOption As vsCommandExecOption, _
      ByRef varIn As Object, _
      ByRef varOut As Object, _
      ByRef handled As Boolean) _
      Implements IDTCommandTarget.Exec
      handled = False
      If (executeOption = vsCommandExecOption.vsCommandExecOptionDoDefault) Then
        If cmdName = "UIMenus.Connect.UIMenus" Then
            handled = True
            Exit Sub
        End If
      End If
    End Sub
```

```
    Public Sub QueryStatus(ByVal cmdName As String, _
        ByVal neededText As vsCommandStatusTextWanted, _
        ByRef statusOption As vsCommandStatus, _
        ByRef commandText As Object) _
        Implements IDTCommandTarget.QueryStatus
        If neededText = _
        EnvDTE.vsCommandStatusTextWanted.vsCommandStatusTextWantedNone Then
            If cmdName = "UIMenus.Connect.UIMenus" Then
                statusOption = CType(vsCommandStatus.vsCommandStatusEnabled + _
                vsCommandStatus.vsCommandStatusSupported, vsCommandStatus)
            Else
                statusOption = vsCommandStatus.vsCommandStatusUnsupported
            End If
        End If
    End Sub
End Class
```

As you have seen in earlier chapters, the Add-in Wizard creates one menu item for you. Now, you need to make some modifications to the code to add two more menu items. Actually, you can add as many menu items as you want to, but practically speaking, that would not make for an ideal UI. Any number of menu items beyond four or five might border on the ridiculous. The changes you make will accomplish the following:

- Add two additional menu items.

- Add code to delete the menu items upon disconnecting the add-in.

- Shorten the name of the applicationObject to oVB.

- Add code to the Click event handler for the menus.

Listing 7-2 shows the code generated by the wizard after the specified changes are made. The changes appear in boldface.

Listing 7-2. Code Modified to Add Menus

```
Imports Microsoft.Office.Core
imports Extensibility
imports System.Runtime.InteropServices
Imports EnvDTE
```

```vb
#Region " Read me for Add-in installation and setup information. "
' When run, the Add-in wizard prepared the registry for the Add-in.
' At a later time, if the Add-in becomes unavailable for reasons such as:
'   1) You moved this project to a computer other than the one it was
'         originally created on.
'   2) You chose 'Yes' when presented with a message asking if you
'         wish to remove the Add-in.
'   3) Registry corruption.
' you will need to re-register the Add-in by building the UIMenusSetup project
' by right-clicking the project in the Solution Explorer, then choosing install.
#End Region

<GuidAttribute("A1DD2ODF-FC66-4E5D-B0C3-1831FF589E42"), _
ProgIdAttribute("UIMenus.Connect")> _
Public Class Connect

    Implements Extensibility.IDTExtensibility2
    Implements IDTCommandTarget

    ' shortened applicationObject to oVB for ease of reading
    Dim oVB As EnvDTE.DTE
    Dim addInInstance As EnvDTE.AddIn
     ' CommandObjs moved to module level so Disconnect can see them
    Dim CommandObj As Command
    Dim CommandObj2 As Command
    Dim CommandObj3 As Command

    Public Sub OnBeginShutdown(ByRef custom As System.Array) _
        Implements Extensibility.IDTExtensibility2.OnBeginShutdown
    End Sub

    Public Sub OnAddInsUpdate(ByRef custom As System.Array) _
        Implements Extensibility.IDTExtensibility2.OnAddInsUpdate
    End Sub

    Public Sub OnStartupComplete(ByRef custom As System.Array) _
        Implements Extensibility.IDTExtensibility2.OnStartupComplete
    End Sub

    Public Sub OnDisconnection(ByVal RemoveMode As _
        Extensibility.ext_DisconnectMode, _
        ByRef custom As System.Array) Implements _
        Extensibility.IDTExtensibility2.OnDisconnection
```

```vbnet
    Try
        CommandObj.Delete()
        CommandObj2.Delete()
        CommandObj3.Delete()
    Catch e As System.Exception
        MsgBox("Error deleting menus: " & e.Message)
    End Try
End Sub

Public Sub OnConnection(ByVal application As Object, _
    ByVal connectMode As Extensibility.ext_ConnectMode, _
    ByVal addInInst As Object, _
    ByRef custom As System.Array) Implements _
    Extensibility.IDTExtensibility2.OnConnection


    oVB = CType(application, EnvDTE.DTE)
    addInInstance = CType(addInInst, EnvDTE.AddIn)


    ' test for type startup, first or subsequent
    If connectMode = _
        Extensibility.ext_ConnectMode.ext_cm_UISetup Or _
        connectMode = _
        Extensibility.ext_ConnectMode.ext_cm_Startup _
        Then
        Dim objAddIn As AddIn = CType(addInInst, AddIn)


        ' When run, the Add-in wizard prepared the registry
        ' for the Add-in.
        ' At a later time, the Add-in or its commands may
        ' become unavailable
        ' for reasons such as:
        '    1) You moved this project to a computer other
        '        than the one it was created on
        '    2) You chose 'Yes' when presented with a message
        '        asking if you wish to remove the add-in
        '    3) You add new commands or modify commands
        '        already defined.
        ' You will need to re-register the Add-in by building the
        ' UIMenusSetup project,
        ' right-clicking the project in the Solution Explorer,
        '  and then choosing install.
        ' Alternatively, you could execute the
        ' ReCreateCommands.reg
```

```
                        ' file the Add-in
                        ' Wizard generated in
                        ' the project directory, or run 'devenv /setup'
                        ' from a command prompt.
                        Try
                            CommandObj = oVB.Commands.AddNamedCommand(objAddIn, _
                                "UIMenus", "UIMenus One", _
                                "Executes the command for UIMenus", _
                                True, 59, Nothing, 1 + 2) _
                                '1+2 == vsCommandStatusSupported+↩
                                vsCommandStatusEnabled
                            CommandObj.AddControl(oVB.CommandBars.Item("Tools"))

                            CommandObj2 = oVB.Commands.AddNamedCommand(objAddIn, _
                                "UIMenus2", "UIMenus Two", _
                                "Executes the command for UIMenus", _
                                True, 60, Nothing, 1 + 2) _
                                '1+2 == vsCommandStatusSupported+↩
                                vsCommandStatusEnabled
                            CommandObj2.AddControl(oVB.CommandBars.Item("Tools"))

                            CommandObj3 = oVB.Commands.AddNamedCommand(objAddIn, _
                                "UIMenus3", "UIMenus Three", _
                                "Executes the command for UIMenus", _
                                True, 62, Nothing, 1 + 2) _
                                '1+2 == vsCommandStatusSupported+↩
                                vsCommandStatusEnabled
                            CommandObj3.AddControl(oVB.CommandBars.Item("Tools"))
                    Catch e As System.Exception
                        MsgBox("Error Adding Menus: " & e.Message)
                    End Try
                End If
            End Sub

            Public Sub Exec(ByVal cmdName As String, _
                ByVal executeOption As vsCommandExecOption, _
                ByRef varIn As Object, _
                ByRef varOut As Object, _
                ByRef handled As Boolean) _
                Implements IDTCommandTarget.Exec
                handled = False
                If (executeOption = vsCommandExecOption.↩
                    vsCommandExecOptionDoDefault) Then
```

```
        If cmdName = "UIMenus.Connect.UIMenus" Then
            handled = True
            MsgBox("Menu one selected.")
        ElseIf cmdName = "UIMenus.Connect.UIMenus2" Then
            MsgBox("Menu two selected.")
        ElseIf cmdName = "UIMenus.Connect.UIMenus3" Then
            MsgBox("Menu three selected.")
        End If
    End If
End Sub


Public Sub QueryStatus(ByVal cmdName As String, _
    ByVal neededText As vsCommandStatusTextWanted, _
    ByRef statusOption As vsCommandStatus, _
    ByRef commandText As Object) _
    Implements IDTCommandTarget.QueryStatus
    If neededText = _
        EnvDTE.vsCommandStatusTextWanted.vsCommandStatusTextWantedNone Then
        If cmdName = "UIMenus.Connect.UIMenus" Or _
            cmdName = "UIMenus.Connect.UIMenus2" Or _
            cmdName = "UIMenus.Connect.UIMenus3" _
            Then
            statusOption = CType(vsCommandStatus.↵
                vsCommandStatusEnabled + _
                vsCommandStatus.vsCommandStatusSupported, ↵
                vsCommandStatus)
        Else
            statusOption = ↵
                vsCommandStatus.vsCommandStatusUnsupported
        End If
    End If
End Sub
End Class
```

The code shown in Listing 7-2 uses two Command methods:
AddNamedCommand and AddControl. Although I illustrated the use of these
methods in earlier chapters, I did not explain them. I will do that now.

The AddNamedCommand object creates a named command that is saved by
the environment and can be made available the next time the environment
starts, even if the add-in is not loaded on environment start-up.

 **NOTE** *Because I always delete the command object(s) in the OnDisconnection method of an add-in, the command(s) do not appear unless the add-in is connected.*

The AddNamedCommand method returns a Command object and has several parameters, which are shown in Table 7-1.

Table 7-1. AddNamedCommand Parameters

PARAMETER	DESCRIPTION
Addin	Required. Refers to the Addin object that is adding the new command.
Name	Required. The nonunique name for the command. AddNamedCommand adds Addins.Progid to make the command unique.
Button Text	Required. This is the caption that will be displayed on the command.
Tool Tip	Required. This is the tool tip that will be displayed as the mouse hovers over the command.
MSOButton	Required. Indicates whether the named command's button picture is a Microsoft Office picture (True = button).
Bitmap	Optional. The integer ID of the bitmap to display. This is a pointer into Office.DLL.
ContextUIGuids	A SafeArray of GUIDs that determines which environment contexts (i.e., debug mode, design mode, and so on) enable the command. (I use Nothing for this parameter.)
DisableFlags	Determines whether the disabled state of the command is invisible or grey when you supply a ContextUIGUID and none are currently active (e.g., `1+2` == `vsCommandStatusSupported` + `vsCommandStatusEnabled`).

Listing 7-3 shows a typical call to the AddNamedCommand method.

Listing 7-3. AddNamedCommand Method Usage

```
CommandObj = oVB.Commands.AddNamedCommand(objAddIn, _
    "UIMenus", "UIMenus One", "Executes the command for UIMenus", _
    True, 59, Nothing, 1 + 2) _
    '1+2 == vsCommandStatusSupported+vsCommandStatusEnabled
CommandObj.AddControl(oVB.CommandBars.Item("Tools"))
```

The returned Command object has a method called AddControl. It is called to set the new command on the toolbar. In this demonstration, the control or Command object is a menu item that is added to the Tools menu. To run the add-in, simply click the Start button or press F5. If you have no compile errors, a second instance of Visual Studio will be automatically started. The add-in should be automatically connected, and the menus should be visible when you click the Tools menu. If they are not, click the Tools menu and then the Add-in Manager menu item to display the Add-in Manager dialog box. Check both check boxes for the UIMenus add-in. When you click OK to close the dialog box, the add-in will connect. Click each of the add-in's menus to see that the event handler is correctly handling the menu clicks. Figure 7-1 shows the Tools menu with the three menu items that have been added by the add-in.

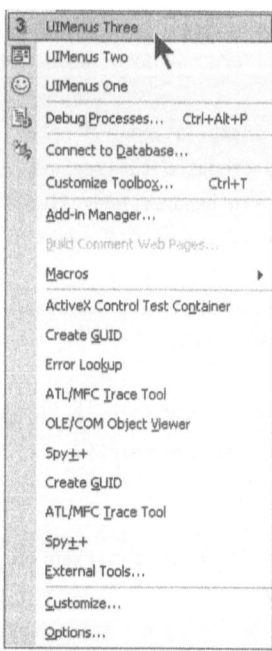

Figure 7-1. UIMenus add-in menu items

 **NOTE** *You can download the code for this book from the Downloads section of the Apress Web site (*`http://www.apress.com`*). You can find the code for this chapter in several directories. You will find one for each add-in created for this chapter under the name of the respective UI topic.*

Adding an Add-in DTE Toolbar

You've seen the simplest and easiest method of presenting a UI. Now let's step up a little more in complexity as well as sophistication of the UI design. In this section, you'll add a new toolbar for the add-in. Listing 7-4 shows the Connect class after it has been enhanced to add a toolbar. Code that was changed or added to create the toolbar appears in boldface.

Listing 7-4. Adding an Add-in Toolbar

```
Imports Microsoft.Office.Core
imports Extensibility
imports System.Runtime.InteropServices
Imports EnvDTE

#Region " Read me for Add-in installation and setup information. "
' When run, the Add-in wizard prepared the registry for the Add-in.
' At a later time, if the Add-in becomes unavailable for reasons such as:
'    1) You moved this project to a computer other than the one it was
'          originally created on.
'    2) You chose 'Yes' when presented with a message asking if
'          you wish to remove the Add-in.
'    3) Registry corruption.
' you will need to re-register the Add-in by building the UIMenusSetup project
' by right-clicking the project in the Solution Explorer, then choosing install.
#End Region

<GuidAttribute("A1DD20DF-FC66-4E5D-B0C3-1831FF589E42"), _
ProgIdAttribute("UIMenus.Connect")> _
Public Class Connect

    Implements Extensibility.IDTExtensibility2
    Implements IDTCommandTarget
```

```
Dim oVB As EnvDTE.DTE
Dim addInInstance As EnvDTE.AddIn
Dim CommandObj As Command
Dim CommandObj2 As Command
Dim CommandObj3 As Command

' moved to module level to make visible to
' AddAddinCmdBar
Dim objAddin As AddIn

' Command Bar commands and object
Dim cmdObj As Command
Dim cmdObj2 As Command
Dim cmdbarobj As Microsoft.Office.Core.CommandBar

Public Sub OnBeginShutdown(ByRef custom As System.Array) _
    Implements Extensibility.IDTExtensibility2.OnBeginShutdown
End Sub

Public Sub OnAddInsUpdate(ByRef custom As System.Array) _
    Implements Extensibility.IDTExtensibility2.OnAddInsUpdate
End Sub

Public Sub OnStartupComplete(ByRef custom As System.Array) _
    Implements Extensibility.IDTExtensibility2.OnStartupComplete
End Sub

Public Sub OnDisconnection(ByVal RemoveMode As _
    Extensibility.ext_DisconnectMode, _
    ByRef custom As System.Array) Implements _
    Extensibility.IDTExtensibility2.OnDisconnection
    Try
        CommandObj.Delete()
        CommandObj2.Delete()
        CommandObj3.Delete()

        ' Delete the toolbar commands
        cmdObj.Delete()
        cmdObj2.Delete()

        ' cmdbarobj.Delete() does not work in RC so
        ' just hide the command bar
        cmdbarobj.Visible = False
```

```
        Catch e As System.Exception
            MsgBox("Error deleting menus: " & e.Message)
        End Try
End Sub

Public Sub OnConnection(ByVal application As Object, _
    ByVal connectMode As Extensibility.ext_ConnectMode, _
    ByVal addInInst As Object, _
    ByRef custom As System.Array) Implements _
    Extensibility.IDTExtensibility2.OnConnection
    Dim iBitmap As Integer

    oVB = CType(application, EnvDTE.DTE)
    addInInstance = CType(addInInst, EnvDTE.AddIn)

    ' test for type startup, first or subsequent
    If connectMode = ↵
        Extensibility.ext_ConnectMode.ext_cm_UISetup Or ↵
        connectMode = ↵
        Extensibility.ext_ConnectMode.ext_cm_Startup Or↵
        connectMode =↵
        Extensibility.ext_ConnectMode.ext_cm_AfterStartup _
        Then
        'Dim objAddIn As AddIn = CType(addInInst, AddIn)
        objAddin = CType(addInInst, AddIn)

        Try
            CommandObj = oVB.Commands.AddNamedCommand(objAddin, _
                "UIMenus", _
                "UIMenus One", _
                "Executes the command for UIMenus", _
                True, 59, Nothing, 1 + 2) _
                '1+2 == vsCommandStatusSupported+↵
                vsCommandStatusEnabled
            CommandObj.AddControl(oVB.CommandBars.Item("Tools"))

            CommandObj2 = oVB.Commands.AddNamedCommand(objAddin, _
                "UIMenus2", _
                "UIMenus Two", _
                "Executes the command for UIMenus", _
                True, 65, Nothing, 1 + 2) _
                '1+2 == vsCommandStatusSupported+↵
                vsCommandStatusEnabled
            CommandObj2.AddControl(oVB.CommandBars.Item("Tools"))
```

```
        CommandObj3 = oVB.Commands.AddNamedCommand(objAddin, _
            "UIMenus3", _
            "UIMenus Three", _
            "Executes the command for UIMenus", _
            True, 73, Nothing, 1 + 2) _
            '1+2 == vsCommandStatusSupported+↵
            vsCommandStatusEnabled
        CommandObj3.AddControl(oVB.CommandBars.Item("Tools"))

        ' call method to add my toolbar
        AddAddinCmdBar()

    Catch e As System.Exception
        MsgBox("Error Adding Menus: " & e.Message)
    End Try
    End If
End Sub


Public Sub Exec(ByVal cmdName As String, _
  ByVal executeOption As vsCommandExecOption, _
  ByRef varIn As Object, _
  ByRef varOut As Object, _
  ByRef handled As Boolean) _
  Implements IDTCommandTarget.Exec
  handled = False
  If (executeOption = vsCommandExecOption.↵
      vsCommandExecOptionDoDefault) _
      Then
      If cmdName = "UIMenus.Connect.UIMenus" Then
          handled = True
          MsgBox("Menu one selected.")
      ElseIf cmdName = "UIMenus.Connect.UIMenus2" Then
          handled = True
          MsgBox("Menu two selected.")
      ElseIf cmdName = "UIMenus.Connect.UIMenus3" Then
          handled = True
          MsgBox("Menu three selected.")
      ElseIf cmdName = "UIMenus.Connect.MyCommand" Then
          handled = True
          MsgBox("Command bar button1 clicked.")
          Exit Sub
      ElseIf cmdName = "UIMenus.Connect.MyCommand2" Then
          handled = True
```

```
                    MsgBox("Command bar button2 clicked.")
                End If
            End If
        End Sub

        Public Sub QueryStatus(ByVal cmdName As String, _
            ByVal neededText As vsCommandStatusTextWanted, _
            ByRef statusOption As vsCommandStatus, _
            ByRef commandText As Object) _
            Implements IDTCommandTarget.QueryStatus
            If neededText = _
                EnvDTE.vsCommandStatusTextWanted. ⏎
                vsCommandStatusTextWantedNone Then
                If cmdName = "UIMenus.Connect.UIMenus" Or _
                    cmdName = "UIMenus.Connect.UIMenus2" Or _
                    cmdName = "UIMenus.Connect.UIMenus3" Or _
                    cmdName = "UIMenus.Connect.MyCommand" Or _
                    cmdName = "UIMenus.Connect.MyCommand2" _
                    Then
                    statusOption = CType(vsCommandStatus. ⏎
                        vsCommandStatusEnabled + _
                        vsCommandStatus.vsCommandStatusSupported, _
                        vsCommandStatus)
                Else
                    statusOption = _
                        vsCommandStatus.vsCommandStatusUnsupported
                End If
            End If
        End Sub

        Sub AddAddinCmdBar()
            ' Add a reference to the Office type library to gain
            ' access to the
            ' CommandBar object.
            Dim cmds As Commands
            Try
                cmds = oVB.Commands

                ' if we have already added the toolbar, set a ptr
                ' to it, otherwise create the commandbar
                Try
                    cmdbarobj = oVB.CommandBars("Mycmdbar")
                Catch
```

```
            cmdbarobj = cmds.AddCommandBar("Mycmdbar", _
                vsCommandBarType.vsCommandBarTypeToolbar)
        End Try
        cmdbarobj.Visible = True

        cmdObj = oVB.Commands.AddNamedCommand(objAddin, _
            "MyCommand", _
            "Button1", _
            "Click for Button1", _
            True, 67, Nothing, 1 + 2)
        cmdObj.AddControl(cmdbarobj)

        cmdObj2 = oVB.Commands.AddNamedCommand(objAddin, _
            "MyCommand2", _
            "Button2", _
            "Click for Button2", _
            True, 68, Nothing, 1 + 2)
        cmdObj2.AddControl(cmdbarobj)
    Catch e As System.Exception
        MsgBox(e.Message)
    End Try
    End Sub
End Class
```

Several changes were made to the code in Listing 7-4 to create the add-in toolbar. First, the code snippet shown in Listing 7-5 simply dimensions the new objects needed for the toolbar. Additionally, objAddin was moved to the module level to make it visible to the new AddAddinCmdBar method.

Listing 7-5. Declaring Toolbar Objects

```
' AddAddinCmdBar
Dim objAddin As AddIn

' Command Bar commands and object
Dim cmdObj As Command
Dim cmdObj2 As Command
Dim cmdbarobj As Microsoft.Office.Core.CommandBar
```

Finally, a whole new method named AddAddinCmdBar was added to the code. Its code is reproduced in Listing 7-6, at the bottom of the class. A call to the AddAddinCmdBar method was added to the OnConnection method.

NOTE *The documentation in the MSDN help file is incorrect on the use of the AddCommandBar method. At least this is the case in the initial release version of the system. The code sequence shown in Listing 7-6 was arrived at by trial and error. Also, in the release version, the Delete method does not work. In fact, if you attempt to delete the toolbar, an error is raised. You can use the RemoveCommandBar method, which will remove the toolbar from the IDE but does not permanently delete it from Visual Studio.*

Listing 7-6. AddAddinCmdBar Method

```
01 Sub AddAddinCmdBar()
02    'Add a reference to the Office type library to gain access to the
03    'CommandBar object.
04    Dim cmds As Commands
05    Try
06        cmds = oVB.Commands
07
08        ' if we have already added the toolbar, set a ptr
09        ' to it, otherwise create the commandbar
10        Try
11            cmdbarobj = oVB.CommandBars("Mycmdbar")
12        Catch
13            cmdbarobj = cmds.AddCommandBar("Mycmdbar", _
14                    vsCommandBarType.vsCommandBarTypeToolbar)
15        End Try
16        cmdbarobj.Visible = True
17
18        cmdObj = oVB.Commands.AddNamedCommand(objAddin, _
19            "MyCommand", _
20            "Button1", _
21            "Click for Button1", _
22            True, 67, Nothing, 1 + 2)
23        cmdObj.AddControl(cmdbarobj)
24
25        cmdObj2 = oVB.Commands.AddNamedCommand(objAddin, _
26            "MyCommand2", _
27            "Button2", _
28            "Click for Button2", _
29            True, 68, Nothing, 1 + 2)
```

```
30      cmdObj2.AddControl(cmdbarobj)
31    Catch e As System.Exception
32        MsgBox(e.Message)
33    End Try
34 End Sub
```

Line 11 attempts to set a CommandBar object. If Line 11 succeeds, it means that you have created the command bar in a previous execution, and you simply need to set a pointer to the existing command bar. If this line fails, it means that you have not created a command bar prior to this execution. In this case, Line 13 is executed, which creates the toolbar.

Line 13 uses the AddCommandBar method of the CommandBarControls object to create the new toolbar. The first parameter to the AddCommandBar method is the name of the new toolbar. The second parameter is the type of command bar. In this case, it is type vsCommandBarTypeToolbar.

Lines 18 through 30 simply use the methods previously described to add two buttons to the command bar.

In the OnDisconnection method in Listing 7-5, you will see that instead of deleting the command bar, you have simply set its Visible property to False to hide it. Figure 7-2 shows the new add-in toolbar that you have created. You can see that you can have picture buttons on the add-in toolbar also. Clicking either of the toolbar buttons will display a message box denoting the respective button that was clicked.

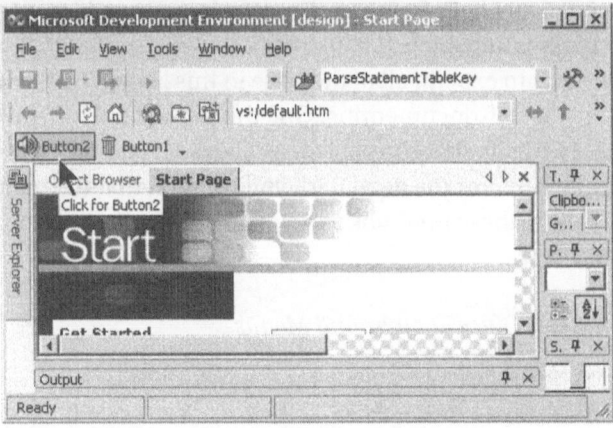

Figure 7-2. Add-in toolbar

Adding Microsoft Office CommandBarControls

Compared to Microsoft Office CommandBarControls, the methods provided by the DTE for creating menus and toolbars are not only primitive, they are also very limited and leave the commands in the registry. In some cases, the commands cannot be deleted, and therefore you can unknowingly clutter the registry. Because the text or captions of the DTE commands are stored in some cryptic manner (probably Unicode), it is also very difficult to find the controls in the registry.

I was extremely pleased to find that the method of creating menus and toolbars in VB 6.0 add-ins is still available in .NET. That method was using the Microsoft Office CommandBarControls. The object model for these commands is very flexible and powerful, and is not overly complex.

NOTE *I have previously demonstrated the use of DTE command bars and menus because they are available and needed to be covered. However, I personally will not use them because the Office Command model is so superior in its power and flexibility.*

Listing 7-7 shows the code for creating a very complete toolbar and menu structure using the Microsoft Office Command object model. This code creates a new add-in named CommandBar. You can create an add-in yourself in the wizard, without any further help from me. Alternately, you can just open the project from the code in this chapter.

I do not attempt to explain all of the code in this listing. First, it is very lengthy. Second, it is self-documenting. One thing that I did for you was create several reusable methods that simplify the process of creating toolbars, buttons, menus, and submenus. For the most part, you will find that the main body of the code is simply calling these methods and passing parameters, such as captions, tool tips, and bitmaps.

Listing 7-7. Microsoft Office Toolbar and Menus

```
'***************************
'* Copyright HHI Software, Inc.
'* All Rights Reserved
'* Date Created: 02/03/2002
'* Author: Les Smith
'***************************
Imports Microsoft.Office.Core
Imports EnvDTE
```

```vbnet
Imports Extensibility
Imports System.Runtime.InteropServices
Imports System.Windows.Forms

#Region " Read me for Add-in installation and setup information. "
' When run, the Add-in wizard prepared the registry for the Add-in.
' At a later time, if the Add-in becomes unavailable for reasons such as:
'    1) You moved this project to a computer other than the one it was
'          originally created on.
'    2) You chose 'Yes' when presented with a message asking if you
'       wish to remove the Add-in.
'    3) Registry corruption.
' you will need to re-register the Add-in by building the CommandBarSetup
project
' by right-clicking the project in the Solution Explorer, then choosing install.
#End Region


<GuidAttribute("D08E0D55-064B-450F-BD32-11A06F17E0DE"), _
ProgIdAttribute("CommandBar.Connect")> _
Public Class Connect

    Implements IDTExtensibility2
    Dim frm As New frmPictures()
    Private oAddin As AddIn
    Dim oVB As EnvDTE.DTE
    Private TBar As Microsoft.Office.Core.CommandBar
    Private mcbBrowseProcs As Microsoft.Office.Core.CommandBarControl
    Private mcbBrowseVars As Microsoft.Office.Core.CommandBarControl
    Private mcbQuikFind As Microsoft.Office.Core.CommandBarControl
    Private mcbExplorer As Microsoft.Office.Core.CommandBarControl
    Private mcbMultiSearch As Microsoft.Office.Core.CommandBarControl
    Private mcbIfAnalyser As Microsoft.Office.Core.CommandBarControl
    Private mcbScanProcs As Microsoft.Office.Core.CommandBarControl
    Private mcbScanVars As Microsoft.Office.Core.CommandBarControl
    Private mcbSetupAbout As Microsoft.Office.Core.CommandBarControl
    Private Kind As Byte

    ' Menu controls
    Dim mnuVBExpoPopup As Microsoft.Office.Core.CommandBarControl
    Dim mnuCompile As Microsoft.Office.Core.CommandBarControl
    Dim mnuBrowse As Microsoft.Office.Core.CommandBarControl
    Dim mnuScan As Microsoft.Office.Core.CommandBarControl
    Dim mnuBrowsePrj As Microsoft.Office.Core.CommandBarControl
```

```
Dim mnuObjBrowse As Microsoft.Office.Core.CommandBarControl
Dim mnuAbout As Microsoft.Office.Core.CommandBarControl
Dim mnuReports As Microsoft.Office.Core.CommandBarControl
Dim mnuSearch As Microsoft.Office.Core.CommandBarControl
Dim mnuIfAnalyzer As Microsoft.Office.Core.CommandBarControl
Dim mnuProjectExplorer As Microsoft.Office.Core.CommandBarControl
Dim mnuQuikFind As Microsoft.Office.Core.CommandBarControl
Dim mnuVarScan As Microsoft.Office.Core.CommandBarControl
Dim mnuVarBrowse As Microsoft.Office.Core.CommandBarControl

'command bar event handler
Public WithEvents mnuScanHandler As EnvDTE.CommandBarEvents
Public WithEvents mnuBrowsePrjHandler As EnvDTE.CommandBarEvents
Public WithEvents mnuVarScanHandler As EnvDTE.CommandBarEvents
Public WithEvents mnuVarBrowseHandler As EnvDTE.CommandBarEvents
Public WithEvents mnuObjBrowseHandler As EnvDTE.CommandBarEvents
Public WithEvents mnuAboutHandler As EnvDTE.CommandBarEvents
Public WithEvents mnuReportsHandler As EnvDTE.CommandBarEvents
Public WithEvents mnuSearchHandler As EnvDTE.CommandBarEvents
Public WithEvents mnuIfAnalyzerHandler As EnvDTE.CommandBarEvents
Public WithEvents mnuProjectExplorerHandler As EnvDTE.CommandBarEvents


Public WithEvents commandBarEvents As EnvDTE.CommandBarEvents
Public WithEvents commandBarEvents2 As EnvDTE.CommandBarEvents
Public WithEvents commandBarEvents3 As EnvDTE.CommandBarEvents
Public WithEvents commandBarEvents4 As EnvDTE.CommandBarEvents
Public WithEvents commandBarEvents5 As EnvDTE.CommandBarEvents
Public WithEvents commandBarEvents6 As EnvDTE.CommandBarEvents
Public WithEvents commandBarEvents7 As EnvDTE.CommandBarEvents
Public WithEvents commandBarEvents8 As EnvDTE.CommandBarEvents
Public WithEvents commandBarEvents9 As EnvDTE.CommandBarEvents
Public WithEvents commandBarEvents10 As EnvDTE.CommandBarEvents
Public WithEvents commandBarEvents11 As EnvDTE.CommandBarEvents
Public WithEvents commandBarEvents12 As EnvDTE.CommandBarEvents
Public WithEvents commandBarEvents13 As EnvDTE.CommandBarEvents
Public WithEvents commandBarEvents14 As EnvDTE.CommandBarEvents
Public WithEvents commandBarEvents15 As EnvDTE.CommandBarEvents
Public WithEvents commandBarEvents16 As EnvDTE.CommandBarEvents
Public WithEvents commandBarEvents17 As EnvDTE.CommandBarEvents
Public WithEvents commandBarEvents18 As EnvDTE.CommandBarEvents
Public WithEvents commandBarEvents19 As EnvDTE.CommandBarEvents
Public WithEvents commandBarEvents20 As EnvDTE.CommandBarEvents
Public WithEvents commandBarEvents21 As EnvDTE.CommandBarEvents
```

```
Public Sub OnBeginShutdown(ByRef custom As System.Array) ↵
   Implements IDTExtensibility2.OnBeginShutdown
End Sub


Public Sub OnAddInsUpdate(ByRef custom As System.Array) ↵
   Implements IDTExtensibility2.OnAddInsUpdate
End Sub


Public Sub OnStartupComplete(ByRef custom As System.Array) ↵
   Implements IDTExtensibility2.OnStartupComplete
End Sub


Public Sub OnDisconnection(ByVal RemoveMode As _
                           ext_DisconnectMode, _
                           ByRef custom As System.Array) _
                           Implements _
                           IDTExtensibility2.OnDisconnection


   On Error Resume Next
   mcbBrowseProcs.Delete()
   mcbBrowseVars.Delete()
   mcbMultiSearch.Delete()
   mcbIfAnalyser.Delete()
   mcbExplorer.Delete()
   mcbScanProcs.Delete()
   mcbSetupAbout.Delete()
   mcbScanVars.Delete()
   mcbQuikFind.Delete()
   TBar.Delete()

   mnuIfAnalyzer.Delete()
   mnuQuikFind.Delete()
   mnuScan.Delete()
   mnuVarScan.Delete()
   mnuVarBrowse.Delete()
   mnuProjectExplorer.Delete()
   mnuSearch.Delete()
   mnuAbout.Delete()
   mnuBrowsePrj.Delete()
   mnuCompile.Delete()
   mnuBrowse.Delete()
   mnuVBExpoPopup.Delete()
End Sub
```

```vb
                Public Sub OnConnection(ByVal application As Object, _
                                ByVal connectMode As ext_ConnectMode, _
                                ByVal addInInst As Object, _
                                ByRef custom As System.Array) _
            Implements IDTExtensibility2.OnConnection
              Dim commandBars As _CommandBars
              Dim toolsCommandBar As Microsoft.Office.Core.CommandBar
              Dim commandBarControls As CommandBarControls
              Dim strCommandBarItem As String = "Tools"

              oVB = CType(application, EnvDTE.DTE)
              oAddin = CType(addInInst, AddIn)

              Try
                  ' load the bitmap container
                  frm.Show()
                  frm.Hide()

                  CreateOfficeToolBar()

                  CreateOfficeToolBarButtons()

                  SetupOfficeMenus()

                  'destroy the bitmap container
                  frm.Dispose()
              Catch ex As System.Exception
                  System.Windows.Forms.MessageBox.Show(ex.ToString())
              End Try
        End Sub

        Private Sub commandBarEvents_Click(&
            ByVal CommandBarControl As Object, _
            ByRef handled As Boolean, _
            ByRef CancelDefault As Boolean) _
            Handles commandBarEvents.Click
            MessageBox.Show("Browse Procedures clicked")
        End Sub
        Private Sub commandBarEvents2_Click(&
            ByVal CommandBarControl As Object, _
            ByRef handled As Boolean, _
            ByRef CancelDefault As Boolean) _
            Handles commandBarEvents2.Click
            MessageBox.Show("Var Browse Clicked")
```

```
   End Sub
   Private Sub commandBarEvents3_Click(↵
      ByVal CommandBarControl As Object, _
      ByRef handled As Boolean, _
      ByRef CancelDefault As Boolean) _
      Handles commandBarEvents3.Click
      MessageBox.Show("Scan Procedures Clicked")
   End Sub
   Private Sub commandBarEvents4_Click(↵
      ByVal CommandBarControl As Object, _
      ByRef handled As Boolean, _
      ByRef CancelDefault As Boolean) _
      Handles commandBarEvents4.Click
      MessageBox.Show("Multi Search Clicked")
   End Sub
   Private Sub commandBarEvents5_Click(↵
      ByVal CommandBarControl As Object, _
      ByRef handled As Boolean, _
      ByRef CancelDefault As Boolean) _
      Handles commandBarEvents5.Click
      MessageBox.Show("Quik Find Clicked")
   End Sub
   Private Sub commandBarEvents6_Click(↵
      ByVal CommandBarControl As Object, _
      ByRef handled As Boolean, _
      ByRef CancelDefault As Boolean) _
      Handles commandBarEvents6.Click
      MessageBox.Show("Control Structure Analyzer Clicked")
   End Sub
   Private Sub commandBarEvents7_Click(↵
      ByVal CommandBarControl As Object, _
      ByRef handled As Boolean, _
      ByRef CancelDefault As Boolean) _
      Handles commandBarEvents7.Click
      MessageBox.Show("Project Explorer Clicked")
   End Sub
   Private Sub commandBarEvents8_Click(↵
      ByVal CommandBarControl As Object, _
      ByRef handled As Boolean, _
      ByRef CancelDefault As Boolean) _
      Handles commandBarEvents8.Click
      MessageBox.Show("Scan variables Clicked")
   End Sub
```

```
            Private Sub commandBarEvents9_Click(⤶
               ByVal CommandBarControl As Object, _
               ByRef handled As Boolean, _
               ByRef CancelDefault As Boolean) _
               Handles commandBarEvents9.Click
               MessageBox.Show("About  Clicked")
            End Sub
            Private Sub commandBarEvents13_Click(⤶
               ByVal CommandBarControl As Object, _
               ByRef handled As Boolean, _
               ByRef CancelDefault As Boolean) _
               Handles commandBarEvents13.Click
               MessageBox.Show("Browse Procs Clicked")
            End Sub
            Private Sub commandBarEvents14_Click(⤶
               ByVal CommandBarControl As Object, _
               ByRef handled As Boolean, _
               ByRef CancelDefault As Boolean) _
               Handles commandBarEvents14.Click
               MessageBox.Show("Browse variables Clicked")
            End Sub
            Private Sub commandBarEvents15_Click(⤶
               ByVal CommandBarControl As Object, _
               ByRef handled As Boolean, _
               ByRef CancelDefault As Boolean) _
               Handles commandBarEvents15.Click
               MessageBox.Show("Multi Search Clicked")
            End Sub
            Private Sub commandBarEvents16_Click(⤶
               ByVal CommandBarControl As Object, _
               ByRef handled As Boolean, _
               ByRef CancelDefault As Boolean) _
               Handles commandBarEvents16.Click
               MessageBox.Show("Control Structure Analyzer Clicked")
            End Sub
            Private Sub commandBarEvents17_Click(⤶
               ByVal CommandBarControl As Object, _
               ByRef handled As Boolean, _
               ByRef CancelDefault As Boolean) _
               Handles commandBarEvents17.Click
               MessageBox.Show("Project Explorer Clicked")
            End Sub
            Private Sub commandBarEvents18_Click(⤶
```

```
        ByVal CommandBarControl As Object, _
        ByRef handled As Boolean, _
        ByRef CancelDefault As Boolean) _
        Handles commandBarEvents18.Click
        MessageBox.Show("Scan Procedures Clicked")
End Sub
Private Sub commandBarEvents19_Click(↵
        ByVal CommandBarControl As Object, _
        ByRef handled As Boolean, _
        ByRef CancelDefault As Boolean) _
        Handles commandBarEvents19.Click
        MessageBox.Show("Setup About Clicked")
End Sub
Private Sub commandBarEvents20_Click(↵
        ByVal CommandBarControl As Object, _
        ByRef handled As Boolean, _
        ByRef CancelDefault As Boolean) _
        Handles commandBarEvents20.Click
        MessageBox.Show("Scan variables Clicked")
End Sub
Private Sub commandBarEvents21_Click(↵
        ByVal CommandBarControl As Object, _
        ByRef handled As Boolean, _
        ByRef CancelDefault As Boolean) _
        Handles commandBarEvents21.Click
        MessageBox.Show("Scan variables Clicked")
End Sub


Private Sub CreateOfficeToolBar()
    ' This method creates the office toolbar
    TBar = AddOfficeToolBar(oVB, _
                            "VBXRTBar", _
                            False)
End Sub


Private Sub CreateOfficeToolBarButtons()
    ' This method calls the low level method that
    ' adds the tool buttons to the toolbar
    Try
        ' note that the bitmap can come from a variety
        ' of places.  Here it is pulled from an imagelist
        ' the next menu pulls from an image control on the form
        mcbBrowseProcs = AddOfficeToolBarButton(oVB, _
```

```
            TBar, _
            "Browse Procedures", _
            frm.ImageList1.Images(0))
        commandBarEvents13 = _
        CType(oVB.Events.CommandBarEvents(↵
        mcbBrowseProcs), EnvDTE.CommandBarEvents)


        mcbBrowseVars = AddOfficeToolBarButton(oVB, _
            TBar, _
            "Browse Variables", _
            frm.pic8.Image)
        commandBarEvents14 = _
            CType(oVB.Events.CommandBarEvents(↵
            mcbBrowseVars), EnvDTE.CommandBarEvents)


        mcbMultiSearch = AddOfficeToolBarButton(oVB, _
            TBar, _
            "Multi Search", _
            frm.pic1.Image)
        commandBarEvents15 = _
            CType(oVB.Events.CommandBarEvents(mcbMultiSearch), _
            EnvDTE.CommandBarEvents)


        mcbIfAnalyser = AddOfficeToolBarButton(oVB, _
            TBar, _
            "Control Structure Analyzer", _
            frm.PictureBox36.Image)
        commandBarEvents16 = _
            CType(oVB.Events.CommandBarEvents(mcbIfAnalyser), _
            EnvDTE.CommandBarEvents)


        mcbExplorer = AddOfficeToolBarButton(oVB, _
            TBar, _
            "Project Explorer", _
            frm.PictureBox32.Image)
        commandBarEvents17 = _
            CType(oVB.Events.CommandBarEvents(mcbExplorer), _
            EnvDTE.CommandBarEvents)


        mcbScanProcs = AddOfficeToolBarButton(oVB, _
            TBar, _
            "Scan Procedures", _
            frm.pic3.Image)
```

```
        commandBarEvents18 = _
            CType(oVB.Events.CommandBarEvents(mcbScanProcs), _
            EnvDTE.CommandBarEvents)


        mcbSetupAbout = AddOfficeToolBarIconAndCaption(oVB, _
            TBar, _
            "About VBXRef", _
            frm.PictureBox33.Image)
        commandBarEvents19 = _
            CType(oVB.Events.CommandBarEvents(mcbSetupAbout), _
            EnvDTE.CommandBarEvents)


        mcbSetupAbout.TooltipText = "Setup Interface"
    Catch e As System.Exception
        MsgBox(e.Message)
    End Try
End Sub


Private Sub SetupOfficeMenus()
    ' This method sets up the office menu, including
    ' the popup and menu item menus
    Dim cmdBar As Microsoft.Office.Core.CommandBarControl

    Try
        cmdBar = oVB.CommandBars("MenuBar").Controls("Tools")

        ' set up top level popup menu
        mnuVBExpoPopup = AddOfficePopupMenu(VBE:=oVB, _
            Menu:=cmdBar, _
            Caption:="&VBXRef2000", _
            sep:=True)

        ' set up submenus
        mnuBrowse = AddOfficePopupMenu(VBE:=oVB, _
            Menu:=mnuVBExpoPopup, _
            Caption:="&Browse Procedures")
        mnuCompile = AddOfficePopupMenu(VBE:=oVB, _
            Menu:=mnuVBExpoPopup, _
            Caption:="Compile Project")

        ' add submenus
        mnuBrowsePrj = AddOfficeMenuItem(VBE:=oVB, _
            Menu:=mnuBrowse, _
```

```
                Caption:="&Procedures", _
                Bitmap:=frm.pic5.Image)
            commandBarEvents = _
                CType(oVB.Events.CommandBarEvents(mnuBrowsePrj), _
                EnvDTE.CommandBarEvents)


            mnuVarBrowse = AddOfficeMenuItem(VBE:=oVB, _
                Menu:=mnuBrowse, _
                Caption:="Variables", _
                Bitmap:=frm.pic5.Image)
            commandBarEvents2 = _
                CType(oVB.Events.CommandBarEvents(mnuVarBrowse), _
                EnvDTE.CommandBarEvents)


            mnuScan = AddOfficeMenuItem(VBE:=oVB, _
                Menu:=mnuCompile, _
                Caption:="&Procedures", _
                Bitmap:=frm.pic1.Image)
            commandBarEvents3 = _
                CType(oVB.Events.CommandBarEvents(mnuScan), _
                EnvDTE.CommandBarEvents)


            mnuSearch = AddOfficeMenuItem(VBE:=oVB, _
                Menu:=mnuVBExpoPopup, _
                Caption:="&Multi-String Search", _
                Bitmap:=frm.pic6.Image)
            commandBarEvents4 = _
                CType(oVB.Events.CommandBarEvents(mnuSearch), _
                EnvDTE.CommandBarEvents)


            mnuQuikFind = AddOfficeMenuItem(VBE:=oVB, _
                Menu:=mnuVBExpoPopup, _
                Caption:="&Quik Find Selection", _
                Bitmap:=frm.PictureBox25.Image)
            commandBarEvents5 = _
                CType(oVB.Events.CommandBarEvents(mnuQuikFind), _
                EnvDTE.CommandBarEvents)


            mnuIfAnalyzer = AddOfficeMenuItem(VBE:=oVB, _
                Menu:=mnuVBExpoPopup, _
                Caption:="CtrlStructure &Analyzer", _
                Bitmap:=frm.PictureBox36.Image)
            commandBarEvents6 = _
```

```
            CType(oVB.Events.CommandBarEvents(mnuIfAnalyzer), _
            EnvDTE.CommandBarEvents)

        mnuProjectExplorer = AddOfficeMenuItem(VBE:=oVB, _
            Menu:=mnuVBExpoPopup, _
            Caption:="&Project Explorer", _
            Bitmap:=frm.PictureBox21.Image)
          commandBarEvents7 = _
            CType(oVB.Events.CommandBarEvents↩
            (mnuProjectExplorer), _
            EnvDTE.CommandBarEvents)

        mnuVarScan = AddOfficeMenuItem(VBE:=oVB, _
            Menu:=mnuCompile, Caption:="&Variables", _
            Bitmap:=frm.PictureBox16.Image)
        commandBarEvents8 = _
            CType(oVB.Events.CommandBarEvents(mnuVarScan), _
            EnvDTE.CommandBarEvents)

        mnuAbout = AddOfficeMenuItem(VBE:=oVB, _
            Menu:=mnuVBExpoPopup, _
            Caption:="&About", _
            Bitmap:=frm.PictureBox32.Image)
        commandBarEvents9 = _
            CType(oVB.Events.CommandBarEvents(mnuAbout), _
            EnvDTE.CommandBarEvents)
        Exit Sub
    Catch e As System.Exception
        MsgBox(e.Message)
    End Try
End Sub


Public Function AddOfficeMenuItem(ByVal VBE As EnvDTE.DTE, _
    ByVal Menu As Microsoft.Office.Core.CommandBarControl, _
    ByVal Caption As String, _
    Optional ByVal pos As Byte = 0, _
    Optional ByVal sep As Boolean = False, _
    Optional ByVal Bitmap As Object = Nothing) _
    As Microsoft.Office.Core.CommandBarControl

    ' This method will add an office menu item
    ' to an existing
```

```vb
                            ' office popupmenu
                            Dim menuItem As Microsoft.Office.Core.CommandBarControl

                            Try
                                If Not (Bitmap Is Nothing) Then
                                    System.Windows.Forms.Clipboard.SetDataObject(Bitmap)
                                End If

                                ' Add menu item to VB menu:
                                If pos = 0 Then pos = Menu.Controls.Count + 1
                                    menuItem = _
                                        Menu.Controls.Add(Type:= _
                                Microsoft.Office.Core.MsoControlType.msoControlButton, _
                                        Before:=pos, _
                                        Temporary:=True)

                                ' Set properties of menu item:
                                menuItem.Caption = Caption
                                If sep Then menuItem.BeginGroup = True
                                If Not (Bitmap Is Nothing) Then
                                    menuItem.Style = _
                                        Microsoft.Office.Core.MsoButtonStyle. ↵
                                        msoButtonIconAndCaption
                                    menuItem.PasteFace()
                                End If
                                Return menuItem
                            Catch e As System.Exception
                                Return menuItem
                            End Try
                        End Function

                    Public Function AddOfficePopupMenu(ByVal VBE As EnvDTE.DTE, _
                        ByVal Menu As Microsoft.Office.Core.CommandBarControl, _
                        ByVal Caption As String, _
                        Optional ByVal pos As Byte = 0, _
                        Optional ByVal sep As Boolean = False) _
                        As Microsoft.Office.Core.CommandBarControl

                        ' This method adds an office popup menu to an existing menu
                        ' The existing menu can be another popup menu.
                        Dim popupMenu As Microsoft.Office.Core.CommandBarControl
```

```
        Try

            ' Add popupMenu menu to VB menu:
            If pos = 0 Then pos = Menu.Controls.Count + 1
            popupMenu = _
                Menu.Controls.Add(Type:= ⏎
        Microsoft.Office.Core.MsoControlType.msoControlPopup, _
                Before:=pos, _
                Temporary:=True)

            ' Set properties of popupMenu menu:
            popupMenu.Caption = Caption
            If sep Then popupMenu.BeginGroup = True
            Return popupMenu
        Catch e As System.Exception
            Return popupMenu
        End Try
    End Function


Public Function AddOfficeToolBar(ByVal VBE As EnvDTE.DTE, _
    ByVal Caption As String, _
    Optional ByVal Floating As Boolean = False) _
    As Microsoft.Office.Core.CommandBar

        ' This method adds an office commandbar (toolbar) to
        ' the IDE.  It will become the container for command buttons.
        Dim Kind As Byte
        Dim toolBar As Microsoft.Office.Core.CommandBar

        Try

            ' Set parameter for pos argument:
            If Floating Then
                Kind = Microsoft.Office.Core.MsoBarPosition.msoBarFloating
            Else
                Kind = Microsoft.Office.Core.MsoBarPosition.msoBarTop
            End If

            ' Add custom toolbar and display it:
            toolBar = VBE.CommandBars.Add(Name:=Caption, _
                                          Position:=Kind, _
                                          Temporary:=True)
            toolBar.Visible = True
```

```
                Return toolBar
        Catch e As System.Exception
                Return toolBar
        End Try
End Function


Public Function AddOfficeToolBarButton(ByVal VBE As EnvDTE.DTE, _
        ByVal ToolBar As Microsoft.Office.Core.CommandBar, _
        ByVal Caption As String, _
        ByVal Bitmap As Object, _
        Optional ByVal pos As Byte = 0, _
        Optional ByVal sep As Boolean = False) _
        As Microsoft.Office.Core.CommandBarControl

        ' Variables:
        Dim cmdBtn As Microsoft.Office.Core.CommandBarControl

        Try
            If Caption = "" Or Bitmap Is Nothing Then Exit Function

            Clipboard.SetDataObject(Bitmap)

            ' Add button to Visual Studio IDE toolbar
            If pos = 0 Then pos = ToolBar.Controls.Count + 1
                cmdBtn = ToolBar.Controls.Add(Type:= ↵
        Microsoft.Office.Core.MsoControlType.msoControlButton, _
                Before:=pos, _
                Temporary:=True)

            ' Set properties of button
            cmdBtn.Caption = Caption
            If sep Then cmdBtn.BeginGroup = True
            cmdBtn.Style = Microsoft.Office.Core.MsoButtonStyle.msoButtonIcon
            cmdBtn.PasteFace()
            Return cmdBtn
        Catch e As System.Exception
            Return cmdBtn
        End Try
End Function


Public Function AddOfficeToolBarIconAndCaption(ByVal VBE As EnvDTE.DTE, _
        ByVal ToolBar As Microsoft.Office.Core.CommandBar, _
        ByVal Caption As String, _
```

```
    ByVal Bitmap As Object, _
    Optional ByVal pos As Byte = 0, _
    Optional ByVal sep As Boolean = False) _
    As Microsoft.Office.Core.CommandBarControl

    ' Variables:
    Dim cmdBtn As Microsoft.Office.Core.CommandBarControl

    Try
        If Caption = "" Or Bitmap Is Nothing Then Exit Function

        Clipboard.SetDataObject(Bitmap)

        ' Add button to VB toolbar:
        If pos = 0 Then pos = ToolBar.Controls.Count + 1
            cmdBtn = ToolBar.Controls.Add(Type:= ↵
    Microsoft.Office.Core.MsoControlType.msoControlButton, _
            Before:=pos, _
            Temporary:=True)

        ' Set properties of button:
        cmdBtn.Caption = Caption
        If sep Then cmdBtn.BeginGroup = True
        cmdBtn.Style = _
            Microsoft.Office.Core.MsoButtonStyle. ↵
            msoButtonIconAndCaption
        cmdBtn.PasteFace()
        Return cmdBtn
    Catch e As System.Exception
        Return cmdBtn
    End Try
    End Function
End Class
```

Creating an Office Toolbar

In Listing 7-8, the first line dimensions the toolbar as CommandBar. The next
lines dimension the individual buttons as CommandBarControl. You are setting
up a toolbar with nine picture buttons on it. The last line declares a variable that
will be used to tell Office the type of command that you want to create.

Listing 7-8. Dimensioning Toolbar and Buttons

```
Private TBar As Microsoft.Office.Core.CommandBar
Private mcbBrowseProcs As Microsoft.Office.Core.CommandBarControl
Private mcbBrowseVars As Microsoft.Office.Core.CommandBarControl
Private mcbQuikFind As Microsoft.Office.Core.CommandBarControl
Private mcbExplorer As Microsoft.Office.Core.CommandBarControl
Private mcbMultiSearch As Microsoft.Office.Core.CommandBarControl
Private mcbIfAnalyser As Microsoft.Office.Core.CommandBarControl
Private mcbScanProcs As Microsoft.Office.Core.CommandBarControl
Private mcbScanVars As Microsoft.Office.Core.CommandBarControl
Private mcbSetupAbout As Microsoft.Office.Core.CommandBarControl
Private Kind As Byte
```

In Listing 7-9, the event handlers for the toolbar buttons are declared. A later code segment will declare the event-handling procedures and also link the event to the handler.

Listing 7-9. Dimensioning Command Bar Events

```
Public WithEvents commandBarEvents As EnvDTE.CommandBarEvents
Public WithEvents commandBarEvents2 As EnvDTE.CommandBarEvents
Public WithEvents commandBarEvents3 As EnvDTE.CommandBarEvents
Public WithEvents commandBarEvents4 As EnvDTE.CommandBarEvents
Public WithEvents commandBarEvents5 As EnvDTE.CommandBarEvents
Public WithEvents commandBarEvents6 As EnvDTE.CommandBarEvents
Public WithEvents commandBarEvents7 As EnvDTE.CommandBarEvents
Public WithEvents commandBarEvents8 As EnvDTE.CommandBarEvents
Public WithEvents commandBarEvents9 As EnvDTE.CommandBarEvents
Public WithEvents commandBarEvents10 As EnvDTE.CommandBarEvents
Public WithEvents commandBarEvents11 As EnvDTE.CommandBarEvents
Public WithEvents commandBarEvents12 As EnvDTE.CommandBarEvents
Public WithEvents commandBarEvents13 As EnvDTE.CommandBarEvents
Public WithEvents commandBarEvents14 As EnvDTE.CommandBarEvents
Public WithEvents commandBarEvents15 As EnvDTE.CommandBarEvents
Public WithEvents commandBarEvents16 As EnvDTE.CommandBarEvents
Public WithEvents commandBarEvents17 As EnvDTE.CommandBarEvents
Public WithEvents commandBarEvents18 As EnvDTE.CommandBarEvents
Public WithEvents commandBarEvents19 As EnvDTE.CommandBarEvents
Public WithEvents commandBarEvents20 As EnvDTE.CommandBarEvents
Public WithEvents commandBarEvents21 As EnvDTE.CommandBarEvents
```

The method calls in Listing 7-10 call some macro methods that are responsible for creating the respective command controls.

Listing 7-10. Calling the Command Creation Methods

```
' load the bitmap container
frm.Show()
frm.Hide()

CreateOfficeToolBar()

CreateOfficeToolBarButtons()

SetupOfficeMenus()

'destroy the bitmap container
frm.Dispose()
```

In order to get pictures (bitmaps) to load into the controls, you simply create a form that is used only to house the bitmaps. The form is shown in Figure 7-3. You create a number of picture controls with images set to various bitmaps. Additionally, you add an ImageList control with many more bitmaps in it. You can go to the property page for the ImageList to view the bitmaps. The methods that actually create the controls and place the pictures on them can use the bitmaps from either source. You could also create a resource file and load the pictures from it, but that process is a little more complex, and resource manipulation is beyond the scope of this book. So, having created the form, you simply load it, hide it, and leave it loaded just long enough to retrieve the pictures from it as you create the controls. After that, you dispose of the form, as it is no longer needed.

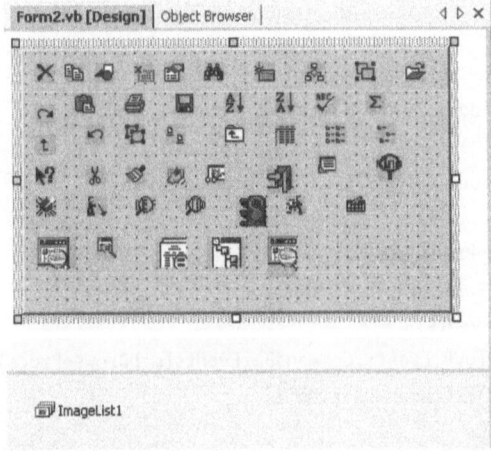

Figure 7-3. Picture container form

In Listing 7-11, you see the methods for calling the low-level methods that will actually communicate with the Microsoft Office object model to create the controls. The code in the CreateOfficeToolBar method calls the AddOfficeToolBar library method to create the toolbar. It will be named VBXRTBar. If you position the client instance of the IDE and step through the code for this add-in, you will see the controls appear to the IDE as they are added. When the ToolBar is first added, it will appear completely blank.

The code in CreateOfficeToolBarButtons consists of paired commands for each button being added to the ToolBar. The first command is a call to AddOfficeToolBarButton, passing the application object, the ToolBar object, a Caption (which actually is a tool tip), and the bitmap that will appear on the button. The second command links the event handler to event for each button added to the ToolBar.

 **NOTE** *The code for creating the toolbar, buttons, and menus was taken directly from one of my commercially available add-ins, VBXRef2000. The bitmaps are not necessarily the same and therefore are not meant to be meaningful in every instance.*

Listing 7-11. Calling the Office Control Creation Methods

```
Private Sub CreateOfficeToolBar()
    ' This method creates the office toolbar
    TBar = AddOfficeToolBar(oVB, _
                            "VBXRTBar", _
                            False)
End Sub


Private Sub CreateOfficeToolBarButtons()
    ' This method adds the tool buttons to the toolbar
    Try
        mcbBrowseProcs = AddOfficeToolBarButton(oVB, _
            TBar, _
            "Browse Procedures", _
            frm.pic5.Image)
        commandBarEvents13 = _
            CType(oVB.Events.CommandBarEvents(mcbBrowseProcs), _
            EnvDTE.CommandBarEvents)

        mcbBrowseVars = AddOfficeToolBarButton(oVB, _
```

```
        TBar, _
        "Browse Variables", _
        frm.pic8.Image)
commandBarEvents14 = _
    CType(oVB.Events.CommandBarEvents(mcbBrowseVars), _
    EnvDTE.CommandBarEvents)


mcbMultiSearch = AddOfficeToolBarButton(oVB, _
    TBar, _
    "Multi Search", _
    frm.pic1.Image)
commandBarEvents15 = _
    CType(oVB.Events.CommandBarEvents(mcbMultiSearch), _
    EnvDTE.CommandBarEvents)


mcbIfAnalyser = AddOfficeToolBarButton(oVB, _
    TBar, _
    "Control Structure Analyzer", _
    frm.PictureBox36.Image)
commandBarEvents16 = CType(oVB.Events.CommandBarEvents(mcbIfAnalyser), _
    EnvDTE.CommandBarEvents)


mcbExplorer = AddOfficeToolBarButton(oVB, _
    TBar, _
    "Project Explorer", _
    frm.PictureBox32.Image)
commandBarEvents17 = CType(oVB.Events.CommandBarEvents(mcbExplorer), _
    EnvDTE.CommandBarEvents)


mcbScanProcs = AddOfficeToolBarButton(oVB, _
    TBar, _
    "Scan Procedures", _
    frm.pic3.Image)
commandBarEvents18 = CType(oVB.Events.CommandBarEvents(mcbScanProcs), _
    EnvDTE.CommandBarEvents)


mcbSetupAbout = AddOfficeToolBarIconAndCaption(oVB, _
    TBar, _
    "About VBXRef", _
    frm.PictureBox33.Image)
commandBarEvents19 = CType(oVB.Events.CommandBarEvents(mcbSetupAbout), _
    EnvDTE.CommandBarEvents)
```

```
        mcbSetupAbout.TooltipText = "Setup Interface"
    Catch e As System.Exception
        MsgBox(e.Message)
    End Try
End Sub
```

You can examine the reusable library methods I have provided for you to see the actual calls to manipulate the Microsoft Office Command object model. You can find them at the end of the code in Listing 7-7. Once the ToolBar has been created, it will appear as shown in Figure 7-4. Clicking any of the buttons will cause a message box to display that indicates which button was clicked.

 **NOTE** *The last tool button is of a different type. Notice that a call is made to the AddOfficeToolBarIconAndCaption method. This method creates a style of button that includes both a picture and a caption.*

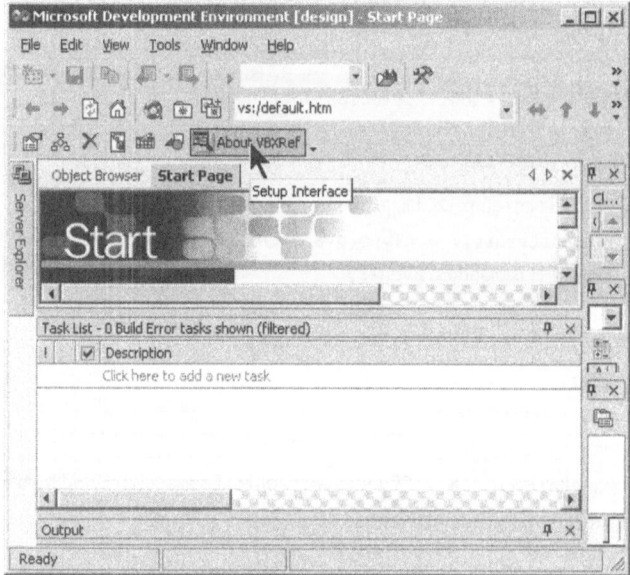

Figure 7-4. Office CommandBar

Creating Office Menus

As I mentioned earlier, I choose to use the Microsoft Office Command object
model because of its power and flexibility. With this model, you can create any
number and level of menus and menu items. In this section, I demonstrate the
creation of a fairly complex menu system. Listing 7-12 shows the code for dimensioning the menu commands and their respective events.

 **NOTE**   *You will notice that all of the menu command controls
in Listing 7-12 are dimensioned as CommandBarControl,
just the same as the buttons in the previous section. Also,
notice that the menu controls are all the same type, regardless
of the type of menu, Popup or MenuItem. That type will be
determined by the specific method called to create the respective type.*

Listing 7-12. Dimensioning Menus and Events

```
' Menu controls
Dim mnuVBExpoPopup As Microsoft.Office.Core.CommandBarControl
Dim mnuCompile As Microsoft.Office.Core.CommandBarControl
Dim mnuBrowse As Microsoft.Office.Core.CommandBarControl
Dim mnuScan As Microsoft.Office.Core.CommandBarControl
Dim mnuBrowsePrj As Microsoft.Office.Core.CommandBarControl
Dim mnuObjBrowse As Microsoft.Office.Core.CommandBarControl
Dim mnuAbout As Microsoft.Office.Core.CommandBarControl
Dim mnuReports As Microsoft.Office.Core.CommandBarControl
Dim mnuSearch As Microsoft.Office.Core.CommandBarControl
Dim mnuIfAnalyzer As Microsoft.Office.Core.CommandBarControl
Dim mnuProjectExplorer As Microsoft.Office.Core.CommandBarControl
Dim mnuQuikFind As Microsoft.Office.Core.CommandBarControl
Dim mnuVarScan As Microsoft.Office.Core.CommandBarControl
Dim mnuVarBrowse As Microsoft.Office.Core.CommandBarControl

'command bar event handler
Public WithEvents mnuScanHandler As EnvDTE.CommandBarEvents
Public WithEvents mnuBrowsePrjHandler As EnvDTE.CommandBarEvents
Public WithEvents mnuVarScanHandler As EnvDTE.CommandBarEvents
Public WithEvents mnuVarBrowseHandler As EnvDTE.CommandBarEvents
Public WithEvents mnuObjBrowseHandler As EnvDTE.CommandBarEvents
Public WithEvents mnuAboutHandler As EnvDTE.CommandBarEvents
```

```
Public WithEvents mnuReportsHandler As EnvDTE.CommandBarEvents
Public WithEvents mnuSearchHandler As EnvDTE.CommandBarEvents
Public WithEvents mnuIfAnalyzerHandler As EnvDTE.CommandBarEvents
Public WithEvents mnuProjectExplorerHandler As EnvDTE.CommandBarEvents
```

In Listing 7-13, you can see the code that creates the menus, both Popup and MenuItem. These methods call the lower level methods that actually manipulate the Microsoft Office command bar object model. You will see that no bitmap parameter is supplied on the pop-up menus (menus that have submenus or menu items under them). A pop-up menu cannot have a picture on it. Only the menu items (lowest level menus) may have bitmaps. If you pass a bitmap parameter to the menu creation method of the Office object, it will simply be ignored.

Listing 7-13. SetupOfficeMenus

```
Private Sub SetupOfficeMenus()
    ' This method sets up the office menu, including
    ' the popup and menu item menus
    Dim cmdBar As Microsoft.Office.Core.CommandBarControl

    Try
        cmdBar = oVB.CommandBars("MenuBar").Controls("Tools")

        ' set up top level popup menu
        mnuVBExpoPopup = AddOfficePopupMenu(VBE:=oVB, _
            Menu:=cmdBar, _
            Caption:="&VBXRef2000", _
            Separator:=True)

        ' set up submenus
        mnuBrowse = AddOfficePopupMenu(VBE:=oVB, _
            Menu:=mnuVBExpoPopup, _
            Caption:="&Browse Procedures")
        mnuCompile = AddOfficePopupMenu(VBE:=oVB, _
            Menu:=mnuVBExpoPopup, _
            Caption:="Compile Project")

        ' add submenus
        mnuBrowsePrj = AddOfficeMenuItem(VBE:=oVB, _
            Menu:=mnuBrowse, _
            Caption:="&Procedures", _
            Bitmap:=frm.pic5.Image)
        commandBarEvents = CType(oVB.Events.CommandBarEvents(mnuBrowsePrj), _
            EnvDTE.CommandBarEvents)
```

```
mnuVarBrowse = AddOfficeMenuItem(VBE:=oVB, _
    Menu:=mnuBrowse, _
    Caption:="Variables", _
    Bitmap:=frm.pic5.Image)
commandBarEvents2 = CType(oVB.Events.CommandBarEvents(mnuVarBrowse), _
    EnvDTE.CommandBarEvents)


mnuScan = AddOfficeMenuItem(VBE:=oVB, _
    Menu:=mnuCompile, _
    Caption:="&Procedures", _
    Bitmap:=frm.pic1.Image)
commandBarEvents3 = CType(oVB.Events.CommandBarEvents(mnuScan), _
    EnvDTE.CommandBarEvents)


mnuSearch = AddOfficeMenuItem(VBE:=oVB, _
    Menu:=mnuVBExpoPopup, _
    Caption:="&Multi-String Search", _
    Bitmap:=frm.pic6.Image)
commandBarEvents4 = CType(oVB.Events.CommandBarEvents(mnuSearch), _
    EnvDTE.CommandBarEvents)


mnuQuikFind = AddOfficeMenuItem(VBE:=oVB, _
    Menu:=mnuVBExpoPopup, _
    Caption:="&Quik Find Selection", _
    Bitmap:=frm.PictureBox25.Image)
commandBarEvents5 = CType(oVB.Events.CommandBarEvents(mnuQuikFind), _
    EnvDTE.CommandBarEvents)


mnuIfAnalyzer = AddOfficeMenuItem(VBE:=oVB, _
    Menu:=mnuVBExpoPopup, _
    Caption:="CtrlStructure &Analyzer", _
    Bitmap:=frm.PictureBox36.Image)
commandBarEvents6 = CType(oVB.Events.CommandBarEvents(mnuIfAnalyzer), _
    EnvDTE.CommandBarEvents)


mnuProjectExplorer = AddOfficeMenuItem(VBE:=oVB, _
    Menu:=mnuVBExpoPopup, _
    Caption:="&Project Explorer", _
    Bitmap:=frm.PictureBox21.Image)
commandBarEvents7 = _
    CType(oVB.Events.CommandBarEvents↵
    (mnuProjectExplorer), _
    EnvDTE.CommandBarEvents)
```

```
mnuVarScan = AddOfficeMenuItem(VBE:=oVB, _
    Menu:=mnuCompile, Caption:="&Variables", _
    Bitmap:=frm.PictureBox16.Image)
commandBarEvents8 = _
    CType(oVB.Events.CommandBarEvents(mnuVarScan), _
    EnvDTE.CommandBarEvents)


mnuAbout = AddOfficeMenuItem(VBE:=oVB, _
    Menu:=mnuVBExpoPopup, _
    Caption:="&About", _
    Bitmap:=frm.PictureBox32.Image)
commandBarEvents9 = _
    CType(oVB.Events.CommandBarEvents(mnuAbout), _
    EnvDTE.CommandBarEvents)
```

Figure 7-5 shows the menu extended. Clicking any one of the menu items will cause a message box to display that denotes the tool button clicked.

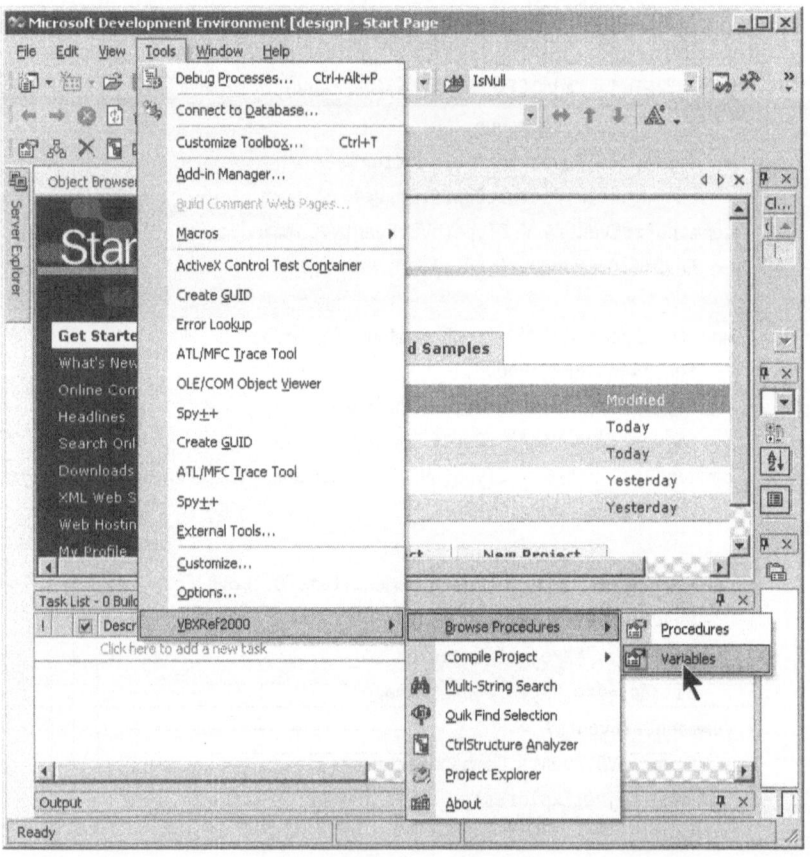

Figure 7-5. Office menu

Interfacing with the Office Command Objects

I have created several low-level methods to use to make the calls to the Microsoft Office Command objects. Without these methods, you would have to have access to the Microsoft Office SDK documentation, and then the interface objects and methods are not intuitive. I do not go over the details of each method; they are straightforward and you can easily follow them. Table 7-1 simply lists each method and describes its purpose.

Table 7-1. Interfacing the Office Command Objects

METHOD	DESCRIPTION
AddOfficeMenuItem	Adds a MenuItem to a Popup menu. A Popup menu is a parent menu and normally acts as a top-level menu. However, it can be the parent of another Popup menu to create a hierarchy of menu items.
AddOfficePopupMenu	Adds a Popup menu to a VSIDE menu or to an existing Popup menu.
AddOfficeToolBar	Adds a new ToolBar (CommandBar) to the VSIDE. It is automatically added below the existing menus. You cannot control where it is placed. This is something that users of your add-in usually request. They want the ToolBar to remember where they left it, but you have no control over its placement.
AddOfficeToolBarButton	Adds ToolBar picture buttons to the Office ToolBar.

Using a TreeView Form for the UI

You have seen the use of the TreeView form in your add-in in Chapters 2 and 3. In this section, you are simply going to correct a problem that you may or may not have discovered in using the add-in created in Chapter 2 and enhanced in Chapter 3. You may have noticed that if you click the same node in the TreeView twice in a row, it does not respond on the second click. You will review this add-in menu again because there is an apparent design flaw in .NET in such controls as the TreeView, ComboBox, and others in which the user makes a selection of an object.

When you select an item in a TreeView, you use the AfterSelect event to determine which node was clicked. In the MSDN help, this is the event that is prescribed for determining the node that was clicked. The problem arises when you click the same node twice in a row. If the node that you click is already selected, the AfterSelect event will not fire. You might think you can use the Click event, because it fires every time a node is clicked, even if you click one that's already selected. In the Click event you could then check the SelectedNode.Text to determine the selected node. No, I'm sorry—it's only when you click one that's already selected that you can get the correct value from SelectedNode.Text in the Click event! The reason is that the Click event fires before the AfterSelect event, and at the time the Click event fires, the new selection has not yet taken place.

So, you have a paradox. The AfterSelect event won't fire when the same node is clicked twice in a row. However, using the Click event only provides the correct node if you click the same node twice in a row. Hopefully, Microsoft will correct this problem before too much frustration occurs. For now, I'll show you how to work around it. You're going to open MyAddinTest1.sln in order to add code to make it work properly.

Once you have opened the add-in solution, add the code shown in Listing 7-14. In the Windows Form Designer, place a Timer control on the form and leave the default name, Timer1, unchanged. Set the Interval property to 50. This will cause the Timer to interrupt 50 milliseconds after it has been enabled.

Listing 7-14. Making the TreeView Work

```
Private Sub tvMenu_AfterSelect(ByVal sender As Object, ByVal e As _
    System.Windows.Forms.TreeViewEventArgs) Handles tvMenu.AfterSelect
    Dim i As Integer
  mbMenuClicked = False
  CallTVSelection(e.Node.Text)
End Sub


Shared Sub CallTVSelection(ByVal tvSelText As String)
    Select Case UCase(tvSelText)
        Case "SMART DESKTOP" 'ignore root clicks
        Case "BLOCK COMMENT"
            Call Connect.BlockComment()
        Case "UNCOMMENT"
            Call Connect.BlockUnComment()
        Case "BLOCK CHANGE"
            Call Connect.BlockChange()
        Case "BLOCK DELETE"
            Call Connect.BlockDelete()
        Case "PROC ERROR HANDLER"
            Call Connect.GenLocalErrorTrap()
        Case "CLONE PROCEDURE"
            Call Connect.CloneProcedure()
        Case Else
```

```
            MsgBox("Please click on a Child Node.", _
                        MsgBoxStyle.Information, "Unknown Request")
        End Select
    End Sub


Private Sub tvMenu_Click(ByVal sender As Object, _
    ByVal e As System.EventArgs) _
    Handles tvMenu.Click
    ' At the time the click event fires, the selection of the just clicked
    ' node has not yet taken place, so if you try to
    ' determine the node clicked in the click event, you
    ' will always find the node which was selected prior
    ' to the click.  To get around this mismatch of event
    ' firing, we start a timer which will fire in 50ms
    ' If the AfterSelect event fires, because a new selection
    ' was made by the user, it will tell the Timer Event to
    ' ignore the interrupt.
    mbMenuClicked = True
    Timer1.Enabled = True
End Sub


Private Sub Timer1_Tick(ByVal sender As System.Object, _
    ByVal e As System.EventArgs)     Handles Timer1.Tick
    ' If the boolean, mbMenuClicked is True, that means the
    ' AfterSelect event did not fire, and the Click Event
    ' has asked us to display the current selection in
    ' the treeview.
    Dim s As String

    If mbMenuClicked Then
        mbMenuClicked = False
        If Not tvMenu.SelectedNode Is Nothing Then
            CallTVSelection(tvMenu.SelectedNode.Text)
        End If
    End If
    Timer1.Enabled = False
End Sub
```

. Move the Select Case construct from the AfterSelect event to the new method named CallTVSelection, so that it can be used from two places without duplicating the code. This new method will call the desired processing method based on the SelectedNode.Text that will be passed to it.

Place a module-level Boolean in the declaration section of the form. You can view it in the code for this section, but it will appear as

```
Private mbNodeClicked As Boolean
```

Remember that the AfterSelect event won't fire if the node that is clicked by the user is already selected. However, the Click event fires on every click of the TreeView. To get around this mismatch of event firing, enable a Timer to interrupt in 50 milliseconds after the Click event fires. You do this in the Click event so that the Timer event will be informed as to whether the AfterSelect event fired or not. In the Click event the Boolean is set to True, denoting that the Click event has fired. The Timer is also enabled at that time.

If the AfterSelect event now fires, it will set the Boolean to False, denoting that the AfterSelect event has fired and handled the click of the TreeView. This will cause the Timer event to ignore the interrupt because the AfterSelect event has already handled the calling of the new selection. If the AfterSelect event does not fire, this means that the user has clicked the same node twice in a row. When the Timer event fires, the Boolean will still be True (set in the Click event) and the Timer event will make a call to CallTVSelection, at the behest of the Click event.

This may all sound very confusing, but it is actually very simple. The Boolean is a simple semaphore telling the Timer event whether or not the AfterSelect event has fired. If it hasn't, the Timer event has to make the call to CallTVSelection. Regardless of who calls CallTVSelection, it is passed the proper value of SelectedNode.Text.

Creating a UI in the System Tray

Not everyone will want to use this, but I will show you how easy it is to create a novel, yet very simple UI in the system tray. Surprisingly, it can be as complex a menu as you want to create, but it is the simplest to create. You can do most of the work right in the Windows Forms Designer.

For this demonstration, you will create another new add-in called UISystray. By now, you should not need any instruction on creating an add-in with the Add-in Wizard. The only difference between this add-in and all of the others you have created is that you do not select the option to have the wizard create a UI menu for you.

Once you've created the add-in, the code for it will be very short and simple, because you did not have a UI built in. The code for the UISystray add-in is shown in Listing 7-15.

Listing 7-15. UISystray Add-in Code Generated by the Wizard

```vb
Imports Microsoft.Office.Core
imports Extensibility
imports System.Runtime.InteropServices
Imports EnvDTE


#Region " Read me for Add-in installation and setup information. "
' When run, the Add-in wizard prepared the registry for the Add-in.
' At a later time, if the Add-in becomes unavailable for reasons such as:
'    1) You moved this project to a computer other than the one it was
'    originally created on.
'    2) You chose 'Yes' when presented with a message asking if you _
'    wish to remove the Add-in.
'    3) Registry corruption.
' you will need to re-register the Add-in by building the _
' UISystraySetup project
' by right-clicking the project in the Solution Explorer, _
' then choosing install.
#End Region


<GuidAttribute("C95EA7C5-2E2E-4A89-BE99-8027DFA3C358"), _
ProgIdAttribute("UISystray.Connect")> _
Public Class Connect

    Implements Extensibility.IDTExtensibility2
    Implements IDTCommandTarget

    Dim applicationObject As EnvDTE.DTE
    Dim addInInstance As EnvDTE.AddIn

    Public Sub OnBeginShutdown(ByRef custom As System.Array) _
        Implements Extensibility.IDTExtensibility2.OnBeginShutdown
    End Sub

    Public Sub OnAddInsUpdate(ByRef custom As System.Array) _
        Implements Extensibility.IDTExtensibility2.OnAddInsUpdate
    End Sub

    Public Sub OnStartupComplete(ByRef custom As System.Array) _
        Implements Extensibility.IDTExtensibility2.OnStartupComplete
    End Sub
```

```
    Public Sub OnDisconnection(ByVal RemoveMode As _
        Extensibility.ext_DisconnectMode, _
        ByRef custom As System.Array) _
        Implements Extensibility.IDTExtensibility2.OnDisconnection
    End Sub

    Public Sub OnConnection(ByVal application As Object, _
        ByVal connectMode As Extensibility.ext_ConnectMode, _
        ByVal addInInst As Object, _
        ByRef custom As System.Array) _
        Implements Extensibility.IDTExtensibility2.OnConnection
        applicationObject = CType(application, EnvDTE.DTE)
        addInInstance = CType(addInInst, EnvDTE.AddIn)
    End Sub
End Class
```

Adding System Tray Code to the Connect Class

You should make several changes and additions to the Connect class code created by the wizard before putting it into Listing 7-15. The changes have been boldfaced in Listing 7-16 for ease of recognition and discussion.

Listing 7-16. Connect Class Code for System Tray Activation

```
Imports Microsoft.Office.Core
imports Extensibility
imports System.Runtime.InteropServices
Imports EnvDTE


#Region " Read me for Add-in installation and setup information. "
' When run, the Add-in wizard prepared the registry for the Add-in.
' At a later time, if the Add-in becomes unavailable for reasons such as:
'    1) You moved this project to a computer other than which is was
'    originally created on.
'    2) You chose 'Yes' when presented with a message asking if you _
'    wish to remove the Add-in.
'    3) Registry corruption.
' you will need to re-register the Add-in by building the _
' UISystraySetup project
' by right-clicking the project in the Solution Explorer, _
' then choosing install.
#End Region
```

```vb
<GuidAttribute("C95EA7C5-2E2E-4A89-BE99-8027DFA3C358"), _
ProgIdAttribute("UISystray.Connect")> _
Public Class Connect

    Implements Extensibility.IDTExtensibility2
    Implements IDTCommandTarget

    Dim oVB As EnvDTE.DTE
    Dim addInInstance As EnvDTE.AddIn
    Dim oFrm As Object

    Public Sub OnBeginShutdown(ByRef custom As System.Array) _
        Implements Extensibility.IDTExtensibility2.OnBeginShutdown
    End Sub

    Public Sub OnAddInsUpdate(ByRef custom As System.Array) _
        Implements Extensibility.IDTExtensibility2.OnAddInsUpdate
    End Sub

    Public Sub OnStartupComplete(ByRef custom As System.Array) _
        Implements Extensibility.IDTExtensibility2.OnStartupComplete
    End Sub

    Public Sub OnDisconnection(ByVal RemoveMode As _
        Extensibility.ext_DisconnectMode, _
        ByRef custom As System.Array) _
        Implements Extensibility.IDTExtensibility2.OnDisconnection
        oFrm.Dispose()
    End Sub

    Public Sub OnConnection(ByVal application As Object, _
        ByVal connectMode As Extensibility.ext_ConnectMode, _
        ByVal addInInst As Object, _
        ByRef custom As System.Array) _
        Implements Extensibility.IDTExtensibility2.OnConnection
        Dim frmIcon As New Form1()
        oVB = CType(application, EnvDTE.DTE)
        addInInstance = CType(addInInst, EnvDTE.AddIn)
        oFrm = frmIcon
    End Sub
End Class
```

First, you make the usual name change from applicationObject to oVB, just to shorten it and in keeping with the convention you've used thus far. Because you're going to add a form to the project, you dimension oFrm as Object. You don't dimension it as New Form1, because doing that will cause the form object to be instantiated too soon in the activation of the add-in and you'll actually instantiate two copies of the form, and therefore have two copies of the add-in's icon in the system tray. You need this object dimensioned at the module level so that the OnDisconnection method can get to it in order to dispose of the form. Next, you'll add the one line of code to the OnDisconnection method that will dispose the form as the add-in is disconnected.

In the OnConnection method, you add several lines of code. You dimension a local object, frmIcon, as New Form1. This is an executable statement in VB .NET, which is different from VB 6.0. When this Dim statement is executed, the instance of Form1 is instantiated; therefore, there is no reason to even "Show" the form. The only other line of code added is to set the module-level object, oFrm, to the local instance of Form1, frmIcon. This creates the module-level object that the OnDisconnection method will use to dispose of the form when the add-in is shut down. The Connect class is now ready to load the form that will actually place the icon in the system tray.

Creating the Icon and Context Menu Form

Now, you will create a form that will place the icon in the system tray. This form will also have a context menu on it that will be displayed by a right-click on the add-in's icon in the system tray.

You start by adding a form to the project. First, select a NotifyIcon control from the Toolbox and place it on the form. Next, add an icon to the project. (I have selected a smiley-face icon.) You can copy any icon you want into the project directory and add it to the project by pressing Ctrl-D. You can also right-click the project in the Solution Explorer and choose Add New Item. Once the icon is in the project, go to the properties page for the NotifyIcon control and set the icon property to point to the icon.

Next, drag a ContextMenu control onto the form. Then add the menus as shown in Figure 7-6. To edit the ContextMenu, simply right-click the ContextMenu control and select the Edit Menu option. Finally, double-click each of the menu items to create an event handler for the respective menu item. Into each resulting menu item event handler, insert a display of a message box. Obviously, this menu is not going to do anything meaningful, but it demonstrates the handling of the Click event for each of the menu items.

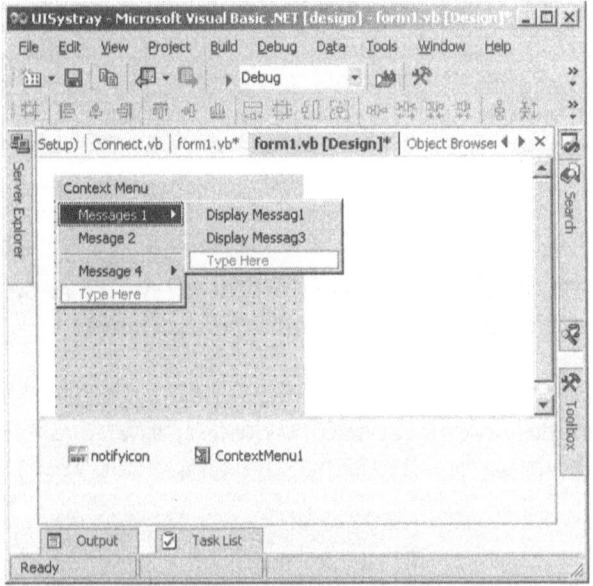

Figure 7-6. Form with a NotifyIcon and a ContextMenu

The completed code for Form1 appears in Listing 7-17.

Listing 7-17. Form1 Code

```vb
Imports System.ComponentModel
Imports System.Drawing
Imports System.Windows.Forms
Imports System.Resources


Public Class Form1
    Inherits System.Windows.Forms.Form
    Private mSmileyDisplayed As Boolean

    Public Sub New()
        MyBase.New()

        Form1 = Me

        'This call is required by the Windows Form Designer.
        InitializeComponent()
```

```vb
            ' we don't use this form so hide it
            Me.Hide()

            'set up the tray icon
            'InitializeNotifyicon()
        End Sub


    Public Sub DisplayMsg1(ByVal sender As Object, ByVal e As System.EventArgs)
        MessageBox.Show("You clicked Display Message1 Menu")
    End Sub

    Public Sub DisplayMsg2(ByVal sender As Object, ByVal e As System.EventArgs)
        MessageBox.Show("You clicked Dispaly Message2 Menu Item")
    End Sub


    'Form overrides dispose to clean up the component list.
    Protected Overloads Overrides Sub Dispose(ByVal disposing As Boolean)
        If disposing Then
            If Not (components Is Nothing) Then
                components.Dispose()
            End If
        End If
        MyBase.Dispose(disposing)
    End Sub
    Private components As System.ComponentModel.IContainer


#Region " Windows Form Designer generated code "

    'Required by the Windows Form Designer

    Dim WithEvents Form1 As System.Windows.Forms.Form

    'NOTE: The following procedure is required by the Windows Form Designer
    'It can be modified using the Windows Form Designer.
    'Do not modify it using the code editor.
    Private WithEvents notifyicon As System.Windows.Forms.NotifyIcon
    Friend WithEvents ContextMenu1 As System.Windows.Forms.ContextMenu
    Friend WithEvents MenuItem1 As System.Windows.Forms.MenuItem
    Friend WithEvents MenuItem2 As System.Windows.Forms.MenuItem
    Friend WithEvents MenuItem3 As System.Windows.Forms.MenuItem
    Friend WithEvents MenuItem5 As System.Windows.Forms.MenuItem
```

```vbnet
Friend WithEvents MenuItem6 As System.Windows.Forms.MenuItem
Friend WithEvents MenuItem4 As System.Windows.Forms.MenuItem
Friend WithEvents MenuItem7 As System.Windows.Forms.MenuItem
Friend WithEvents MenuItem8 As System.Windows.Forms.MenuItem
Private Sub InitializeComponent()
    Me.components = New System.ComponentModel.Container()
    Dim resources As System.Resources.ResourceManager = New _
        System.Resources.ResourceManager(GetType(Form1))
    Me.notifyicon = New System.Windows.Forms.NotifyIcon(Me.components)
    Me.ContextMenu1 = New System.Windows.Forms.ContextMenu()
    Me.MenuItem1 = New System.Windows.Forms.MenuItem()
    Me.MenuItem5 = New System.Windows.Forms.MenuItem()
    Me.MenuItem6 = New System.Windows.Forms.MenuItem()
    Me.MenuItem2 = New System.Windows.Forms.MenuItem()
    Me.MenuItem3 = New System.Windows.Forms.MenuItem()
    Me.MenuItem4 = New System.Windows.Forms.MenuItem()
    Me.MenuItem7 = New System.Windows.Forms.MenuItem()
    Me.MenuItem8 = New System.Windows.Forms.MenuItem()
    '
    'notifyicon
    '
    Me.notifyicon.ContextMenu = Me.ContextMenu1
    Me.notifyicon.Icon = CType(resources.GetObject("notifyicon.Icon"), _
        System.Drawing.Icon)
    Me.notifyicon.Text = "Right-click for menu"
    Me.notifyicon.Visible = True
    '
    'ContextMenu1
    '
    Me.ContextMenu1.MenuItems.AddRange(New System.Windows.Forms. ↵
MenuItem() {Me.MenuItem1, Me.MenuItem2, Me.MenuItem3, Me.MenuItem4})
    '
    'MenuItem1
    '
    Me.MenuItem1.Index = 0
    Me.MenuItem1.MenuItems.AddRange(New System.Windows.Forms. ↵
        MenuItem() {Me.MenuItem5, Me.MenuItem6})
    Me.MenuItem1.Text = "Messages 1"
    '
    'MenuItem5
    '
    Me.MenuItem5.Index = 0
    Me.MenuItem5.Text = "Display Messag1"
```

```vbnet
'
'MenuItem6
'
Me.MenuItem6.Index = 1
Me.MenuItem6.Text = "Display Messag3"
'
'MenuItem2
'
Me.MenuItem2.Index = 1
Me.MenuItem2.Text = "Mesage 2"
'
'MenuItem3
'
Me.MenuItem3.Index = 2
Me.MenuItem3.Text = "-"
'
'MenuItem4
'
Me.MenuItem4.Index = 3
Me.MenuItem4.MenuItems.AddRange(New System.Windows.Forms. ↵
    MenuItem() {Me.MenuItem7, Me.MenuItem8})
Me.MenuItem4.Text = "Message 4"
'
'MenuItem7
'
Me.MenuItem7.Index = 0
Me.MenuItem7.Text = "Display Msg5"
'
'MenuItem8
'
Me.MenuItem8.Index = 1
Me.MenuItem8.Text = "Display Msg6"
'
'Form1
'
Me.AccessibleRole = System.Windows.Forms.AccessibleRole.None
Me.AutoScaleBaseSize = New System.Drawing.Size(5, 13)
Me.ClientSize = New System.Drawing.Size(200, 168)
Me.ControlBox = False
Me.Enabled = False
Me.FormBorderStyle = System.Windows.Forms.FormBorderStyle.None
Me.MaximizeBox = False
Me.MinimizeBox = False
```

```vbnet
        Me.Name = "Form1"
        Me.Opacity = 0
        Me.ShowInTaskbar = False
        Me.SizeGripStyle = System.Windows.Forms.SizeGripStyle.Hide
        Me.StartPosition = System.Windows.Forms.FormStartPosition.Manual

    End Sub

#End Region

    Private Sub ContextMenu1_Popup(ByVal sender As System.Object, _
        ByVal e As System.EventArgs) Handles ContextMenu1.Popup

    End Sub

    Private Sub MenuItem1_Click(ByVal sender As System.Object, _
        ByVal e As System.EventArgs) Handles MenuItem1.Click
    End Sub

    Private Sub MenuItem2_Click(ByVal sender As System.Object, _
        ByVal e As System.EventArgs) Handles MenuItem2.Click
        MsgBox("Display msg2")
    End Sub

    Private Sub MenuItem4_Click(ByVal sender As System.Object, _
        ByVal e As System.EventArgs)
        notifyicon.Visible = False
        Me.Close()
    End Sub

    Private Sub MenuItem5_Click(ByVal sender As System.Object, _
        ByVal e As System.EventArgs) Handles MenuItem5.Click
        MsgBox("You clicked to display Msg1")
    End Sub

    Private Sub MenuItem6_Click(ByVal sender As System.Object, _
        ByVal e As System.EventArgs) Handles MenuItem6.Click
        MsgBox("You clicked to display Msg3")
    End Sub

    Private Sub MenuItem7_Click(ByVal sender As System.Object, _
        ByVal e As System.EventArgs) Handles MenuItem7.Click
        MsgBox("You clicked to display Msg5")
```

```
    End Sub

    Private Sub MenuItem8_Click(ByVal sender As System.Object, _
        ByVal e As System.EventArgs) Handles MenuItem8.Click
        MsgBox("You clicked to display Msg6")
    End Sub

End Class
```

Summary

In this chapter you explored several ways of creating a user interface for an add-in. You learned how to create toolbars and menus using objects inherent in .NET extensibility. You also learned how to create sophisticated menus and toolbars using the Microsoft Office Command object model. Although .NET extensibility offers the ability to create toolbars and menus, using the Microsoft Office Command object model offers a much more powerful and flexible tool for creating an interface. Finally, you learned a novel, yet simple way to create a UI that is activated from the system tray.

In Chapter 8 you will discover how to use the Macro Explorer and Macros IDE to test code that you can use in an add-in. The Macro Explorer and Macros IDE are new to Visual Studio and provide a very powerful addition to the IDE.

CHAPTER 8

The Macro Explorer and the Macros IDE

"Potential just means you ain't done it yet."
—Darrell Royal, football coach, University of Texas

WHILE DEVELOPING CODE in Visual Studio, you'll often find yourself repeatedly performing a particular process or series of keystrokes. In previous versions of Visual Studio, with the exception of Visual C++, the only way to do this was to perform the tedious actions over and over again. But now in Visual Studio .NET, you can automate the process by using macros. If you've used Microsoft Word or Microsoft Excel, you're probably familiar with macros. A *macro* is a set of instructions saved in a file (.Vsmacros) that can be executed later. You can either create the macro manually by typing the code in the Macros IDE, or you can have the environment record a macro for you automatically as you type and click.

 **TIP** *Clicks on menu options are recorded, but clicks in the Text Editor window are not.*

After you've created a macro, you can run it from the Macro Explorer, the Find/Command box, or the Macros IDE. You can even use a keyboard shortcut to execute the macro.

In this chapter, I refer to the complex of features surrounding macros as the *macro facility*. This encompasses the macro recorder, the Macro Explorer, and the Macros IDE. In many ways, this facility will reduce the number of features that you might want to put into an add-in. Certainly, you can develop some things in a macro quicker than you can put them into an add-in. However, as the tasks become more complex, the tendency and requirement to develop an add-in feature becomes greater. In my estimation, once a feature has been placed into an add-in, it will always be easier to execute that functionality from the add-in than from the macro facility. In other words, it will take fewer keystrokes or

mouse clicks to get to it. You will also find that much of the extensibility functionality can only be executed in an add-in and will not execute in a macro.

The most powerful thing that the macro facility provides to the add-in developer is the ability to debug add-in functionality in the macro facility without
having to compile and debug it in the add-in. Compiling an add-in, running
a second instance of Visual Studio, and connecting to the add-in, only to find that
your new code does not work, can become tedious after a while. This is especially
true if you only need to change one line of code, but you have to start the process
all over again for each change. Here is where the macro facility can really help you.

The Macro Explorer

The Macro Explorer is the primary tool for managing and running macros. It is
a window in the main Visual Studio .NET integrated development environment
(IDE) that you can view by pressing Alt-F8. You can also access it by selecting
Tools ➤ Macros ➤ Macro Explorer. Additionally, you can arrange your IDE so that
tool windows open and close automatically as you move your mouse over them
or move your mouse away from them. The Macro Explorer is just another tool
window. The primary tasks associated with managing macros are as follows:

- *Creating new macro projects and modules.* Macros exist as commands
  (Subs or Functions) in a module. You can place multiple modules in
  a macro project. You can create a new macro project by right-clicking the
  Macros node and choosing New Project. To create a new macro module,
  you should right-click a project and choose New Module.

- *Loading and unloading existing macro projects.* To load an existing macro
  project in the Macro Explorer, you should right-click the Macros node
  and choose Load Project. Next, browse to the macro project file and then
  choose Open. To unload a macro project from the Macro Explorer, right-
  click the macro project you want to unload and choose Unload Project.

- *Deleting macro projects and modules.* To unload a macro from the Macro
  Explorer, right-click the macro project you want to unload and choose
  Unload Project. To delete a macro module or command from the Macro
  Explorer, select the item and press the Delete button or right-click the
  module and choose Delete.

- *Renaming macro projects, modules, and commands.* To rename a macro
  project, module, or command, right-click it and choose Rename. Next,
  type the new name and press Enter.

The macro facility has several features. Macros are stored in special modules. The Macro Explorer window lists all macros available in the current solution. The macros are listed in a TreeView form. You can view a list of each macro's modules by expanding the module name. You can open modules by double-clicking their names or by right-clicking their names and choosing Edit. Macro modules are opened in the Macros IDE, which is discussed in the "The Macros IDE" section later in this chapter.

> **NOTE** *You can save macros as either binary or text files. Binary is the default format for macros and uses the .Vsmacros extension. You can also choose, however, to save the macro as Unicode text (.txt). Saving a macro as a binary file makes it convenient to distribute several macros in a project as a single file. Saving a macro as a text file enables you, for example, to open the file outside of Visual Studio .NET, copy a single command from it, and then e-mail it to someone.*

You can find the Macros menu options on the Tools menu. Figure 8-1 shows the Macros menu. It will serve you well to memorize the shortcut keys for getting to various components of the macro facility. Table 8-1 lists the various features and their associated shortcut keys.

Table 8-1. Macro Facility Shortcut Keys

FEATURE	SHORTCUT KEYS
Record TemporaryMacro	Ctrl-Shift-R
Run TemporaryMacro	Ctrl-Shift-P
Macro Explorer	Alt-F8
Macros IDE	Alt-F11

In order to record and run a macro, you will normally need to have a project open. What you want to do with the macro determines the amount of code and/or controls you may need to have in the project. For now, you will create a new Windows application project called "Chap 8 Sample Project1". Creating the project automatically creates Form1. Add three command buttons as shown in Figure 8-2.

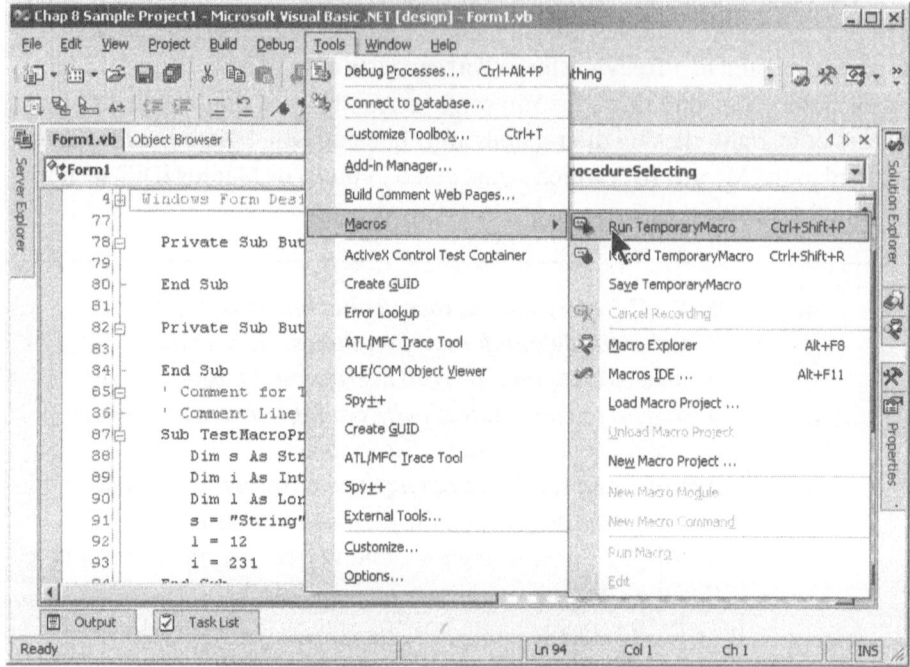

Figure 8-1. Macros menu

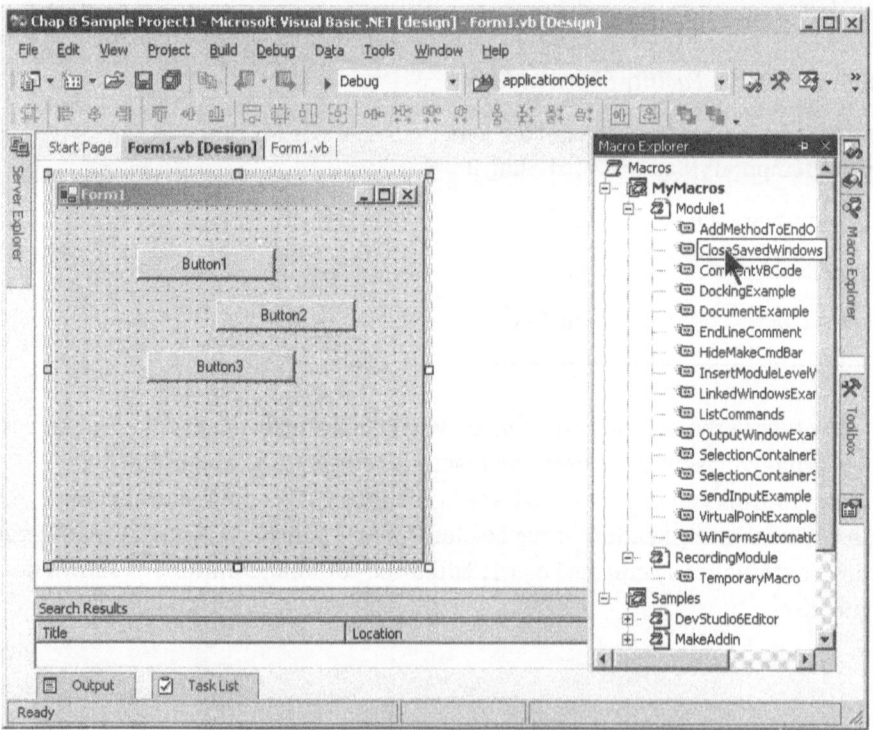

Figure 8-2. Form1 and controls

The Macro Explorer window is also displayed in Figure 8-2. Notice that it has a TreeView that, when expanded, reveals two root nodes. One is called MyMacros and the other is called Samples. The Samples macros are provided with Visual Studio .NET and can be extremely helpful in learning how the IDE performs certain operations. During this chapter, you will explore several of the macros in the Samples set. You will notice that I have even added some extra macros to the Samples set. I have saved all of the macros that I discuss in this chapter and more in Module.vb with the code for this chapter. You can store your macros anywhere you want to.

If you right-click a macro in the Macro Explorer, a pop-up menu will display, as shown in Figure 8-3. Clicking the Run option will actually run the selected macro. Double-clicking the desired macro in the Macro Explorer will also run the macro. Clicking the Edit option will display the Macros IDE, which is covered in detail later in this chapter.

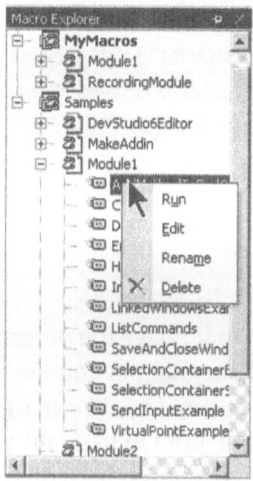

Figure 8-3. Macro Explorer pop-up menu

Now you will run a macro from the Macro Explorer. Figure 8-2 shows the Visual Studio IDE with the Form1 designer open. The code window is also open. The macro in Listing 8-1 will close all saved windows. You will see that a macro is encapsulated in a Sub/End Sub construct, just like any normal code for a procedure.

As you recall from add-in code, you have to reference objects within the IDE by qualifying them with a DTE object instance. In the code for a macro, you reference the DTE object directly. That's because the macro is actually executed inside the DTE. Other than that, the code is exactly as it would be coded in an add-in. Conversely, once you have debugged a section of code in a macro and then want to move it to an add-in, you simply substitute the add-in's applicationObject (oVB in the case of my add-ins) for DTE. That's normally all there is to it, and your code is ready to run in an add-in.

The code in Listing 8-1 is very simple. I simply set up a For/Next loop through the Documents collection. I test the Saved status of the window before attempting to close it. I also protect the code with On Error Resume Next to ensure that no type of error will stop the macro. I chose not to use a Try/Catch construct here, because if an error occurred, the code would exit without closing the remaining windows.

Listing 8-1. CloseSavedWindows Macro

```
Sub CloseSavedWindows()
    ' Close all saved documents.
    Dim i As Integer

    With DTE
        On Error Resume Next
        For i = .Documents.Count To 1 Step -1
            If .Documents.Item(i).Saved Then
                .Documents.Item(i).Close(vsSaveChanges.vsSaveChangesPrompt)
            End If
        Next i
    End With
End Sub
```

In Figure 8-2, you will see that I have the mouse positioned over the CloseSavedWindows macro. I am going to double-click the name of the macro in the Explorer that will cause it to run. I could also right-click the desired macro and then choose the Run option, but I'm basically a "double-clicker." Figure 8-4 shows that the macro has run and closed both of the windows previously named.

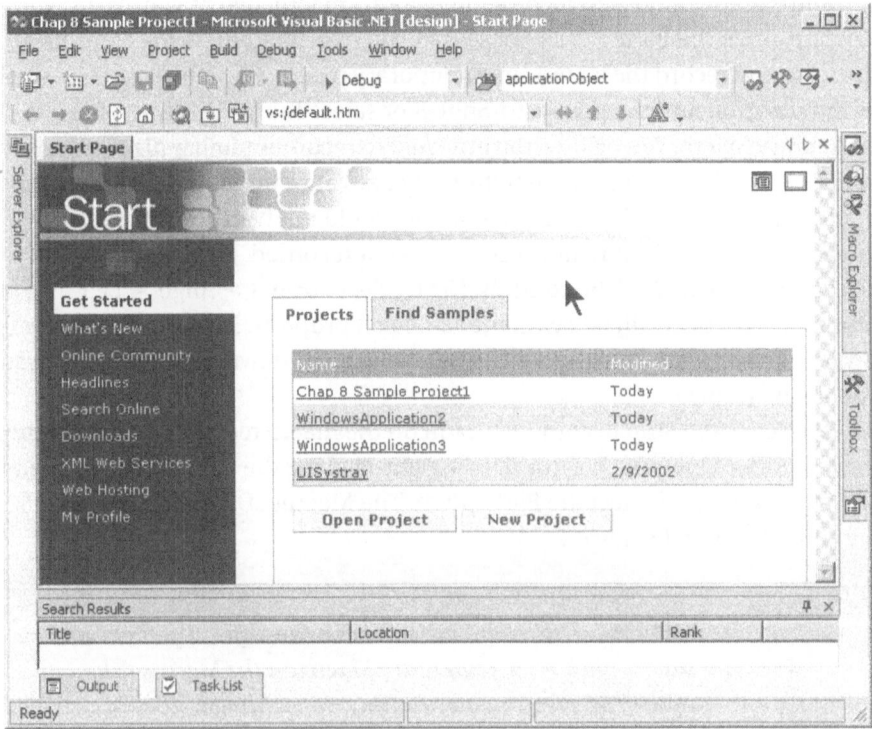

Figure 8-4. Windows closed by macro

Recording a Macro

Recording macros is the simplest and most common way to create macros. Alternatively, you can manually create macros without recording them. You can think of the macro recorder as a VCR recorder. If you have a VCR recorder hooked to your television, you can record television programs. Macro recording simply "remembers" actions you performed in the environment, similar to the way a VCR records a television program. When you press the Record button on a VCR, all the sound and pictures are stored on the VCR tape until you press Stop. Recording a macro is a virtually identical process. When you click the Record button, the tasks you perform, the windows and tools used, and so on are recorded as macro code. You can also use Ctrl-Shift-R to start or stop recording a macro.

Unlike recording a television program, however, after you record a macro, you can examine the recording and even change it. If the macro does not do exactly what you want it to do, or if you want to add additional functionality, you can edit it after recording and customize the code.

You will use the macro recorder to record a macro. Before you start to record a macro, open the Form1 designer so that you can manipulate the controls on the form and record the actions in a temporary macro. With the Form1 Designer as the active document, press Ctrl-Shift-R or select Tools ➤ Macro ➤ Record Temporary Macro. You will see the little macro recorder toolbar display. Next, you could select all three command buttons by drawing a box completely around them with the mouse. However, this action would not be recorded, because mouse clicks in the Text Editor window are not recorded. Instead, select Edit ➤ Select All to select all of the controls. Next, select Format ➤ Align ➤ Left. The buttons now have been aligned with the same Left property. Next, while holding the Ctrl key down, press in sequence the right arrow, the down arrow, the left arrow, and the up arrow.

Now click the Stop Recording button on the macro recorder toolbar to stop the recording. Open the Macros IDE by right-clicking the temporary macro in the Macro Explorer and select the Edit option. The Macros IDE opens and reveals the code shown in Listing 8-2.

CAUTION *The macro has not been saved yet. If you want to save it, click Save Temporary Macro on the Macros submenu of the Tools menu. Alternatively, you can right-click TemporaryMacro and choose Rename. This allows you to rename the macro and prevent it from being overwritten by the next new macro.*

Because the majority of macros are used only for a short time and then discarded, TemporaryMacro is overwritten each time a macro is recorded. If you want to reuse the macro later, you can rename TemporaryMacro to prevent it from being overwritten by the next recorded macro.

NOTE *If you accidentally start recording a macro, you can prevent deletion of your previous temporary macro by canceling the macro recording. If you do this, Visual Studio reverts back to your previous macro code in TemporaryMacro.*

While recording a macro, you can pause the recording and then resume it later. Typically, you'll do this to make preparations in the environment that will be required by the macro, but that you do not want to record. To cancel recording of a macro, either click the Cancel Recording button on the Recording toolbar or click the spinning cassette icon in the status bar.

Listing 8-2. Temporary Macro

```
Sub TemporaryMacro()
    DTE.ExecuteCommand("Edit.SelectAll")
    DTE.ExecuteCommand("Format.AlignLefts")
    DTE.ExecuteCommand("Edit.MoveControlRight")
    DTE.ExecuteCommand("Edit.MoveControlDown")
    DTE.ExecuteCommand("Edit.MoveControlLeft")
    DTE.ExecuteCommand("Edit.MoveControlUp")
End Sub
```

In order to test the macro, go back to the Visual Studio IDE and move the buttons around to get them unaligned. Figure 8-5 shows the position of my buttons prior to running the macro. You can see that the mouse is positioned over the temporary macro.

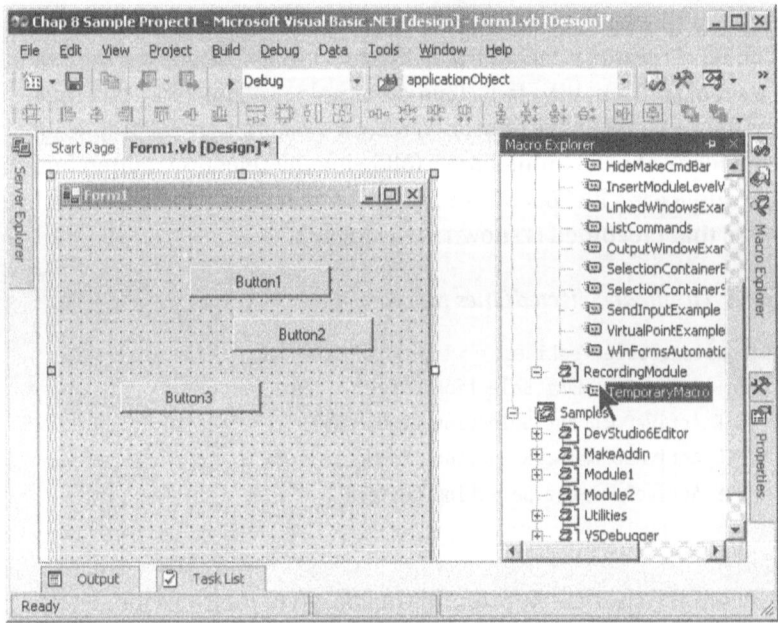

Figure 8-5. Form1 with buttons randomly placed

Next, double-click TemporaryMacro to run it. If you do this, you will see the buttons align and then they will seem to jump around momentarily. This is because they are actually moving in a 360-degree circle. Figure 8-6 shows that the buttons have been realigned.

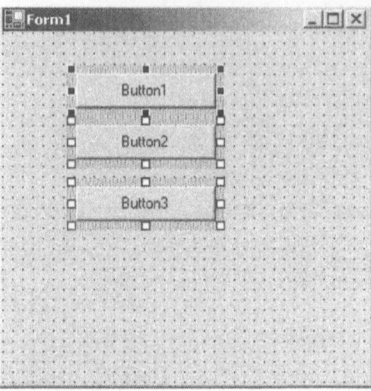

Figure 8-6. Form1 with buttons realigned

Assigning Shortcut Keys to a Macro

Once you have created a macro that you expect to use often, you may want to assign a set of shortcut keys to it. This is a simple process. First, you must record and rename a macro. I have chosen to record a macro that will duplicate a selected block of code immediately following the selection. I often find that I need to duplicate a line of code or a block of code and then modify it slightly. The macro that I recorded is shown in Listing 8-3.

Listing 8-3. DuplicateSelectedLines Macro

```
Sub DuplicateSelectedLines()
    DTE.ActiveDocument.Selection.Copy()
    DTE.ActiveDocument.Selection.LineDown()
    DTE.ActiveDocument.Selection.LineUp()
    DTE.ActiveDocument.Selection.Paste()
End Sub
```

To record the shortcut keys for this macro, go to the Tools menu and click Options. The Options dialog box will open. In the Environment folder, click Keyboard. In the Commands list box, find the desired macro and click it to select it. In this case, it is listed as Macros, MyMacros, Module1, DuplicateSelectedLines. In the Press Shortcut key(s) box, press Ctrl-Shift-A. In the Use New Shortcut Key in box, select TextEditor. Finally, click the Assign and OK buttons to save the shortcut keys.

Running Existing Macros

As you develop in .NET, you will most likely develop a project and modules of macros. Additionally, you will notice that Visual Studio comes with sample macro projects. You should take time to examine the numerous macro commands in the Samples set of macros. You can learn how to do things in a macro and in an add-in that otherwise might be very elusive. I certainly appreciate the code samples not only in the Samples set, but also throughout the MSDN help system.

Next, you'll learn how to manipulate code in a code window before you examine the Macros IDE. Listing 8-4 shows a macro command for commenting a selected block of Visual Basic code.

Listing 8-4. Commenting Visual Basic Code with a Macro

```
Sub CommentVBCode()
    Dim sel As TextSelection = DTE.ActiveDocument.Selection()
    Dim stpt As EditPoint = sel.TopPoint.CreateEditPoint()
    Dim endpt As TextPoint = sel.BottomPoint

    Try
        Do While (stpt.LessThan(endpt))
            stpt.Insert("'")
            stpt.LineDown()
            stpt.StartOfLine()
        Loop
    Catch
    End Try
End Sub
```

To run the macro, first select a block of code in the code window. Next, display the Macro Explorer by clicking its icon. Finally, right-click the CommentVBCode macro command in the Explorer. Figure 8-7 shows the selected code just before it is commented by the macro.

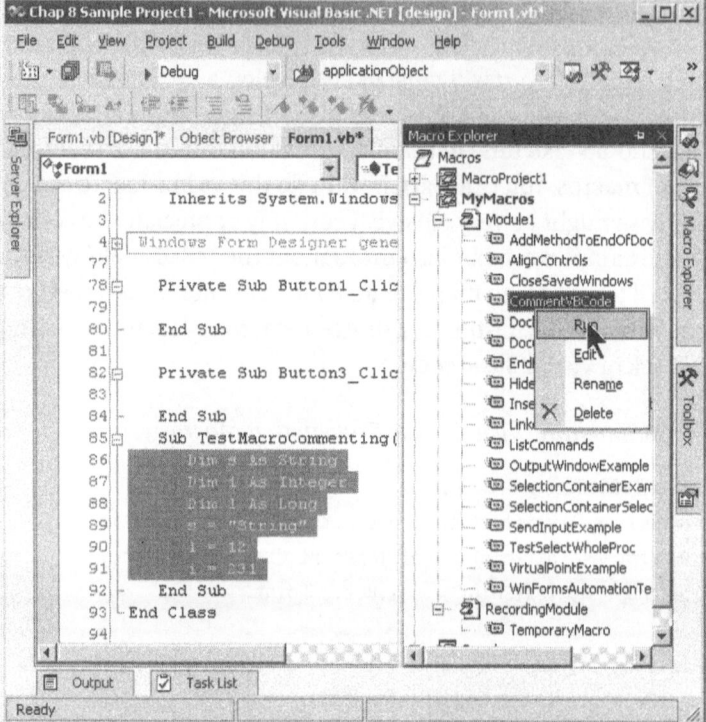

Figure 8-7. Code block before commenting

Next, click the Run menu option. You could double-click the command in the Macro Explorer to execute the command. Figure 8-8 shows the code block immediately after the macro has been run and has commented the code.

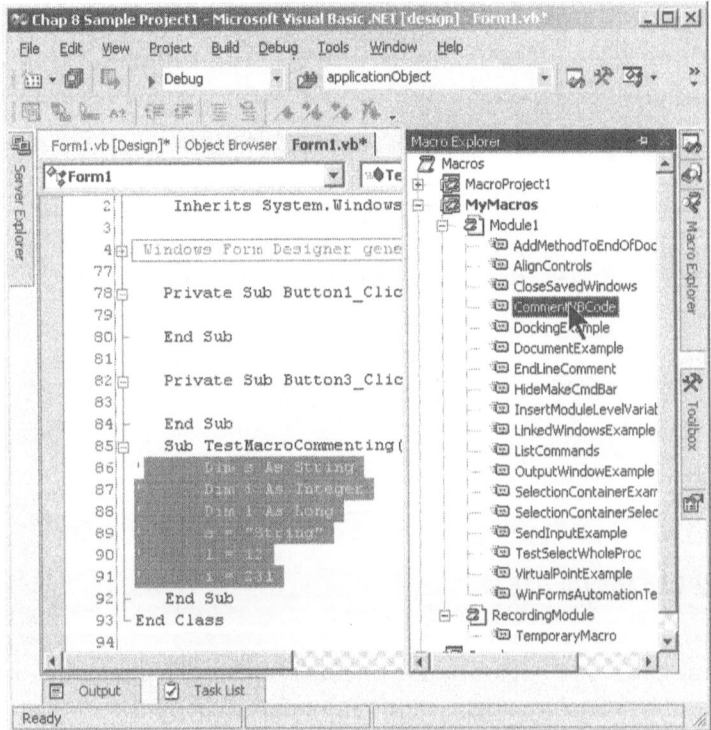

Figure 8-8. Code block commented by the macro command

The Macros IDE

Once you record a macro, you will probably want to edit the macro's code to add, change, or delete functionality. You may want to manually create your own macro rather than record one. If you write a complex macro, you will undoubtedly need to debug the macro. The Macros IDE is the tool that allows you to accomplish these tasks. The Macros IDE appears and functions very much like the regular IDE. If you right-click a module or a macro command in the Macro Explorer and select the Edit option, the Macros IDE will open as a separate window on top of the regular IDE.

For example, if you right-click the CommentVBCode macro command in Module1 of MyMacros and select the Edit option, the Macros IDE will be displayed as shown in Figure 8-9.

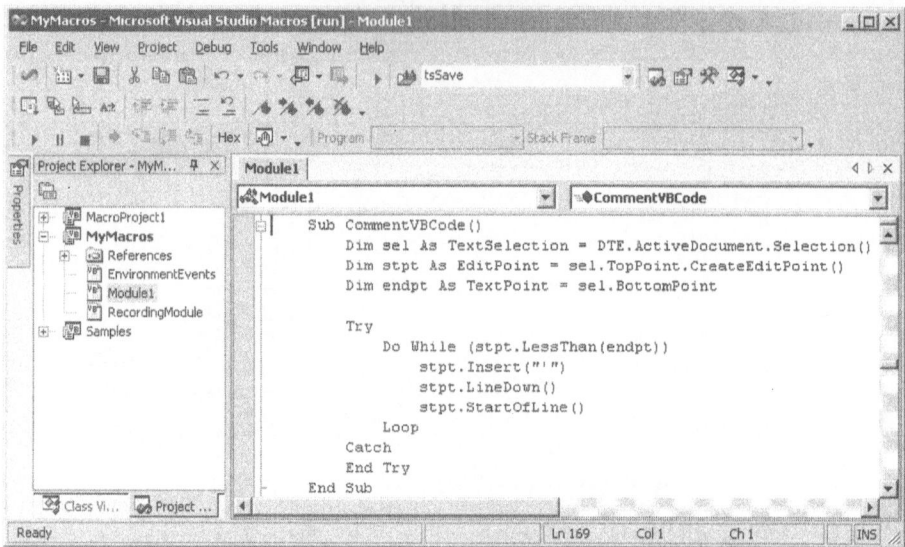

Figure 8-9. The Macros IDE

In some cases, you might want to manually create a macro rather than record one. In the Macro Explorer, right-click Module1 and choose New Macro Command. Insert the code shown in Listing 8-5. Press Ctrl-S to save your macro. You can now run the macro as you would any other macro.

Listing 8-5. Manually Created Macro

```
Sub MyNewMacro()
    MessageBox.Show("Good morning Les.")
End Sub
```

Debugging Macros

When errors occur in your macros, you can debug the code in the Macros IDE by setting breakpoints, watch variables, and so forth. By now, you should be familiar with debugging procedures in .NET, but if you aren't, you can see details about debugging in the MSDN topic "Debugging."

 **TIP** *The default keys for stepping through the debugger are F10 for Step Over and F11 for Step Into. I had to be reminded of this the first time I tried using F8 to step through a macro. Also, the reason that I was expecting F8 to step is that I have set my keystrokes to use the Microsoft Visual Basic Keystroke option in the Options dialog box. I have to confess that because I have been using such keys as F8 for debugging, I have a hard time moving to F11 and F10. You can set the keyboard to respond to VB 6.0 shortcut keys by selecting Tools ➤ Options and then selecting the Keyboard option. Click the Keyboard Mapping Scheme combo box and select Visual Basic 6. This will make the shortcut keys the same as they were in VB 6.0.*

To catch runtime errors in the Macros IDE and to be able to navigate to lines that contain errors, you must either run with debugging enabled, which requires starting the macro by pressing F5, or choose Start on the Debug menu. If you start the macro by using Ctrl-F5 or by choosing Start Without Debugging on the Debug menu, runtime errors will be ignored.

Whether or not debugging is enabled depends on how a macro is executed. If you click inside a macro and press F5 or choose Start on the Debug menu, the macro is run with debugging enabled. If you click inside a macro and press Ctrl-F5 or choose Start Without Debugging on the Debug menu, the macro is run without debugging enabled. If the insertion point is not inside a macro and you press F5 or choose Start on the Debug menu, the Macros IDE goes into Run mode with debugging enabled. Additionally, if you set a breakpoint anywhere in your macro code, debugging is automatically enabled.

I now want to show you how to create a fairly complex macro that will provide a great improvement on a procedure you created in an earlier chapter. That procedure was designed to capture a block of code that the user has selected. The procedure worked fine, except that sometimes the user wants to use an add-in feature that requires a whole procedure to be selected. In this case, the user was required to select the whole proc and was responsible for doing it correctly prior to invoking an add-in feature such as CloneProcedure. This was not only an extra burden for the user, but it was also a place where errors could occur if the user was not careful in selecting every line of the procedure.

Therefore, I needed to develop a procedure for automatically picking up the whole procedure when the user simply places the cursor within the procedure but does not select anything. I have this kind of functionality in VBCommander in VB 6.0. The problem is that VB 6.0 provides high-level methods for facilitating such functionality. My challenge was to find the objects that could accomplish the same functionality in VB .NET, where the classes and objects are not as intuitive as was VB 6.0.

Because my ultimate goal was to produce a debugged procedure for use in an add-in, I elected to write the procedure as a Function that will return the string containing the whole procedure. In the Macro Explorer, Functions do not show up in the listing of macro commands that can be executed.

NOTE *The fact that a macro Function does not show in the Macro Explorer does not mean that you cannot debug Functions in the Macros IDE. Rather, it means that they cannot be called directly from the Macro Explorer. The Macro Explorer only lists Sub commands. Therefore, you debug a macro Function by calling it from a macro Sub.*

Because macro Functions are not listed or executable from the Macro Explorer, I created a test Sub macro command for calling the macro Function that I want to develop. This Sub macro command is shown in Listing 8-6. Its sole reason for existence is to provide a callable interface to the GetWholeProc function.

Listing 8-6. Testing GetWholeProc

```
Sub TestGetWholeProc()
    Dim s As String
    s = GetWholeProc()
    Debug.WriteLine(s)
End Sub
```

Listing 8-8 shows the code for retrieving the whole procedure, in which the cursor resides at the time the user invokes an add-in feature that needs to work on a whole procedure. The only one that I have implemented thus far is CloneProcedure, but I implement others in Chapter 12.

Developing this function took a series of debugging sessions in the Macros IDE. I had several requirements to fulfill to accomplish the design goals of the function. These requirements are outlined here:

- Determine the starting point of the procedure.

- Determine the ending point of the procedure.

- Determine if there are any comment lines preceding the procedure definition line. If so, they belong to the procedure also.

- Select the whole procedure, including preceding comment lines.

Remember that there are over 3,400 classes in the .NET Framework and the biggest challenge is to ferret out the one(s) that will provide the functionality that you need at a given time. In order to create the new procedure, the first thing that I needed was some code that would position the cursor at the top and bottom of the procedure in which the user has placed the cursor. This is where the sample macros that Microsoft has provided are so helpful. In the VSEditor module of the Samples node, I found a macro command named OneFunctionView.

In the OneFunctionView macro command (see Listing 8-7), I found the two lines that I was looking for that would locate the beginning and end of the procedure in which the user positioned the cursor. Obviously, there are support lines, such as the dimension of the objects that are used by these two lines, and I picked them up also.

Listing 8-7. OneFunctionView Macro from the Sample Macro Projects

```
Sub OneFunctionView()
        Dim ts As TextSelection = ActiveWindow().Selection
        Dim tsSave As EditPoint = ts.ActivePoint.CreateEditPoint
        Dim ep As EditPoint = ts.ActivePoint.CreateEditPoint
        '' Get the start and outline to start of doc.
        ep.MoveToPoint(ep.CodeElement(EnvDTE. ⏎
            vsCMElement.vsCMElementFunction) ⏎
            .GetStartPoint(vsCMPart.vsCMPartWhole))
        ep.LineUp()
        Debug.WriteLine(ep.Line)
        ts.MoveToPoint(ep, False)
        ts.StartOfDocument(True)
        ts.OutlineSection()
        ep.LineDown()
        '' Move ep back in function and outline from end to end of doc.
        ep.MoveToPoint(tsSave)
        ep.MoveToPoint(ep.CodeElement(EnvDTE. ⏎
            vsCMElement.vsCMElementFunction) ⏎
            .GetEndPoint(vsCMPart.vsCMPartWhole))
        ep.LineDown()
        Debug.WriteLine(ep.Line)
        ts.MoveToPoint(ep, False)
        ts.EndOfDocument(True)
        ts.OutlineSection()
        ts.MoveToPoint(tsSave)
    End Sub
```

Having found the major code lines that I needed in the OneFunctionView macro, I began to construct the code shown in Listing 8-8. Next, I added lines of code that back up from the top of the procedure to determine whether there are comment lines preceding the procedure definition line. If there are, they actually belong to the procedure also.

So now having assembled the procedure shown in Listing 8-8, I began to debug it. At this point, I will not show images depicting the various debugging sessions that I went through to arrive at the desired procedure—that would take up too much time and space. Needless to say, it took several iterations through the code in the debugger in the Macros IDE to arrive at the finished code.

There were a couple of final details that I had to take into consideration. First, I had to make a determination as to whether the user had already selected the whole procedure before invoking the add-in. That is entirely possible and a viable option that I must account for. Second, if the cursor is not positioned within the procedure, the GetStartPoint method will raise an exception. It will not work if the cursor is positioned on the procedure definition line. Therefore, I had to protect the code with structured error handling.

Listing 8-8. GetWholeProc Macro Function

```
01  Function GetWholeProc() As String
02      Dim ts As TextSelection = ActiveWindow().Selection
03      Dim ep As EditPoint = ts.ActivePoint.CreateEditPoint
04      Dim sLine As String
05      Dim i As Integer
06
07      Try
08          ' if the user has selected the whole proc, then just return it
09          ' otherwise select it for them...
10          If Len(ts.Text) > 0 Then
11              If (InStr(1, ts.Text, "Sub ", 1) > 0 Or _
12                  InStr(1, ts.Text, "Function ", 1) > 0) And _
13                  (InStr(1, ts.Text, "End Sub", 1) > 0 Or _
14                  InStr(1, ts.Text, "End Function", 1) > 0) _
15                  Then
16                      Return ts.Text
17              End If
18              GoTo SelectTheProc
19          Else
20 SelectTheProc:
21              '' Get the start of the proc
22              ep.MoveToPoint(ep.CodeElement(EnvDTE.vsCMElement. ⤶
23                  vsCMElementFunction).GetStartPoint(vsCMPart.vsCMPartWhole))
24
```

```
25            ' move selection start point to top of proc
26            ts.MoveToPoint(ep, False)
27
28            ' back up to previous line looking for comments
29            i = 0
30            Do
31                ep.LineUp()
32                ts.MoveToPoint(ep, False)
33                ts.SelectLine()
34                sLine = ts.Text
35                If Left(Trim(sLine), 1) <> "'" Then
36                    ep.LineDown()
37                    ts.MoveToPoint(ep, False)
38                    Exit Do
39                End If
40                i = i + 1
41            Loop
42
43            ' if the count of comment lines > 0  the ts point is set
44            ' else we must move it back to the original
45            ep.LineDown(i + 1)
46
47            ' move to bottom of proc
48            ep.MoveToPoint(ep.CodeElement(EnvDTE.vsCMElement. ↵
49                    vsCMElementFunction).GetEndPoint(vsCMPart.vsCMPartWhole))
50
51            ' select the proc
52            ts.MoveToPoint(ep, True)
53            Return ts.Text
54        End If
55    Catch
56            System.Windows.Forms.MessageBox.Show↵
57            ("You must either select the whole ↵
58            procedure or your cursor must↵
59            be within the procedure to be selected.")
60        Return ""
61    End Try
62 End Function
```

In the procedure, lines 02 through 10 dimension the objects required by the procedure. Line 02 sets a pointer to the whole of the selection if the user has selected the procedure prior to invoking the add-in feature that will call this function. If the user has not selected any code block, but has positioned the cursor within the procedure to be selected, the TextSelection (ts) object will simply point to the position of the cursor within the procedure to be retrieved. Line 03 creates an EditPoint object pointing to the current cursor position. This EditPoint (ep) and the TextSelection (ts) objects will also be moving as I progress through the code.

Lines 10 and 11 are simply testing for the presence of code first and then for the presence of the beginning and ending lines of the procedure. If these tests are positive, the function returns the selected procedure.

CAUTION *If there were comments preceding the procedure definition line, but the user did not select them, and they are needed for some feature (such as a procedure-documenting feature), then this test is not sufficient. You should remember that double-clicking in the left margin of a procedure will automatically select the whole procedure, but it will not select comments preceding that procedure, even though comments immediately preceding a procedure definition line actually are a part of that procedure rather than the previous procedure.*

If the tests in line 10 or 11 fail, then control passes to line 22, where I'll begin the process of selecting the desired procedure. Line 22 is a complex line that begins by calling a method of the EditPoint object. It uses the EditPoint object's MoveToPoint method, which will actually move to the beginning of the procedure. To do this, it references the EditPoint object's CodeElement property. The CodeElement property returns the code element at the location of a TextPoint or EditPoint. A code element can be any fragment of code, but generally there's a CodeElement object for each definition or declarative syntax in a language. This means that for most top-level definitions or declarations in a file, or for any syntactic form in a class definition, there's an associated CodeElement object. Because the CodeElement property is an object (remember, everything is an object), it has a method called GetStartPoint. This method is passed a constant specifying the type of CodeElement to return. In this case, it is requesting the start point of the procedure. The result of this complex line is that the EditPoint (ep) is moved to the beginning of the procedure.

Having moved the EditPoint, line 26 moves the TextSelection point to the same position as the EditPoint. I do this so that when the desired EditPoint is reached, I will be ready to select the block of text.

Lines 29 through 41 are fairly straightforward. They back up the EditPoint and TextSelection point, looking for comment lines immediately preceding the procedure definition line. The Integer (i) is a count of the lines that I have moved above the procedure definition line. Line 31 moves the EditPoint backward and line 32 keeps the TextSelection point in sync. I do this so that I can select the current line to examine its text for a comment delimiter. If at line 35 I do not find the comment delimiter, I am finished moving backward and must move the EditPoint and TextSelection point down one line. This will either place the TextSelection point at the procedure definition line if there were no comments found or at the first comment line belonging to the procedure being selected.

Line 45 moves the EditPoint back into the procedure. Remember that the cursor must be within the procedure to prevent raising an error in the GetStartPoint or GetEndPoint methods of the CodeElement property.

Line 48 uses the same mechanism to find the end of the procedure as line 22 did to find the start of the procedure. The only difference is that it calls the GetEndPoint method of the CodeElement property. Having found the end of the procedure, line 52 does the actual selection of the whole procedure. If the second parameter of the MoveToPoint method of the TextSelection object is True, the MoveToPoint method will select all text from the current TextSelection point to the point to which it is being moved.

To run the completed macro command, I place the cursor anywhere inside of the procedure to be selected. In this case, it is the procedure named TestMacroProcedureSelection. Next, I double-click the TestSelectWholeProc command in the Macro Explorer. Figure 8-10 shows the result of running the macro.

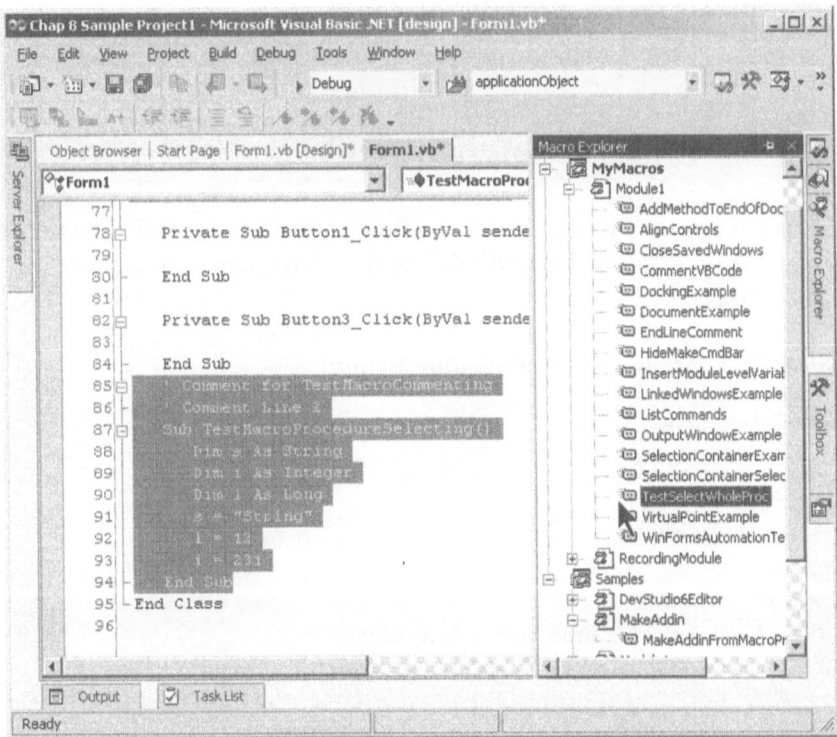

Figure 8-10. Automatic selection of a whole procedure by a macro

Obviously, this new function, GetWholeProc, is a valuable addition to your library of reusable procedures. You will find that it has many uses, especially in features such as CloneProcedure, which was developed in an earlier chapter.

Enhancing the Smart Desktop Add-in

Now you're going to use the new function that I just created in the Smart Desktop add-in that you've been developing thus far in the book. First, use the new procedure in the CloneProcedure feature, so that the developer will not have to select the whole procedure before invoking the add-in. This will make it easier and faster to use and, after all, the primary reason for writing add-ins is to increase the developer's productivity. You can find the code for these new features in MyAddinTest1 in the code for Chapter 8. If you're following along with me, load the project into Visual Studio .NET.

To use this new procedure, perform the following tasks:

1. Add the new GetWholeProc method to the Connect class.

2. Change the call from GetCodeFromWindow to GetWholeProc.

3. Introduce some new features to the add-in that will use the GetWholeProc method.

Enhancing CloneProcedure

Listing 8-8 shows the CloneProcedure method of the Connect class. The only line changed is in bold. The call to GetCodeFromWindow changed to a call to GetWholeProc.

Listing 8-8. The Modified CloneProcedure Method

```
Shared Sub CloneProcedure()
    Dim s As String
    Dim i As Integer
    Dim rs As String

    Try
        ' get selected proc from active window
        s = GetWholeProc() ' GetCodeFromWindow()
```

```
        If InStr(1, s, " Sub ", 0) = 0 And _
            InStr(1, s, " Function ", CompareMethod.Binary) = 0 Then
            MsgBox("Please select a whole Procedure↵
                to be cloned.", MsgBoxStyle.Exclamation)
            Exit Sub
        End If
        Dim oFrm As New CloneProc()
        rs = oFrm.Display(s)
        oFrm.Dispose()
        If rs <> "" Then
            AddMethodToEndOfDocument(rs)
        End If
    Catch e As System.Exception
        'MsgBox("Error: " & e.Message, MsgBoxStyle.Critical, "Clone Procedure")
        Exit Sub
    End Try
End Sub
```

Next, you add the new method, GetWholeProc, to the Connect class. Copy it from the macro module into the Connect class and place it at the end of the class. You make two changes to the method when you move it. First, you add the keyword Shared to the function definition line. This will allow it to be seen from anywhere in the project. Second, you substitute the object oVB for DTE in the one line where it is used. Listing 8-9 displays the new method with the changed lines in bold.

Listing 8-9. The GetWholeProc Method Modified for Use in the Add-in

```
Shared Function GetWholeProc() As String
    Dim ts As TextSelection = oVB.ActiveWindow().Selection
    Dim ep As EditPoint = ts.ActivePoint.CreateEditPoint
    Dim sLine As String
    Dim i As Integer

    Try
        ' if the user has selected the whole proc,
        ' then just return it
        ' otherwise select it for them...
        If Len(ts.Text) > 0 Then
            If (InStr(1, ts.Text, "Sub ", 1) > 0 Or _
                InStr(1, ts.Text, "Function ", 1) > 0) And _
                (InStr(1, ts.Text, "End Sub", 1) > 0 Or _
                InStr(1, ts.Text, "End Function", 1) > 0) _
```

```
            Then
                Return ts.Text
            End If
            GoTo SelectTheProc
        Else
SelectTheProc:
            '' Get the start of the proc
            ep.MoveToPoint(ep.CodeElement(EnvDTE.vsCMElement. ⏎
                vsCMElementFunction).GetStartPoint(vsCMPart.vsCMPartWhole))

            ' move selection start point to top of proc
            ts.MoveToPoint(ep, False)

            ' back up to previous line looking for comments
            i = 0
            Do
                ep.LineUp()
                ts.MoveToPoint(ep, False)
                ts.SelectLine()
                sLine = ts.Text
                If Left(Trim(sLine), 1) <> "'" Then
                    ep.LineDown()
                    ts.MoveToPoint(ep, False)
                    Exit Do
                End If
                i = i + 1
            Loop

            ' if the count of comment lines > 0  the ts point is set properly
            ' else we must move it back to the original
            ep.LineDown(i + 1)

            ' move to bottom of proc
            ep.MoveToPoint(ep.CodeElement(EnvDTE.vsCMElement ⏎
                .vsCMElementFunction).GetEndPoint(vsCMPart.vsCMPartWhole))

            ' select the proc
            ts.MoveToPoint(ep, True)
            Return ts.Text
        End If
    Catch
        System.Windows.Forms.MessageBox.Show⏎
            ("You must either select the whole⏎
```

```
            procedure or your cursor must be within⤶
            the procedure to be selected.")
        Return ""
    End Try
End Function
```

Running the Modified CloneProcedure Feature

Now that you've made all of the changes to use the new and improved method for retrieving a procedure, run the add-in to test the changes. Because you already have the add-in (MyAddinTest1 from the Chapter 8 code) loaded into Visual Studio, simply press F5 to test the add-in. Assuming that you've made the changes correctly and have no compile errors, the second copy (add-in client) of Visual Studio .NET should start automatically. When it does, select Chap 8 Sample Project1 from the code for Chapter 8 as the project to run. When the sample project is loaded into the client copy of Visual Studio, open the Add-in Manager dialog box, check both boxes for MyFirstAddin1, and click OK to close the dialog box. This will connect the add-in.

From the Tools menu, select the Smart Desktop menu option. It should be the top menu item on the Tools menu. This will cause the add-in's UI form to appear. Open the TreeView. If Form1.vb (code window) is not already open in the client copy of Visual Studio .NET, open it and place the cursor anywhere in the TestMacroProcedureSelecting method. Next, click the CloneProcedure node in the TreeView. The code for the selected procedure will be retrieved and displayed in the Clone Procedure form, as shown in Figure 8-11.

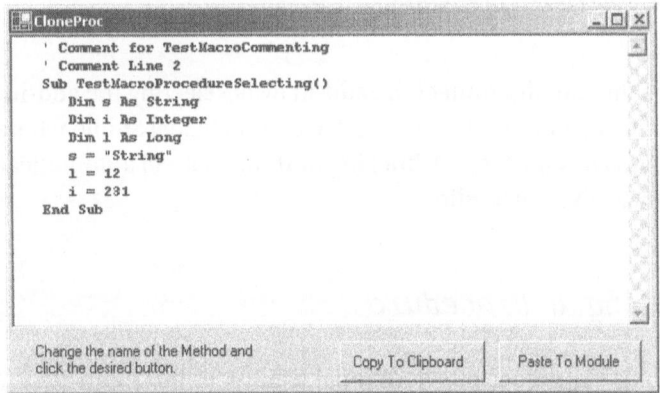

Figure 8-11. Clone procedure display form

At this point, you're going to change the name of the procedure in the CloneProc form to NewTestProc. Finally, click the PasteToModule button on the form. This causes the form to paste the cloned procedure back to the client code window. The cloned procedure is shown in Figure 8-12.

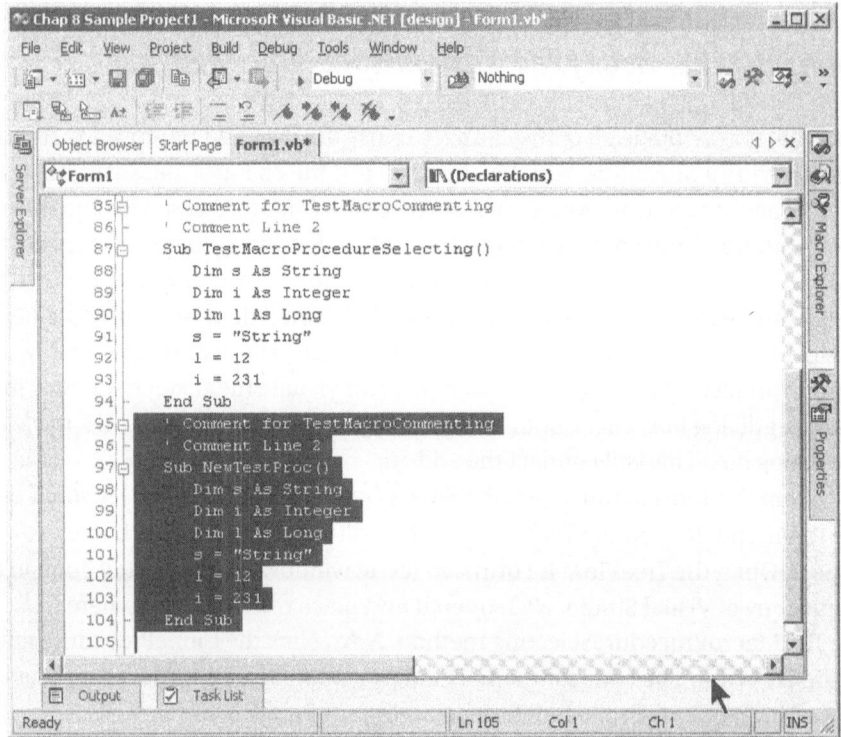

Figure 8-12. New cloned procedure

To close the test, disconnect the add-in by deselecting the add-in in the Add-in Manager dialog box. Next, return to the copy of Visual Studio where the add-in is running and click the Stop Debugging button. This will automatically close the client instance of Visual Studio.

Documenting a Procedure

In this section, I introduce one additional feature for the Smart Desktop add-in that will use the GetWholeProc method. This feature can retrieve the comments that are immediately before and following a procedure definition line. It takes those comments, extracts the parameters, and applies a document template to the extracted data. It formalizes the programmer-supplied comments, adds some additional data, and creates a formal-looking documentation template. It then puts the procedure back into the module.

Obviously, many of the data parameters and the template itself are hard-coded in this add-in. In a real add-in, the template would be read from a file, which could be customized. The user name and company name would be retrieved from the registry.

The code in Listing 8-10 does the work of reading through the captured procedure and applying the formal document template to the procedure. I don't explain this code in detail, mainly due to its length and because it's very straight-forward in what it does. At a high level, it does the following things:

- Extracts comment lines before and following the procedure definition line

- Extracts the parameters from the procedure definition line

- Extracts the return value if the procedure is a function

- Substitutes live values for keywords found in the template, such as Copyright, Created By, Created Date, and so forth

- Concatenates all the template data and places it into the procedure

- Returns the procedure to the module

In addition to adding this code to the Connect class, you should add a new node to the TreeView in Form1 and name the node Document Procedure. You'll see the new node when you execute the add-in. I'm sure that by now you're famil-iar with how to add a node to the TreeView, so I won't go through that process.

Listing 8-10. DocTemplate Method

```
Shared Sub DocTemplate()
    ' Apply a formal template to the captured procedure
    Dim i As Long
    Dim iPtr As Integer
    Dim nL As Integer
    Dim bParameters As Boolean
    Dim bPurpose As Boolean
    Dim sOut As String
    Dim sLine As String
    Dim bFoundSub As Boolean
    Dim sDocTemplate As String
    Dim sWord As String
```

```vb
            Dim sTempParams As String
            Dim cComStr As String
            Dim sPar As String
            Dim sRetVal As String
            Dim sProcToCopy As String
            Dim sProcType As String
            Dim j As Integer
            Dim k As Integer
            Const sPurpose = "Purpose:"
            Const sParameters = "Parameters:"
            Const sDateCreated = "Date Created:"
            Const sAuthor = "Author:"
            Const sUserName = "Les Smith"
            Const sCopyright = "Copyright:"
            Const sCompanyName = "HHI Software, Inc."
            Const sReturns = "Returns:"
            Dim s As String

            Try
                ' create the doc template
                ' In a production add-in this would be read from a file
                ' so that the file could be customized...
                s = "'*************************************" & vbCrLf
                s = s & "'* Name: ProcName" & vbCrLf
                s = s & "'* Purpose:" & vbCrLf
                s = s & "'*" & vbCrLf
                s = s & "'* " & vbCrLf
                s = s & "'* Parameters:" & vbCrLf
                s = s & "'*" & vbCrLf
                s = s & "'* Returns:" & vbCrLf
                s = s & "'*" & vbCrLf
                s = s & "'* Author: " & vbCrLf
                s = s & "'* Date Created:" & vbCrLf
                s = s & "'* CopyRight: " & vbCrLf
                s = s & "'* Date Last Changed: " & vbCrLf
                s = s & "'*************************************" & vbCrLf
                sDocTemplate = s

                ' if user selected the text prior to clicking the
                ' button, get that code

                sProcToCopy = ""
                sProcToCopy = GetWholeProc()
```

```
sOut = ""
sDocTemplate = ""

bFoundSub = False


' find out some stuff about the template
bPurpose = (InStr(1, sDocTemplate, sPurpose, 1) > 1)
bParameters = (InStr(1, sDocTemplate, sParameters, 1) > 1)

nL = MLCount(sProcToCopy, 0)
cComStr = ""

For i = 1 To nL
    sLine = MemoLine(sProcToCopy, 0, i)
    If Not bFoundSub Then
        If InStr(sLine, "Sub ") > 0 Or _
            InStr(sLine, "Function ") > 0 Then
            sOut = sOut & sLine & vbCrLf
            bFoundSub = True

            ' get sub name
            Do While Trim$(sLine) <> ""
                sWord = GetToken(sLine, "")
                If InStr("Sub_Function", sWord) > 0 Then Exit Do
                sProcType = sWord
            Loop

            ' get sub name
            sWord = GetToken(sLine, "_")

            'get parameters if applicable
            If bParameters Then
                sRetVal = ""
                sTempParams = ""
                j = CountOccurrences(",", sLine)
                For k = 1 To j
                    ' the next parm
                    sPar = Left$(sLine, InStr(sLine, ",") - 1)
                    ' remove it from sline
                    sLine = Mid$(sLine, InStr(sLine, ",") + 1)
                    sTempParams = sTempParams & "'*    " & _
                            Trim(sPar) & vbCrLf
```

```
            Next k
            ' get last parm
            k = InStr(sLine, ")") - 1
            If k > 0 Then
                sPar = Left$(sLine, InStr(sLine, ")") - 1)
                sTempParams = sTempParams & "'*    " & _
                               Trim(sPar) & vbCrLf
            End If
            sLine = Mid$(sLine, InStr(sLine, ")"))
            sPar = Trim$(GetToken(sLine, " _"))
            If Left$(sPar, 3) = "As " Then
                sRetVal = Mid$(sPar, 4)
            End If
        End If


        ' now get any comments after the proc def line
        Do While i <= nL
            i = i + 1
            sLine = MemoLine(sProcToCopy, 0, i)
            ' if this is a comment line let's uncomment it and
            ' put in cComStr, if a blank, skip it...
            If Left$(Trim$(sLine), 2) = "'*" Then
                If InStr(sLine, "***") > 1 Or _
                    InStr(sLine, "--") > 1 Or _
                    InStr(sLine, "$$$") > 1 Or _
                    InStr(sLine, "___") > 1 Then
                Else
                    sLine = Trim$(sLine)
                    sLine = Mid$(sLine, 3)
                    sLine = Trim$(sLine)
                    cComStr = cComStr & "'*    " & sLine & vbCrLf
                End If
            ElseIf Left$(Trim$(sLine), 1) = "'" Then
                If InStr(sLine, "***") > 1 Or _
                    InStr(sLine, "--") > 1 Or _
                    InStr(sLine, "$$$") > 1 Or _
                    InStr(sLine, "___") > 1 Then
                Else
                    sLine = Trim$(sLine)
                    sLine = Mid$(sLine, 2)
                    sLine = Trim$(sLine)
                    cComStr = cComStr & "'*    " & sLine & vbCrLf
                End If
            End If
```

```
      ElseIf Trim$(sLine) = "" Then
          ' discard blank lines before Sub/Function
      Else
          Exit Do
      End If
Loop

If Trim$(cComStr) <> "" Then
    ' strip the last crlf so we don't get a blank line
    iPtr = InStrRev(cComStr, vbCrLf)
    If iPtr > 0 Then
        cComStr = Left$(cComStr, iPtr - 1)
    End If
End If

If Trim$(sTempParams) <> "" Then
    ' strip the last crlf so we don't get a blank line
    iPtr = InStrRev(sTempParams, vbCrLf)
    If iPtr > 0 Then
        sTempParams = Left$(sTempParams, iPtr - 1)
    End If
End If

' substitute into the template
sDocTemplate = Replace(sDocTemplate, _
                        "ProcName", sWord)
sDocTemplate = Replace(sDocTemplate, _
                        sCopyright, _
                        sCopyright & " " & _
                        sCompanyName)
sDocTemplate = Replace(sDocTemplate, _
                        sDateCreated, _
                        sDateCreated & " " & _
                        TodaysDate)
sDocTemplate = Replace(sDocTemplate, _
                        sAuthor, _
                        sAuthor & " " & _
                        sUserName)
If bPurpose And Trim$(cComStr) <> "" Then
    sDocTemplate = Replace(sDocTemplate, _
                            sPurpose, _
                            sPurpose & " " & _
                            vbCrLf & cComStr)
```

```
                    End If
                    If bParameters And Trim$(sTempParams) <> "" Then
                        sDocTemplate = Replace(sDocTemplate, _
                                               sParameters, _
                                               sParameters & " " & _
                                               vbCrLf & sTempParams)
                    End If
                    If sRetVal <> "" Then
                        sDocTemplate = Replace(sDocTemplate, _
                                               sReturns, _
                                               sReturns & " " & sRetVal)
                    ElseIf sProcType = "Sub" Then
                        sDocTemplate = Replace(sDocTemplate, sReturns, "")
                    Else
                        sDocTemplate = Replace(sDocTemplate, _
                                               sReturns, _
                                               sReturns & _
                                               " Return Value not specified")
                    End If
                    sOut = sOut & sDocTemplate
                    sOut = sOut & sLine & vbCrLf
                Else
                    ' we have not found the proc def line yet
                    ' if this is a comment line let's uncomment it and
                    ' put in cComStr, if a blank, skip it...
                    If Left$(Trim$(sLine), 2) = "'*" Then
                        If InStr(sLine, "***") > 1 Or _
                            InStr(sLine, "--") > 1 Or _
                            InStr(sLine, "$$$") > 1 Or _
                            InStr(sLine, "___") > 1 Then
                        Else
                            sLine = Trim$(sLine)
                            sLine = Mid$(sLine, 3)
                            sLine = Trim$(sLine)
                            cComStr = cComStr & "'*    " & sLine & vbCrLf
                        End If
                    ElseIf Left$(Trim$(sLine), 1) = "'" Then
                        If InStr(sLine, "***") > 1 Or _
                            InStr(sLine, "--") > 1 Or _
                            InStr(sLine, "$$$") > 1 Or _
                            InStr(sLine, "___") > 1 Then
                        Else
                            sLine = Trim$(sLine)
```

```
                        sLine = Mid$(sLine, 2)
                        sLine = Trim$(sLine)
                        cComStr = cComStr & "'*    " & sLine & vbCrLf
                    End If
                ElseIf Trim$(sLine) = "" Then
                    ' discard blank lines before Sub/Function
                Else
                    sOut = sOut & sLine & vbCrLf
                End If
            End If
        Else
            sOut = sOut & sLine & vbCrLf
        End If
    Next


    ' paste the code back to the window
    PutCodeBack(sOut)


    Exit Sub
  Catch e As System.Exception
  End Try
End Sub
```

Listing 8-11 shows a helper function called by DocTemplate. It simply counts occurrences of an expression in a string.

Listing 8-11. CountOccurrences Helper Method

```
Shared Function CountOccurrences(ByVal rsExp As String, _
                                 ByVal rsStr As Object) As Long
  ' Returns the number of occurrences of rsExp (expression)
  ' found in rsStr (string)
  ' Returns 0 of no occurrences found.
  Dim pPos As Integer
  Dim lPos As Integer
  Dim nPos As Integer
  Dim nFirst As Integer
  Dim lCnt As Integer


  Try


    pPos = 0 ' previous find
    lPos = 0 ' return position of right char
```

```
            nPos = 1 ' position of next right most char
            nFirst = 1
            lCnt = 0

            ' loop thru every char in string until we
            ' find the last occurrence
            Do
                lPos = InStr(nPos, rsStr, rsExp, 1)
                If lPos > 0 Then
                    nPos = lPos + 1
                    pPos = lPos
                    lCnt = lCnt + 1
                Else
                    Exit Do
                End If
            Loop

        Return lCnt
    Catch e As System.Exception
    End Try
End Function
```

Listing 8-12 shows the code added to the TreeView event handler in Form1.vb. The new code is in boldface. It calls the DocTemplate method of the Connect class to retrieve and document the selected procedure.

Listing 8-12. AfterSelect Event of TreeView

```
Private Sub tvMenu_AfterSelect(ByVal sender As Object, _
    ByVal e As System.Windows.Forms.TreeViewEventArgs) _
    Handles tvMenu.AfterSelect
    Dim i As Integer

    Select Case UCase$(e.Node.Text)
        Case "SMART DESKTOP" 'ignore root clicks
        Case "BLOCK COMMENT"
            Call Connect.BlockComment()
        Case "UNCOMMENT"
            Call Connect.BlockUnComment()
        Case "BLOCK CHANGE"
            Call Connect.BlockChange()
        Case "BLOCK DELETE"
            Call Connect.BlockDelete()
```

```
        Case "PROC ERROR HANDLER"
            Call Connect.GenLocalErrorTrap()
        Case "CLONE PROCEDURE"
            Call Connect.CloneProcedure()
        Case "DOCUMENT PROCEDURE"
            Call Connect.DocTemplate()
        Case Else
            MsgBox("Please click on a Child Node.", _
                MsgBoxStyle.Information, "Unknown ↵
                Request")
    End Select
End Sub
```

Now I have shown all of the code that has been added to retrieve and document the selected procedure. To run the add-in, follow the normal procedure of debugging: Press F5. When the second copy of the Visual Studio opens, connect the add-in by going to the Add-in Manager and checking both boxes representing MyAddinTest1.

You should open Chap 8 Sample Project1 and open the Form1.vb code module. Place the cursor anywhere in the TestMacroProcedureSelecting procedure. Display the add-in's TreeView menu form and select the Document Procedure node. Listing 8-13 shows the procedure before it has been documented.

Listing 8-13. Procedure Before Being Documented

```
' Comment for TestMacroCommenting
' Comment Line 2
Sub TestMacroProcedureSelecting()
    Dim s As String
    Dim i As Integer
    Dim l As Long
    s = "String"
    l = 12
    i = 231
End Sub
```

After the code has been documented and placed back into the module, it will appear as shown in Figure 8-13.

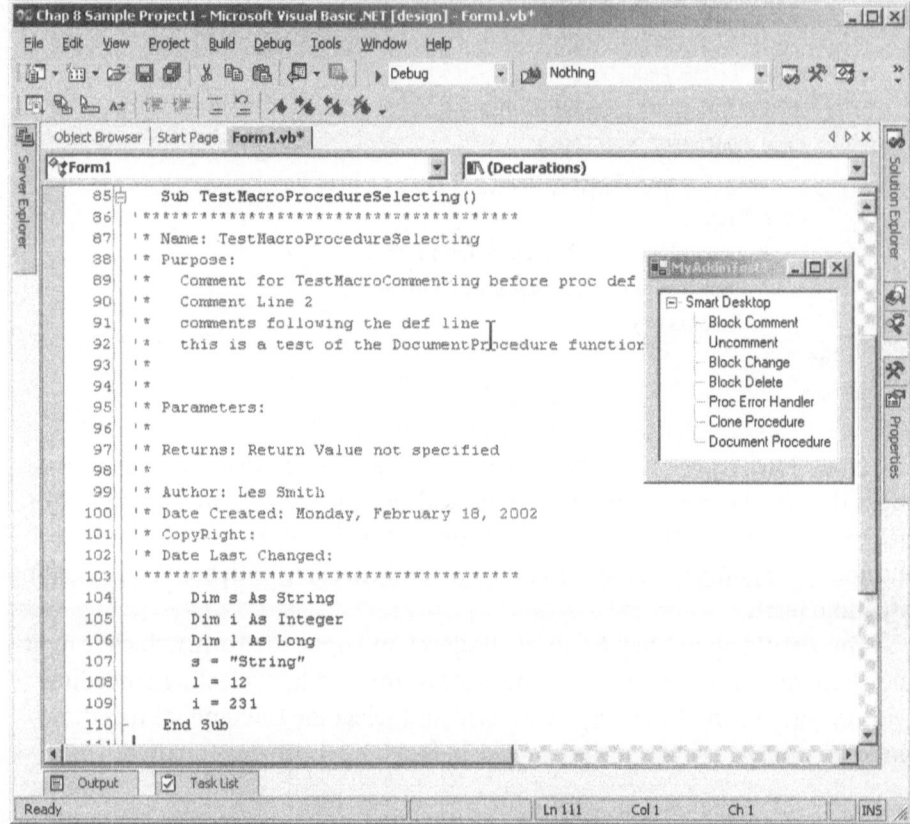

Figure 8-13. Documented code

Summary

In this chapter you saw how to record, run, write, and debug macros. You saw that the Macros IDE is an excellent place to learn some extensibility tricks from the sample macros. You also discovered that the Macros IDE provides a simple and fast way to test new code for an add-in without having to compile and run an add-in, with its inherent use of two instances of Visual Studio.

You enhanced an existing feature, CloneProcedure, in the Smart Desktop add-in to use the new GetWholeProc method that you developed in the Macros IDE. You also added a new feature, Document Procedure, to the add-in.

In Chapter 9, I discuss the manipulation of projects. With automation objects, you can manipulate projects programmatically, just as the developer can in the IDE. You can create new projects, add items to the project, and even build a project from an add-in.

CHAPTER 9

Manipulating Projects

Hank Aaron, while at bat, was asked by Yogi Berra, "Can't you read? Your bat's upside down." Aaron hit the ball over the fence, turned to Berra, and said, "Didn't come up here to read. Came up here to hit."

AT THIS POINT IN THE BOOK, you have seen how to manipulate forms and their associated controls. You have seen how to manipulate code in the Text Editor window. You have learned how to perform these actions through the use of macros and in an add-in. In this chapter you'll learn how to manipulate the solution and its project(s). At the end of the chapter, you'll explore some of the other items within the IDE, such as the ToolBox and TaskList objects.

The Visual Studio .NET automation model provides objects and collections that allow you to control both the solution and the projects, and the project items within the solution. The Solution object and the Solution.Projects collection contain all of the projects in the current solution.

Only one solution can be open in the Visual Studio .NET IDE at one time. That solution must contain at least one project. You certainly are not limited to one project. In VB 6.0, if you wanted to debug one or more DLLs, you had to have an instance of the client application that called the first DLL. Additionally, you had to have another instance of the IDE for each DLL that would be called in a series. In Visual Studio .NET, you can have numerous projects in a solution. Therefore, you can debug a client application calling a series of DLLs in one instance of the IDE. Obviously then, the projects can be of various types. Furthermore, they can be written in various languages. For example, a solution might contain a Visual Basic .NET Windows application project and a Visual C# class library (DLL) project. Each project contains one or more project items, such as classes, modules, forms, and so forth.

The Solution object is the key object that facilitates the manipulation of all of these objects. Using the Solution object you can do the following:

- Create a new solution.

- Add new projects to the solution using a Visual Studio .NET template.

- Add existing projects to the solution.

- Remove a project from the solution.

- Open, save, close, and build the solution.

Visual Studio .NET provides a generic project model. By this I mean that an add-in written in any of the Visual Studio .NET languages that support the automation model can manipulate the project model. The project model is composed of the objects listed in Table 9-1.

Table 9-1. Project Object Model

OBJECT NAME	OBJECT DESCRIPTION
Projects collection	A collection of all projects in the solution
Project object	Represents one project in the Projects collection or the solution
ProjectItems collection	Collection of all of the items in a project
ProjectItem object	Represents an item, such as a class, form, and so forth, in a specified project

These objects allow you to build an add-in using any Visual Studio .NET language. In the add-in, you can create a new project, save or delete an existing project, and add or remove project items to and from a project.

In addition to the generic project objects available to all languages, each language provides its own custom project objects. These are the VBProject, VCProject, and CsharpProject objects, which represent their respective languages (VB, C++, and C#).

You can reference these language-specific objects by a reference such as DTE.VBProjects or DTE.GetObject("VBProjects") to retrieve the VB-specific project object.

The Solution Object

The Solution object is the collection of all the projects in the current instance of the Visual Studio IDE. The Solution object also contains all solution-wide properties, such as build configurations. The Solution object contains a project object for every project in the solution.

NOTE *Because you have learned either from this book or prior experience how to use the Macro Explorer to execute code that can manipulate the extensibility objects, you will use the Macro Explorer to run many of the code examples in this chapter. It is easier to demonstrate many of the procedures that I will show you in the Macro Explorer than to take the time to build them into an add-in. Again, if you want to move code from a macro to an add-in, any references to the DTE object must be replaced with a reference to the application object (oVB in my add-ins).*

You can reference the Solution object by using DTE.Solution. In this section, you will create a solution, add a project to the solution, remove the solution, and close the solution.

Creating a solution is very simple. Listing 9-1 shows the code for creating a new solution in an IDE that has just been opened. After the solution is created (which only takes three lines of code), the code adds a Windows application project to the solution.

Listing 9-1. Creating a Solution and Project

```
Sub CreateSolution1()
    Dim sln As Solution
    Dim prj As Project
    'Create a reference to the solution.
    sln = DTE.Solution

    ' Create a new solution.
    sln.Create("c:\vsprojs", "MyNewSolution")

    MsgBox("Solution has been created.")

    ' Create a new windows application project in the solution
    prj = sln.AddFromTemplate("C:\Program Files\Microsoft " & _
        "Visual Studio " & _
        ".NET\Vb7\VBProjects\windowsapplication.vsz", _
        "c:\vsprojs\Chap9 Solution1", "My New Project", True)

    MsgBox("Windows Application has been added to solution.")

    sln.SaveAs("c:\vsProjs\MyNewSolution.sln")

    MsgBox("Solution has been saved.")
End Sub
```

To run the code in Listing 9-1, import the macro project from the Chapter 9 code. In the Macro Explorer, double-click the CreateSolution1 macro.

> **CAUTION** *Before you run this macro on your computer, ensure that the path to the place you want to save projects is correct. If it isn't, you should change the path in the sln.Create statement to a path where you save projects on your computer. If, by chance, the path to the Windows application template is not the same as the one hard-coded in the macro, you'll have to change that also.*

The macro is highlighted in Figure 9-1. The IDE has no solution open at the time the macro is run.

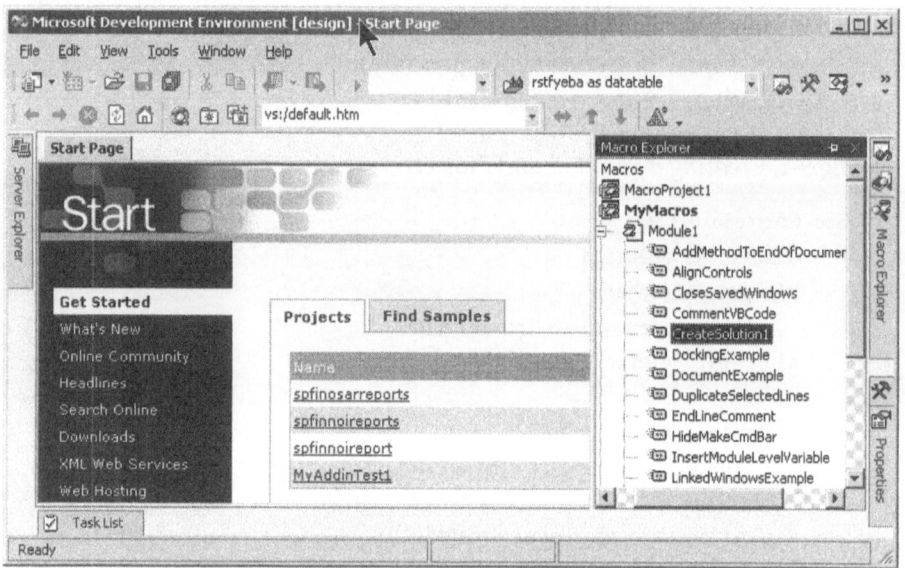

Figure 9-1. Running the CreateSolution1 macro

When the macro is invoked, the solution is created and a message box displays the fact that the IDE now has an empty solution open. Next, the code adds a Windows application to the solution; the AddFromTemplate method of the Solution object does this. As the macro runs, you can tell that the project is being opened when the Form Designer displays Form1.vb. You will recall that when a project is created, a form is automatically added to the project.

 **NOTE** *When the project is added to the solution, a Save dialog box will appear asking if you want to save the solution. You can click the No button, as the project will be saved by the automation code.*

The macro will display two additional messages. One will display when the project has been added, and the other will display when the project has been saved. Figure 9-2 shows the project that has been created. The Solution Explorer is open, showing the structure of the project. If you go to the Windows Explorer and look in the directory where the solution was stored, you should see the normal solution and project structure of directories and files displayed, just as if you had done it manually in the IDE.

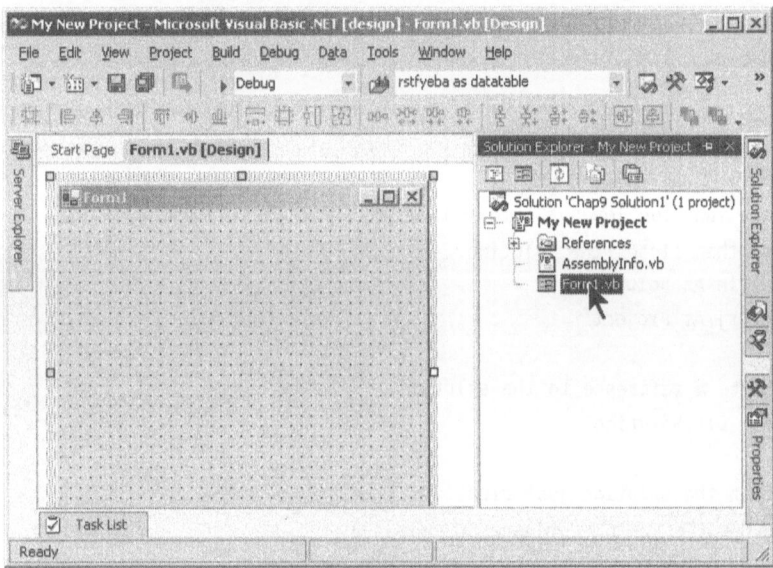

Figure 9-2. New Windows application project

Next, you'll close the solution manually and reopen it programmatically. The macro in Listing 9-2 will perform this operation. First, you must create a DTE.Solution object. Then you can use the Open method of the Solution object to open the project by simply specifying the path where the solution was created.

Listing 9-2. OpenExistingSolution1 Macro

```
Sub OpenExistingSolution1()
    Dim sln As Solution
    'Create a reference to the solution.
    sln = DTE.Solution

    ' Open the solution just created.
    sln.Open("c:\vsProjs\MyNewSolution.sln")

    MsgBox("Solution has been reopened")

End Sub
```

Finally, you'll close the solution manually and then execute a macro to programmatically reopen the solution. The macro will remove the project from the solution and then close the solution. Listing 9-3 shows the code for this set of operations.

Listing 9-3. RemoveProjectFromSolution Macro

```
Sub RemoveProjectFromSolution()
    'This function loads a solution, deletes the first project,
    'and then closes the solution.
    Dim sln As Solution
    Dim prj As Project

    'Create a reference to the solution.
    sln = DTE.Solution

    ' Open the solution just created.
    sln.Open("c:\vsProjs\MyNewSolution.sln")

    ' Delete the newly created VB Console application project in
    'this solution.
    prj = sln.Projects.Item(1)
    sln.Remove(prj)
    MsgBox("Project was deleted from the solution, &
            click Ok to close the solution)

    ' Close the solution from the IDE.
    sln.Close()
End Sub
```

The Project Object

Visual Studio .NET projects are used as containers to help you organize and manipulate the items that you are developing to build your application. The projects exist within a solution to manage, debug, and build the items that make up your application. A Visual Studio .NET project can contain many more types of items than you would normally find in a VB 6.0 project. In addition to the normal types of files, such as classes, forms, and modules, you may now find bitmaps, icons, and other graphic files, along with other items.

You can make a project as simple or as complex as you need to perform the task of building your application. A project can be made as simple as containing one form for a Windows application or a class for a DLL. You can also build complex projects that include many forms, modules, and classes, plus database scripts, stored procedures, and so forth.

All languages in the Visual Studio .NET environment provide several predefined project templates. With a project template, you can create a basic project container and an initial set of items that you would need to develop an application of the type specified by the template. You have already used a project template in this chapter to programmatically create a Visual Basic Windows application. There are also templates available to do the same thing in Visual C++ and Visual C#.

In addition to the templates that create a project, there are templates that allow you to add additional items to your project. Project templates allow you to concentrate on the "business" functionality that you want to develop rather than concern yourself with the housekeeping tasks that would have been associated with earlier development environments.

Listing ProjectItems Programmatically

Items within the project are called ProjectItems. The ProjectItems collection represents all of the classes, forms, documents, and any other type of item that is included in the project. The collection may be a simple, flat list of items or a hierarchical structure of ProjectItems collections. You can reference the collection by using Solution.Item(n).ProjectItems. Because the ProjectItems object is a collection, it follows that the items within the collection are ProjectItem objects, each of which may itself be a collection. Listing 9-4 shows the code for listing the items in the ProjectItem collection. This listing includes two macro commands (Subs). I have done this in order to make the second macro, ShowOneProjectItemCollection, a recursive procedure. This allows the macro to call itself when it determines that one of the ProjectItems is itself a collection. When you run the first macro, it calls the second.

Listing 9-4. Listing the ProjectItems Collection

```
Sub ShowProjectItems()
    Dim prj As Project = DTE.ActiveSolutionProjects(0)
    ShowOneProjectItemCollection(prj.ProjectItems(), 0)
End Sub


Sub ShowOneProjectItemCollection(ByVal PrjItems As↵
    ProjectItems, ↵
    ByVal CallLevel As Integer)
    Dim prjItem As ProjectItem ' object
    For Each prjItem In PrjItems
        If prjItem.Collection Is PrjItems Then
            MsgBox("Item Name = " & prjItem.Name & Chr(10) & _
                    "Item Level = " & CallLevel.ToString & _
                    Chr(10) & _
                    "Item Count = " & _
                    prjItem.Collection.Count.ToString, _
                    MsgBoxStyle.OKOnly, )

            ' call me if this item has subitems...
            Dim prjItems2 As ProjectItems
            prjItems2 = prjItem.ProjectItems
            Dim bColl As Boolean = Not (prjItems2 Is Nothing)
            If bColl Then
                ShowOneProjectItemCollection(prjItems2, _
                    CallLevel + 1)
            End If
        End If
    Next
End Sub
```

When the second macro encounters a form file, you will see that it displays
a message for Form1.vb and then recourses to display a message for Form1.resx.
Figure 9-3 shows the message box display for Form1.vb.

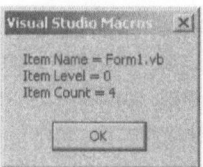

Figure 9-3. ProjectItem for Form1.vb

The message box displays the item name, the call level, and the number of items in the current collection. While the level number is 0, the ProjectItem collection is at the top level. When the level number is 1 or greater, the ProjectItem collection is a child of the top or parent level. Figure 9-4 shows the message box display for Form1.resx, which is a child item of Form1.vb.

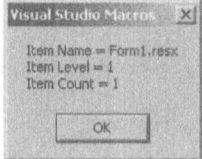

Figure 9-4. ProjectItem for Form1.resx

Adding New Items to the Project

I showed you earlier how to use a template to create a Windows application project for use with the Visual Basic language. There are templates provided for Visual C++ and Visual C#. You can use them in an add-in written in Visual Basic to create projects for the other languages and vice versa.

In addition to templates for the creation of projects, there are also templates provided for adding the standard file items to the project, such as classes, forms, and modules. Listing 9-5 shows the code for adding a module, form, and class to the project previously created by the code in Listing 9-1, which is the CreateSolution1 macro command.

NOTE *If you have not run the CreateSolution1 macro from Listing 9-1, the project is included with the code for this chapter. Also, be aware that the various macros developed thus far in the chapter will modify the original solution created by the CreateSolution1 macro. If you run all of them in sequence, you will delete the project from the solution. If that is the case, you should delete the solution and then rerun CreateSolution1. At that point, you should have the project needed to run this macro.*

Listing 9-5. Adding Items to the Project

```
01  Sub AddItemToSolution()
02      Dim sln As Solution
03      Dim prj As Project
04      Dim bas As Object
05      Dim frm As Object
06      'Create a reference to the solution.
07      sln = DTE.Solution
08
09      ' Open the solution just created.
10      sln.Open("c:\vsProjs\Chap9 Solution1\MyNewSolution.sln")
11
12          MsgBox("Solution has been reopened; ↵
13              new form will be added.")
14
15      ' get pointer to the project
16      prj = sln.Projects.Item(1)
17      bas = prj.ProjectItems.AddFromTemplate(↵
18              "C:\Program Files\Microsoft ↵
19              Visual Studio .NET\Vb7\VBProjectItems\↵
20              module.vsz", "Module1.vb")
21
22      MsgBox("Module1 has been added to the project.")
23
24      frm = prj.ProjectItems.AddFromTemplate(↵
25          "C:\Program Files\Microsoft ↵
26 Visual Studio .NET\Vb7\VBProjectItems\↵
27              winform.vsz", "Form2.vb")
28
29      MsgBox("Form2  has been added to the project.")
30
31      frm = prj.ProjectItems.AddFromTemplate(↵
32          "C:\Program Files\Microsoft ↵
33          Visual Studio .NET\Vb7\VBProjectItems\↵
34          Class.vsz", "Class1.vb")
35
36      MsgBox("Class1 has been added to the project.")
37 End Sub
```

Figure 9-5 displays the project just after the Module1.vb object has been added to the project. Line 17 in Listing 9-5 uses the AddFromTemplate method of the ProjectItems object to add the module. The AddFromTemplate method requires two parameters. The first is the path and file name of the desired template. The path to the templates is the same for all three items being added, but the template file name is changed. The second parameter is the name of the object being added. It is used by the object method to name the new module.

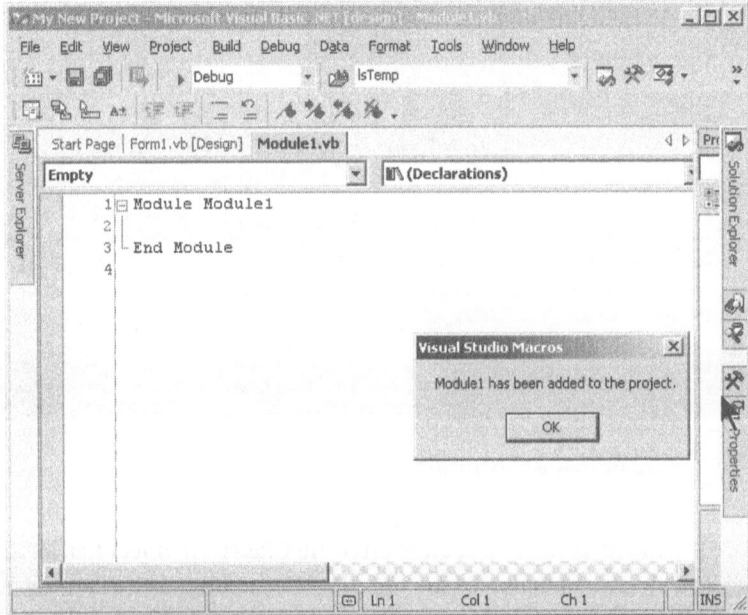

Figure 9-5. Module1 added to the project

Figure 9-6 displays the project just after the Form2.vb object has been added to the project. Line 24 in Listing 9-5 is the same as line 17, except that the file name of the template has been changed to point to the WinForm.vsz template. Additionally, the parameter supplying the name has been changed.

CAUTION   *You will not be able to run this macro twice in a row without first deleting the solution and then recreating it by using the CreateSolution1 macro. Otherwise, the modules would already be in the project and could not be added again. This implies that if you are writing an add-in that is adding items, you will have to loop through the ProjectItems collection enumerating the names of the type of item that you want to add to the project. This will ensure that you are not adding an item that is already in the project.*

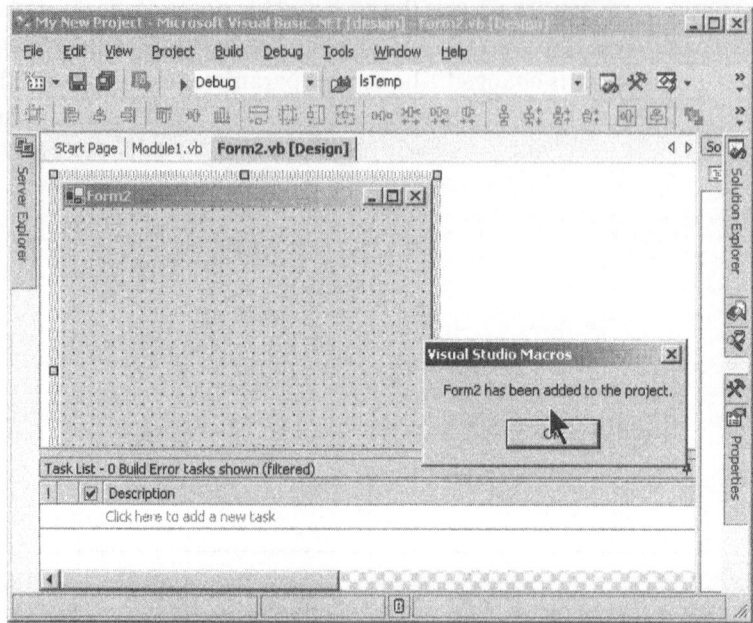

Figure 9-6. Form2 added to the project

Figure 9-7 displays the project just after the Class1.vb object has been added to the project. Again, the name of the template has changed to Class.vsz. Also, the name parameter has been changed to reflect the name of the new class.

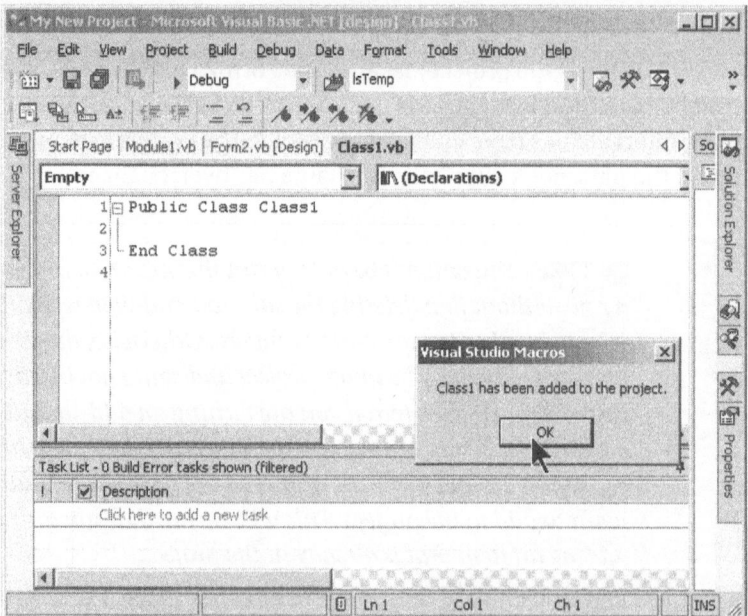

Figure 9-7. Class1 added to the project

Maintaining Build Rules

Build rules are simply processes that can be run before and after a developer builds a solution. These processes can be executable programs or even files, as long as the file type is a registered file type. In this section, I demonstrate an add-in that will allow you to maintain a set of pre- and postbuild rules or processes. This simply means that you can have a set of processes run automatically for you just before the solution build process starts and/or finishes.

> **NOTE** *A registered file type example is a .txt file. When a .txt file is double-clicked in the Windows Explorer, it causes Notepad.exe to be automatically launched.*

Before I show you the new add-in, I discuss the object through which these build rules can be maintained across sessions of the Visual Studio .NET IDE. This object is the Globals object.

The Globals Object

Visual Studio .NET uses a cache object for storing data throughout each session. It can even save data across sessions. This object is the Globals object. The Globals object can be used by macros. The object can also be used by an add-in because, once connected, an add-in is virtually part of the IDE. Therefore, macros can have global variables whose values persist between executions of the macro. The Globals object can be used to allow a macro to implement a default value instead of requiring the user to enter a repeating value each time the macro is executed. The variable could also be used to change the behavior of the macro after it has been executed a certain number of times. Add-ins can have global variables that persist between sessions of the IDE.

The Globals object stores data in name/variant value pairs. These pairs can optionally be saved on disk. The VariablePersists property of the Globals object can be used to allow the macro or add-in to maintain state between different sessions of Visual Studio. The Globals object can also be used to save to and retrieve from a solution (.sln) file.

> **NOTE** *Object variables cannot be saved in the Globals object unless they can be saved as a string. The length of a variable name to be saved in the Globals object cannot exceed 31 characters.*

The VariablePersists property is used with the following types of Globals objects:

- *DTE.Globals:* Used to persist values between sessions of the environment. The values are stored in the User Profiles directory.

- *Solutions.Globals:* Used to persist values in the solution (.sln) file so that the data is saved when the solution is closed and reloaded when the solution is reloaded. If you want to save values with a particular solution, use the DTE.Solution.Globals object.

- *Project.Globals:* Allows persistence of values in the project file.

Any variables saved will overwrite previously saved values. To remove a variable from the saved file, set the VariablePersists property to False. The environment will remove its value during the next Save operation. Values can be saved and retrieved by using the VariableValue property. The use of the Globals object and its properties will be demonstrated in the MaintainBuildRules add-in.

MaintainBuildRules Add-in

In this section I demonstrate the use of the Globals object as well as the processing of build rules before and after a solution is built. This demonstration also introduces the use of DTE events processing, which Chapter 11 explores in more detail.

In order to demonstrate these objects and events, I have created a new add-in. I have named the add-in MaintainBuildRules. I built this add-in using the Add-in Wizard, but I will not bore you by documenting that process again. Once the wizard created the base code for the add-in, I made numerous modifications and additions to the Connect class. Listing 9-6 shows the code for the Connect class after the modifications. The new code is shown in bold.

Listing 9-6. Enhanced Connect Class

```
Imports Microsoft.Office.Core
imports Extensibility
imports System.Runtime.InteropServices
Imports EnvDTE
Imports System.IO
Imports System
```

```vbnet
#Region " Read me for Add-in installation and setup information. "
' When run, the Add-in wizard prepared the registry for the Add-in.
' At a later time, if the Add-in becomes unavailable for
' reasons such as:
'    1) You moved this project to a computer other than
'       the one it was
'       originally created on.
'    2) You chose 'Yes' when presented with a message asking
'       if you wish
'       to remove the Add-in.
'    3) Registry corruption.
'       you will need to re-register the Add-in by building the
'       MaintainBuildRulesSetup project
'       by right-clicking the project in the Solution Explorer,
'       then choosing install.
#End Region

<GuidAttribute("19125D5B-4728-42B6-8206-7B69784E9217"), _
ProgIdAttribute("MaintainBuildRules.Connect")> _
Public Class Connect

    Implements Extensibility.IDTExtensibility2
    Implements IDTCommandTarget
    Dim CommandObj As Command
    Dim WithEvents bldevents As BuildEvents
    Dim form1 As MaintainBuildRules
    Dim rules As String()
    Dim oVB As EnvDTE.DTE
    Dim addInInstance As EnvDTE.AddIn

    Public Sub OnBeginShutdown(ByRef custom As System.Array) _
        Implements Extensibility.IDTExtensibility2.OnBeginShutdown
    End Sub

    Public Sub OnAddInsUpdate(ByRef custom As System.Array) _
        Implements Extensibility.IDTExtensibility2.OnAddInsUpdate
    End Sub

    Public Sub OnStartupComplete(ByRef custom As System.Array) _
        Implements Extensibility.IDTExtensibility2.OnStartupComplete
    End Sub
```

```vbnet
Public Sub OnDisconnection(ByVal RemoveMode As _
    Extensibility.ext_DisconnectMode, _
    ByRef custom As System.Array) _
    Implements Extensibility.IDTExtensibility2.OnDisconnection
    If Not CommandObj Is Nothing Then
        oVB.CommandBars.Item("Tools").Controls.↵
            Item(CommandObj.Name).Delete()
        CommandObj.Delete()
    End If
    bldevents = Nothing
End Sub


Public Sub OnConnection(ByVal application As Object, _
    ByVal connectMode As Extensibility.ext_ConnectMode, _
    ByVal addInInst As Object, _
    ByRef custom As System.Array) _
    Implements Extensibility.IDTExtensibility2.OnConnection

    oVB = CType(application, EnvDTE.DTE)
    addInInstance = CType(addInInst, EnvDTE.AddIn)
    Dim objAddIn As AddIn = CType(addInInst, AddIn)

    Try
        CommandObj = oVB.Commands.AddNamedCommand(objAddIn, _
            "MaintainBuildRules", "MaintainBuildRules", _
            "Executes the command for MaintainBuildRules", _
            True, 59, Nothing, 1 + 2)
        CommandObj.AddControl(oVB.CommandBars.Item("Tools"))
        bldevents = CType(oVB.Events.BuildEvents, ↵
            EnvDTE.BuildEvents)
    Catch e As System.Exception
    End Try
End Sub


Public Sub Exec(ByVal cmdName As String, _
    ByVal executeOption As vsCommandExecOption, _
    ByRef varIn As Object, _
    ByRef varOut As Object, _
    ByRef handled As Boolean) _
    Implements IDTCommandTarget.Exec
    handled = False
    If (executeOption = ↵
        vsCommandExecOption↵
```

```
            .vsCommandExecOptionDoDefault) Then
        If cmdName = ⏎
            "MaintainBuildRules.Connect⏎
            .MaintainBuildRules" Then
            form1 = New MaintainBuildRules(oVB)
            form1.ShowDialog()
            handled = True
            Exit Sub
        End If
    End If
End Sub


Public Sub QueryStatus(ByVal cmdName As String, _
    ByVal neededText As vsCommandStatusTextWanted, _
    ByRef statusOption As vsCommandStatus, _
    ByRef commandText As Object) _
    Implements IDTCommandTarget.QueryStatus
    If neededText = ⏎
        EnvDTE.vsCommandStatusTextWanted.⏎
        vsCommandStatusTextWantedNone _
        Then
        If cmdName = ⏎
            "MaintainBuildRules.Connect.⏎
            MaintainBuildRules" Then
            statusOption = ⏎
                CType(vsCommandStatus.⏎
                vsCommandStatusEnabled + _
                vsCommandStatus.⏎
                vsCommandStatusSupported, vsCommandStatus)
        Else
            statusOption = ⏎
                vsCommandStatus.vsCommandStatusUnsupported
        End If
    End If
End Sub


Private Sub bldevents_OnBuildDone(ByVal Scope As⏎
    EnvDTE.vsBuildScope, ⏎
    ByVal Action As EnvDTE.vsBuildAction) ⏎
    Handles bldevents.OnBuildDone
    'apply postbuild rules when the build event is done
    Dim i As Integer = 0
    Dim tmps As String
```

```vb
        Dim glosb As Globals
        glosb = oVB.Solution.Globals

        'go through rules saved in solution.globals,
        ' parse them and then execute
        While glosb.VariableExists("SolutionPostBuildRule" & _
            i.ToString()) = True
            If glosb.VariableValue("SolutionPostBuildRule" & _
                i.ToString()) <> "" Then
                tmps = glosb.VariableValue("SolutionPostBuildRule" & _
                    i.ToString())
                bldRules = Split(tmps, " ", 2)
                bldRules(0).Replace("\", "\\")
                If bldRules.Length = 2 Then
                    System.Diagnostics.Process. ↩
                        Start(bldRules(0), bldRules(1))
                Else
                    System.Diagnostics.Process.Start(bldRules(0))
                End If
            End If
            i = i + 1
        End While
End Sub

Private Sub bldevents_OnBuildBegin(ByVal Scope As ↩
        EnvDTE.vsBuildScope, ↩
        ByVal Action As ↩
        EnvDTE.vsBuildAction) ↩
        Handles bldevents.OnBuildBegin
    ' apply prebuild rules when solution starts to build
    Dim i As Integer = 0
    Dim tmps As String
    Dim glosb As Globals
    glosb = oVB.Solution.Globals

    'go through rules saved in solution.globals,
    ' parse them and then execute
    While glosb.VariableExists("SolutionPreBuildRule" & ↩
        i.ToString()) = True
        If glosb.VariableValue("SolutionPreBuildRule" & ↩
            i.ToString()) <> "" Then
            tmps = glosb.VariableValue("SolutionPreBuildRule" & ↩
                i.ToString())
```

```
                bldRules = Split(tmps, " ", 2)
                bldRules(0).Replace("\", "\\")
                If bldRules.Length = 2 Then
                    System.Diagnostics.Process.Start(bldRules(0), ↵
                        bldRules(1))
                Else
                    System.Diagnostics.Process.Start(bldRules(0))
                End If
            End If
            i = i + 1
        End While
    End Sub
End Class
```

I have made the usual changes to the Connect class, such as changing the name of the applicationObject, changing the scope of the command object, and so forth. In addition to these changes and additions to the methods created by the Add-in Wizard, you will notice that there are two new event handlers. They are named bldevents_OnBuildBegin and bldevents_OnBuildDone, and you can see them at the end of the class. These two methods handle the OnBuildBegin and OnBuildDone events. These methods will fire when the solution build begins and finishes. They check to see if there are any pre- and postbuild rules, respectively. If any rules are found in the Globals object, in either of the events, the rules (processes) are executed using the Start method of the System.Diagnostics.Process object. This method simply launches the specified process (file, executable, and so forth). The method accepts either one or two parameters. The first is the name of the process and the second is an optional command line parameter to be placed on the command line call to the process. Starting a process by specifying its file name and arguments is analogous to typing the file name and command line arguments in the Run dialog box of the Windows Start menu. For this reason, the file name does not need to represent an executable file. It can use any file whose extension has become associated with an application installed on the system.

In addition to the Connect class, the add-in has a form that is used to load and maintain the build rules. I display this form later in the chapter when I show the execution of the add-in. For now, Listing 9-10 shows the code for the form.

Listing 9-10. Maintain Build Rules Form

```
Option Strict Off
Imports System.IO
Imports System.Diagnostics
Imports System.Runtime.InteropServices
Imports process = System.Diagnostics.Process
```

```vb
<ComVisible(False)> Public Class MaintainBuildRules

    Inherits System.Windows.Forms.Form
    Dim appObject As EnvDTE.DTE
    Dim mbDirty As Boolean
    Const PreBuild = "SolutionPreBuildRule"
    Const PostBuild = "SolutionPostBuildRule"

#Region " Windows Form Designer generated code "

    Public Sub New()
        MyBase.New()

        'This call is required by the Windows Form Designer.
        InitializeComponent()

        'Add any initialization after the InitializeComponent() call

    End Sub

    Public Sub New(ByVal applicationObject As EnvDTE.DTE)
        MyBase.New()
        appObject = applicationObject
        'This call is required by the Windows Form Designer.
        InitializeComponent()

        'Add any initialization after the InitializeComponent() call
    End Sub

    'Form overrides dispose to clean up the component list.
    Protected Overloads Overrides Sub Dispose(ByVal disposing As↵
            Boolean)
        If disposing Then
            If Not (components Is Nothing) Then
                components.Dispose()
            End If
        End If
        MyBase.Dispose(disposing)
    End Sub
    Friend WithEvents Addnewruletextbox As System.Windows.Forms.TextBox
    Friend WithEvents MoveDown As System.Windows.Forms.Button
    Friend WithEvents MoveUp As System.Windows.Forms.Button
    Friend WithEvents OK As System.Windows.Forms.Button
```

```
Friend WithEvents RemoveButton As System.Windows.Forms.Button
Friend WithEvents AddButton As System.Windows.Forms.Button
Friend WithEvents Addanewrule As System.Windows.Forms.Label
Friend WithEvents MyPostBuildRule As System.Windows.Forms.Label
Friend WithEvents MaintainBuildRuleListBox As System.Windows.Forms.ListBox


Friend WithEvents btnSaveRules As System.Windows.Forms.Button
'Required by the Windows Form Designer
Private components As System.ComponentModel.Container


'NOTE: The following procedure is required by the
'Windows Form Designer
'It can be modified using the Windows Form Designer.
'Do not modify it using the code editor.
Friend WithEvents GroupBox1 As System.Windows.Forms.GroupBox
Friend WithEvents RadioButton1 As System.Windows.Forms.RadioButton
Friend WithEvents rbPreBuild As System.Windows.Forms.RadioButton
<System.Diagnostics.DebuggerStepThrough()> _
Private Sub InitializeComponent()
    Me.OK = New System.Windows.Forms.Button()
    Me.Addanewrule = New System.Windows.Forms.Label()
    Me.Addnewruletextbox = New System.Windows.Forms.TextBox()
    Me.MaintainBuildRuleListBox = New ⏎
        System.Windows.Forms.ListBox()
    Me.MoveUp = New System.Windows.Forms.Button()
    Me.AddButton = New System.Windows.Forms.Button()
    Me.MoveDown = New System.Windows.Forms.Button()
    Me.MyPostBuildRule = New System.Windows.Forms.Label()
    Me.RemoveButton = New System.Windows.Forms.Button()
    Me.GroupBox1 = New System.Windows.Forms.GroupBox()
    Me.btnSaveRules = New System.Windows.Forms.Button()
    Me.btnLoadRules = New System.Windows.Forms.Button()
    Me.RadioButton1 = New System.Windows.Forms.RadioButton()
    Me.rbPreBuild = New System.Windows.Forms.RadioButton()
    Me.GroupBox1.SuspendLayout()
    Me.SuspendLayout()
    '
    'OK
    '
    Me.OK.Location = New System.Drawing.Point(291, 267)
    Me.OK.Name = "OK"
    Me.OK.Size = New System.Drawing.Size(80, 24)
    Me.OK.TabIndex = 2
```

```vb
Me.OK.Text = "&OK"
'
'Addanewrule
'
Me.Addanewrule.Font = _
   New System.Drawing.Font("Microsoft Sans Serif", 8.25!, _
   System.Drawing.FontStyle.Regular, _
   System.Drawing.GraphicsUnit.Point, CType(0, Byte))
Me.Addanewrule.Location = New System.Drawing.Point(10, 215)
Me.Addanewrule.Name = "Addanewrule"
Me.Addanewrule.Size = New System.Drawing.Size(100, 16)
Me.Addanewrule.TabIndex = 4
Me.Addanewrule.Text = "Add a new rule"
'
'Addnewruletextbox
'
Me.Addnewruletextbox.Location = ↵
   New System.Drawing.Point(10, 231)
Me.Addnewruletextbox.Name = "Addnewruletextbox"
Me.Addnewruletextbox.Size = New System.Drawing.Size(256, 20)
Me.Addnewruletextbox.TabIndex = 3
Me.Addnewruletextbox.Text = ""
'
'MaintainBuildRuleListBox
'
Me.MaintainBuildRuleListBox.Location = ↵
   New System.Drawing.Point(10, 32)
Me.MaintainBuildRuleListBox.Name = "MaintainBuildRuleListBox"
Me.MaintainBuildRuleListBox.Size = ↵
   New System.Drawing.Size(256, 134)
Me.MaintainBuildRuleListBox.TabIndex = 0
'
'MoveUp
'
Me.MoveUp.Location = New System.Drawing.Point(17, 176)
Me.MoveUp.Name = "MoveUp"
Me.MoveUp.Size = New System.Drawing.Size(80, 24)
Me.MoveUp.TabIndex = 2
Me.MoveUp.Text = "Move &Up"
'
'AddButton
'
Me.AddButton.Location = New System.Drawing.Point(290, 231)
```

```
Me.AddButton.Name = "AddButton"
Me.AddButton.Size = New System.Drawing.Size(80, 24)
Me.AddButton.TabIndex = 2
Me.AddButton.Text = "&Add Rule"
'
'MoveDown
'
Me.MoveDown.Location = New System.Drawing.Point(102, 176)
Me.MoveDown.Name = "MoveDown"
Me.MoveDown.Size = New System.Drawing.Size(80, 24)
Me.MoveDown.TabIndex = 2
Me.MoveDown.Text = "Move &Down"
'
'MyPostBuildRule
'
Me.MyPostBuildRule.Font = New _
    System.Drawing.Font("Microsoft Sans Serif", 8.25!, _
    System.Drawing.FontStyle.Regular, _
     System.Drawing.GraphicsUnit.Point, CType(0, Byte))
Me.MyPostBuildRule.Location = New System.Drawing.Point(10, 8)
Me.MyPostBuildRule.Name = "MyPostBuildRule"
Me.MyPostBuildRule.Size = New System.Drawing.Size(112, 16)
Me.MyPostBuildRule.TabIndex = 1
Me.MyPostBuildRule.Text = "Build Rules"
'
'RemoveButton
'
Me.RemoveButton.Location = New System.Drawing.Point(186, 176)
Me.RemoveButton.Name = "RemoveButton"
Me.RemoveButton.Size = New System.Drawing.Size(80, 24)
Me.RemoveButton.TabIndex = 2
Me.RemoveButton.Text = "&Remove"
'
'GroupBox1
'
Me.GroupBox1.Controls.AddRange↵
  (New System.Windows.Forms.Control()↵
  {Me.btnSaveRules, Me.btnLoadRules, ↵
  Me.RadioButton1, Me.rbPreBuild})
Me.GroupBox1.Location = New System.Drawing.Point(274, 9)
Me.GroupBox1.Name = "GroupBox1"
Me.GroupBox1.Size = New System.Drawing.Size(124, 152)
Me.GroupBox1.TabIndex = 7
```

```
Me.GroupBox1.TabStop = False
Me.GroupBox1.Text = "Load  &&  Save"
'
'btnSaveRules
'
Me.btnSaveRules.Location = New System.Drawing.Point(18, 107)
Me.btnSaveRules.Name = "btnSaveRules"
Me.btnSaveRules.Size = New System.Drawing.Size(80, 24)
Me.btnSaveRules.TabIndex = 10
Me.btnSaveRules.Text = "&Save Rules"
'
'btnLoadRules
'
Me.btnLoadRules.Location = New System.Drawing.Point(19, 75)
Me.btnLoadRules.Name = "btnLoadRules"
Me.btnLoadRules.Size = New System.Drawing.Size(80, 24)
Me.btnLoadRules.TabIndex = 9
Me.btnLoadRules.Text = "&Load Rules"
'
'RadioButton1
'
Me.RadioButton1.Location = New System.Drawing.Point(9, 47)
Me.RadioButton1.Name = "RadioButton1"
Me.RadioButton1.Size = New System.Drawing.Size(102, 16)
Me.RadioButton1.TabIndex = 8
Me.RadioButton1.Text = "PostBuild Rules"
'
'rbPreBuild
'
Me.rbPreBuild.Checked = True
Me.rbPreBuild.Location = New System.Drawing.Point(8, 21)
Me.rbPreBuild.Name = "rbPreBuild"
Me.rbPreBuild.Size = New System.Drawing.Size(99, 16)
Me.rbPreBuild.TabIndex = 7
Me.rbPreBuild.TabStop = True
Me.rbPreBuild.Text = "PreBuild Rules"
'
'MaintainBuildRules
'
Me.AutoScaleBaseSize = New System.Drawing.Size(5, 13)
Me.ClientSize = New System.Drawing.Size(410, 301)
Me.Controls.AddRange(New System.Windows.Forms.Control() ⏎
    {Me.GroupBox1, ⏎
```

```vbnet
                Me.MyPostBuildRule, Me.Addanewrule, Me.AddButton, ⏎
                Me.RemoveButton, Me.OK,
                Me.MoveDown, Me.MoveUp, Me.MaintainBuildRuleListBox, _
                Me.Addnewruletextbox})
            Me.FormBorderStyle = ⏎
                System.Windows.Forms.FormBorderStyle.FixedSingle
            Me.Name = "MaintainBuildRules"
            Me.Text = "Build Rules Maintenance"
            Me.GroupBox1.ResumeLayout(False)
            Me.ResumeLayout(False)

    End Sub


#End Region

    Private Sub MaintainBuildRules_Load(ByVal sender As⏎
        System.Object, ⏎
        ByVal e As System.EventArgs) Handles MyBase.Load
        mbDirty = False
    End Sub
    Private Sub GetSelectedBuildRules()
        Dim i As Integer = 0
        Dim globs As EnvDTE.Globals
        Dim s As String
        If Me.rbPreBuild.Checked Then
            s = PreBuild
        Else
            s = PostBuild
        End If
        globs = appObject.Solution.Globals
        MaintainBuildRuleListBox.Items.Clear()

        'load postbuild rules save in solution.globals to the form
        While (globs.VariableExists(s & i.ToString()) = True)
            If globs.VariableValue(s & i.ToString()) <> "" Then
                MaintainBuildRuleListBox.⏎
                Items.Add(globs.VariableValue(s & ⏎
                    i.ToString()))
                MaintainBuildRuleListBox.SetSelected(i, True)
            End If
            i = i + 1
        End While
    End Sub
```

```
'move the selected item in the rule list down
Private Sub MoveDown_Click(ByVal sender As System.Object, _
    ByVal e As System.EventArgs) _
    Handles MoveDown.Click
    Dim temp As Object
    Dim index As Integer
    mbDirty = True

    If ((MaintainBuildRuleListBox.SelectedIndex = _
        (MaintainBuildRuleListBox.Items.Count - 1)) Or _
        (MaintainBuildRuleListBox.SelectedItem = Nothing)) _
        Then
        Exit Sub
    End If
    index = MaintainBuildRuleListBox.SelectedIndex + 1
    temp = MaintainBuildRuleListBox.SelectedItem

    MaintainBuildRuleListBox.Items.↵
        RemoveAt(MaintainBuildRuleListBox.↵
        SelectedIndex)
    MaintainBuildRuleListBox.Items.Insert(index, temp)
    MaintainBuildRuleListBox.SetSelected(index, True)

End Sub

'remove the selected item from the rule list
Private Sub RemoveButton_Click(ByVal sender As System.Object, _
    ByVal e As System.EventArgs) Handles RemoveButton.Click
    Dim sindex As Integer
    mbDirty = True
    If (MaintainBuildRuleListBox.Items.Count = 0) Then
        Exit Sub
    Else
        sindex = MaintainBuildRuleListBox.SelectedIndex
        MaintainBuildRuleListBox.Items.↵
            RemoveAt(MaintainBuildRuleListBox.↵
            SelectedIndex)
        If (sindex <> 0) Then
            MaintainBuildRuleListBox.SetSelected(sindex - 1, True)
        End If
    End If

End Sub
```

```
'add a rule to the rule list
Private Sub AddButton_Click(ByVal sender As System.Object, _
   ByVal e As System.EventArgs) Handles AddButton.Click
   If ((Addnewruletextbox.Text = "") Or _
      (Addnewruletextbox.Text.IndexOf(" ") = 0)) _
      Then
      Addnewruletextbox.Clear()
      Exit Sub
   End If
   mbDirty = True
   MaintainBuildRuleListBox.Items.Add(Addnewruletextbox.Text)
   MaintainBuildRuleListBox.SetSelected↵
      (MaintainBuildRuleListBox.↵
      Items.Count - 1, True)
   Addnewruletextbox.Clear()
End Sub


'move the selected item in the rule list up
Private Sub MoveUp_Click(ByVal sender As System.Object, _
   ByVal e As System.EventArgs) _
   Handles MoveUp.Click
   Dim temp As Object
   Dim index As Integer
   If ((MaintainBuildRuleListBox.SelectedIndex = 0) Or _
      (MaintainBuildRuleListBox.SelectedItem = Nothing)) Then
      Exit Sub
   End If
   mbDirty = True
   If ((MaintainBuildRuleListBox.SelectedIndex - 1) < 0) Then
      index = 0
   Else
      index = MaintainBuildRuleListBox.SelectedIndex - 1
   End If
   temp = MaintainBuildRuleListBox.SelectedItem

   MaintainBuildRuleListBox.Items.RemoveAt↵
      (MaintainBuildRuleListBox.SelectedIndex)
   MaintainBuildRuleListBox.Items.Insert(index, temp)
   MaintainBuildRuleListBox.SetSelected(index, True)

End Sub
```

```vb
'click OK button on the form
Private Sub OK_Click(ByVal sender As System.Object, _
    ByVal e As System.EventArgs) Handles OK.Click
    If mbDirty Then
        If MsgBox("Rules have been changed, " & _
            "do you want to close without saving?", _
            MsgBoxStyle.YesNo, _
            "Confirm Closing") = _
            MsgBoxResult.Yes Then
            Exit Sub
        End If
    End If
    Close()
End Sub

Private Sub SaveRules()
    Dim i As Integer = 0
    Dim globs As EnvDTE.Globals
    Dim s As String

    If Me.rbPreBuild.Checked Then
        s = PreBuild
    Else
        s = PostBuild
    End If

    globs = appObject.Solution.Globals

    'clean up the solution.globals variables
    While (globs.VariableExists(s & i.ToString()) = True)
        globs.VariableValue(s & i.ToString()) = ""
        globs.VariablePersists(s & i.ToString()) = False
        i = i + 1
    End While

    'write the rules from the form to solution.globals variables
    For i = 0 To MaintainBuildRuleListBox.Items.Count - 1
        globs.VariableValue(s & i.ToString()) = _
            MaintainBuildRuleListBox.Items.Item(i)
        globs.VariablePersists(s & i.ToString()) = True
    Next
```

```
        ' show no save pending
        mbDirty = False
    End Sub


    Private Sub btnLoadRules_Click(ByVal sender As System.Object, _
        ByVal e As System.EventArgs) Handles btnLoadRules.Click
        GetSelectedBuildRules()
    End Sub
    Friend WithEvents btnLoadRules As System.Windows.Forms.Button

    Private Sub btnSaveRules_Click(ByVal sender As System.Object, _
        ByVal e As System.EventArgs) Handles btnSaveRules.Click
        SaveRules()
    End Sub
End Class
```

The form whose code is shown in Listing 9-10 is a fairly simple maintenance form. It allows you to add pre- and postbuild rules and save them in the DTE.Globals object. It also has buttons for removing and reordering the rules. Option buttons determine which rules, prebuild or postbuild, are to be loaded into the list box and saved from the List Box.

The form is loaded from the Connect class when the user clicks the add-in's menu option. The application object (oVB) is passed to the form via the overload Sub New. This allows the form to have a pointer to the IDE's DTE object so that it can reference the DTE.Globals object.

Now, I load a Windows application project into the IDE. I also connect the MaintainBuildRules add-in. Next, I click the add-in's menu item, which will cause the MaintainBuildRules form to be loaded as shown in Figure 9-8.

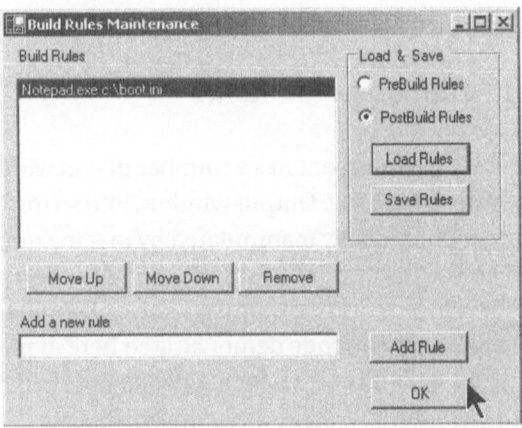

Figure 9-8. Adding a postbuild rule

You can see in Figure 9-8 that I have entered a postbuild rule. This is a simple load of Notepad.exe, passing it a command line parameter specifying the file to be loaded. I have also entered a prebuild rule that simply loads Notepad.exe without passing it a file to load. After closing the form, I start a build of the solution by selecting Build ➢ Build Solution. Immediately, Notepad will be loaded before the build does anything. Because loading Notepad will not stop the build process, the build will be done and a second instance of Notepad will be loaded when the build process completes. In Figure 9-9, you can see that I have positioned the last instance of Notepad over the first. This depicts the order in which the two instances of Notepad were loaded. This is the way that I scheduled their loading by setting them up as pre- and postbuild processes.

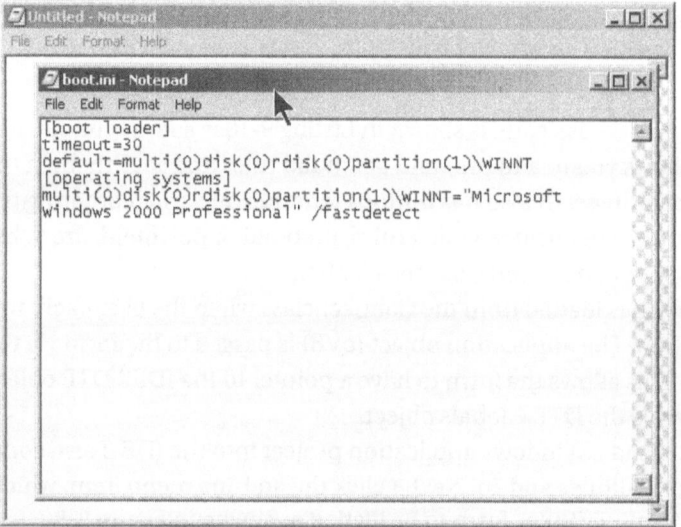

Figure 9-9. Notepad loaded as pre- and postbuild processes

Manipulating IDE Tool Windows

The Visual Studio .NET environment has a number of tool windows, such as the Task List, Toolbox, Clipboard Ring, Output window, and so forth. Most of these windows can be programmatically manipulated by macro commands and add-ins. In this section I discuss some of the objects that allow you to control the operation of these windows. I also demonstrate the use of the objects by macro commands. Remember that any code demonstrated here in macros can be converted to run in an add-in by simply changing the keyword DTE to the name of the application object in the add-in.

The TaskList Object

The Task List in Visual Studio .NET is an automated to-do list. Among other things, Visual Studio automatically places an item in the Task List for every line of code that will not compile. The user can add, delete, and check off the Task List items manually. Additionally, add-ins and macros can also manipulate the Task List programmatically using the TaskList object. The TaskList object represents the items in the Task List window in the IDE.

The code in Listing 9-11 adds two items to the Task List and then deletes one of them.

Listing 9-11. TaskListManipulation

```
01  Sub TaskListManipulation()
02      Dim win As Window = DTE.Windows.Item(Constants.vsWindowKindTaskList)
03      Dim tskList As TaskList = win.Object
04      Dim tlItem As TaskItem
05
06      ' Add a couple of tasks to the Task List.
07      tlItem = tskList.TaskItems.Add(" ", " ", _
08          "Test task 1. Delete this by right-
09          clicking and select Delete.",
10          vsTaskPriority.vsTaskPriorityHigh,
11          vsTaskIcon.vsTaskIconUser, True, , 10, , )
12      tlItem = tskList.TaskItems.Add(" ", " ",
13          "Test task 2. Delete this by right
14          clicking and select Delete.", _
15          vsTaskPriority.vsTaskPriorityLow, _
16          vsTaskIcon.vsTaskIconComment, , 20, , )
17
18      ' List the total number of task list items after adding
19      ' the new task items.
20      MsgBox("Task Item 1 description: " & _
21          tskList.TaskItems.Item(2).Description)
22      MsgBox("Total number of task items: " &
23          tskList.TaskItems.Count)
24
25          ' Remove the second task item. The items list
26          'in reverse numeric order.
27      MsgBox("Deleting the second task item")
28      tskList.TaskItems.Item(1).Delete()
29      MsgBox("Total number of task items: " &
30          tskList.TaskItems.Count)
31  End Sub
```

In lines 02 and 03, the macro command gets an object representing the Task List window. In lines 07 and 12, it uses the TaskItems.Add method to add the two text items to the Task List. Line 20 displays the description of the specified TaskList item. Line 22 simply enumerates the number of TaskItems in the TaskList object. Line 28 deletes the first TaskList item, and line 29 displays the count after the item is deleted.

In order to see items added programmatically, you must set the Task List Show Task options to Show All. You can do this by right-clicking the caption bar of the Task List and selecting Show Tasks ➤ All.

Figure 9-10 shows the Task List after the macro command has been run.

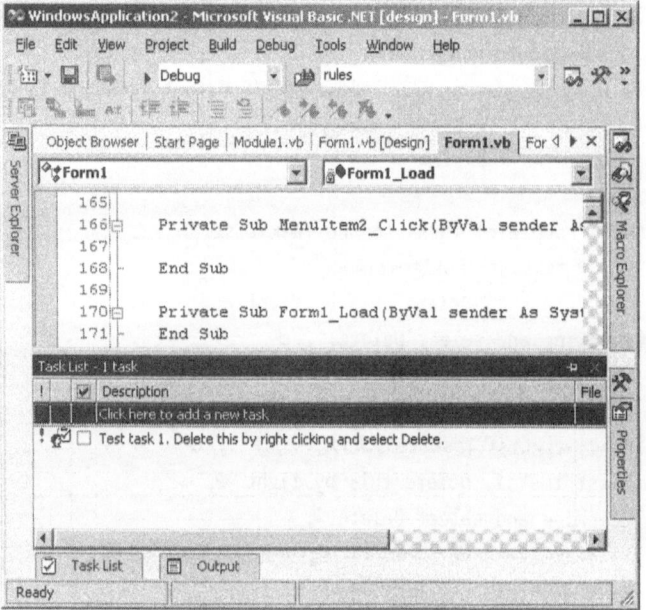

Figure 9-10. Adding items to the Task List programatically

The ToolBox Object

The ToolBox object represents the Toolbox in the Visual Studio .NET environment. The Toolbox is a container for WinForms components when a Forms Designer is the active window. It is also the container for the Clipboard Ring when a code editor is the active window.

A Window object represents the Toolbox's window. The ToolBox contains a collection of ToolBoxTab objects. The tab object is list of Components when the Forms Designer is the active window. The tab object may be the Clipboard Ring when a code editor is the active window. ToolBoxItem objects represent individual items in the ToolBoxTabs collection.

You can programmatically add your own tabs to the Toolbox. For an example of this, you'll create a new tab named "My Code Snippets." You probably have a few sets of code, each of which consists of one to five lines that you use over and over. A simple example of this is code to fill a DataTable from a database. Obviously, you could use the Clipboard Ring for storing these snippets, but because the Clipboard Ring always maintains the last 15 text items cut or copied, your code snippets would soon be pushed off the Ring. Creating your own ToolBox tab for storing your code snippets alleviates the problem of losing them during the session of the IDE.

If you run the code shown in Listing 9-12 in an add-in rather than in a macro command, you could automatically load your snippets each time a new session of the IDE is started. Obviously, if you had a number of code snippets, you would probably read them from a text file and load them into the newly created ToolBox tab.

Listing 9-12. CreateMyCodeSnippets Macro

```
Sub CreateMyCodeSnippets()
    Dim objToolbox As ToolBox
    Dim colTbxTabs As ToolBoxTabs
    Dim objTab As ToolBoxTab
    Dim colTbxItems As ToolBoxItems
    Dim objTbxItem As ToolBoxItem
    Const CS1 = "Dim dbCMD as New OledbCommand" & vbCrLf & _
            "Dim dt As New DataTable" & vbCrLf & _
            "Dim da as New OleDBDataAdapter" & vbCrLf & _
            "dbCmd.CommandText = Sql" & vbCrLf & _
            "dbCmd.Connection = CurrentConnection" & vbCrLf & _
            "da = New OleDBDataAdapter(dbCMD)" & vbCrLf & _
            "da.Fill(dt)" & vbCrLf
    Const CS2 = "' This code does nothing but demo " & ↵
        vbCrLf & _
                "Dim s As String = " & Chr(34) & "ABC" & ↵
        Chr(34) & vbCrLf & _
                "Dim i As Integer = 1" & vbCrLf & _
                "s = s & i.ToString()" & vbCrLf


    ' Create an object reference to the IDE's ToolBox object.
    objToolbox = ↵
        DTE.Windows.Item(Constants.↵
        vsWindowKindToolbox).Object
    colTbxTabs = objToolbox.ToolBoxTabs
```

```
' Add a new tab to the ToolBox.
objTab = colTbxTabs.Add("My Code Snippets")
colTbxTabs = objToolbox.ToolBoxTabs

' Use the ToolBoxItems collection to access
' all the items under a
' ToolBoxTab.
colTbxItems = objTab.ToolBoxItems

' Add a couple new ToolboxItem objects to the
' new tab we added above.
objTbxItem = objTab.ToolBoxItems.Add("Fill Datatable", CS1)
objTbxItem = objTab.ToolBoxItems.Add("Code Item2 ", CS2)
objTbxItem = objTab.ToolBoxItems.Add("Code Item3", _
    "Hello world Line2" & vbCrLf & "Hello world Line3" & _
        vbCrLf)
objTbxItem = objTab.ToolBoxItems.Add("Code Item4", _
        "Hello world Line4" & vbCrLf & "Hello world Line3" & _
        vbCrLf)

' List number of ToolBoxItems in a ToolBoxTab.
MsgBox("Number of items in ToolBox tab: " & _
    colTbxItems.Count)

' Select the fourth item in the ToolBoxItems
' collection and delete it.
' the tab is the first item in the collection
colTbxItems.Item(4).Select()
If (MsgBox("Delete second ToolBox item?", vbYesNo) = ↵
        vbYes) Then
        colTbxItems.SelectedItem.Delete()
End If
End Sub
```

The code for manipulating the ToolBox is much like the code for manipulating the TaskList object. There is one exception. The new tab itself, "My Code Snippets," is the first item in the collection. Therefore, the first code item (CS1) is actually item 2 in the ToolBox tab. Figure 9-11 shows the Toolbox after the macro has run and created the new code snippets tab. In the picture, I have just right-clicked the first code snippet and I will select the Copy menu option.

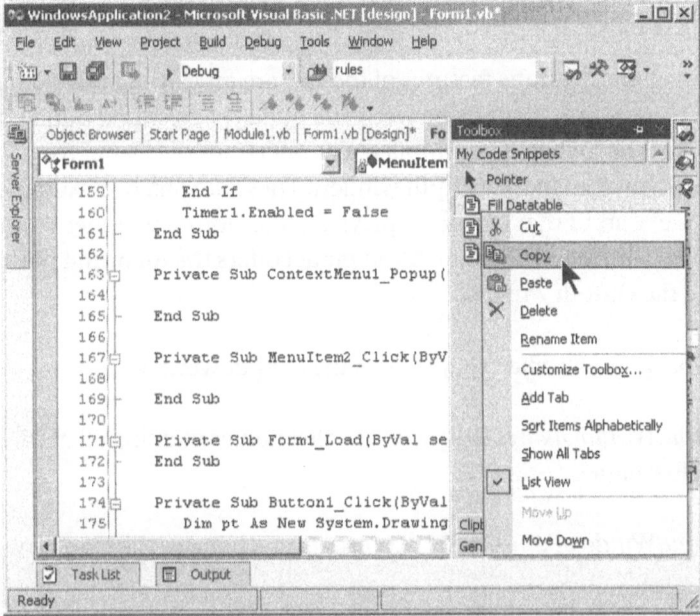

Figure 9-11. Copying a code snippet

In Figure 9-12, you will see that I have pasted the code from the My Code Snippets tab of the ToolBox to the code editor window. The code that you see in the window was copied from the code item labeled "Fill DataTable."

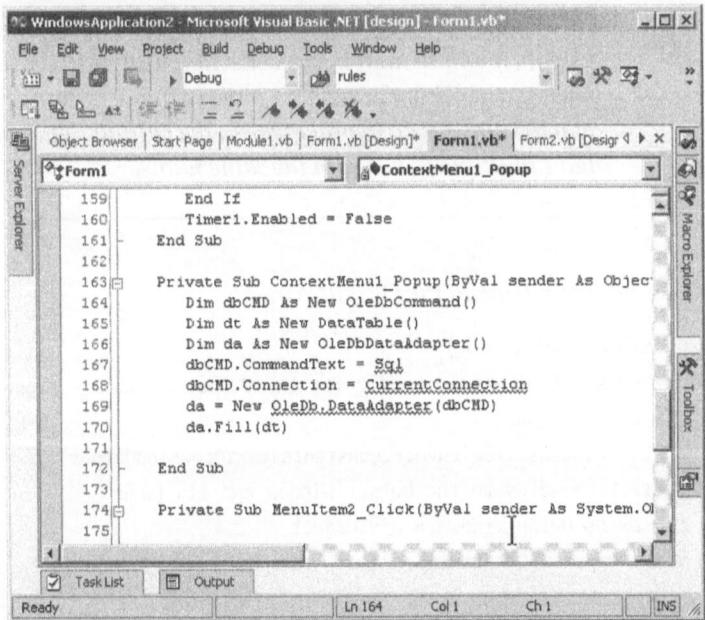

Figure 9-12. Pasting the code snippet

The Output Window

Status messages for various features of the IDE are displayed in the Output window. The most prominent of these would be build progress and build errors if a project has errors when it is compiled. Outputs from the Debug.WriteLine() method are displayed in the Output window. These are just two examples of the many types of output that can be displayed in the Output window.

The Visual Studio .NET automation model offers the following objects for controlling the Output window:

- *OutputWindow object:* Represents the Output window

- *OutputWindowPanes collection:* A collection containing all of the Output window panes

- *OutputWindowPane object:* Represents one pane in the Output window

The Output window displays text output from various IDE processes. It is possible that each process might use a different Output window pane. Panes are selected with a drop-down box at the top of the window. For example, build errors go to the Build Errors pane, and each external command tool potentially goes to its own distinct Output window pane.

The code in Listing 9-13 adds a new pane to the Output Window collection and then adds some text to the new pane.

NOTE *Once you add a pane to the OutputWindowPanes collection, it will remain in the collection until the IDE session is terminated. Also, if you add a pane with the same name, it will be duplicated. In other words, the Output window can have multiple panes with the same name.*

Listing 9-13. Adding a Pane to the Output Window

```
Sub OutputWindowPaneDemo()
    ' Create a tool window handle for the Output window.
    Dim win As Window = _
        DTE.Windows.Item(EnvDTE.Constants.vsWindowKindOutput)
    ' Create handles to the Output window and its panes.
    Dim ow As OutputWindow = win.Object
    Dim owPane As OutputWindowPane
```

```
    ' Add a new pane to the Output window
    Try
        owPane = ow.OutputWindowPanes.Add("My New Pane")
    Finally
    End Try

    ' Add a line of text to the new pane.
    ow.OutputWindowPanes.Item("My New Pane").Activate()
    owPane.OutputString("Some Text")
    If MsgBox("Clear the Output Window current pane?", _
        MsgBoxStyle.YesNo) = _
        MsgBoxResult.Yes Then
            owPane.Clear()
    End If
End Sub
```

After you run the macro in Listing 9-13, the Output window will appear as shown in Figure 9-13. If you answer Yes to the message box that prompts you as to whether the Output window is to be cleared, the currently active pane will be cleared.

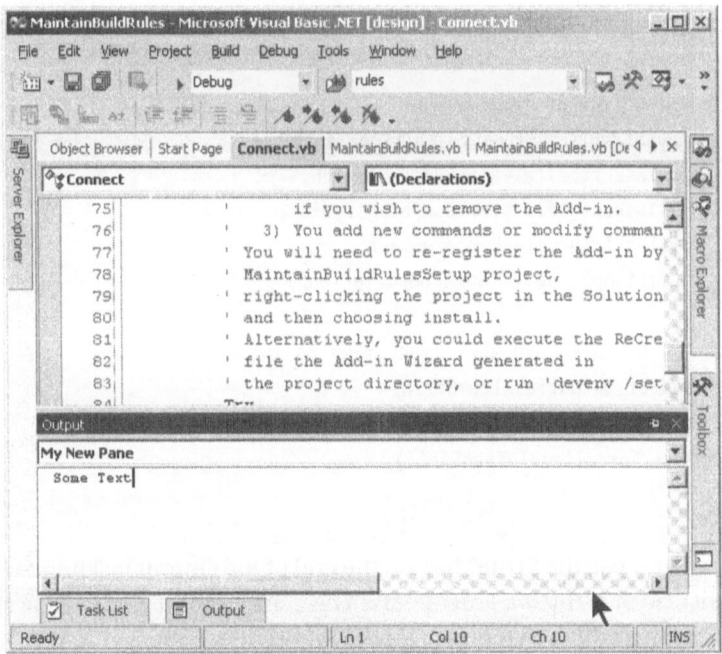

Figure 9-13. New pane in the Output window

It is possible to place text into a pane of the Output window and into the Task List at the same time using the OutputTaskItemString method. This method adds a corresponding item to the Task List. The code in Listing 9-14 demonstrates this functionality.

Listing 9-14. OutputTaskItemString Example

```
Sub OutputTaskItemStringDemo()
    ' Create a tool window handle for the Output window.
    Dim win As Window = _
        DTE.Windows.Item(EnvDTE.Constants.vsWindowKindOutput)
    ' Create handles to the Output window and its panes.
    Dim ow As OutputWindow = win.Object
    Dim owPane As OutputWindowPane

    ' Activate previously created pane
    Try
        owPane = ow.OutputWindowPanes.Item("My New Pane")
        owPane.Activate()
    Catch e As System.Exception
        MsgBox("You must run OutputWindowPaneDemo " & _
            "before running this command.")
        Exit Sub
    End Try

    ' Add a line of text to the new pane and to the Task List.
    owPane.OutputTaskItemString("Some task", _
        vsTaskPriority.vsTaskPriorityHigh, _
        vsTaskCategories.vsTaskCategoryMisc, _
        vsTaskIcon.vsTaskIconComment, _
        "C:\temp", 100, "Some description")

    ' You can also use the 'True' flag on the
    ' end of OutputTaskItemString
    ' rather than using the next line (ForceItemsToTaskList).
    owPane.ForceItemsToTaskList()
End Sub
```

You can also use the "True" flag on the end of the OutputTaskItemString method instead of using the ForceItemsToTaskList method. Figure 9-14 shows the item that was added to the Task List, in addition to placing it in the Output window. Notice the Priority and Icon options that were added to the Task List item by specifying these options on the OutputTaskItemString method.

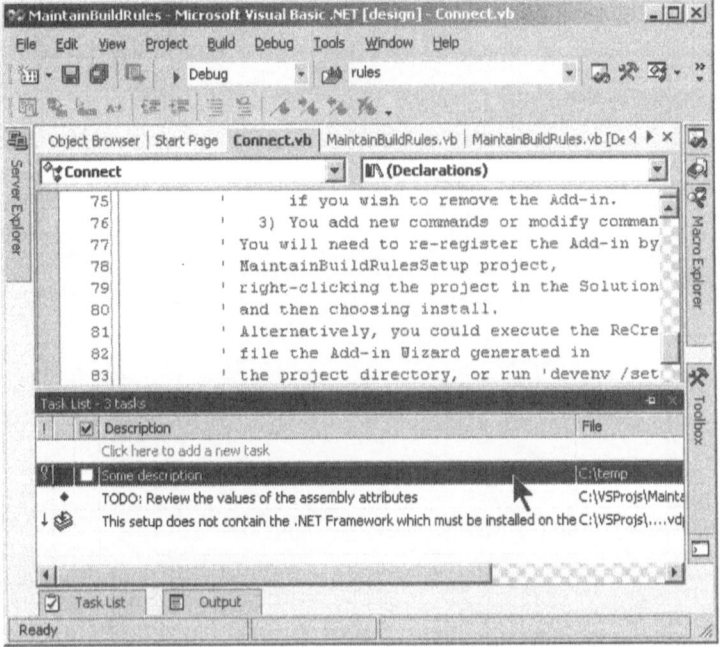

Figure 9-14. ForceItemsToTaskList example

Summary

In this chapter you saw how to manipulate the Solution and Project objects. You learned how to add a project to the solution. Additionally, you saw how to use the templates in Visual Studio .NET to add forms, classes, and modules to a project programmatically.

This chapter covered a number of different, and in some ways, unrelated topics. However, I wanted to show that even the tool windows that you might not think about controlling can be manipulated from a macro command or an add-in.

In the next chapter you'll learn how to enhance your add-ins to recognize that the user may be using a language other than Visual Basic and adjust the features accordingly. In other words, your add-ins will be able to handle code written in multiple languages.

Multiple Languages in Add-ins

"One of the worst traps a person can fall into is to become obsessed with his own exceptional moments of inspiration."
—Oswald Chambers

IN THIS CHAPTER I discuss several options that Microsoft has provided in Visual Studio .NET to allow you to expand on the languages that are initially provided with .NET. I also demonstrate how to write add-ins in other languages and how to mix languages in an add-in. Finally, I demonstrate how to alter the operation of an add-in based on the language being used in the IDE's Active Document window.

The .NET programming platform includes three languages at this time: Visual Basic .NET, Visual C#, and Visual C++. Microsoft has intimated that there will be other languages from Microsoft as well as other languages from various vendors that will use the .NET Framework. This is possible because of the set of unified classes provided by .NET Framework. Visual Studio .NET classes provide a consistent method of using the Framework's functionality, regardless of the base language that you choose. Once you learn to use the class library, you no longer need to learn different API calling sequences to write applications.

The programming language you choose depends on your experience and the needs of the application you are writing. In most situations, you can use any or all of the Microsoft programming languages. Each of the Visual Studio .NET programming languages has its strengths. It may well be a matter of preference that determines the language you choose.

In addition to the languages that Microsoft has already released with .NET and those it plans to release in the future, there are other avenues for introducing more languages and tools into .NET. Several of these avenues are discussed in the following sections.

NOTE *Microsoft has partnered with a number of companies to bring additional languages to the .NET platform. Some of the languages Microsoft documents in MSDN are COBOL, Pascal, Perl, Fortran, Smalltalk, and Eiffel, just to name a few. To find out more about these languages and others, you should contact the vendor for the specific language in which you are interested.*

Visual Studio Integrator Program

For most of us, the use of add-ins, macros, and wizards will provide the functionality to meet the majority of our programming needs in Visual Studio .NET. However, some users will want to go beyond the automation model provided by Visual Studio .NET. Some users may want to introduce a new programming language and associated compiler, or a new text editor.

Microsoft created the Visual Studio Integrator Program (VSIP) to allow advanced users to accomplish this. VSIP provides the tools and information needed to integrate a new product through a collection of System Development Kits (SDKs). If you are interested in exploring the possibilities, you can find out more about this functionality by going to the Microsoft Web site and looking up the VSIP program.

External Tools

Third-party tool developers have added numerous tools over the years to allow you to launch external tools or programs from the operating system and from programs that you use often. Visual Studio .NET provides this functionality through the External Tools dialog box, which you can access from the Tools menu. Using the External Tools dialog box, you can add programs or tools to the Tools menu.

You can add items to the Tools menu that allow you to launch external tools from within Visual Studio. Figure 10-1 shows the External Tools dialog box. The tools that are already available for launching are shown in the dialog box's list box.

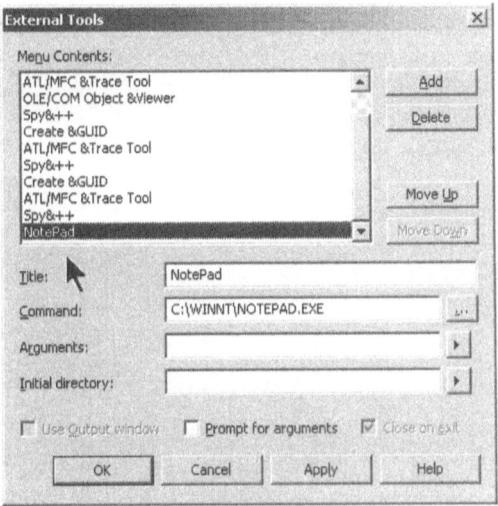

Figure 10-1. External Tools dialog box

To add an external tool to the Tools menu, follow these steps:

1. On the Tools menu, click the External Tools option.

2. In the External Tools dialog box, click the Add button and enter a name in the Title box. This name will be displayed on the Tools menu to access your new external tool.

3. In the Command box, enter the path to the file that you want to launch. You can also browse to locate the file or program (click the button with the ellipses to the right of the Command box to browse). You can launch such file types as .exe, .bat, .com, .cmd, and .pif.

4. Click OK to close the dialog box and add the new tool to the Tools menu.

NOTE *The Output window option is only available for use with .com and .bat file types.*

Once the new tool has been added to the Tools menu, you can launch it by clicking the Tools menu and then selecting the menu item for the new tool. Figure 10-2 shows the tool that I added (NotePad).

Figure 10-2. Launching an external tool

The menu items beginning with Create GUID and ending with NotePad are all external tools that can be launched by clicking the respective menu. They can all be edited or deleted from the External Tools dialog box.

In addition to the options that I described, you can also set up the following options for external tools:

- Pass variables to external tools upon launch.

- Add accelerator keys.

- Set up predefined arguments.

Selecting the Automation Methodology

Before I go into the use of multiple languages in add-ins, I want to look at the automation methods that I have discussed and provide you with a matrix for determining which methodology to use.

There are basically three methods for automating functionality in the IDE: macros, add-ins, and wizards. The method that you should consider using can be determined by the answers to one or more of the following questions:

- *Is the code for your use only, or do you want to distribute it to others?* If you need to distribute the code, you can use a macro without setup or registration by just exporting your macros. If you need to distribute a compiled application, you must use an add-in or a wizard. Add-ins and wizards protect your code, but you will need to have a deployment method.

- *What language do you want to use for automation development?* If you want to stick with Visual Basic, you can create macros, add-ins, or wizards. If you want to use other languages, you can create add-ins or wizards. Macros must be written in Visual Basic.

- *Do you need to prompt the user for input?* If no input is required, a macro or add-in can be used. If you need a small amount of input, a macro, add-in, or wizard will work. If a large or complex input is required, a wizard may be the best choice.

- *What is the level of complexity of the automation task?* If the task is simple, a macro is the easiest way to do it. If the automation task is complicated, an add-in or a wizard may be appropriate.

- *How do you want the user to start the automation process?* If you want to provide a menu or command bar user interface, you can use an add-in. A keyboard shortcut or the Macro Explorer can start a macro. If you are adding a new project or new item to a project, a wizard is probably the best way.

- *What is the lifetime of your application?* If you just want to use it today, use a macro if possible. For the long term, any of the three methods may be appropriate.

- *What functionality are you developing?* If you are automating a task in the IDE, then you can use macros, add-ins, or wizards. If you need to create a custom tool window, an add-in will support your development.

Using Multiple Languages in Add-ins

Thus far, you have only used Visual Basic in the code for your add-ins. Now, I am going to show you how to use another language provided by Visual Studio .NET. This language is C#, the latest addition to Visual Studio. In my years in Windows applications development, I have stuck primarily to Visual Basic. With the advent of .NET, I determined to not only take the paradigm switch to VB .NET, but also to learn the newest language, C#.

To those of you who have invested a lot of time in learning and using C++, C# offers a big advantage in that you do not have to discard what you have already learned in order to learn this new language. There are some new concepts and techniques, and a new class library to learn, but the syntax is similar to C++.

If you have majored in Visual Basic as I have, C# appears to have been built on the Visual Basic programming model, as you will see in the code comparison in the next section. In actuality, C# draws from the C family of languages and Visual Basic, and the result is a language that is somewhere in the middle of the two. The way I look at it is that C# looks like Visual Basic with the addition of semicolons and braces from C and C++.

Comparing Visual Basic to C#

To see how similar C# is to Visual Basic, you're going to develop a simple Windows application in both of the languages and compare the code. This example is somewhat of an oversimplification, and it certainly does not represent the overall C# language model, but it illustrates the point. The application that you'll develop is a digital clock application. You'll develop and run the application first in C# and then in Visual Basic.

C# Clock Application

You are familiar with the creation of projects by now, but I will step you through this one because you are using a C# project for the first time in this book.

NOTE   *If you are experienced with C# development, you can ignore this section of the chapter.*

There isn't a lot of difference between the clock application written in C# and the clock application written in Visual Basic. For this reason, I will lead you through the creation of the C# application and then you can simply follow the same steps for creating the Visual Basic application and make a few minor changes to the code.

1. To create a new project in C#, select New Project ➤ Visual C# Projects ➤ Windows Application. Name the project **Ch10ClockCS** and click OK to create the project. Your project will be created and Form1.cs will be added to your project.

2. In the Forms Designer, add two Label controls to the form. Also, double-click the Timer control in the Toolbox to place a timer on the form. Size the form and position and size the Label controls as shown in Figure 10-3.

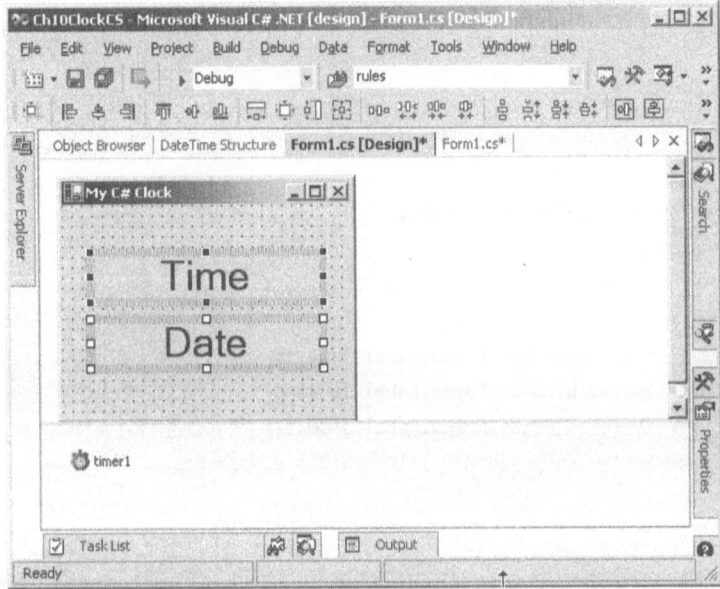

Figure 10-3. C# Form1

3. Select both Label controls on the form. In the Properties window, set the font size of the Label controls to 24.

4. Double-click the Timer control in the form designer to open the event handler for the timer. Place the call to the ResetClock function, as shown at the bottom of Listing 10-1.

5. Duplicate the code for the ResetClock function into the code for the form just after the code for the Timer1 tick event.

6. In the Form1 function, add the code to start the timer and reset the clock labels.

Listing 10-1. C# Code for Form1

```csharp
using System;
using System.Drawing;
using System.Collections;
using System.ComponentModel;
using System.Windows.Forms;
using System.Data;

namespace Ch10ClockCS
{
    /// <summary>
    /// Summary description for Form1.
    /// </summary>
    public class Form1 : System.Windows.Forms.Form
    {
        private System.Windows.Forms.Timer timer1;
        private System.Windows.Forms.Label lblTime;
        private System.Windows.Forms.Label lblDate;
        private System.ComponentModel.IContainer components;

        public Form1()
        {
            //
            // Required for Windows Form Designer support
            //
            InitializeComponent();

            //
            // TODO: Add any constructor code after
            // InitializeComponent call
            //
            timer1.Start();
            ResetClock();
        }

        /// <summary>
        /// Clean up any resources being used.
        /// </summary>
        protected override void Dispose( bool disposing )
        {
            if( disposing )
            {
```

```
            if (components != null)
            {
                components.Dispose();
            }
        }
        base.Dispose( disposing );
    }


#region Windows Form Designer generated code
/// <summary>
/// Required method for Designer support - do not modify
/// the contents of this method with the code editor.
/// </summary>
private void InitializeComponent()
{
    this.components = new System.ComponentModel.Container();
    this.lblTime = new System.Windows.Forms.Label();
    this.lblDate = new System.Windows.Forms.Label();
    this.timer1 = new ⤸
        System.Windows.Forms.Timer(this.components);
    this.SuspendLayout();
    //
    // lblTime
    //
    this.lblTime.Font = new System.Drawing.Font("Microsoft
        Sans Serif", 24F, System.Drawing.FontStyle.Regular,
        System.Drawing.GraphicsUnit.Point, ((System.Byte)(0)));
    this.lblTime.Location = new System.Drawing.Point(26, 40);
    this.lblTime.Name = "lblTime";
    this.lblTime.Size = new System.Drawing.Size(180, 32);
    this.lblTime.TabIndex = 0;
    this.lblTime.Text = "label1";
    this.lblTime.TextAlign = ⤸
        System.Drawing.ContentAlignment.MiddleCenter;
    //
    // lblDate
    //
    this.lblDate.Font = new System.Drawing.Font⤸
        ("Microsoft Sans ⤸
        Serif", 24F, System.Drawing.FontStyle.Regular, ⤸
        System.Drawing.GraphicsUnit.Point, ⤸
        ((System.Byte)(0)));
    this.lblDate.Location = new System.Drawing.Point(26, 92);
```

```
            this.lblDate.Name = "lblDate";
            this.lblDate.Size = new System.Drawing.Size(180, 32);
            this.lblDate.TabIndex = 1;
            this.lblDate.Text = "label2";
            this.lblDate.TextAlign = ⏎
                System.Drawing.ContentAlignment.MiddleCenter;
            //
            // timer1
            //
            this.timer1.Interval = 1000;
            this.timer1.Tick += new System.EventHandler⏎
                (this.timer1_Tick);
            //
            // Form1
            //
            this.AutoScaleBaseSize = new System.Drawing.Size(5, 13);
            this.ClientSize = new System.Drawing.Size(232, 165);
            this.Controls.AddRange(new System.Windows.Forms.⏎
                Control[] {
                  this.lblDate,
                  this.lblTime});
            this.Name = "Form1";
            this.Text = "My C# Clock";
            this.ResumeLayout(false);

        }
        #endregion

        /// <summary>
        /// The main entry point for the application.
        /// </summary>
        [STAThread]
        static void Main()
        {
            Application.Run(new Form1());
        }

        private void timer1_Tick(object sender, System.EventArgs e)
        {
            ResetClock();
        }
        protected void ResetClock()
        {
```

```
        string s = DateTime.Now.ToString();
        int i = s.IndexOf(" ");
        this.lblTime.Text=s.Substring(i+1);
        this.lblDate.Text=s.Substring(0,i);
    }
  }
}
```

Build and run the application by clicking the Debug Start tool button. If you have no compile errors, your application should run and the digital clock should appear as shown in Figure 10-4. You will soon learn that C# does not do some of the things that Visual Basic programmers take for granted. In some respects, it is not as "user-friendly." The following list presents just a few of the things that you will encounter immediately if you are a Visual Basic programmer just learning C#:

- C# is *very* case sensitive. Among other things, this means that IntelliSense does not work unless you use the proper case when typing object names. For example, if you type **system.**, IntelliSense will not pop up the properties for the System object. You must enter **System.** to get it to work.

- C# will not automatically insert parentheses () after a method or function call as Visual Basic does. If you do not enter (), the compiler will bark at you.

- In order to have IntelliSense list controls on a form for you, you must use the keyword "this" instead of "Me". Note that "this" is lowercase.

- Indenting by the C# editor is automatic as you enter new code, but if you disturb the spacing of the indenting, C# does not automatically correct the indenting for you as Visual Basic does.

- The C# editor does not immediately list errors in the Task List when you code a line that will produce a compiler error. Visual Basic does this dynamically when you enter a line of code with an error in it. In C#, you must compile before the error lines will be placed into the Task List.

- The C# editor does not dynamically remove the "underline" from a line of code that is in error when you correct the error. Again, you must compile to ensure that the line of code has been corrected and that it will now compile without error.

Figure 10-4. Running the C# digital clock

Visual Basic Clock Application

To create the Visual Basic clock application, follow the same steps that I outlined for the C# project. The only things that change are shown in Listing 10-2. The changes are only in the Timer1 tick event and the code for the ResetClock procedure. On the form, change the Text property of the form to "My VB Clock". You will notice that the code is almost identical except for the following five things:

1. The semicolons have been removed.

2. The braces have been removed.

3. "this." was changed to "Me.".

4. C# does not use or allow continuation marks. On the other hand, C# does not need the continuation marks in order to continue a line to one or more lines. You can simply press the Enter key at a reasonable line length. This will allow you to control the length of long lines and make your code more readable.

5. The use of Dim has replaced the C# typing method.

Listing 10-2. Visual Basic Code Changes

```
Private Sub Timer1_Tick(ByVal sender As System.Object, _
                        ByVal e As System.EventArgs) _
                        Handles Timer1.Tick
    ResetClock()
End Sub
Protected Sub ResetClock()
    Dim s As String = Now.ToString
    Dim i As Short = s.IndexOf(" ")
```

```
    Me.lblTime.Text = s.Substring(i + 1)
    Me.lblDate.Text = s.Substring(0, i)
End Sub
```

If you now compile and run the Visual Basic application, you will see no difference in the appearance of the forms. The WinForms model is the same, regardless of the base language behind it.

Creating a C# Add-in

In this section you are going to create an add-in in C#. Up to this point in the book, you have built all of the add-ins using Visual Basic as the base language. Anything that can be done in Visual Basic can also be done in C#. To create a C# add-in, you will use the Add-in Wizard. You will select the exact same options you would select for a Visual Basic add-in, except for the base language option: You will select C# as the base language for the add-in rather than Visual Basic. Once the wizard has created the basic add-in, the generated code will appear as shown in Listing 10-3.

The code generated by the wizard is basically the same as the code you have seen generated for a Visual Basic add-in, except for the basic syntax differences ({} ;). However, C# does something neat that Visual Basic does not do.

Visual Studio .NET provides a special feature in C# that allows you to document your C# code using XML. You will notice that there are some new lines of comments. However, these special comment lines have three slashes instead of two, which is the normal C/C++/C# comment delimiter. I have highlighted the first few sets of these comments in boldface. This special comment is eXtensible Markup Language (XML) documentation of the functions. You will notice the XML keyword <summary> followed by the comment and terminated by </summary>. At some time in the future, you can extract the XML comments and place them into an XML file.

NOTE *Although the compiler initially placed these XML comments in front of every function, I have removed most of them from the code for the add-in in order to save space. You can still see the code as originally created by downloading the book's code from the Downloads section of the Apress Web site (*http://www.apress.com*) and looking at the code for this section.*

The C# text editor will automatically produce these comments for you as you code a new function. After you enter a new function, position the cursor to a blank line just above the function definition line. Enter three slashes (///) and press Enter. The editor will automatically enter the XML comments documenting the function and any parameters that you may have entered in the function definition line.

I have made a few simple changes to the code for the add-in in Listing 10-3 that I normally make to the code generated by the Add-in Wizard. I have highlighted each of the changes and summarized them in the following list:

1. I added a module-level command object so that it would be in scope for the OnDisconnection method.

2. I added another condition to the test for connect mode to the OnConnection method.

3. I added a message box display to report any error encountered while attempting to load the menu in the OnConnection method.

4. I added code to remove the add-in menu in the OnDisconnection method. I also added error-handling code in case an error is encountered when removing the menu.

Listing 10-3. C# Add-in Code Created by the Add-in Wizard

```csharp
namespace Chap10AddinCS
{
using System;
using Microsoft.Office.Core;
using Extensibility;
using System.Runtime.InteropServices;
using EnvDTE;

/// <summary>
///    The object for implementing an Add-in.
/// </summary>
/// <seealso class='IDTExtensibility2' />
[GuidAttribute("8133C305-7BB5-4BC0-9FBD-172BE4A40BB3"), ⏎
    ProgId("Chap10AddinCS.Connect")]
public class Connect : Object, Extensibility.IDTExtensibility2, ⏎
    IDTCommandTarget
{
    Command command;
```

```
/// <summary>
///        Implements the constructor for the Add-in object.
///        Place your initialization code within this method.
/// </summary>
public Connect()
{
}


/// <summary>
///        Implements the OnConnection method of the I
///        DTExtensibility2 interface.
///        Receives notification that the Add-in is being loaded.
/// </summary>
/// <param term='application'>
///        Root object of the host application.
/// </param>
/// <param term='connectMode'>
///        Describes how the Add-in is being loaded.
/// </param>
/// <param term='addInInst'>
///        Object representing this Add-in.
/// </param>
/// <seealso class='IDTExtensibility2' />
public void OnConnection(object application,
    Extensibility.ext_ConnectMode connectMode,
    object addInInst, ref System.Array custom)
{
    applicationObject = (_DTE)application;
    addInInstance = (AddIn)addInInst;
    if(connectMode ==
      Extensibility.ext_ConnectMode.ext_cm_UISetup ||
        connectMode ==
        Extensibility.ext_ConnectMode.ext_cm_AfterStartup)
    {
        object []contextGUIDS = new object[] { };
        Commands commands = applicationObject.Commands;
        _CommandBars commandBars =
            applicationObject.CommandBars;

        try
        {
            Command command =
                commands.AddNamedCommand(addInInstance, ⏎
```

```
                    "Chap10AddinCS", "Chap10AddinCS", ↵
                    "Executes the command for Chap10AddinCS", true, ↵
                    59, ref contextGUIDS,
                    (int)vsCommandStatus.vsCommandStatusSupported+↵
                    (int)vsCommandStatus.vsCommandStatusEnabled);
                CommandBar commandBar = ↵
                    (CommandBar)commandBars["Tools"];
                CommandBarControl commandBarControl = ↵
                        command.AddControl(commandBar, 1);
            }
        catch(System.Exception e)
        {
            MessageBox.Show("Error setting command " +
                e.Message);
        }
    }


    public void OnDisconnection(Extensibility.ext_DisconnectMode
        disconnectMode, ref System.Array custom)
    {
        try
        {
            command.Delete();
        }
        catch(System.Exception e)
        {
            MessageBox.Show("Error removing command " +
                e.Message);
        }
        }
    public void OnAddInsUpdate(ref System.Array custom)
    {
    }


    public void OnStartupComplete(ref System.Array custom)
    {
    }


    public void OnBeginShutdown(ref System.Array custom)
    {
    }
```

```csharp
public void QueryStatus(string commandName,
    EnvDTE.vsCommandStatusTextWanted neededText,
    ref EnvDTE.vsCommandStatus status,
    ref object commandText)
{
    if(neededText ==
        EnvDTE.vsCommandStatusTextWanted.
        vsCommandStatusTextWantedNone)
    {
        if(commandName ==
            "Chap10AddinCS.Connect.Chap10AddinCS")
        {
            status =
                (vsCommandStatus)vsCommandStatus.
                vsCommandStatusSupported|222
                vsCommandStatus.
                vsCommandStatusEnabled;
        }
    }
}


public void Exec(string commandName,
    EnvDTE.vsCommandExecOption executeOption,
    ref object varIn,
    ref object varOut,
    ref bool handled)
{
    handled = false;
    if(executeOption ==
        EnvDTE.vsCommandExecOption.vsCommandExecOptionDoDefault)
    {
        if(commandName ==
            "Chap10AddinCS.Connect.Chap10AddinCS")
        {
            MessageBox.Show ("You Rang?");
            handled = true;
            return;
        }
    }
}
    private _DTE applicationObject;
    private AddIn addInInstance;


}
}
```

Using Multiple Languages in the Add-in

Having created an add-in in C#, you are going to create a simple example of using multiple languages within the add-in. You are going to add a new project to the add-in. It will be a Visual Basic DLL and you will call it from the C# add-in's Exec method. It will also pass the application object (IDE instance) to the Visual Basic code so that it can reference the extensibility objects.

Adding a Visual Basic DLL to the Project

In order to add a new project to the add-in solution, right-click the solution in the Solution Explorer. In the pop-up menu, select Add ➤ New Project. Visual Studio will display the New Projects dialog box, which you have seen numerous times before. Select the Visual Basic Projects folder and single-click the Class Library icon.

> **NOTE** *The class library is the type of project that you need to select to create a dynamic link library (DLL). One of the great things about Visual Studio .NET is its capability to debug any number of DLLs in series within the single solution.*

Single-click the icon to select the project type, because you want to enter a name for the project rather than let Visual Studio use a default project name. Then click the OK button to create the new DLL project and add it to the solution. You are adding it to the solution instead of creating a new one so that you can debug the DLL by calling it from the add-in. Once the project is created, the Solution Explorer will appear as shown in Figure 10-5. You add references to the EnvDTE and Extensibility namespaces by right-clicking the References folder in the new project. You then select Add ➤ New Reference in the pop-up menu. When the References dialog box appears, select the respective items.

In order for the C# project to call the Visual Basic DLL, you add a reference in the C# project to the Visual Basic project. Again, right-click the References folder in the C# project and select Add ➤ New Reference in the pop-up menu. This time, you need to choose the Projects tab in the References dialog box. Figure 10-6 shows the Projects tab and the Visual Basic project. You must reference the project because the DLL has not yet been built and will therefore not appear in the .NET tab of the dialog box. Click the Visual Basic project, and click the Select and OK buttons to add a reference to the DLL.

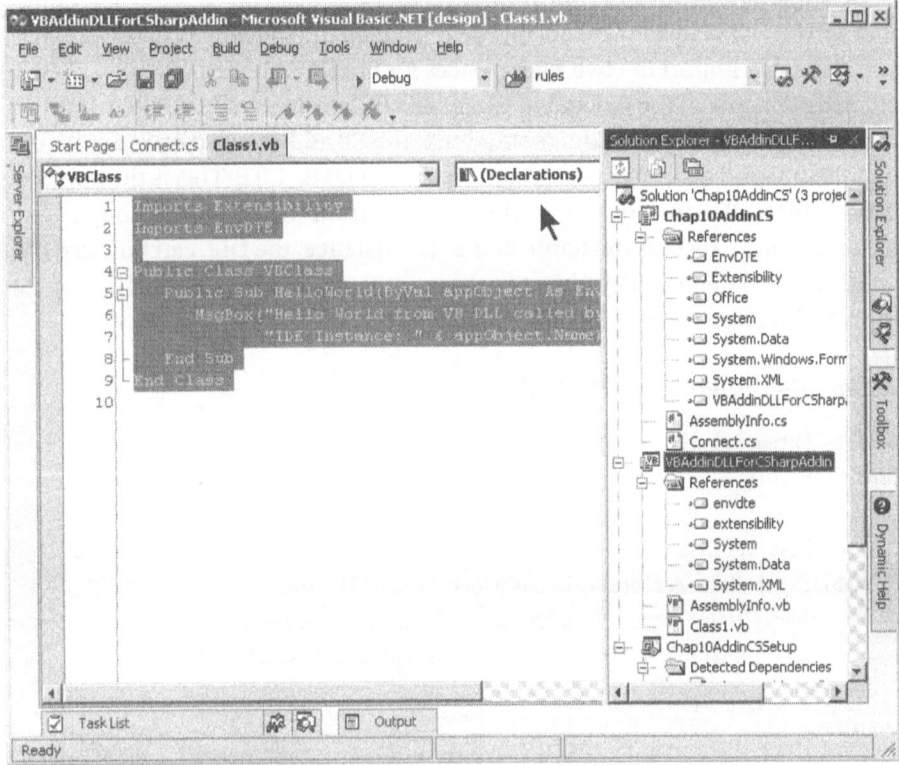

Figure 10-5. DLL project added to the add-in solution

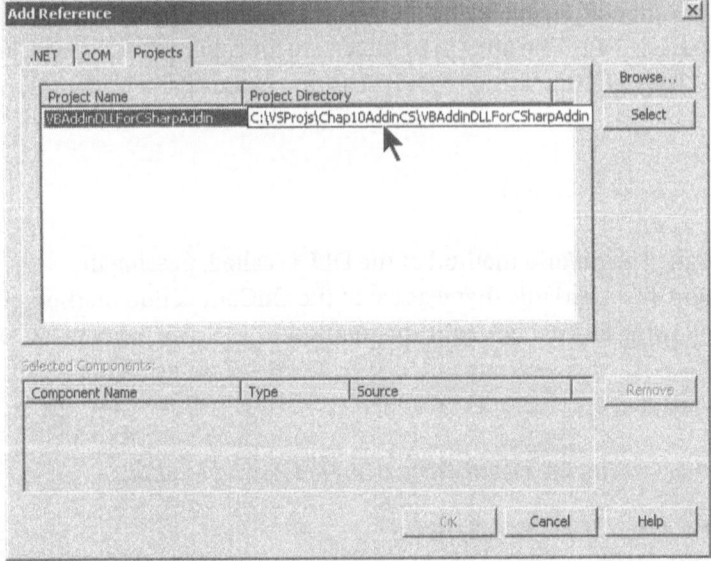

Figure 10-6. Adding a reference to the DLL project

Listing 10-4 shows the code for the Visual Basic class and associated method that will be called by the C# add-in. Having added the references to the project, you also must import the two namespaces for EnvDTE and Extensibility. First, change the name of the generated Class1 to VBClass. Next, add a Public method named HelloWorld. This is the method that the C# add-in will call. You will notice that the method expects a parameter of type EnvDTE._DTE. This is the application object (IDE instance) that will be passed from the add-in. Although you are only going to access the name of the IDE instance, the DLL can now use the appObject to reference any object in the automation model, just as if it were the original Connect class in the add-in.

Listing 10-4. Visual Basic DLL Code

```
Imports Extensibility
Imports EnvDTE

Public Class VBClass
    Public Sub HelloWorld(ByVal appObject As EnvDTE._DTE)
        MsgBox("Hello World from VB DLL called by C# Add-in." & _
                Chr(10) & "IDE Instance: " & appObject.Name)
    End Sub
End Class
```

Calling the Visual Basic DLL from the Add-in

Listing 10-5 shows the modifications that you make to the C# Exec method to call the Visual Basic DLL. The lines in boldface are for calling the DLL within an error-protected Try/Catch construct. The DLL is first instantiated by the following line of code:

```
VBClass ovb = new VBClass();
```

Next, the HelloWorld method of the DLL is called, passing the applicationObject variable that was set in the OnConnection method of the add-in. The following line of code calls the method:

```
ovb.HelloWorld(applicationObject);
```

Listing 10-5. Calling the Visual Basic DLL HelloWorld Method

```
public void Exec(string commandName, ⏎
        EnvDTE.vsCommandExecOption executeOption, ⏎
        ref object varIn, ⏎
```

```
            ref object varOut, ⤶
            ref bool handled)
{
    handled = false;
    if(executeOption == ⤶
        EnvDTE.vsCommandExecOption.vsCommandExecOptionDoDefault)
    {
        if(commandName == "Chap10AddinCS.Connect.Chap10AddinCS")
        {
        MessageBox.Show ("You Rang?");
            try
            {
                VBClass ovb = new VBClass();
                    ovb.HelloWorld(applicationObject);
            }
            catch(System.Exception e)
            {
                MessageBox.Show("Error calling VBDLL " +
                    e.Message);
            }
            handled = true;
            return;
        }
    }
}
```

Running the Add-in to Call the DLL

You have now completed the code for the new DLL written in Visual Basic.
Although it is about as simple as a DLL can be, it is nevertheless a complete DLL
that is capable of referencing any object in the IDE automation model. You have
also added the code to the C# add-in that will call the DLL. This completes the
coding for using multiple languages in an add-in or for any other type of Visual
Studio .NET application.

To run the add-in, click the Debug Start button in the IDE for the add-in. This
will automatically start a second instance of Visual Studio .NET. When the second
instance of the IDE opens, open the Add-in Manager dialog box from the Tools
menu. Check both boxes for the CH10AddinCS add-in, and then close the dialog
box. At this time, the add-in will be connected and its menu item will be added to
the Tools menu. If you select Tools ➤ CH10AddinCS, the C# add-in will display
two message boxes. The first is from the add-in itself. The second comes from the
Visual Basic DLL and will appear as shown in Figure 10-7.

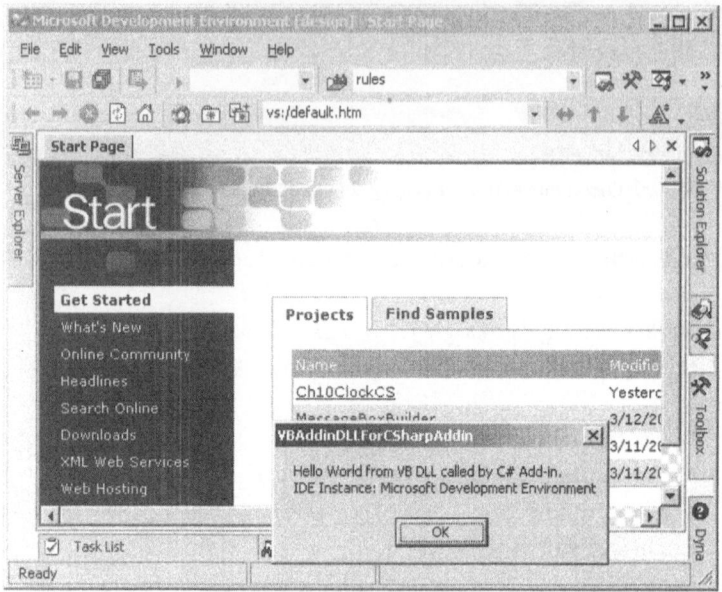

Figure 10-7. Message displayed from the Visual Basic DLL

Handling Multiple Languages in an Add-in

If you or other developers within your team are using more than one of the languages supplied with Visual Studio .NET, you certainly want your add-in functionality to support the developers, regardless of the language in which they may be programming. Additionally, as I have just demonstrated, a developer may be using multiple languages in a single solution. In this section you will learn how to enhance some of the add-in features you have previously developed so that they can handle multiple languages.

Reorganizing the Add-in Code

In this section, you'll make a copy of the code from Chapter 7. Next, you'll want to reorganize some of the code that you've already developed. You'll move the reusable functions from the Connect class of MyFirstAddin1 that are not normally associated with the Connect class. You would have done this earlier in the book, but I wanted to keep the code as simple as possible. The features of the add-in have grown, both in number and complexity, and now it is time to get organized.

The first thing you'll do is create two new classes named CodeManipulation and Utilities. You'll move all of the "business logic" code from the Connect.vb class to the CodeManipulation class. Next, you'll move the utility functions to the Utilities class. Once you do this, you'll immediately have to make some changes. Because all of the methods that are being moved will now be in separate classes, the code that calls them will have to instantiate an instance of the respective class before the methods can be called. Another problem that arises is that the application object (oVB) must be made available to the new classes so that their respective methods can make references to the IDE instance and to its automation objects.

Since the advent of Visual Studio .NET brought constructors and destructors (New and Finalize) to Visual Basic classes, it is possible to pass parameters to the constructor method New. To add a parameter to the New method after the class is added to the project, you should click the drop-down list of methods. In the drop-down list, select the New method. Visual Studio will create a method that looks like the following code snippet:

```
Public Sub New()
    oVB = roVB
End Sub
```

Now you can add one or more parameters to the method definition line, as shown in the code snippet in Listing 10-6. In this case, you want to pass the application object (oVB) to the class when it is instantiated.

Listing 10-6. Sample Constructor Usage

```
Imports EnvDTE
Imports Extensibility
Public Class CodeManipulation
    Dim oVB As DTE
    ' any number of lines of code that constitute the
    ' code for the class

    Public Sub New(roVB As DTE)
        oVB = roVB
    End Sub
End Class
```

To instantiate the class and pass the application object to it, you'll use the following line of code:

```
Dim oCM As New CodeManipulation(oVB)
```

When the object is instantiated by the previous line of code, the New method is called and the application object is set into a module-level variable of the class. This will allow any code anywhere in the class to have access to the extensibility objects in the current instance of the Visual Studio IDE.

At this point, a word to the wise is in order. Because methods of the CodeManipulation object will be calling methods of the Utilities class, that class will have to be instantiated by the CodeManipulation class. You might think that it would be a neat trick to do this by the code highlighted in boldface in Listing 10-7. It is a great idea, but it won't work. The code compiles with no problem, but at execution time the Dim of oUtil executes before the constructor is executed. Consequently, the Utilities class gets instantiated and the new object is set into the variable oUtil, but the variable oVB is set to Nothing at the time of the instantiation of the new object. Again, this is true because the constructor for the CodeManipulation class has not yet been called.

Listing 10-7. Sample Constructor Usage

```
Imports EnvDTE
Imports Extensibility
Public Class CodeManipulation
    Dim oVB As DTE
    Dim oUtil As New Utilities(oVB)

    ' any number of lines of code that constitute the
    ' code for the class

    Public Sub New(roVB As DTE)
        oVB = roVB
    End Sub
End Class
```

In order to pass the application object variable after it has been set in the oUtil object, you must change the code to appear as shown in Listing 10-8. Now, when the new instance of the Utilities class is instantiated, the application object variable has been properly set and can be safely passed.

Listing 10-8. Sample Constructor Usage

```
Imports EnvDTE
Imports Extensibility
Public Class CodeManipulation
    Dim oVB As DTE
    Public Sub SomeMethod()
        Dim sText As String
```

```
        Dim oUtil As New Utilities(oVB)
        SText = "some text"
        oUtil.PutCodeBack(sText)
    End Sub
    Public Sub New(roVB As DTE)
        oVB = roVB
    End Sub
End Class
```

Determining the Language Type

You have learned that a developer could be working with code in one or more languages in one instance of the Visual Studio IDE. To make the add-in features that you have developed work in multiple languages, you must determine the type of file that is represented by the active document. You are going to develop two different methods. The first, GetFileType, will return a Short value denoting the file type. In some scenarios you will use it to determine how or even if you will attempt to process a file. At other times, such as in commenting a block of code, you will use the file type to determine the comment character. That is where the second method, GetCommentChar, will be used.

 **TIP**   *The EndsWith method of the string class is a neat new feature of the .NET Framework. It returns True when the string object ends with the quoted expression passed to EndsWith. Note that the method is case sensitive.*

In the GetFileType method, shown in Listing 10-9, you are simply testing for the source file extensions that you want to attempt to handle. In the C++ extensibility model, you can use the Language property of the Document object. However, the EnvDTE.Constants collection does not include constants for Visual Basic and C# file types.

Listing 10-9. Determining the File Type

```
Function GetFileType(ByVal doc As Document) As Integer
    ' Pass this function the document that you wish
    ' to get information for.
    ' Return value:
    ' 0 Unknown file type
    ' 1 C-related file, this includes .c, .cpp, .cxx,
    '.h, .hpp, .hxx
```

```
' 2 Java-related file, this includes .jav, .java
' 3 ODL-style file, .odl, .idl
' 4 Resource file, .rc, .rc2
' 7 Def-style file, .def
' 8 VB, .vb
' 9 C#, .cs
' 10 Batch, .bat

Dim pos As Integer
Dim ext As String

ext = doc.Name.ToUpper
If ext.EndsWith(".rc") Or ext.EndsWith(".rc2") Then
    Return 4
ElseIf ext.EndsWith(".CPP") Or _
        ext.EndsWith(".C") Or _
        ext.EndsWith(".H") Or _
        ext.EndsWith(".HPP") Then
    Return 1
ElseIf ext.EndsWith(".JAV") Or ext.EndsWith(".JAVA") Then
    Return 2
ElseIf ext = ".def" Then
    Return 7
ElseIf ext.EndsWith(".vb") Then
    Return 8
ElseIf ext.EndsWith(".cs") Then
    Return 9
ElseIf ext.EndsWith(".bat") Then
Else
    Return 0
End If
End Function
```

Once you have called GetFileType, you can use the return value to call the GetCommentChars to get the comment character for the respective language, as shown in Listing 10-10.

Listing 10-10. GetCommentChars

```
Public Function GetLanguageCommentChars(ByVal FileType _
    As Short) As String       Select Case FileType
        Case 1, 2, 9 : Return "//" ' C languages and java
        Case 8, 6 : Return "'*" ' VB
```

```
      Case 4,10 : Return ";" ' rc, bat files
    End Select
End Function
```

In case you just want to get the comment character(s), regardless of file type, you can use the method I have developed that is shown in Listing 10-11. If the document type is not recognized by the function, an empty string is returned.

Listing 10-11. GetCommentCharForDoc Method

```
Function GetCommentCharForDoc(Optional ByVal doc As Document = Nothing) _
As String
    If (doc Is Nothing) Then
        doc = oVB.ActiveDocument
    End If

    Dim ext As String = doc.Name
    If (ext.EndsWith(".cs")) Then
        Return "//"
    ElseIf (ext.EndsWith(".cpp")) Then
        Return "//"
    ElseIf (ext.EndsWith(".h")) Then
        Return "//"
    ElseIf (ext.EndsWith(".vb")) Then
        Return "'*"
    ElseIf (ext.EndsWith(".idl")) Then
        Return "//"
    Else
        Return ""
    End If
End Function
```

Enhancing the CodeManipulation Methods

Now that you have functions that will tell you the type of file residing in the Active Document, you can modify the methods of the CodeManipulation class. I have divided the code for this class into two listings. Listing 10-12 contains all of the methods that have to do with block commenting and uncommenting. These methods have been enhanced to handle code manipulation for Visual Basic, C#, and C++. The changes made to provide this new functionality are highlighted in boldface.

The highlighted changes accomplish the following things:

- Instantiate an instance of the Utilities class.

- Determine the file type of the Active Document.

- Prefix Utilities class method calls with an object variable.

- Retrieve and use the respective comment characters.

- Destroy the instance of the Utilities class upon completion.

Listing 10-12. CodeManipulation Class Commenting Methods

```vb
Imports Microsoft.Office.Core
Imports Extensibility
Imports System.Runtime.InteropServices
Imports EnvDTE


Public Class CodeManipulation
    Shared UserName As String = "Les Smith"
    Shared TodaysDate As String
    Public oVB As DTE
    Const UnknownDoc = "Unrecognizible document type."
    Const DocVB = 8
    Const DocCSharp = 9
    Const DocCPP = 1
    Private sCommentChar As String
    Public Sub BlockComment()
        Dim iNL As Integer ' number of lines in block
        Dim sIN As String ' input selection
        Dim sOUT As String ' commented output
        Dim i As Integer
        Dim n As Short ' number of chars before first non
                       ' blank in first line
        Dim s As String
        Dim oUtil As New Utilities(oVB)

        Try
            sCommentChar = ↵
              oUtil.GetCommentCharForDoc(oVB.ActiveDocument)
            If Len(sCommentChar) = 0 Then
               MsgBox(UnknownDoc)
               Exit Sub
            End If
```

```vb
        ' Get selected text from active window
        sIN = oUtil.GetCodeFromWindow()

        ' ensure the user selected something
        If sIN.Length < 1 Then
            MsgBox("Please select block to be commented.", _
                vbExclamation, "BlockComment")
            Exit Sub
        End If
        ' get the number of lines in the text
        iNL = oUtil.MLCount(sIN, 0)

        ' comment the block
        For i = 1 To iNL
            s = oUtil.MemoLine(sIN, 0, i)
            If i = 1 Then
                n = oUtil.CountSpacesBeforeFirstChar(s)
                sOUT = CType(IIf(n = 0, "", Space(n)), String) & _
                    sCommentChar & " Block Commented by " & _
                    UserName & " on " & _
                    TodaysDate & vbCrLf
            End If

            sOUT = sOUT & Space(n) & sCommentChar & s & vbCrLf

        Next i

        ' now end the block
        sOUT = sOUT & CType(IIf(n = 0, "", Space(n)), String) & _
            sCommentChar & " End of Block Commented by " & _
            UserName & vbCrLf

        ' now put the code back
        oUtil.PutCodeBack(sOUT)
    Catch e As System.Exception
        MsgBox("Error: " & e.Message, vbCritical, "BlockComment")
    End Try
    oUtil = Nothing
End Sub

Public Sub BlockDelete()
    ' Insert a deletion comment block around a block
    ' that is about to be deleted
```

```vb
Dim sCC As String
Dim sText As String
Dim sLine As String
Dim i As Long
Dim nL As Integer
Dim sTmpText As String
Dim liCnt As Integer
Dim oUtil As New Utilities(oVB)
' get the selected code from the code window
Try
    sCommentChar = _
        oUtil.GetCommentCharForDoc(oVB.ActiveDocument)
    If Len(sCommentChar) = 0 Then
        MsgBox(UnknownDoc)
        Exit Sub
    End If

    sText = oUtil.GetCodeFromWindow()
    If Trim$(sText) = "" Then
        MsgBox("No deletion text selected!")
        Exit Sub
    End If

    ' we have the text that is to be deleted
    ' comment it to delete it
    sTmpText = ""
    nL = oUtil.MLCount(sText, 0)
    For i = 1 To nL
        sLine = oUtil.MemoLine(sText, 0, i)
        If i = 1 Then
            liCnt = oUtil.CountSpacesBeforeFirstChar(sLine)
        End If
        sTmpText = sTmpText & IIf(liCnt > 0, Space(liCnt), "") _
                & sCommentChar & " " & sLine & vbCrLf
    Next i

    sCC = IIf(liCnt > 0, Space(liCnt), "") & sCommentChar & _
            " Block Deleted by " & UserName & " on " & _
            TodaysDate & vbCrLf
    sCC = sCC & sTmpText
    sCC = sCC & IIf(liCnt > 0, Space(liCnt), "") & _
            sCommentChar & _
            " End of Block Deleted by " & UserName & " on " & _
            TodaysDate & vbCrLf
```

```vb
            oUtil.PutCodeBack(sCC)
        Catch e As System.Exception
            MsgBox("Error in Block Delete: " & e.Message)
        End Try
        oUtil = Nothing
        Exit Sub
End Sub


Public Sub BlockChange()
    Dim sText As String
    Dim sCC As String
    Dim liCnt As Integer
    Dim lsLine As String
    Dim oUtil As New Utilities(oVB)


    Try
        sCommentChar = _
          oUtil.GetCommentCharForDoc(oVB.ActiveDocument)
        If Len(sCommentChar) = 0 Then
            MsgBox(UnknownDoc)
            Exit Sub
        End If


        sText = oUtil.GetCodeFromWindow()


        If Trim$(sText) = "" Then
            MsgBox("No change text selected!")
            Exit Sub
        End If
        liCnt = oUtil.MLCount(sText, 0)
        If liCnt > 0 Then
            lsLine = oUtil.MemoLine(sText, 0, 1)
            liCnt = oUtil.CountSpacesBeforeFirstChar(lsLine)
        Else
            liCnt = 0
        End If


        sCC = vbCrLf & IIf(liCnt > 0, Space(liCnt), "") & _
                sCommentChar & _
                " Block Changed by " & UserName & " on " & _
                TodaysDate & vbCrLf
        sCC = sCC & sText & vbCrLf
        sCC = sCC & IIf(liCnt > 0, Space(liCnt), "") & _
```

```vb
                    sCommentChar & _
                    " End of Block Changed by " & UserName & " on " & _
                    TodaysDate & vbCrLf & vbCrLf
            oUtil.PutCodeBack(sCC)
            Exit Sub
        Catch e As System.Exception
            MsgBox("Error in Block Change: " & e.Message)
        End Try
        oUtil = Nothing
    End Sub


    Public Sub BlockUnComment()
        Dim iNL As Integer ' number of lines in block
        Dim sIN As String ' input selection
        Dim sOUT As String ' commented output
        Dim i As Integer
        Dim n As Short ' number of chars before first non blank
                        ' in first line
        Dim n2 As Short ' nbr chars before first nb char
                        ' subsequent lines
        Dim s As String
        Dim lsCD As String
        Dim oUtil As New Utilities(oVB)

        Try
            sCommentChar = _
              oUtil.GetCommentCharForDoc(oVB.ActiveDocument)
            If Len(sCommentChar) = 0 Then
                MsgBox(UnknownDoc)
                Exit Sub
            End If
            lsCD = sCommentChar & " "

            ' Get selected text from active window
            sIN = oUtil.GetCodeFromWindow()

            ' ensure the user selected something
            If sIN.Length < 1 Then
                MsgBox("Please select block to be commented.", _
                    vbExclamation, "BlockComment")
                Exit Sub
            End If
            ' get the number of lines in the text
            iNL = oUtil.MLCount(sIN, 0)
```

```
        ' comment the block
        For i = 1 To iNL
            s = oUtil.MemoLine(sIN, 0, i)
            ' look for commented lines
            Select Case True
                Case Left(Trim(s), 8) = sCommentChar & " Block"
                    ' comment header, dont write to output
                Case Left(Trim(s), 15) = sCommentChar & _
                    " End of Block"
                    ' comment footer, don't write to output
                Case Left(Trim(s), 3) = lsCD
                    sOUT = sOUT & Replace(s, lsCD, "", , 1) & vbCrLf
                Case Left(Trim(s), 1) = "'"
                    sOUT = sOUT & Replace(s, lsCD, "", , 1) & vbCrLf
            End Select
        Next i

        ' now put the code back
        oUtil.PutCodeBack(sOUT)

    Catch e As System.Exception
        MsgBox("Error: " & e.Message, vbCritical, _
                "BlockUnComment")
    End Try
    oUtil = Nothing
End Sub

Public Sub New(ByVal roVB As DTE)
    oVB = roVB
    ' set up today's date for use in all methods
    TodaysDate = Format(Now(), "Long Date")
End Sub
End Class
```

I have not taken the time to modify the other two methods of the CodeManipulation class to handle multiple languages. If you are adept at C# and C++, you might want to go ahead and do that yourself. I have protected them so that they will not work if the Active Document does not contain Visual Basic code. I have done this by calling the GetFileType method of the Utilities class and ensuring that the code is Visual Basic. If it is not, I inform the user that these functions are valid for Visual Basic only and then exit from the method. Again, the code that performs this functionality is highlighted in boldface in Listing 10-13.

Listing 10-13. CodeManipulation Methods for Visual Basic Only

```
Public Sub GenLocalErrorTrap()
    Dim sLine As String
    Dim sTemp As String
    Dim sTemp2 As String
    Dim sWord As String
    Dim i As Long
    Dim nL As Integer
    Dim bFound As Boolean
    Dim sTempLine As String
    Dim sProcType As String
    Dim sProcName As String
    Dim bFoundDefLine As Boolean
    Const EM = "   MsgBox(Error in "
    Dim oUtil As New Utilities(oVB)

    Try
        If oUtil.GetFileType(oVB.ActiveDocument) <> DocVB Then
            MsgBox("GenLocalErrorTrap only works for VB Code.")
            Exit Sub
        End If
        sTemp = oUtil.GetCodeFromWindow()

        sTemp2 = ""

        nL = oUtil.MLCount(sTemp, 0)
        bFound = False

        For i = 1 To nL

            ' look for the first line of code
            sLine = oUtil.MemoLine(sTemp, 0, i)

            ' get the procname to make the goto label unique
            If Not bFoundDefLine Then
                If InStr(sLine, "Sub ") > 0 Then
                    sProcType = "Sub"
                ElseIf InStr(sLine, "Function ") > 0 Then
                    sProcType = "Function"
                Else
                    sTemp2 = sTemp2 & sLine & vbCrLf
                    GoTo JustOutPutThisLine
```

```
            End If
            bFoundDefLine = True
            sTempLine = sLine
            Do While Trim$(sTempLine) <> ""
                sWord = oUtil.GetToken(sTempLine, "_")
                ' when we find the Proc type, term the loop
                ' and retrieve the name next below
                If sWord = "Sub" Or sWord = "Function" Then _
                    Exit Do
                If Trim$(sWord) = "" Then Exit Do
                sProcName = sWord
            Loop
            sProcName = oUtil.GetToken(sTempLine, "_")
        End If


    If Not bFound Then
        If InStr(sLine, "Sub ") > 0 Or _
            InStr(sLine, "Function ") > 0 Or _
            InStr(sLine, "Global ") > 0 Or _
            InStr(sLine, "Const ") > 0 Or _
            InStr(sLine, "Dim ") > 0 Then
            sTemp2 = sTemp2 & sLine & vbCrLf
        ElseIf Left$(Trim$(sLine), 1) = "'" Then
            sTemp2 = sTemp2 & sLine & vbCrLf
        ElseIf Trim$(sLine) = "" Then
            sTemp2 = sTemp2 & sLine & vbCrLf
        Else
            bFound = True
            sTemp2 = sTemp2 & vbCrLf & "      Try" & vbCrLf
            If Trim$(sLine) <> "End " & sProcType Then
                sTemp2 = sTemp2 & sLine & vbCrLf
            Else
                sTemp2 = sTemp2 & _
                "      Catch e as System.Exception" & vbCrLf
                sTemp2 = sTemp2 & _
                "          MsgBox(" & Chr(34) & _
                "Error in " & sProcName & _
                ": " & Chr(34) & _
                " & e.Message) " & vbCrLf
                sTemp2 = sTemp2 & "      End Try" & vbCrLf
                sTemp2 = sTemp2 & sLine & vbCrLf
            End If
        End If
    Else
```

```
                    If InStr(sLine, "End " & sProcType) > 0 Then
                        sTemp2 = sTemp2 & "          Catch e as↵
                            System.Exception" & vbCrLf
                        sTemp2 = sTemp2 & "              MsgBox(" & ↵
                            Chr(34) & "Error in " & _
                            sProcName & ": " & Chr(34) & ↵
                            " & e.Message)" & vbCrLf
                        sTemp2 = sTemp2 & "          End Try" & vbCrLf
                        sTemp2 = sTemp2 & sLine & vbCrLf
                        Exit For
                    Else
                        sTemp2 = sTemp2 & sLine & vbCrLf
                    End If
                End If
JustOutPutThisLine:
            Next

            ' now the proc with err code added is ready to paste
            oUtil.PutCodeBack(sTemp2)
            oUtil = Nothing
            Exit Sub
        Catch e As System.Exception
            MsgBox("Error in GenLocalErrorTrap: " & e.Message)
        End Try
    End Sub
    Public Sub CloneProcedure()
        Dim s As String
        Dim i As Integer
        Dim rs As String
        Dim oUtil As New Utilities(oVB)
        Dim iFileType As Short
        Try
            ' get selected proc from active window
            iFileType = oUtil.GetFileType(oVB.ActiveDocument)
            If iFileType = DocVB Then
                s = oUtil.GetWholeProc()
            Else
                s = oUtil.GetCodeFromWindow()
            End If

            If s = "" Then Exit Sub
            If iFileType = DocVB Then
                If InStr(1, s, " Sub ", 0) = 0 And _
```

```
                InStr(1, s, " Function ", CompareMethod.Binary) ↵
                = 0 Then
                MsgBox("Please select a whole Procedure to↵
                        be cloned.", _
                    MsgBoxStyle.Exclamation)
                Exit Sub
            End If
        End If

        Dim oFrm As New CloneProc(oVB)
        rs = oFrm.Display(s)
        oFrm.Dispose()
        If rs <> "" Then
            oUtil.AddMethodToEndOfDocument(rs)
        End If
    Catch e As System.Exception
        MsgBox("Error: " & e.Message, MsgBoxStyle.Critical, ↵
                "Clone Procedure")
        Exit Sub
    End Try
    oUtil = Nothing
End Sub
```

Utilities Class

The new Utilities class contains the following methods. They are all general-purpose methods that can be used by all CodeManipulation methods.

- GetToken

- MLCount

- MemoLine

- CountSpacesBeforeFirstChar

- GetFileType

- AddMethodToEndOfDocument

- GetCodeFromWindow

- GetCommentCharForDoc

- GetLanguageCommentChars

- PutCodeBack

- GetWholeProc

A couple of methods have been changed, and I list only the ones that have changed. The first is PutCodeBack. I have simply modified that method to put the code back into the document without using the Clipboard so that it does not destroy the contents of the Clipboard. Listing 10-14 shows the old code commented out and the new code inserted.

Listing 10-14. PutCodeBack Method

```
Public Sub PutCodeBack(ByVal s As String)
    Dim selCodeBlock As TextSelection
    Dim datobj As New System.Windows.Forms.DataObject()

    Try
        selCodeBlock = CType(oVB.ActiveDocument.Selection(), _
            EnvDTE.TextSelection)
        'datobj.SetData(System.Windows.Forms.DataFormats.Text, s)
        'System.Windows.Forms.Clipboard.SetDataObject(datobj)

        'selCodeBlock.Paste()
        selCodeBlock.Delete()
        selCodeBlock.Insert(s, 1)
    Catch e As System.Exception
        MsgBox("Could not put code back in window.", _
            MsgBoxStyle.Critical, _
            "PutCodeBackInWindow")
    End Try
End Sub
```

The second method changed in the Utilities class is GetWholeProc. Listing 10-15 shows the changes made to this method. The code for selecting the proc if the user has not completely selected it only works for Visual Basic code windows. Therefore, the method guarantees that the user has selected some code if the file type is not Visual Basic.

Listing 10-15. GetWholeProc Method

```
Public Function GetWholeProc() As String
    Dim ts As TextSelection = oVB.ActiveWindow().Selection
    Dim ep As EditPoint = ts.ActivePoint.CreateEditPoint
    Dim sLine As String
    Dim i As Integer
    Dim sCommentChar As String

    Try
        sCommentChar = Me.GetCommentCharForDoc(oVB.ActiveDocument)
        sCommentChar = Left(sCommentChar, 1)
        If sCommentChar = "/" Then
            If Len(ts.Text) = 0 Then
                MsgBox("For a C#/C++ project you must select the⤶
                        whole proc.")
                Return ""
            End If
        End If

        ' if the user has selected the whole proc,
        ' then just return it
        ' otherwise select it for them...
        If Len(ts.Text) > 0 Then
            If (InStr(1, ts.Text, "Sub ", 1) > 0 Or _
                InStr(1, ts.Text, "Function ", 1) > 0) And _
                (InStr(1, ts.Text, "End Sub", 1) > 0 Or _
                InStr(1, ts.Text, "End Function", 1) > 0) _
                Then
                Return ts.Text
            End If
            GoTo SelectTheProc
        Else
SelectTheProc:
            '' Get the start of the proc
            ep.MoveToPoint(ep.CodeElement(EnvDTE.vsCMElement.⤶
                vsCMElementFunction).GetStartPoint⤶
                (vsCMPart.vsCMPartWhole))

            ' move selection start point to top of proc
            ts.MoveToPoint(ep, False)
```

```
        ' back up to previous line looking for comments
        i = 0
        Do
            ep.LineUp()
            ts.MoveToPoint(ep, False)
            ts.SelectLine()
            sLine = ts.Text
            If Left(Trim(sLine), 1) <> sCommentChar Then
                ep.LineDown()
                ts.MoveToPoint(ep, False)
                Exit Do
            End If
            i = i + 1
        Loop

        ' if the count of comment lines > 0  the
        ' ts point is set properly
        ' else we must move it back to the original
        ep.LineDown(i + 1)

        ' move to bottom of proc
        ep.MoveToPoint(ep.CodeElement(EnvDTE.vsCMElement.⤶
            vsCMElementFunction).GetEndPoint⤶
            (vsCMPart.vsCMPartWhole))

        ' select the proc
        ts.MoveToPoint(ep, True)
        Return ts.Text
      End If
    Catch e As System.Exception
      System.Windows.Forms.MessageBox.Show(⤶
          "You must either select " & _
          "the whole procedure or your cursor must" & _
          " be within the procedure " & _
          "to be selected.   " & e.Message)
      Return ""
    End Try
  End Function
```

Finally, I changed the AddMethodToEndOfDocument method. The bold-faced code in Listing 10-16 was added to check for the type of file. C# classes always begin with a namespace, and therefore there are two terminating braces

(}) above which the new procedure must be positioned. If the file type is C#, I simply move up one additional line before inserting the code at the end of the class.

Listing 10-16. AddMethodToEndOfDocument Method

```
Public Sub AddMethodToEndOfDocument(ByVal NewMethod As String)
    Dim objTD As TextDocument = oVB.ActiveDocument.Object
    Dim objEP As EditPoint = objTD.EndPoint.CreateEditPoint

    ' We are past the end of the last line of the document
    ' move back in front of the End Module/Class
    objEP.LineUp(1)

    ' if a c# file, we must get within the namespace
    ' and the class braces
    If Me.GetFileType(oVB.ActiveDocument) = 9 Then
        objEP.LineUp(1)
    End If
    objEP.Insert(NewMethod)
End Sub
```

Running the Code for Multiple Languages

You have completed the modifications to the add-in to handle multiple languages. Next you will run just a couple of the features to show the results of the enhancements. Now most of the features in the add-in can do their respective jobs regardless of the type of code in which the user is programming.

Block Commenting C# Code

You have already seen that the add-in can comment blocks of Visual Basic code. Now you will see the results of running the code when the user is programming in C#. Put the add-in in debug mode so that a second instance of the Visual Studio IDE will be automatically started. When it opens, open a C# Windows application and select some lines for commenting. After connecting the add-in by going to the Add-in Manager, click the add-in's menu item to display the SmartDesktop UI form. Next, click the Block Comment node of the TreeView and the C# code is commented as shown in Figure 10-8.

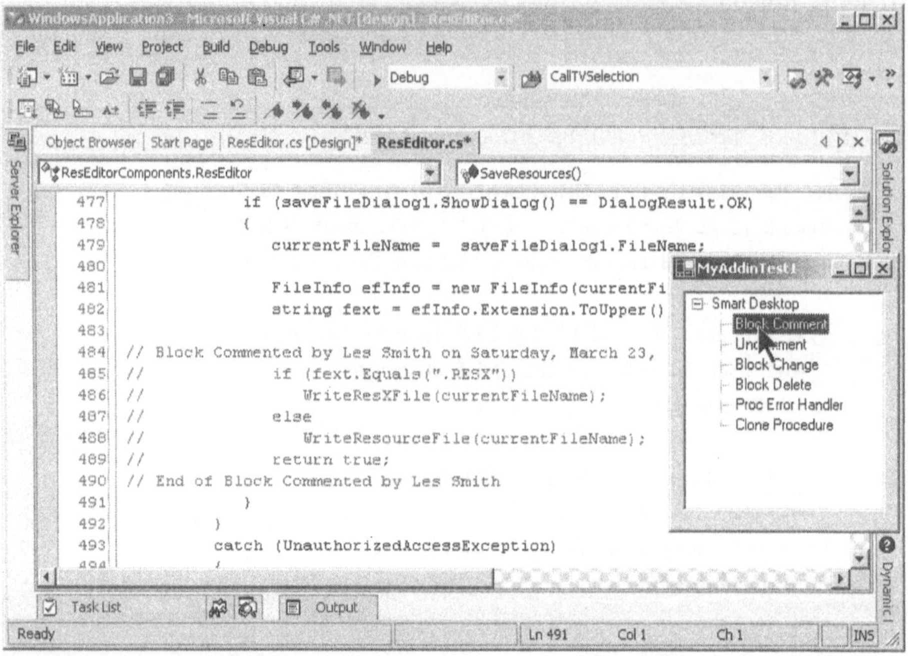

Figure 10-8. C# block commented code

Cloning a Proc in C# Code

Admittedly, this feature is not as useful in C# as it is in Visual Basic, but nevertheless, the code works the same as it does for a user programming in Visual Basic. The only caveat is that the user must select the whole procedure in C# prior to clicking the Clone Procedure option in the add-in's UI. Figure 10-9 shows the code in the CloneProc form after I have changed the name by appending "Cloned" to the end of the name.

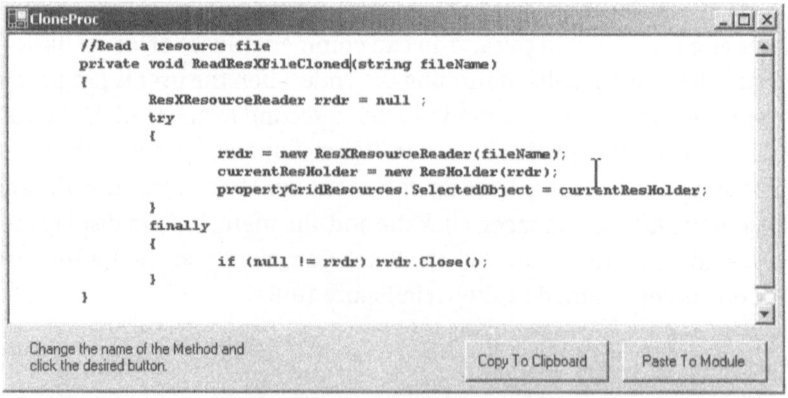

Figure 10-9. CloneProc form with the C# procedure being cloned

Once you have changed the name, click the Paste To Module button and the cloned C# method is inserted at the end of the class. Figure 10-10 shows the cloned code.

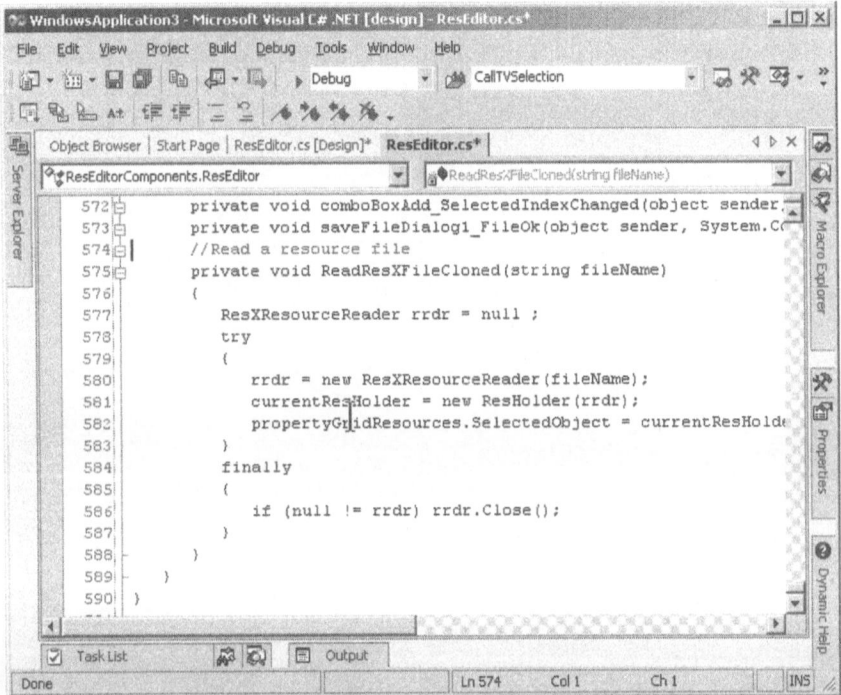

Figure 10-10. Cloned C# procedure inserted in the class

Summary

In this chapter you reviewed the alternate methods for automating tasks and saw some possible guidelines for their respective uses. You learned how to add external tools to the IDE. You saw that you can code an add-in in any of the current Visual Studio .NET development languages, and you can also mix the usage of these languages within an add-in. Finally, you learned how to detect the presence of different languages in the IDE and react accordingly in your add-in.

In Chapter 11, you will see how to respond to the events that occur within the Visual Studio .NET IDE as the developer is adding files and components, saving files, and so forth. You will see that there are some neat things that can be done as the various events fire.

Handling Automation Events

"Modern science is so enamored with its ability to create that it takes no time to consider whether it is right to create."
—Les Smith

GONE ARE THE DAYS when you could think of an application as a series of procedures that would execute in sequence. Since the advent of Windows programming, applications programming has become event driven. This means that the developer cannot tightly control the execution flow of an application. In Windows programming, the sooner that a developer learns that the user will determine how an application will flow (if you use the word "flow" loosely), the better off he or she will be. In Windows programming, the developer must program the application to respond to anything and everything the user can do. This is one of the things that makes Windows programming so interesting. The developer must learn to anticipate, think ahead, and plan for any type of user action.

This type of programming is called *event-driven programming*. An *event* is notification to an application that something important has occurred. When the developer using Visual Studio .NET does anything—almost literally *anything*, such as clicking a mouse, entering a keystroke, and so on—an event is likely to occur. This is especially true if focus changes from one window in the integrated development environment (IDE) to another. It also happens when the developer presses the Enter key in a Text Editor window.

In this chapter, I show you how to trap in an add-in the IDE events as they occur.

Trapping IDE Events

A number of top-level EnvDTE events can be trapped simply by declaring an event object variable using the WithEvents keyword and then providing and setting an event handler. However, by no means do they represent all of the events that can occur. They are simply the ones that are obvious and easy to trap. These top-level events are as follows:

- EnvDTE.ProjectsEvents

- EnvDTE.WindowEvents

- EnvDTE.TextEditorEvents

- EnvDTE.TaskListEvents

- EnvDTE.SolutionEvents

- EnvDTE.SelectionEvents

- EnvDTE.OutputWindowEvents

- EnvDTE.FindEvents

- EnvDTE.DTEEvents

- EnvDTE.DocumentEvents

- EnvDTE.DebuggerEvents

- EnvDTE.CommandEvents

- EnvDTE.BuildEvents

- EnvDTE.ProjectItemsEvents

Two additional events that pertain to the VSLangProj namespace are as follows:

- VSLangProj.ReferencesEvents

- VSLangProj.ImportsEvents

Associating an Event with a Handler

Before you can trap events, you have to associate the event with a handler. The WithEvents statement and the Handles clause are used to declare event handlers. The WithEvents statement is used to declare an object that can raise events. The event can be handled by a subroutine with a Handles clause that names the event. The Handles clause is a static method of linking the event object to the event handler at compile time.

The AddHandler and RemoveHandler are used to dynamically link and unlink the events with one or more event handlers at runtime. These clauses do not require the use of the WithEvents clause to declare an event object.

When you are working in a regular Windows application, Visual Studio .NET will automatically create an empty event handler and associate it with an event. An example of this would be when you double-click a Label control in design mode. Visual Basic .NET will create an empty event handler. Additionally, it will create a WithEvents object variable for the Label. Examples of these two code snippets are as follows:

```
Friend WithEvents lblDate As System.Windows.Forms.Label

Private Sub lblDate_Click(ByVal sender As System.Object, _
            ByVal e As System.EventArgs) Handles lblDate.Click
End Sub
```

In case you are programming in Visual C#, the compiler will create an empty event handler and associate it with an event. However, it does not use the WithEvents keyword to declare the event. Rather, it uses the following code. The empty event handler is listed below the event object.

```
this.lblDate.Click += new System.EventHandler(this.lblDate_Click);
private void lblDate_Click(object sender, System.EventArgs e)
{

}
```

Four separate snippets of code are involved in the trapping of IDE events in Visual Basic. First, an event object variable must be declared as shown in the following line of code:

```
Public WithEvents eventWindows As EnvDTE.WindowEvents
```

Next, an event handler must be coded. You can do anything you want to in the event handler, but I am simply writing a record of the occurrence in the

Output window. The OWP object is assumed to have been created by another
process that will be shown later in this chapter.

 **NOTE** *The Output window of the client instance of the IDE is
used for displaying information passed to the respective event
handlers throughout this chapter. In a production add-in,
you would not want to do this. Instead, you could write to the
Debug window of the add-in for use while in debug mode.*

```
Private Sub eventWindows_WindowActivated(ByVal GotFocus As↵
    EnvDTE.Window, _
    ByVal LostFocus As EnvDTE.Window) ↵
    Handles eventWindows.WindowActivated
    OWP.OutputString("WindowEvents.WindowActivated" & vbCrLf)
    OWP.OutputString(vbTab & "Window getting focus: " & _
        GotFocus.Caption & vbCrLf)
    OWP.OutputString(vbTab & _
        "Window losing focus: " & _
        LostFocus.Caption & vbCrLf)
End Sub
```

Now that you have an event handler, you need to link the event object variable, eventWindows, to the event handler. To do that, use the following line
of code:

```
eventWindows = CType(events.WindowEvents(Nothing), ↵
    EnvDTE.WindowEvents)
```

When the add-in is terminating, destroy the event object by placing the following line of code in the OnDisconnection method:

```
eventWindows = Nothing
```

In the following topics I use an add-in to demonstrate the handling of events.
I also describe each of the previously listed events.

 **NOTE** *It is not my intention to go into great detail with
respect to each type of event described in the following
sections. The intent here is to present a high-level overview of
the various events occurring in the IDE. Please refer to MSDN
for further detail.*

Event Handling Add-in

I am going to create a new add-in and use code from it as I describe the various events raised by the IDE. Once again, I will use the Add-in Wizard to create the framework for the add-in. The add-in will be named Chap11EventHandling and will be based on Visual Basic code. It will be just like all of the Visual Basic add-ins that I created previously in the book, except that it will not have a user interface (UI). If you are creating an add-in instead of simply running the code, don't check the box to have the wizard create a user interface.

As I describe the events raised by the various event objects, I will describe the object, list its events, and show you the respective event handlers from the add-in. For that reason, I will not show the Connect class assembled together. However, if you were to take all of the code from each event topic and place it into the Connect class, you would have all of the code for the class.

You will note that each of the event handlers is calling the WriteOutputWindow method of the ow object. This is a class that is used to insert text into the Output window of the client instance of the IDE. The code for this class is shown in Listing 11-1.

ProjectsEvents

The ProjectsEvents object raises events when a project is added, removed, or renamed in a solution. It also can raise the same events when an item is added, removed, or renamed in a project. The ProjectsEvents object can raise three possible events, which are described in Table 11-1. The code for the events is shown in Listing 11-1.

Table 11-1. ProjectsEvents

EVENT	DESCRIPTION
ItemAdded	Raised when a project is added to a solution or when an item is added to a project
ItemRemoved	Raised when a project is removed from a solution or when an item is removed from a project
ItemRenamed	Raised when a project is renamed in a solution or an item in a project is renamed

Listing 11-1. ProjectsEvents Event Handlers

```
Private Sub prjEvents_ItemAdded(↵
    ByVal Project As EnvDTE.Project) ↵
    Handles prjEvents.ItemAdded
    ow.WriteOutputWindow("ProjectsEvents::ItemAdded", ↵
        vbTab & "Project: " & Project.Name)
End Sub
Private Sub prjEvents_ItemRemoved(ByVal Project As ↵
    EnvDTE.Project) _
    Handles prjEvents.ItemRemoved
    ow.WriteOutputWindow("ProjectsEvents::ItemRemoved", ↵
        vbTab & "Project: " & Project.Name)
End Sub
Private Sub prjEvents_ItemRenamed(↵
    ByVal Project As EnvDTE.Project, ↵
    ByVal OldName As String) ↵
    Handles prjEvents.ItemRenamed
    ow.WriteOutputWindow("ProjectsEvents::ItemRenamed", ↵
        vbTab & "OldProjectName: " & OldName, ↵
        vbTab & "NewProjectName: " & Project.Name)
End Sub
```

WindowEvents

The WindowEvents object provides events for changes made to Windows in the environment. These events fire when the user clicks a different window other than the currently active window. It also raises events when a window is closed or opened. It has four events, which are described in Table 11-2.

Table 11-2. WindowEvents

EVENT	DESCRIPTION
WindowActivated	Raised when a window receives focus
WindowClosing	Raised just before a window is closed
WindowCreated	Raised when a new window is created
WindowMoved	Raised when a window is removed or resized

The code for handing the WindowEvents object events is shown in Listing 11-2.

Listing 11-2. WindowEvents Event Handlers

```
Private Sub eventWindows_WindowActivated(ByVal GotFocus As EnvDTE.Window, _
    ByVal LostFocus As EnvDTE.Window) Handles ⤶
        eventWindows.WindowActivated
    ow.WriteOutputWindow("WindowEvents::WindowActivated", ⤶
        vbTab & "Window receiving focus: " & ⤶
        GotFocus.Caption, ⤶
        vbTab & "Window that lost focus: " & ⤶
        LostFocus.Caption)
End Sub
Private Sub winEvents_WindowClosing(⤶
    ByVal Window As EnvDTE.Window) ⤶
    Handles eventWindows.WindowClosing
    ow.WriteOutputWindow("WindowEvents::WindowClosing", ⤶
        vbTab & "Window: " & Window.Caption)
End Sub
Private Sub winEvents_WindowCreated(⤶
    ByVal Window As EnvDTE.Window) ⤶
    Handles eventWindows.WindowCreated
    ow.WriteOutputWindow("WindowEvents::WindowCreated", ⤶
        vbTab & "Window: " & Window.Caption)
End Sub
Private Sub winEvents_WindowMoved(⤶
    ByVal Window As EnvDTE.Window, ⤶
    ByVal Top As Integer,⤶
    ByVal Left As Integer,⤶
    ByVal [Width] As Integer, ⤶
    ByVal Height As Integer) Handles eventWindows.WindowMoved
    ow.WriteOutputWindow("WindowEvents::WindowMoved", ⤶
        vbTab & "Window: " & Window.Caption, ⤶
        vbTab & "Location: (" & Top.ToString() & ⤶
        " , " & Left.ToString() & ⤶
        " , " & Width.ToString() & ⤶
        " , " & Height.ToString() & ")")
End Sub
```

TextEditorEvents

The TextEditorEvents object provides events for changes made in the Text/Code Editor. Something as simple as pressing the Enter key in the Editor will cause the object to raise an event. The TextEditorEvents object has one event: the LineChanged event. The LineChanged event is raised when changes are made to a line in the Text/Code Editor that move the insertion point. The event provides both a TextPoint and an EndPoint object. Chapter 5 discussed these objects. Listing 11-3 shows the code for handling the TextEditorEvents object.

Listing 11-3. TextEditorEvents Object Event Handler

```
Private Sub textEditorEvents_LineChanged(↵
    ByVal StartPoint As ↵
    EnvDTE.TextPoint, ↵
    ByVal EndPoint As EnvDTE.TextPoint, ↵
    ByVal Hint As Integer) _
    Handles textEditorEvents.LineChanged
    Dim textChangedHint As EnvDTE.vsTextChanged = CType(↵
        Hint, ↵
        EnvDTE.vsTextChanged)
    ow.WriteOutputWindow("TextEditorEvents::LineChanged", ↵
        vbTab & "Document: " & ↵
        StartPoint.Parent.Parent.Name, ↵
        vbTab & "Change hint: " & ↵
        textChangedHint.ToString())
End Sub
```

TaskListEvents

The TaskListEvents object provides events for changes made to the Task List. It raises four events, which are described in Table 11-3. The code for handling the events of the TaskListEvents object is shown in Listing 11-4.

Table 11-3. TaskListEvents

EVENT	DESCRIPTION
TaskAdded	Raised when a new item is added to the Task List
TaskModified	Raised when a Task List item is modified
TaskNavigated	Raised immediately before you navigate to the source of an item in the Task List
TaskRemoved	Raised when a Task List item is removed from the Task List

Listing 11-4. TaskListEvents Object Event Handler

```
Private Sub taskListEvents_TaskAdded(ByVal TaskItem As EnvDTE.TaskItem) _
    Handles taskListEvents.TaskAdded
    ow.WriteOutputWindow("TaskListEvents::TaskAdded", ↵
        vbTab & "Task description: " ↵
        & TaskItem.Description)
End Sub
Private Sub taskListEvents_TaskModified(↵
    ByVal TaskItem As EnvDTE.TaskItem, ↵
    ByVal ColumnModified As EnvDTE.vsTaskListColumn) ↵
    Handles taskListEvents.TaskModified
    ow.WriteOutputWindow("TaskListEvents::TaskModified", ↵
        vbTab & ↵
        "Task description: " & TaskItem.Description)
End Sub
Private Sub taskListEvents_TaskNavigated(↵
    ByVal TaskItem As EnvDTE.TaskItem, ↵
    ByRef NavigateHandled As Boolean) ↵
    Handles taskListEvents.TaskNavigated
    ow.WriteOutputWindow("TaskListEvents::TaskNavigated", ↵
        vbTab & "Task description: " & ↵
        TaskItem.Description)
End Sub
Private Sub taskListEvents_TaskRemoved(↵
    ByVal TaskItem As EnvDTE.TaskItem) ↵
    Handles taskListEvents.TaskRemoved
    ow.WriteOutputWindow("TaskListEvents::TaskRemoved", ↵
        vbTab & "Task description: " & ↵
        TaskItem.Description)
End Sub
```

SolutionEvents

The SolutionEvents object raises events when changes are made to the
solution. The object can raise eight events, which are described in Table 11-4.
Listing 11-5 shows the code to handle the events raised by the SolutionEvents
object.

Table 11-4. SolutionEvents

EVENT	DESCRIPTION
AfterClosing	Raised after a solution is closed
BeforeClosing	Raised before a solution is closed
Opened	Raised after a solution is opened
ProjectAdded	Raised after a project is added to a solution
ProjectRemoved	Raised after a project is removed from a solution
ProjectRenamed	Raised after a project is renamed
QueryCloseSolution	Raised before the BeforeClosing event
Renamed	Raised after the solution is renamed

Listing 11-5. SolutionEvents Object Event Handler

```
Private Sub solutionEvents_AfterClosing() ⤸
    Handles solutionEvents.AfterClosing
    ow.WriteOutputWindow("SolutionEvents::AfterClosing")
End Sub
Private Sub solutionEvents_BeforeClosing() ⤸
    Handles solutionEvents.BeforeClosing
    ow.WriteOutputWindow("SolutionEvents::BeforeClosing")
End Sub
Private Sub solutionEvents_Opened() ⤸
    Handles solutionEvents.Opened
    ow.WriteOutputWindow("SolutionEvents::Opened")
End Sub
Private Sub solutionEvents_ProjectAdded(⤸
    ByVal Project As EnvDTE.Project) ⤸
    Handles solutionEvents.ProjectAdded
    ow.WriteOutputWindow("SolutionEvents::ProjectAdded", ⤸
        vbTab & "Project: "⤸
        & Project.UniqueName)
End Sub
Private Sub solutionEvents_ProjectRemoved(⤸
    ByVal Project As EnvDTE.Project) ⤸
    Handles solutionEvents.ProjectRemoved
    ow.WriteOutputWindow("SolutionEvents::ProjectRemoved", ⤸
        vbTab & "Project: "⤸
        & Project.UniqueName)
End Sub
```

```
Private Sub solutionEvents_ProjectRenamed(↵
    ByVal Project As EnvDTE.Project, _
    ByVal OldName As String) ↵
    Handles solutionEvents.ProjectRenamed
    ow.WriteOutputWindow("SolutionEvents::ProjectRenamed", ↵
        vbTab & "Project: "↵
        & Project.UniqueName)
End Sub
Private Sub solutionEvents_QueryCloseSolution(↵
    ByRef fCancel As Boolean) ↵
    Handles solutionEvents.QueryCloseSolution
    ow.WriteOutputWindow("SolutionEvents::QueryCloseSolution")
End Sub
Private Sub solutionEvents_Renamed(↵
    ByVal OldName As String) ↵
    Handles solutionEvents.Renamed
    ow.WriteOutputWindow("SolutionEvents::Renamed")
End Sub
Private Sub selectionEvents_OnChange() ↵
    Handles selectionEvents.OnChange
    OWP.OutputString("SelectionEvents::OnChange" & vbCrLf)
    Dim count As Integer = oVB.SelectedItems.Count
    Dim i As Integer
    For i = 1 To oVB.SelectedItems.Count
        ow.WriteOutputWindow("Item name: " & _
            oVB.SelectedItems.Item(i).Name)
    Next
End Sub
```

SelectionEvents

The SelectionEvents object provides events for changes to a selection. Whenever something is selected in the development environment, a model of what the user has selected is created. A change in this model causes the OnChanged event to occur. The following code snippet is the event handler for the OnChanged event:

```
Private Sub selectionEvents_OnChange() ↵
    Handles  selectionEvents.OnChange
    ow.WriteOutputWindow("SelectionEvents::OnChange")
    Dim count As Integer = oVB.SelectedItems.Count
    Dim i As Integer
    For i = 1 To oVB.SelectedItems.Count
```

```
        ow.WriteOutputWindow("Item name: " & ↵
            oVB.SelectedItems.Item(i).Name)
    Next
End Sub
```

OutputWindowEvents

Numerous IDE tools use the Output window for display of output text. Initially, the IDE has two basic Output window panes: Debug and Build. However, it is possible for each tool in the IDE to use a different Output window pane. For example, build errors could go to the Build Errors pane and debug messages could go to the Debug pane. You can select panes with the drop-down box at the top of the Output window. The Output window raises three events, as described in Table 11-5. Listing 11-6 shows the code for the OutputWindowEvents object events.

CAUTION *You must be careful if you are attempting to write to the Output window from the PaneUpdated event of the OutputWindow. You can cause a recursion loop if you do not protect against it.*

Table 11-5. OutputWindowEvents Events

EVENT	DESCRIPTION
PaneAdded	Raised when a new pane is added to the OutputWindow object
PaneClearing	Raised just before an Output window pane is cleared
PaneUpdate	Raised when text is added to the Output window

TIP *When a new pane is added to the OutputWindow object, it will remain there until the IDE is closed. However, the Debug and Build panes are closed when the solution is closed.*

Listing 11-6. OutputWindowEvents Event Handlers

```
Private Sub outputWindowEvents_PaneAdded(⤶
    ByVal pane As EnvDTE.OutputWindowPane)⤶
    Handles outputWindowEvents.PaneAdded
    ow.WriteOutputWindow("OutputWindowEvents::PaneAdded", ⤶
        vbTab & "Pane: " & pane.Name)
End Sub
Private Sub outputWindowEvents_PaneClearing(⤶
    ByVal pane As EnvDTE.OutputWindowPane)⤶
    Handles outputWindowEvents.PaneClearing
    ow.WriteOutputWindow("OutputWindowEvents::PaneClearing", ⤶
        vbTab & "Pane: " & pane.Name)
End Sub
Private Sub outputWindowEvents_PaneUpdated(⤶
    ByVal pPane As EnvDTE.OutputWindowPane)⤶

    Handles outputWindowEvents.PaneUpdated
    Static Busy As Boolean
    'If Busy Then Exit Sub
    'Busy = True
    'Don't want to do this one, causes too much output
    'ow.WriteOutputWindow("OutputWindowEvents::PaneUpdated", ⤶
    '    vbTab & "Pane: " & pPane.Name)
    'Busy = False
End Sub
```

FindEvents

The FindEvents object provides events for Find-in-Files operations. The FindEvents object raises only one event, the FindDone event. The FindDone event is raised after a Find-in-Files with a results list operation completes. The following code snippet handles the code for the FindEvents object:

```
Private Sub findEvents_FindDone(⤶
    ByVal Result As EnvDTE.vsFindResult, ⤶
    ByVal Cancelled As Boolean) Handles findEvents.FindDone
    ow.WriteOutputWindow("FindEvents::FindDone")
End Sub
```

```
Private Sub dteEvents_ModeChanged(↵
    ByVal LastMode As EnvDTE.vsIDEMode) ↵
    Handles dteEvents.ModeChanged
    ow.WriteOutputWindow("DTEEvents::ModeChanged", ↵
        "LastMode: " & LastMode.ToString)
End Sub
```

DTEEvents

The DTEEvents object raises events relating to the state of the environment. The DTEEvents object raises four events, which are described in Table 11-6. Listing 11-7 shows the code for handling the events of the DTEEvents object.

Table 11-6. DTEEvents Object Event Handlers

EVENT	DESCRIPTION
ModeChanged	Raised when the mode of the development environment (build, run, or debug) is changed. The LastMode is passed to the ModeChanged event.
OnBeginShutdown	Raised when the development environment is closing.
OnMacrosRuntimeReset	Raised when the macro runtime execution engine resets. When this happens, all global variable data and all event connections are lost.
OnStartupComplete	Raised when the development environment has completed initialization.

Listing 11-7. DTEEvents Object Event Handlers

```
Private Sub dteEvents_OnBeginShutdown() ↵
    Handles dteEvents.OnBeginShutdown
    ow.WriteOutputWindow("DTEEvents::OnBeginShutdown")
End Sub
Private Sub dteEvents_OnMacrosRuntimeReset() ↵
    Handles dteEvents.OnMacrosRuntimeReset
    ow.WriteOutputWindow("DTEEvents::OnMacrosRuntimeReset")
End Sub
Private Sub dteEvents_OnStartupComplete() ↵
    Handles dteEvents.OnStartupComplete
    ow.WriteOutputWindow("DTEEvents::OnStartupComplete")
End Sub
```

DocumentEvents

The DocumentEvents object raises four events relating to activity in the Documents object. These events are described in Table 11-7. Listing 11-8 shows the code for handling the events of the DocumentEvents object.

Table 11-7. DocumentEvents Object Events

EVENT	DESCRIPTION
DocumentClosing	Raised just before a document is closed. Passes the document that is being closed.
DocumentOpening	Raised just before a document is opened. Passes the document that is being opened along with a parameter denoting whether the document is read-only.
DocumentOpened	Raised after a document is opened. Passed the document that was opened.
DocumentSaved	Raised after a document is saved. Passed the document that was saved.

Listing 11-8. DocumentEvents Object Event Handlers

```
Private Sub documentEvents_DocumentClosing(↵
    ByVal Document As EnvDTE.Document)↵
    Handles documentEvents.DocumentClosing
        ow.WriteOutputWindow("DocumentEvents::DocumentClosing", ↵
            vbTab & "Document: " & Document.Name)
End Sub
Private Sub documentEvents_DocumentOpened(↵
    ByVal Document As EnvDTE.Document)↵
    Handles documentEvents.DocumentOpened
        ow.WriteOutputWindow("DocumentEvents::DocumentOpened", ↵
            vbTab & "Document: " & Document.Name)
End Sub
Private Sub documentEvents_DocumentOpening(↵
    ByVal DocumentPath As String, ↵
    ByVal [ReadOnly] As Boolean) ↵
    Handles documentEvents.DocumentOpening
        ow.WriteOutputWindow("DocumentEvents::DocumentOpening", ↵
            vbTab & "Path: " & DocumentPath)
End Sub
Private Sub documentEvents_DocumentSaved(↵
```

```
        ByVal Document As EnvDTE.Document)⏎
        Handles documentEvents.DocumentSaved
        ow.WriteOutputWindow("DocumentEvents::DocumentSaved", ⏎
            vbTab & "Document: " & Document.Name)
    End Sub
```

DebuggerEvents

The DebuggerEvents object provides events supported by the debugger.
Table 11-8 describes the six events that are raised by the DebuggerEvents object.
Listing 11-9 shows the code for handling the events for the DebuggerEvents
object.

Table 11-8. DebuggerEvents Object Events

EVENT	DESCRIPTION
OnContextChanged	Raised whenever the current process, program, thread, or stack is changed through either the user interface or the automation model.
OnEnterBreakMode	Raised when the debugger enters break mode regardless of how the break mode was established.
OnEnterDesignMode	Raised when run mode is terminated and design mode is reentered.
OnEnterRunMode	Raised when run mode is entered. This event may not fire when stepping.
OnExceptionNotHandled	Raised before OnEnterBreakMode. Setting the ExceptionAction parameter allows the handler to affect the development environment's user interface when the handler exits.
OnExceptionThrown	Thrown before OnEnterBreakMode. Setting the ExecuteAction parameter allows the handler to affect the development environment's user interface when the handler exits.

Listing 11-9. DebuggerEvents Object Event Handlers

```
    Private Sub debuggerEvents_OnContextChanged(⏎
        ByVal NewProcess As EnvDTE.Process,⏎
        ByVal NewProgram As EnvDTE.Program, ⏎
        ByVal NewThread As EnvDTE.Thread, ⏎
        ByVal NewStackFrame As EnvDTE.StackFrame) ⏎
```

```
        Handles debuggerEvents.OnContextChanged
        ow.WriteOutputWindow("DebuggerEvents::OnContextChanged")
End Sub
Private Sub debuggerEvents_OnEnterBreakMode( ⏎
    ByVal Reason As EnvDTE.dbgEventReason, ⏎
    ByRef ExecutionAction As ⏎
    EnvDTE.dbgExecutionAction) ⏎
    Handles debuggerEvents.OnEnterBreakMode
    ExecutionAction = ⏎
        EnvDTE.dbgExecutionAction.dbgExecutionActionDefault
    ow.WriteOutputWindow("DebuggerEvents::OnEnterBreakMode")
End Sub
Private Sub debuggerEvents_OnEnterDesignMode( ⏎
    ByVal Reason As ⏎
    EnvDTE.dbgEventReason) ⏎
    Handles debuggerEvents.OnEnterDesignMode
    ow.WriteOutputWindow("DebuggerEvents::OnEnterDesignMode")
End Sub
Private Sub debuggerEvents_OnEnterRunMode( ⏎
    ByVal Reason As _
    EnvDTE.dbgEventReason) ⏎
    Handles debuggerEvents.OnEnterRunMode
    ow.WriteOutputWindow("DebuggerEvents::OnEnterRunMode")
End Sub
Private Sub debuggerEvents_OnExceptionNotHandled ⏎
    (ByVal ExceptionType As String, _
    ByVal [Name] As String, ByVal Code As Integer, ⏎
    ByVal Description As String, ⏎
    ByRef ExceptionAction As EnvDTE.dbgExceptionAction) ⏎
    Handles debuggerEvents.OnExceptionNotHandled
    ExceptionAction = ⏎
        EnvDTE.dbgExceptionAction.dbgExceptionActionDefault
    ow.WriteOutputWindow("DebuggerEvents::OnExceptionNotHandled")
End Sub
Private Sub debuggerEvents_OnExceptionThrown( ⏎
    ByVal ExceptionType As String, ⏎
    ByVal [Name] As String, ByVal Code As Integer, ⏎
    ByVal Description As String, _
    ByRef ExceptionAction As EnvDTE.dbgExceptionAction) ⏎
    Handles debuggerEvents.OnExceptionThrown
    ExceptionAction = ⏎
        EnvDTE.dbgExceptionAction.dbgExceptionActionDefault
    ow.WriteOutputWindow("DebuggerEvents::OnExceptionThrown")
End Sub
```

CommandEvents

The CommandEvents object provides events for the Command object to automation clients. This object raises two events, BeforeExecute and AfterExecute, which are raised just before and after the command is executed, respectively. Listing 11-10 shows the code for handling the CommandEvents object.

Listing 11-10. CommandEvents Object Event Handlers

```
Private Sub commandEvents_AfterExecute(↵
    ByVal Guid As String, ↵
    ByVal ID As Integer, ByVal CustomIn As Object, ↵
    ByVal CustomOut As Object) ↵
    Handles commandEvents.AfterExecute
    Dim commandName As String
    Try
        commandName = oVB.Commands.Item(Guid, ID).Name
    Catch excep As System.Exception
    End Try
    ow.WriteOutputWindow("CommandEvents::AfterExecute")
    If (commandName <> "") Then
        ow.WriteOutputWindow(vbTab & "Command name: "↵
            & commandName)
    End If
    ow.WriteOutputWindow(vbTab & "Command GUID/ID: " & ↵
        Guid & ", " & ID.ToString())
End Sub
Private Sub commandEvents_BeforeExecute(↵
    ByVal Guid As String, ↵
    ByVal ID As Integer, ByVal CustomIn As Object, ↵
    ByVal CustomOut As Object, ↵
    ByRef CancelDefault As Boolean) ↵
    Handles commandEvents.BeforeExecute
    Dim commandName As String
    Try
        commandName = oVB.Commands.Item(Guid, ID).Name
    Catch excep As System.Exception
    End Try
    ow.WriteOutputWindow("CommandEvents::BeforeExecute")
    OWP.OutputString("CommandEvents::BeforeExecute" & ↵
        vbCrLf)
    If (commandName <> "") Then
```

```
    ow.WriteOutputWindow(vbTab & ↵
        "Command name: " & commandName)
  End If
  ow.WriteOutputWindow(vbTab & "Command GUID/ID: " & ↵
      Guid & ", " & ID.ToString())
End Sub
```

BuildEvents

The BuildEvents object raises events for solution builds. Table 11-9 describes the four events raised by the BuildEvents object. Listing 11-11 shows the code for handling the events of the BuildEvents object. The BuildEvents object was described and exploited in Chapter 9.

Table 11-9. BuildEvents Object Events

EVENT	DESCRIPTION
OnBuildBegin	Raised just before a project, solution, or batch build begins. Passed variables representing the scope and type of build taking place.
OnBuildDone	Raised after a build is complete. Passed variables representing the scope and type of build that has completed.
OnBuildProjConfigBegin	Raised when a project configuration build begins.
OnBuildProjConfigDone	Raised when a project configuration build is completed.

Listing 11-11. BuildEvents Object Event Handlers

```
Private Sub buildEvents_OnBuildBegin(↵
    ByVal Scope As EnvDTE.vsBuildScope, ↵
    ByVal Action As EnvDTE.vsBuildAction) ↵
    Handles buildEvents.OnBuildBegin
    ow.WriteOutputWindow("BuildEvents::OnBuildBegin")
End Sub
Private Sub buildEvents_OnBuildDone(↵
    ByVal Scope As EnvDTE.vsBuildScope, ↵
    ByVal Action As EnvDTE.vsBuildAction) ↵
    Handles buildEvents.OnBuildDone
    ow.WriteOutputWindow("BuildEvents::OnBuildDone")
End Sub
```

```
Private Sub buildEvents_OnBuildProjConfigBegin(↵
    ByVal Project As String, ↵
    ByVal ProjectConfig As String, ↵
    ByVal Platform As String, ↵
    ByVal SolutionConfig As String) ↵
    Handles buildEvents.OnBuildProjConfigBegin
    ow.WriteOutputWindow(↵
        "BuildEvents::OnBuildProjConfigBegin", ↵
        vbTab & "Project: " & Project, ↵
        vbTab & "Project Configuration: " & ProjectConfig, ↵
        vbTab & "Platform: " & Platform, ↵
        vbTab & "Solution Configuration: " & SolutionConfig)
End Sub
Private Sub buildEvents_OnBuildProjConfigDone(↵
    ByVal Project As String, ↵
    ByVal ProjectConfig As String, ↵
    ByVal Platform As String, ↵
    ByVal SolutionConfig As String, ↵
    ByVal Success As Boolean) ↵
    Handles buildEvents.OnBuildProjConfigDone
    ow.WriteOutputWindow(↵
        "BuildEvents::OnBuildProjConfigDone", ↵
        vbTab & "Project: " & Project, ↵
        vbTab & "Project Configuration: " & ProjectConfig, ↵
        vbTab & "Platform: " & Platform, ↵
        vbTab & "Build success: " & Success.ToString())
End Sub
```

ProjectItemsEvents

The ProjectItemsEvents object provides the base interface from which the various project types derive their specific project item event interfaces. The ProjectItemsEvents object raises three events. Table 11-10 describes the events for the ProjectItemsEvents object. Listing 11-12 shows the code for handling the events of the ProjectItemsEvents object.

Table 11-10. ProjectItemsEvents Object Events

EVENT	DESCRIPTION
ItemAdded	Raised immediately after adding a project to a solution or an item to a project
ItemRemoved	Raised immediately after removing a project from a solution or a project item from a project
ItemRenamed	Raised immediately after renaming a project in a solution or a project item in a project

Listing 11-12. ProjectItemsEvents Object Event Handlers

```
Private Sub prjEvents_ItemAdded(↵
    ByVal Project As EnvDTE.Project) ↵
    Handles prjEvents.ItemAdded
    ow.WriteOutputWindow("ProjectsEvents::ItemAdded", ↵
        vbTab & "Project: " & Project.Name)
End Sub
Private Sub prjEvents_ItemRemoved(↵
    ByVal Project As EnvDTE.Project) ↵
    Handles prjEvents.ItemRemoved
    ow.WriteOutputWindow("ProjectsEvents::ItemRemoved", ↵
        vbTab & "Project: " & Project.Name)
End Sub
Private Sub prjEvents_ItemRenamed(↵
    ByVal Project As EnvDTE.Project, _
    ByVal OldName As String) ↵
    Handles prjEvents.ItemRenamed
    ow.WriteOutputWindow("ProjectsEvents::ItemRenamed", ↵
        vbTab & "OldProjectName: " & OldName, ↵
        vbTab & "NewProjectName: "↵
        & Project.Name)
End Sub
```

Connect Class

The remainder of the Connect class is shown in Listing 11-13. You have already seen the event handlers in Listings 11-1 through 11-11. The event objects are declared and associated with the event handlers in the OnConnection method of the class. The event objects are set to Nothing in the OnDisconnection method of the class as the add-in is being shut down. The code for connecting and destroying the events is highlighted in boldface font.

Listing 11-13. Connect Class Declaration Section

```
Imports Microsoft.Office.Core
Imports Extensibility
Imports System.Runtime.InteropServices
Imports EnvDTE

<GuidAttribute("65DCDC37-6A98-4862-A91C-81F8B5B83073"), ↵
    ProgIdAttribute("Chap11EventHandling.Connect")> _
Public Class Connect

    Implements Extensibility.IDTExtensibility2

    Dim ow As WinOutput
    Dim oVB As EnvDTE.DTE
    Dim addInInstance As EnvDTE.AddIn
    Public WithEvents refEvents As VSLangProj.ReferencesEvents
    Public WithEvents importEvents As VSLangProj.ImportsEvents
    Public WithEvents prjEvents As EnvDTE.ProjectsEvents
    Public WithEvents eventWindows As EnvDTE.WindowEvents
    Public WithEvents textEditorEvents As EnvDTE.TextEditorEvents
    Public WithEvents taskListEvents As EnvDTE.TaskListEvents
    Public WithEvents solutionEvents As EnvDTE.SolutionEvents
    Public WithEvents selectionEvents As EnvDTE.SelectionEvents
    Public WithEvents outputWindowEvents As ↵
        EnvDTE.OutputWindowEvents
    Public WithEvents findEvents As EnvDTE.FindEvents
    Public WithEvents dteEvents As EnvDTE.DTEEvents
    Public WithEvents documentEvents As EnvDTE.DocumentEvents
    Public WithEvents debuggerEvents As EnvDTE.DebuggerEvents
    Public WithEvents commandEvents As EnvDTE.CommandEvents
    Public WithEvents buildEvents As EnvDTE.BuildEvents
    Public WithEvents solutionItemsEvents As EnvDTE.ProjectItemsEvents

    Public Sub OnBeginShutdown(ByRef custom As System.Array) ↵
        Implements Extensibility.IDTExtensibility2.OnBeginShutdown
    End Sub

    Public Sub OnAddInsUpdate(ByRef custom As System.Array) ↵
        Implements Extensibility.IDTExtensibility2.OnAddInsUpdate
    End Sub
```

```vbnet
Public Sub OnStartupComplete(ByRef custom As System.Array) ↵
    Implements Extensibility.IDTExtensibility2.OnStartupComplete
End Sub


Public Sub OnDisconnection(ByVal RemoveMode As ↵
    Extensibility.ext_DisconnectMode, ↵
    ByRef custom As System.Array) ↵
    Implements ↵
    Extensibility.IDTExtensibility2.OnDisconnection
    eventWindows = Nothing
    textEditorEvents = Nothing
    taskListEvents = Nothing
    solutionEvents = Nothing
    selectionEvents = Nothing
    outputWindowEvents = Nothing
    findEvents = Nothing
    dteEvents = Nothing
    documentEvents = Nothing
    debuggerEvents = Nothing
    commandEvents = Nothing
    buildEvents = Nothing
    solutionItemsEvents = Nothing
    ow = Nothing
End Sub


Public Sub OnConnection(ByVal application As Object, ↵
    ByVal connectMode As ↵
    Extensibility.ext_ConnectMode, ↵
    ByVal addInInst As Object, ↵
    ByRef custom As System.Array) ↵
    Implements ↵
    Extensibility.IDTExtensibility2.OnConnection

    oVB = CType(application, EnvDTE.DTE)
    addInInstance = CType(addInInst, EnvDTE.AddIn)
    ' set up my output window object
    ow = New WinOutput(oVB)

    Dim events As EnvDTE.Events
    events = oVB.Events
    eventWindows = CType(events.WindowEvents(Nothing), EnvDTE.WindowEvents)
    textEditorEvents = ↵
    CType(events.TextEditorEvents(Nothing), ↵
```

```
                EnvDTE.TextEditorEvents)
        taskListEvents = CType(events.TaskListEvents(""), ↵
        EnvDTE.TaskListEvents)
        solutionEvents = CType(events.SolutionEvents, ↵
            EnvDTE.SolutionEvents)
        selectionEvents = CType(events.SelectionEvents, ↵
            EnvDTE.SelectionEvents)
        outputWindowEvents = ↵
            CType(events.OutputWindowEvents(""), ↵
            EnvDTE.OutputWindowEvents)
        findEvents = CType(events.FindEvents, EnvDTE.FindEvents)
        dteEvents = CType(events.DTEEvents, EnvDTE.DTEEvents)
        documentEvents = CType(events.DocumentEvents(Nothing), _
            EnvDTE.DocumentEvents)
        debuggerEvents = CType(events.DebuggerEvents, ↵
            EnvDTE.DebuggerEvents)
        commandEvents = ↵
            CType(events.CommandEvents(↵
            "{00000000-0000-0000-0000-000000000000}", ↵
            0), EnvDTE.CommandEvents)
        buildEvents = CType(events.BuildEvents, EnvDTE.BuildEvents)
        solutionItemsEvents = CType(events.SolutionItemsEvents, ↵
            EnvDTE.ProjectItemsEvents)
    End Sub
End Class
```

WinOutput Class

The WinOutput class handles the insertion of text into the IDE's Output window. It has six overloaded methods named WriteOutputWindow. The event handlers in the Connect class write information about their respective event into the Output window by calling these methods. The only difference between these methods is the number of parameters passed to the respective methods.

NOTE *The Overloads keyword is new to Visual Basic developers in Visual Studio .NET. It has been in Visual C++ for a long time. It allows you to have multiple procedures with the same name differentiated by the number or type of parameters passed to the procedure.*

Listing 11-13. WinOutput Class

```
Imports EnvDTE
Public Class WinOutput
    Private OWP As OutputWindowPane
    Public Overloads Sub WriteOutputWindow(ByVal s1 As String)
        OWP.OutputString(s1 & vbCrLf)
    End Sub
    Public Overloads Sub WriteOutputWindow(ByVal s1 As String, ⏎
        ByVal s2 As String)
        OWP.OutputString(s1 & vbCrLf)
        OWP.OutputString(s2 & vbCrLf)
    End Sub
    Public Overloads Sub WriteOutputWindow(ByVal s1 As String, ⏎
        ByVal s2 As String, _
        ByVal s3 As String)
        OWP.OutputString(s1 & vbCrLf)
        OWP.OutputString(s2 & vbCrLf)
        OWP.OutputString(s3 & vbCrLf)
    End Sub
    Public Overloads Sub WriteOutputWindow(⏎
        ByVal s1 As String, ⏎
        ByVal s2 As String, ⏎
        ByVal s3 As String, ⏎
        ByVal s4 As String)
        OWP.OutputString(s1 & vbCrLf)
        OWP.OutputString(s2 & vbCrLf)
        OWP.OutputString(s3 & vbCrLf)
        OWP.OutputString(s4 & vbCrLf)
    End Sub
    Public Overloads Sub WriteOutputWindow(⏎
        ByVal s1 As String, ⏎
        ByVal s2 As String, ⏎
        ByVal s3 As String, ⏎
        ByVal s4 As String, ⏎
        ByVal s5 As String)
        OWP.OutputString(s1 & vbCrLf)
        OWP.OutputString(s2 & vbCrLf)
        OWP.OutputString(s3 & vbCrLf)
        OWP.OutputString(s4 & vbCrLf)
        OWP.OutputString(s5 & vbCrLf)
    End Sub
    Public Overloads Sub WriteOutputWindow(⏎
```

```
        ByVal s1 As String, ⏎
        ByVal s2 As String, ⏎
        ByVal s3 As String, ⏎
        ByVal s4 As String, ⏎
        ByVal s5 As String, ⏎
        ByVal s6 As String)
        OWP.OutputString(s1 & vbCrLf)
        OWP.OutputString(s2 & vbCrLf)
        OWP.OutputString(s3 & vbCrLf)
        OWP.OutputString(s4 & vbCrLf)
        OWP.OutputString(s5 & vbCrLf)
        OWP.OutputString(s6 & vbCrLf)
    End Sub
    Public Sub New(ByRef oVB As EnvDTE.DTE)
        Dim outputWindow As OutputWindow
        outputWindow = ⏎
            CType(oVB.Windows.Item⏎
            (Constants.vsWindowKindOutput).Object, ⏎
            EnvDTE.OutputWindow)
        OWP = outputWindow.OutputWindowPanes. ⏎
            Add("DTE Event Information")
    End Sub
End Class
```

Making Good Use of DTE Events

Now that you have seen how to set up and trap the major events within the IDE,
you may be asking what you can do with the information. In this section, you are
going to add code to some of the event handlers that will allow you to provide
useful features to an add-in. This will not be an exhaustive study of the events,
but it should spark your thinking and cause you to look for ways to use the information provided by the events.

Using the WindowActivated Event

The WindowActivated event is raised each time a window receives focus. This
gives you an opportunity to enforce a small, but significant standard. When
a new class, module, or form is added to the project, the first thing that you
should do is change the default name of the file from Module1, Class1, or Form1
to some more meaningful name that will describe its contents or purpose. Yet,
many times in the heat of the battle, developers forget to do simple things like

this. Later on, they find themselves wondering where some code is located. Giving meaningful names to files and methods, which provides developers a good head start on organizing their code, could have solved that problem.

In the WindowActivated event, I have called the CkForRemindOfDefaultName of the CReminder class. This method looks for forms, modules, and classes whose names have never been changed from the default name provided when they were initially added to the project.

NOTE *Visual Studio .NET makes it easy for the user to change a default name. At the time that a new item is added to the project, the Add New Item dialog box is displayed to allow the user to choose or confirm the type of item to be added. At the same time, the default name is highlighted in the Name text box. All developers have to do is to start typing the name of the new item. Therefore, you should not worry about reminding them if they did not take advantage of that option when adding the new item.*

If you implement such a feature in your add-in, you might consider having a way to turn this feature off, as it may become annoying to developers who choose not to change the name. However, this feature can be used to enforce a standard of changing to a meaningful name. With this feature activated, developers will probably change the name just so they will not have to keep clicking the OK button on the message box.

Listing 11-14 shows the new code for the WindowActivated event handler. It calls a method of the Creminder class that is shown in Listing 11-17.

Listing 11-14. Using the WindowActivated Event

```
Private Sub eventWindows_WindowActivated(ByVal GotFocus As EnvDTE.Window, _
    ByVal LostFocus As EnvDTE.Window) ⤶
    Handles eventWindows.WindowActivated
    ' Let's do something useful
    ' if the window name is a default name, e.g, Form(n),
    ' Module(n) or Class(n)
    ' suggest to the user that they need to rename it
    oRemind.CkForRemindOfDefaultName(GotFocus.Caption)
    ' task item removed does not always fire because of
    ' multiple events firing, so place the calls in this
    ' event to force the closing of the task list
```

```
      If GotFocus.Caption.StartsWith("Task List") Then
          oRemind.CkForClosingTaskList()
      End If
      If LostFocus.Caption.StartsWith("Task List") Then
          oRemind.CkForClosingTaskList()
      End If
  End Sub
```

Figure 11-1 shows a display of the message box reminding the user to change the default name of Form1.

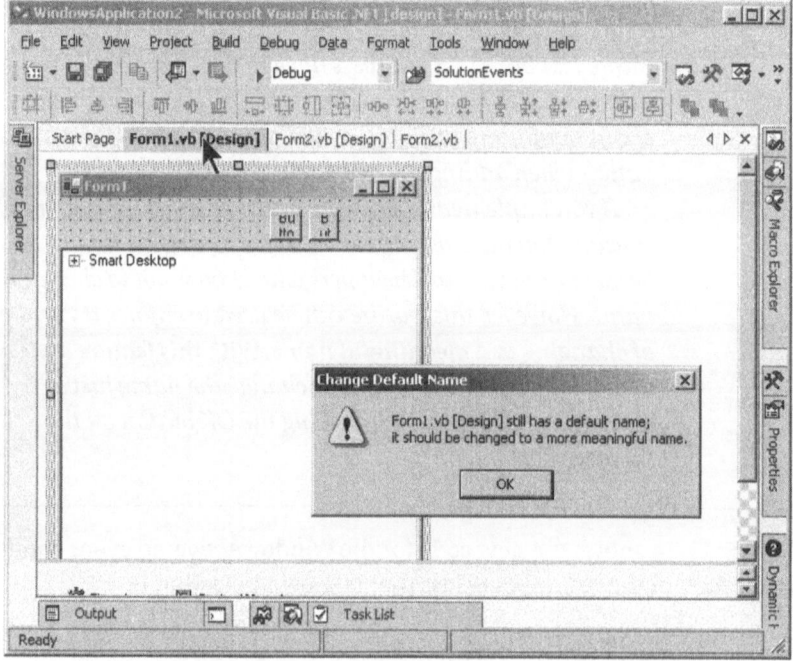

Figure 11-1. Reminding the user to change the name of Form1

Using the TaskList Object's ItemAdded Event

When you enter a line of code into the Text Editor that will generate a compile error, a to-do item is automatically placed into the Task List.

NOTE *A to-do item is placed automatically in the Task List in Visual Basic only. This is not done in Visual C# until you compile the project.*

Although I do not want to have to answer a message box, it would be nice for the Task List to automatically open and remain open to remind me to correct the problem immediately. Sometimes I may have to enter some other code before the error is cleared up. This would be the case if I enter a call to a procedure that does not yet exist. Even in this case, I may need to be reminded to code that procedure. Having the Task List automatically open to show the to-do item seems to me to be a nice touch.

I have added special code to the TaskAdded event handler. This code automatically opens the Task List when an item is added to the Task List. In addition to opening the window, I have set the AutoHides property to False. This will keep me from ignoring the error and attempting to compile the program only to find, to my surprise, that I have one or more errors. Along with the code that I have added to the TaskRemoved event handler, the window will stay open until I have corrected all of the lines with errors in them.

TIP *If you implement this feature in your add-in, you might consider having a way to disable it. This feature may annoy the developer that uses your add-in and it does not enforce any standards—it is simply a quick reminder of errors being created as the developer is coding.*

Listing 11-15 shows the code for the new ItemAdded event of the TaskListEvents object.

Listing 11-15. TaskListEvents ItemAdded Event

```
Private Sub taskListEvents_TaskAdded(ByVal TaskItem As EnvDTE.TaskItem) _
    Handles taskListEvents.TaskAdded
    ow.WriteOutputWindow("TaskListEvents::TaskAdded", _
        vbTab & "Task description: ⏎
        " & TaskItem.Description)
    oRemind.ActivateTaskList()
End Sub
```

Using the TaskRemoved Event

Listing 11-16 shows the new code for the ItemRemoved event of the TaskListEvents object. This code calls the CkForClosingTaskList method of the CReminder class. That method checks the count of items in the Task List, and if it is zero, it automatically hides the Task List window.

Listing 11-16. New TaskRemoved Event

```
Private Sub taskListEvents_TaskRemoved(↵
    ByVal TaskItem As EnvDTE.TaskItem) ↵
    Handles taskListEvents.TaskRemoved
    ow.WriteOutputWindow("TaskListEvents::TaskRemoved", ↵
        vbTab & "Task description: " & ↵
        TaskItem.Description)
    ORemind.CkForClosingTaskList()
End Sub
```

NOTE *You cannot always depend on the sequence of the firing of events, and in fact, you cannot always depend on certain events firing if other events are firing at the same time, which is often the case. For that reason, the ItemRemoved event of the TaskListEvents object does not always fire. Therefore, the CkForClosingTaskList method may not always be called. In testing, I have found this sequence to be erratic at best. For that reason, I have placed calls to the CReminder class in the WindowActivated event handler. Placing these extra calls helps get the Task List closed.*

Figure 11-2 shows a display of the Task List that has been activated because an item has been added to the Task List. You will note that Task List already has some error items in it. Even if the developer closes the Task List with errors in it, it will pop up again if another error is entered into the Task List.

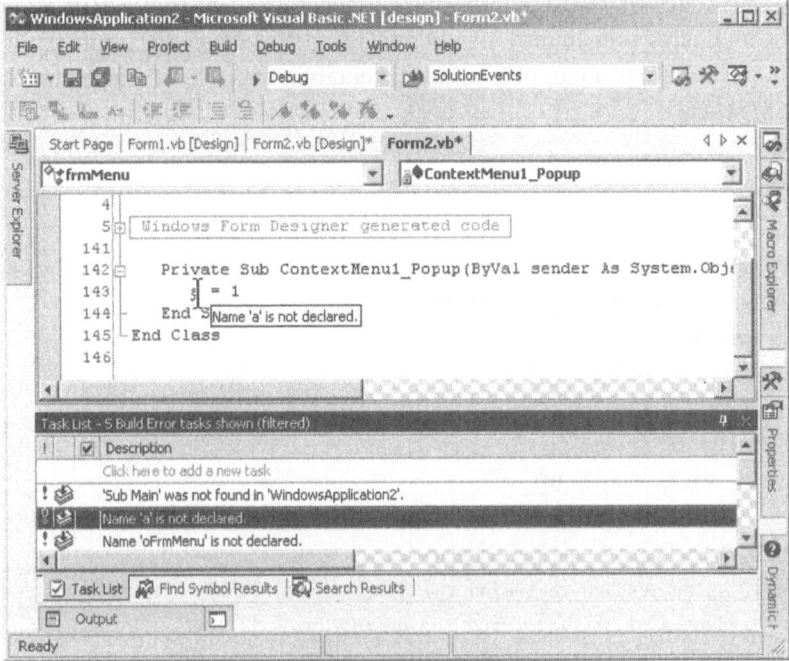

Figure 11-2. Task List activated by code with errors

CReminder Class

I have created a new class called the CReminder class. Initially it contains only three public methods that perform the functions described in the two previous sections. However, this class provides the container for other methods and functionality that you can add as you think through some of the features that you would like to trigger upon the occurrence of a DTE event. Listing 11-17 shows the code for this class.

> **NOTE** *In the CkForRemindOfDefaultName method I keep a record of the files that have been passed to the method. I did this so that I will not display the reminder message every time the window is activated. That would be a little too annoying to developers. It will remind them once per instance of the IDE.*

You will notice that I am using the StringBuilder object at the beginning of the CkForRemindOfDefaultName method. The StringBuilder object is new to

Visual Basic .NET. It creates a mutable (changeable) string that can be appended to without having to recreate a new string as it does when you simply use a String variable. The StringBuilder object, sb, is created in the constructor of the CReminder class.

Listing 11-17. CReminder Class

```
Imports Microsoft.Office.Core
Imports Extensibility
Imports System.Runtime.InteropServices
Imports EnvDTE
Public Class CReminders
    Private DefaultName As String
    Private sb As System.Text.StringBuilder
    Private oVB As EnvDTE.DTE


    Public Sub CkForRemindOfDefaultName(ByVal winCaption As String)
        ' Display message to remind the developer to change
        ' the name of the file from the default name if they
        ' have not already done so.  However, don't do it but
        ' once per instance of the IDE.
        ' DefaultName is a string variable which simply contains
        ' the winCaption parameter concatenated with all previous
        ' names, separated by "_".

        ' if the name is extant in the string, don't put it
        ' there again or notify the user.
        If sb.ToString.IndexOf(winCaption) > -1 Then Exit Sub
        If (Left(winCaption, 4) = "Form" And _
            winCaption.EndsWith("[Design]")) Or _
            Left(winCaption, 6) = "Module" Or _
            Left(winCaption, 5) = "Class" _
            Then
            MsgBox(winCaption & " still has a default name;" & _
                vbLf & _
                "it should be changed to a more meaningful name.", _
                MsgBoxStyle.Exclamation, "Change Default Name")
            sb.Append(winCaption & "_")
        End If
    End Sub


    Public Sub ActivateTaskList()
        Dim win As Window = _
```

```
        oVB.Windows.Item(Constants.vsWindowKindTaskList)
      win.Activate()
      win.AutoHides = False
   End Sub
   Public Sub CkForClosingTaskList()
      Dim win As Window = ⏎
         oVB.Windows.Item(Constants.vsWindowKindTaskList)
      Dim tskList As TaskList = win.Object
      If tskList.TaskItems.Count = 0 Then
         win.AutoHides = True
      End If
      win.Activate()
   End Sub
   Public Sub New(ByVal roVB As EnvDTE.DTE)
      oVB = roVB
      sb = New System.Text.StringBuilder()
   End Sub
End Class
```

Summary

In this chapter you saw how to declare events, associate those events with event
handlers, and handle the various events of the integrated development environment (IDE) in an add-in. You also saw how to use the events to accomplish useful
functions upon the occurrence of specific events.

   In Chapter 12 you are going to take examples of all the features and potential
features discussed in Chapters 1 through 11 and put them together to build
a powerful add-in that you can use in your everyday development activities.

CHAPTER 12

Putting It Together: Let's Build a Real Add-in

"When you have to make a choice and don't make it, that is in itself a choice."
—*William James*

FOR 11 CHAPTERS, I have shown you how to develop various features in an add-in. You have seen code manipulation, control manipulation, window manipulation, and how to trap and respond to events that are raised in the IDE. In each subsequent chapter since Chapter 1, you have added some new feature that illustrated the subject described in that respective chapter. As you think back over all that has been covered, you may be wondering how to put all that you have learned together into one useful add-in. That is the purpose of this chapter.

In this chapter you'll create what I believe to be the best user interface (UI). In Chapter 7, I introduced several different methods for creating a UI, but I did not tell you which one I personally prefer. You'll draw on one of the methodologies that I've already shown you and introduce an additional feature that will make the UI truly appear to be part of the IDE.

You will incorporate most of the technology that you have explored and the features that you have developed into a new add-in. Additionally, I introduce new features that use the technology and methods I have shown you. This should give you seed thoughts for coming up with ideas of your own for features that you may develop in the future.

You will walk through the creation of a simple UserControl. Although this book is not on the subject of UserControls, I want to use one on the About box of the add-in for this chapter. Therefore, you will build a very simple UserControl so that you can see how easy the process is in Visual Basic .NET.

Where applicable and feasible, you will make the add-in work for any of the three currently installed .NET languages: Visual Basic, Visual C#, and Visual C++.

In addition to providing many features for the developer to use proactively, you will incorporate IDE event handling, described in Chapter 11, to implement the reminder features developed there. You will be adding new functionality in this area also.

Finally, you will attempt to modularize this new add-in and organize the code into classes that will promote ease of maintenance and enhancement in the future. Until this point, you have not been too concerned about that because you were covering new ground in each subsequent chapter. In this chapter you will use objects that you have already seen to build the final add-in of this book.

Creating the NET Desktop Add-in

As always, you will create the framework (Connect class) of the new add-in using the Add-in Wizard. Create the add-in with the name "NET Desktop." Do not have the wizard create a user interface menu item, and do not have it create an About box. You will be creating both of these manually in the add-in.

I will not describe the steps of the Add-in Wizard because I did that in detail in Chapter 2. You may refer back to that chapter if you have any questions about using the wizard. If you do not want to create this add-in as I describe it, you can simply open the add-in for this chapter from the book's code, which is provided in the Downloads section of the Apress Web site (http://www.apress.com).

Although you've seen the Connect class generated by the wizard numerous times before, Listing 12-1 shows it again. You can see from this listing that when you don't let the wizard create a user interface command, there's very little code generated by the wizard. The only changes I made were to shorten the name of the application object and place continuation marks so that the code would fit on the page. I've highlighted the changes to the application object in boldface font.

Listing 12-1. Connect Class for the NET Desktop Add-in

```
Imports Microsoft.Office.Core
imports Extensibility
imports System.Runtime.InteropServices
Imports EnvDTE


<GuidAttribute("F555EECD-3A41-4925-A564-75B2FC619333"), _
ProgIdAttribute("NetDesktop.Connect")> _
Public Class Connect

    Implements Extensibility.IDTExtensibility2


    Dim oVB As EnvDTE.DTE
    Dim addInInstance As EnvDTE.AddIn
```

```vb
Public Sub OnBeginShutdown(ByRef custom As System.Array) _
    Implements Extensibility.IDTExtensibility2.OnBeginShutdown
End Sub


Public Sub OnAddInsUpdate(ByRef custom As System.Array) _
    Implements Extensibility.IDTExtensibility2.OnAddInsUpdate
End Sub


Public Sub OnStartupComplete(ByRef custom As System.Array) _
    Implements Extensibility.IDTExtensibility2.OnStartupComplete
End Sub


Public Sub OnDisconnection(ByVal RemoveMode As _
    Extensibility.ext_DisconnectMode, _
    ByRef custom As System.Array) _
    Implements Extensibility.IDTExtensibility2.OnDisconnection
End Sub


Public Sub OnConnection(ByVal application As Object, _
    ByVal connectMode As Extensibility.ext_ConnectMode, _
    ByVal addInInst As Object, ByRef custom As System.Array) _
    Implements Extensibility.IDTExtensibility2.OnConnection

    oVB = CType(application, EnvDTE.DTE)
    addInInstance = CType(addInInst, EnvDTE.AddIn)
End Sub
End Class
```

Adding the User Interface

I am going to assume that you have either created a new add-in by now or that
you have opened the one that I have provided for you in the code for this chapter
that you can download from the Apress Web site (http://www.apress.com).

The first thing you'll want to do is add the user interface to the add-in. Recall
that I advised you not to have the Add-in Wizard create a user interface menu for
you. In Chapter 7, I said that I recommend using the Microsoft Office Command
object model rather than using the .NET-provided interface methods. I feel that
the Office model offers more flexibility and the commands are not stored in the
registry like the .NET commands are.

NOTE *Commands created through the .NET Command object are somehow stored in the registry. However, the methodology for storing them is not documented, and they are obviously encrypted or at least stored in Unicode format. Therefore, a search of the registry will not yield a find on any of the .NET commands. This makes them very difficult to locate, and if you are not careful, you will clutter the registry with these commands with no apparent way of cleaning them out of the registry. For that reason, I do not recommend their use unless your add-in needs only one or two menus.*

For the NET Desktop add-in you are moving away from the use of the TreeView control that you have used in previous add-ins. You are going to use the Office CommandBar and associated buttons for the top-level menu. You are going to use context pop-up menus for the drop-down menus for each major menu. You have to do this because the Office DropDown menu style from a tool button is not implemented for Visual Basic add-ins. However, I am going to show you how to make the Windows Forms perform as drop-down menus and appear just as they would if you were able to use the DropDown style.

NOTE *If you do not care for this fairly complex method of creating a user interface, I suggest that you use the Office menu controls shown in Chapter 7. You can add multilevel menus to the Tools menu by using the code presented in that chapter.*

In order to create this menu scheme, you must first decide how many tool buttons and submenus you are going to have. Obviously, as you add new functionality to an application, including an add-in, you will think of features that you did not design in at the inception of development. However, let's attempt to anticipate all of the features that this add-in will have up front, so that the initial user interface will accurately show the features you will have in the final add-in.

Setting Up the Toolbar

The NET Desktop add-in is going to have its own toolbar. The toolbar will have several tool buttons on it. Each tool button will have its own drop-down menu. To set up the toolbar, you will add some new code to the OnConnection method of the Connect class. This code will make calls on methods to create the toolbar and to add the tool buttons to the toolbar. Listing 12-2 shows the updated OnConnection method.

Several lines of code have been added to the method. This code, which is highlighted in boldface font, accomplishes the following things:

- Instantiates an instance of the CUserInterface class.

- Loads a form that has the images in it. It is immediately hidden because it is used only to retrieve images.

- Creates the toolbar by calling CreateOfficeToolBar.

- Creates the tool buttons by calling CreateOfficeToolBarButtons.

- Disposes of the image form as it is no longer needed and adds a call to the DoEvents method so that the form will have time to unload before execution resumes.

The frm referenced in the code in Listing 12-2 has been dimensioned in the declarations section of the Connect class with the following line of code:

```
Dim frm As New frmPictures()
```

Listing 12-2. OnConnection Method Updated to Create a Toolbar

```
Public Sub OnConnection(ByVal application As Object, _
    ByVal connectMode As Extensibility.ext_ConnectMode, _
    ByVal addInInst As Object, ByRef custom As System.Array) _
    Implements Extensibility.IDTExtensibility2.OnConnection

    oVB = CType(application, EnvDTE.DTE)
    addInInstance = CType(addInInst, EnvDTE.AddIn)
    Try
        oUI = New CUIToolbar()

        ' load the form with the pictures on it
        frm.Show()
        frm.Hide()
        System.Windows.Forms.Application.DoEvents()

        ' create the add-in's toolbar
        CreateOfficeToolBar()
```

```
                              ' Add the tool buttons to the add-in toolbar
                              CreateOfficeToolBarButtons()


                              ' don't need the form anymore, destroy it
                              frm.Dispose()


                      Catch e As System.Exception
                          MsgBox(e.Message)
                      End Try
                  End Sub
```

Listing 12-3 shows the code for the methods that create the toolbar and the associated tool buttons. These two methods will call methods of the CUserInterface class to do the actual calls to the Microsoft Office Command methods.

The CreateOfficeToolBar method will cause a completely new toolbar to be added to the IDE. This is called an *add-in toolbar*, and it will house the four tool buttons that will be created by the CreateOfficeToolBarButtons method.

Listing 12-3. Creating the Toolbar and Tool Buttons

```
Private Sub CreateOfficeToolBar()
    ' This method creates the office toolbar
    TBar = oUI.AddOfficeToolBar(oVB, _
                        "NETDesktopTBar", _
                        False)
End Sub
Private Sub CreateOfficeToolBarButtons()
    ' This method calls the low level method that
    ' adds the tool buttons to the toolbar
    ' The paired commands do two things.
    ' 1) create the toolbar or button
    ' 2) link the command event to the event handler.
    Try
        ' note that the bitmap can come from a variety
        ' of places.  Here it is pulled from an imagelist
        mcbComment = oUI.AddOfficeToolBarButton(oVB, _
            TBar, "Comment Menus", frm.ImageList1.Images(78))
        mnuCommentHandler = _
            CType(oVB.Events.CommandBarEvents(mcbComment), _
            EnvDTE.CommandBarEvents)
```

```
        mcbWindows = oUI.AddOfficeToolBarButton(oVB, _
            TBar, "Windows Menu", frm.ImageList1.Images(81))
        mnuWindowsHandler = _
            CType(oVB.Events.CommandBarEvents(mcbWindows), _
            EnvDTE.CommandBarEvents)

        mcbDesigner = oUI.AddOfficeToolBarButton(oVB, _
            TBar, "Designers", frm.ImageList1.Images(80))
        mnuDesignerHandler = _
            CType(oVB.Events.CommandBarEvents(mcbDesigner), _
            EnvDTE.CommandBarEvents)

        mcbSetupAbout = oUI.AddOfficeToolBarIconAndCaption(oVB, _
            TBar, "About NET Desktop", frm.ImageList1.Images(90))
        mnuSetupAboutHandler = _
            CType(oVB.Events.CommandBarEvents(mcbSetupAbout), _
            EnvDTE.CommandBarEvents)

    Catch e As System.Exception
        MsgBox(e.Message)
    End Try
End Sub
```

I have created two new classes that contain the methods for creating
Microsoft Office toolbars, tool buttons, menus, and pop-up menus. I have placed
the methods for creating toolbars and tool buttons in a class called CUIToolBar.
This class is shown in Listing 12-4. The CUIToolBar class has three methods. The
first method, AddOfficeToolBar, creates the add-in toolbar. The other two methods create the two different types of tool buttons used in this add-in. The three
icon buttons are created using the AddOfficeToolBarButton method. This
type of button contains an icon and displays a tool tip if the mouse pointer
is held over it. The fourth tool button is called an *icon and caption–type*
tool button. It not only displays an icon, but it also displays a caption. I like
to use this type of button to display the About box for the add-in. The
AddOfficeToolBarIconAndCaption method is used to create this type of tool
button.

Listing 12-4. CUIToolBar Class

```
Imports Microsoft.Office.Core
Imports Extensibility
Imports System.Runtime.InteropServices
Imports EnvDTE
Imports System.Windows.Forms
```

```vb
Public Class CUIToolBar
    Public Function AddOfficeToolBar(ByVal VBE As EnvDTE.DTE, _
        ByVal Caption As String, _
        Optional ByVal Floating As Boolean = False) _
        As Microsoft.Office.Core.CommandBar

        ' This method adds an office commandbar (toolbar) to
        ' the IDE.  It will become the container for command buttons.
        Dim Kind As Byte
        Dim toolBar As Microsoft.Office.Core.CommandBar

        Try

            ' Set parameter for pos argument:
            If Floating Then
                Kind = _
                    Microsoft.Office.Core.MsoBarPosition.msoBarFloating
            Else
                Kind = Microsoft.Office.Core.MsoBarPosition.msoBarTop
            End If

            ' Add custom toolbar and display it:
            toolBar = VBE.CommandBars.Add(Name:=Caption, _
                                    Position:=Kind, _
                                    Temporary:=True)
            toolBar.Visible = True
            Return toolBar
        Catch e As System.Exception
            Return toolBar
        End Try
    End Function

    Public Function AddOfficeToolBarButton(↵
        ByVal VBE As EnvDTE.DTE, _
        ByVal ToolBar As Microsoft.Office.Core.CommandBar, _
        ByVal Caption As String, _
        ByVal Bitmap As Object, _
        Optional ByVal pos As Byte = 0, _
        Optional ByVal sep As Boolean = False) _
        As Microsoft.Office.Core.CommandBarControl

        ' Variables:
        Dim cmdBtn As Microsoft.Office.Core.CommandBarControl
```

```
    Try
        If Caption = "" Or Bitmap Is Nothing Then Exit Function

        Clipboard.SetDataObject(Bitmap)

        ' Add button to Visual Studio IDE toolbar
        If pos = 0 Then pos = ToolBar.Controls.Count + 1
        cmdBtn = _
            ToolBar.Controls.Add(Type:=Microsoft.Office.Core. ↵
            MsoControlType.msoControlButton, _
                                    Before:=pos, _
                                    Temporary:=True)


        ' Set properties of button
        cmdBtn.Caption = Caption
        If sep Then cmdBtn.BeginGroup = True
        cmdBtn.Style = _
            Microsoft.Office.Core.MsoButtonStyle.msoButtonIcon
        cmdBtn.PasteFace()
        Return cmdBtn
    Catch e As System.Exception
        Return cmdBtn
    End Try
End Function


Public Function AddOfficeToolBarIconAndCaption(↵
    ByVal VBE As EnvDTE.DTE, _
    ByVal ToolBar As Microsoft.Office.Core.CommandBar, _
    ByVal Caption As String, _
    ByVal Bitmap As Object, _
    Optional ByVal pos As Byte = 0, _
    Optional ByVal sep As Boolean = False) _
    As Microsoft.Office.Core.CommandBarControl
    Dim cmdBtn As Microsoft.Office.Core.CommandBarControl
    Try
        If Caption = "" Or Bitmap Is Nothing Then Exit Function
        Clipboard.SetDataObject(Bitmap)
        ' Add button to VB toolbar:
        If pos = 0 Then pos = ToolBar.Controls.Count + 1
            cmdBtn = _
                ToolBar.Controls.Add(Type:=Microsoft.Office.Core. ↵
                MsoControlType.msoControlButton, _
                                    Before:=pos, _
                                    Temporary:=True)
```

```
                        ' Set properties of button:
                        cmdBtn.Caption = Caption
                        If sep Then cmdBtn.BeginGroup = True
                        cmdBtn.Style = _
                            Microsoft.Office.Core.MsoButtonStyle. ⤶
                            msoButtonIconAndCaption
                        cmdBtn.PasteFace()
                        Return cmdBtn
                    Catch e As System.Exception
                        Return cmdBtn
                    End Try
                End Function
            End Class
```

The methods to create Microsoft Office menus and pop-up menus will not be used in this add-in, and I do not show the code for them in this chapter. I have placed the code for creating these type menus in a class named CUIMenus. This class is in the add-in and you can view it in the code for this chapter that is available for download from the Apress Web site (http://www.apress.com).

Toolbar Event Handlers

In addition to declaring and associating event handlers for each of the tool buttons, you must also create the event handlers. Listing 12-5 shows the code for the event handlers. Although there are four tool buttons, there is only one event handler. You are able to handle all of the tool button Click events with one event handler because of the Handles keyword. Regardless of the tool button that is clicked, the mnuCommentHandler Click event will receive control. In this handler, you use a Select Case construct to determine which tool button was clicked by examining the CommandBarControl.Name property. This code will be placed at the end of the Connect class.

Listing 12-5. Tool Button Event Handler

```
    Private Sub mnuCommentHandler_Click(ByVal CommandBarControl As Object, _
        ByRef handled As Boolean, _
        ByRef CancelDefault As Boolean) _
        Handles mnuCommentHandler.Click, _
                mnuWindowsHandler.Click, _
                mnuDesignerHandler.Click, _
                mnuSetupAboutHandler.Click
        Dim oFH As New CMenuHandler()
```

```
    Try
        Select Case CommandBarControl.caption
            Case "Comment Menu"
                Dim oFRM As New frmComment(oVB)
                oFH.LoadMenuForm(oVB, mcbComment, oFRM)
            Case "Windows Menu"
                Dim oFRM As New frmWindowsMenu(oVB)
                oFH.LoadMenuForm(oVB, mcbWindows, ofrm)
            Case "Designers"
                Dim oFRM As New frmDesignerMenu(oVB)
                oFH.LoadMenuForm(oVB, mcbDesigner, ofrm)
            Case "About NET Desktop"
                Dim oFRM As New frmAbout(oVB)
                oFH.LoadMenuForm(oVB, mcbClone, oFRM)
        End Select
        handled = True
    Catch e As System.Exception
        MsgBox(e.Message)
    End Try
End Sub
```

Setting Up the Menus

I have shown you the code for creating the toolbar for the add-in, and for creating
the respective tool buttons and their event handlers. Now you are going to create
a set of menu forms that will be displayed when you click the respective tool
button.

> **NOTE** *You might think that you could use context menus, or
> PopupMenus as they were known in VB 6.0, but you can't.
> A context menu must be placed relative to a control on
> a Windows form. The Microsoft Office CommandBarControl
> does not meet that criterion, and therefore context menus
> cannot be used. Also, it is not possible to cast
> a CommandBarControl to a Windows form control.*

Comment Menu

Add a small form to the project and name it frmComment. This form will be
loaded when you click the Comment tool button. Figure 12-1 shows the Windows
Forms Designer with this newly designed form. To the form, add five Label controls that will be the menu items. Also add a Panel control between the fourth
and fifth labels to act as a separator. Finally, add a Timer control that will be used
to automatically unload (Dispose) the form.

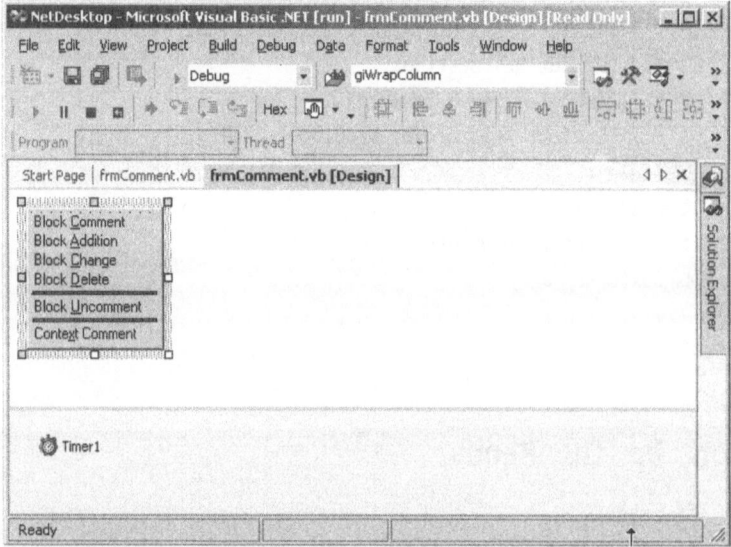

Figure 12-1. Comment menu form

Listing 12-6 shows the code for frmComment. I have deleted the Designer-
generated code that creates the form and its components for the sake of space.
You have seen this code before, and you can view it in the code for this chapter
that is available for download from the Apress Web site (http://www.apress.com)
if you want to see the details of how the components are being created.

Listing 12-6. Code for frmComment

```
Public Class frmComment
    Inherits System.Windows.Forms.Form
    Private miTimerStart As Integer
    Private miTimeToUnload As Short
#Region " Windows Form Designer generated code "
    Public Sub New()
        MyBase.New()
```

```
            'This call is required by the Windows Form Designer.
            InitializeComponent()

            'Add any initialization after the InitializeComponent() call
            miTimeToUnload = 5
            miTimerStart = Microsoft.VisualBasic.DateAndTime.Timer
            Me.Timer1.Interval = 500
            Me.Timer1.Enabled = True
        End Sub
    ' Code intentionally deleted by author
    #End Region

        Private Sub lblComment_MouseLeave(ByVal sender As Object, _
            ByVal e As System.EventArgs) _
            Handles lblComment.MouseLeave, _
                    lblAddition.MouseLeave, _
                    lblDelete.MouseLeave, _
                    lblChange.MouseLeave, _
                    lblUncomment.MouseLeave, _
                    lblContextComment.MouseLeave
            Dim ofh As New CMenuHandler()
            ofh.HandleMouseLeave(sender, miTimerStart, miTimeToUnload)
        End Sub

        Private Sub lblComment_Click(ByVal sender As Object, _
            ByVal e As System.EventArgs) _
            Handles lblComment.Click, _
                    lblAddition.Click, _
                    lblDelete.Click, _
                    lblChange.Click, _
                    lblUncomment.Click, _
                    lblContextComment.Click
            Dim lbl As System.Windows.Forms.Label
            Dim oCM As New CodeManipulation(oVB)
            lbl = CType(sender, System.Windows.Forms.Label)
            Me.Dispose()
            DoEvents()
            Select Case lbl.Name
                Case "lblComment"
                    oCM.BlockComment()
                Case "lblAddition"
                    oCM.BlockAddition()
                Case "lblDelete"
```

```vb
                oCM.BlockDelete()
            Case "lblChange"
                oCM.BlockChange()
            Case "lblUncomment"
                oCM.BlockUnComment()
            Case "lblContextComment"
                oCM.EnterContextComments()
        End Select
    End Sub


    Private Sub lblComment_MouseMove(ByVal sender As Object, _
        ByVal e As System.Windows.Forms.MouseEventArgs) _
        Handles lblComment.MouseMove, _
                lblAddition.MouseMove, _
                lblDelete.MouseMove, _
                lblChange.MouseMove, _
                lblUncomment.MouseMove, _
                lblContextComment.MouseMove
        Dim oMH As New CMenuHandler()
        oMH.HandleMouseMove(sender, miTimerStart, miTimeToUnload)
    End Sub


    Private Sub Timer1_Tick(ByVal sender As Object, _
        ByVal e As System.EventArgs) Handles Timer1.Tick
        If Microsoft.VisualBasic.DateAndTime.Timer - miTimerStart > _
            miTimeToUnload Then
            Me.Dispose()
        End If
    End Sub


    Private Sub frmComment_MouseMove(ByVal sender As Object, _
        ByVal e As System.Windows.Forms.MouseEventArgs) _
        Handles MyBase.MouseMove
        miTimerStart = Microsoft.VisualBasic.DateAndTime.Timer
        miTimeToUnload = 30
    End Sub


    Private Sub frmComment_MouseLeave(ByVal sender As Object, _
        ByVal e As System.EventArgs) _
        Handles MyBase.MouseLeave
        miTimerStart = Microsoft.VisualBasic.DateAndTime.Timer
        miTimeToUnload = 0.5
    End Sub
```

```
    Private Sub Panel1_MouseLeave(ByVal sender As Object, _
        ByVal e As System.EventArgs) _
        Handles Panel1.MouseLeave, _
                Panel2.MouseLeave
        miTimerStart = Microsoft.VisualBasic.DateAndTime.Timer
        miTimeToUnload = 0.5
    End Sub

    Private Sub Panel1_MouseMove(ByVal sender As Object, _
        ByVal e As System.Windows.Forms.MouseEventArgs) _
        Handles Panel1.MouseMove, _
                Panel2.MouseMove
        miTimerStart = Microsoft.VisualBasic.DateAndTime.Timer
        miTimeToUnload = 30
    End Sub
End Class
```

I have left the code for the form constructor (New) in the listing because I needed to add some code to it. At the top of the class, I have added two module-level variables. They are highlighted in boldface font. The two variables are used to tell the Timer_Tick event when to unload the form in case the user does not click a menu item.

Basically, the way the form works is as follows. When the form loads, the timer is set to automatically unload in 5 seconds if the user does not move the mouse pointer over the form. This means that the user has 5 seconds to move the mouse over the Comment menu or it will be automatically unloaded. It is a logical assumption that the user will normally move fairly quickly down a menu once it drops down.

Once the mouse pointer moves over a Label control, the MouseMove event will fire. You can see by examining the MouseMove event that it instantiates an instance of the CMenuHandler class. It then calls the HandleMouseMove method of the class. This will cause the Label control (menu item) to be highlighted. It also causes the timer to be reset to allow the user another 30 seconds to click a menu item.

This CMenuHandler class basically handles highlighting and unhighlighting the menus as the user moves from one item to the next. The CMenuHandler class is shown in Listing 12-7. At that point I will describe its operation.

As the user moves the pointer from one menu item to the next, the MouseLeave event will fire. This causes the Label control (menu item) to be unhighlighted. It also causes the timer to be set to unload the form in 1 second. In case the user moves the mouse off of the menu form completely, it will be unloaded almost immediately. However, if the user simply moves from one menu item to the next, the form will be displayed indefinitely or until the user clicks one of the menu items. At that point, the menu form is unloaded immediately and the desired feature is invoked to perform the functionality desired by the user.

You will notice that the MouseMove and MouseLeave events have Handles clauses that list all five Label names associated with their MouseMove and MouseLeave events. Visual Basic .NET does not allow control arrays, as did Visual Basic 6.0. Therefore, the event handler does not receive an Index to denote which control is forcing the event to fire. However, Visual Basic .NET provides the Handles keyword, which allows you to delegate the events of multiple controls to one event handler. This essentially replaces the control array for event handling.

You do the same thing in the Click event. You use the Handles keyword to list all of the menu item events so that the one handler event can process the event regardless of which control was clicked. You then cast the Sender object to a Label control so that you can retrieve the name of the label that was clicked. At this point, it is simple to use the name in a Select Case construct to determine which feature to invoke.

In the Click event, you instantiate an instance of the CodeManipulation class. You created this class in Chapter 10. It contains all of the methods for commenting and uncommenting code blocks. One of its methods will be called based on the outcome of the Select Case construct.

> **NOTE** *You can see the CodeManipulation class in the code for this chapter that is available for download from the Apress Web site (*http://www.apress.com*), but I do not show it in this chapter in order to save space. Also note that the Utilities class is instantiated by the CodeManipulation class. That class was also created in Chapter 10 and is included with the code for this chapter that is available for download from the Apress Web site. I do not show it in this chapter in order to save space.*

CMenuHandler Class

The code for the CMenuHandler class is shown in Listing 12-7. The event handlers of frmComment call the methods of this class. The other menu forms that will be created to display the menus for the remaining tool buttons will also call these methods.

Listing 12-7. CMenuHandler Class

```vb
Imports System.Runtime.InteropServices
Imports EnvDTE
Imports System.Windows.Forms
Public Class CMenuHandler
    Public Sub LoadMenuForm(ByRef oVB As EnvDTE.DTE, _
        ByVal btn As Microsoft.Office.Core.CommandBarControl, ByVal oFrm As Form)
        Dim x As Integer
        Dim y As Integer

        x = btn.Left
        y = btn.Top + btn.Height
        oFrm.Visible = False
        oFrm.Show()
        oFrm.Left = x
        oFrm.Top = y
        oFrm.Visible = True
        oFrm.TopMost = True
        System.Windows.Forms.Application.DoEvents()
    End Sub
    Public Sub HandleMouseMove(ByVal Sender As Object, _
                            ByRef TimerStart As Integer, _
                            ByRef TimeToUnload As Short)
        Dim lbl As System.Windows.Forms.Label
        lbl = CType(Sender, System.Windows.Forms.Label)
        lbl.ForeColor = System.Drawing.SystemColors.Window
        lbl.BackColor = System.Drawing.SystemColors.ActiveCaption
        TimerStart = Microsoft.VisualBasic.DateAndTime.Timer
        TimeToUnload = 30
    End Sub
    Public Sub HandleMouseLeave(ByVal Sender As Object, _
                            ByRef TimerStart As Integer, _
                            ByRef TimeToUnload As Short)
        Dim lbl As System.Windows.Forms.Label
        lbl = CType(Sender, System.Windows.Forms.Label)
        lbl.BackColor = System.Drawing.SystemColors.Control
        lbl.ForeColor = System.Drawing.SystemColors.WindowText
        TimerStart = Microsoft.VisualBasic.DateAndTime.Timer
        TimeToUnload = 1
    End Sub
End Class
```

The CMenuHandler class has three methods. The first one, LoadMenuForm, is called to load the specified form. Thus far, I have only shown you frmComment and its menu items. I list the other two forms and describe their respective menus, but in order to save space I do not show you the code for each individual form. They will all work essentially the same as frmComment. In LoadMenuForm you have to compute where to load the form to make it look like a menu that has dropped down from the selected tool button. It is a very simple computation based on the position of the specified button that was clicked. Notice that the TopMost property of the form is set to True. This will cause the menu form to stay on top of the IDE.

The MouseMove method is used to highlight the menu that the mouse is positioned over. It also sets the timer to allow another 30 seconds before auto-matically unloading the form. Consequently, each time the mouse is moved over a menu, you guarantee that you have at least 30 more seconds to make a decision about the option to select.

The MouseLeave method is used to return the unselected menu to its default colors and to tell the timer to unload the form in 1 second. Because the Label controls are set against each other, the MouseLeave method is followed immedi-ately by the MouseMove event. If the user is moving the mouse pointer up or down on the menu form, the form will remain displayed indefinitely.

NOTE *The form must have a timer on it because it will not go away if the user simply clicks somewhere else on the screen, as would a context menu. There is another way to cause the form to go away without the timer: You would have to use an API to capture mouse clicks. If the user clicked away the menu form, you could check the coordinates and upon find-ing that the mouse click was not within the form, you could unload the form and then use another API to release control of the mouse. I will leave you with that task if you desire to take it to that point.*

Using the Comment Menu

Before you create the other menu forms, run the add-in to show the new toolbar and the first drop-down menu form. If you have done your job well, the form will have the look and feel of a real drop-down menu. Figure 12-2 shows the first menu displayed after I clicked the Comment tool button. You will see that I have also selected a block of code to comment.

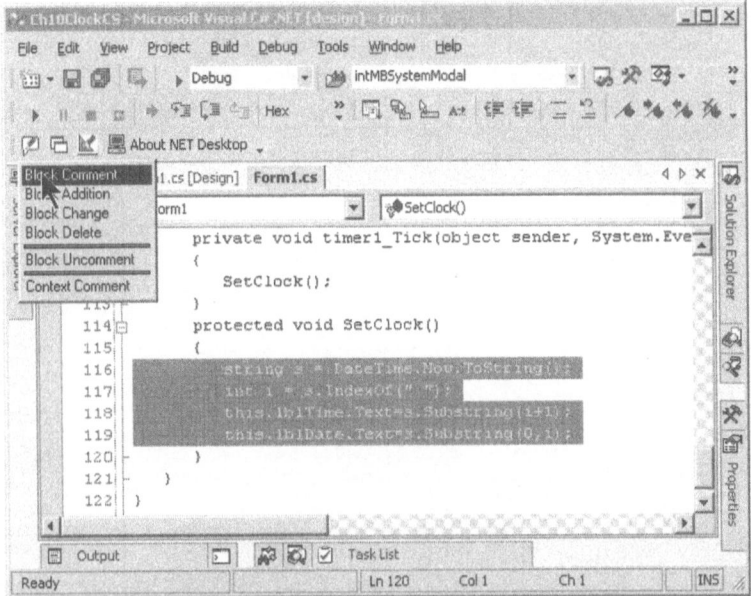

Figure 12-2. Displaying the Comment menu form

Next, I have clicked the Block Comment option to comment the selected block of code. Figure 12-3 shows that the menu form has been unloaded and the selected block of code has been commented.

> **NOTE** *This add-in is sensitive to the type of language in which the user is developing. Remember that the add-in itself is written in Visual Basic, but the application that currently has the add-in connected is being developed in C#. Therefore, the commenting that is shown is done using the C# comment characters.*

In Chapters 3 and 5 you saw most of the commenting features, so I will not bore you with the code for them or with more figures showing those features being executed. You can view the code for the chapter and see all of the code for those features. You can find them all in the CodeManipulation class.

However, I have added a new commenting feature called Context Comment. You can see the menu item at the bottom of the Comment menu in Figure 12-2. I discuss that feature in the following section.

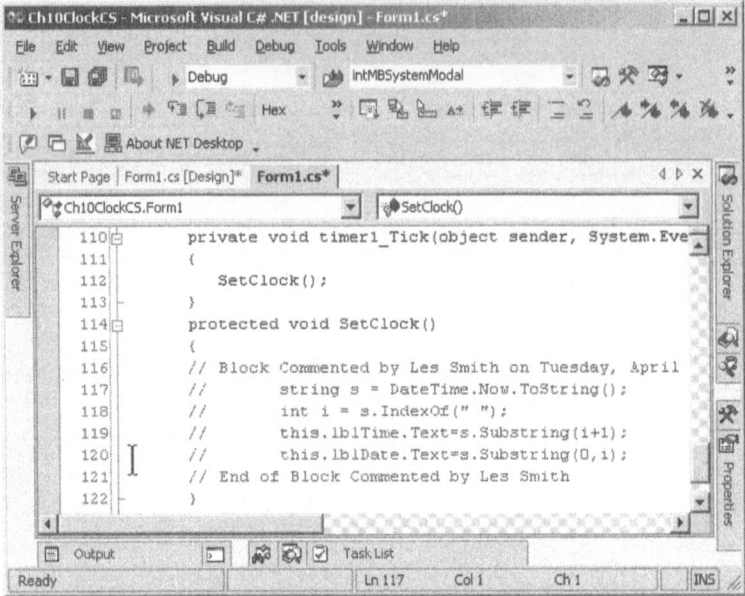

Figure 12-3. The selected block has been commented.

Context Comment Feature

Many times you encounter situations where you have comments in the code of a procedure and you find that you need to change the comments. It is always a hassle to change, delete, and insert words and lines into a block of comments and have them come out looking like they were originally composed in just one sitting. The Context Comment feature is designed to allow you to write a block of comments and insert them into the code. They will be word wrapped so that they are nicely formatted, and you can select the length of the comment lines. At a later time, when you need to change them, you can simply select them and bring them into a mini-editor. When you finish your changes and save the comments back to the code, they will look just like you entered them for the first time and you did it with a smart editor.

To create such a feature, two separate areas of code are involved. I have placed a new method in the CodeManipulation class named EnterContextComments. Listing 12-8 shows the code for this new method. This method uses several of the methods of the Utilities class, and there is no need to explain them again.

Listing 12-8. EnterContextComments Method

```
Public Sub EnterContextComments()
      Dim sCC As String
      Dim l As Long
      Dim sText As String
      Dim liCnt As Integer
      Dim lsLine As String
      Dim iNL As Integer
      Dim sOUT As String
      Dim i As Long
      Dim oUtil As New Utilities(oVB)
      Dim iFT As Integer

      iFT = oUtil.GetFileType(oVB.ActiveDocument)
      sOUT = ""
      sText = oUtil.GetCodeFromWindow()
      Dim oFrm As New frmGetComments(oVB)
      sText = oFrm.Display("Enter Context Comments", sText)
      If sText = "" Then Exit Sub

      iNL = oUtil.MLCount(sText, Connect.giWrapColumn)
      For i = 1 To iNL
          lsLine = oUtil.MemoLine(sText, Connect.giWrapColumn, i)
          If iFT = 8 Then ' vb
              If oUtil.LastLineWrapped Then
                  sOUT.Append("'`" & " " & lsLine & vbCrLf)
              Else
                  sOUT.Append("''" & " " & lsLine & vbCrLf)
              End If
          Else
              If oUtil.LastLineWrapped Then
                  sOUT.Append("//`" & " " & lsLine & vbCrLf)
              Else
                  sOUT.Append("//'" & " " & lsLine & vbCrLf)
              End If
          End If
      Next i
      oUtil.PutCodeBack(sOUT.ToString())
   End Sub
```

The EnterContextComments method calls the Display method of a new
form, frmGetComments. This form is shown in use in Figure 12-4. You will also

notice that the code is appending either ' ' or ' ` to the front of the lines as they are put into the output string. If the code editor contains C# or C++ code, then you see that I am appending //' or //` to the front of the lines. I explain this in more detail later, but suffice it to say that these varying character pairs tell frmGetComments whether or not the lines were word wrapped the next time they are picked up for editing.

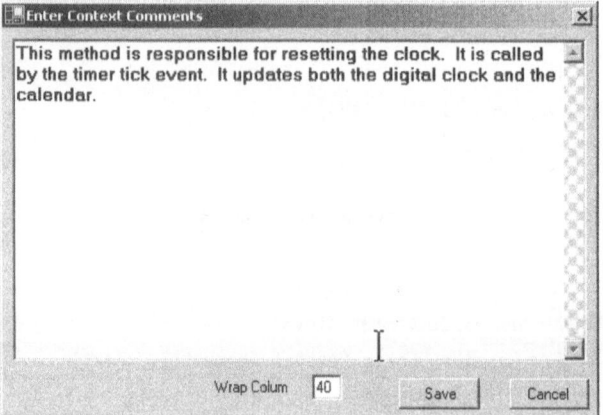

Figure 12-4. Entering context comments

You can see that the form allows you to enter any amount of comments. You can also set a new line length for word wrapping the lines. If you set a new length, it will be saved in the registry and will be the default the next time that you use the form.

Figure 12-5 shows the comments in the code editor after they have been saved. You should simply place the cursor in the left margin at the point where you want to insert the new comments when you are inserting comments. If you want to change a set of existing comments, you should select that block of comments and click the Context Comment menu item.

NOTE   *The Context Comment feature can also handle the Visual Basic, C#, and C++ languages. This comment is placed into a Visual Basic code editor.*

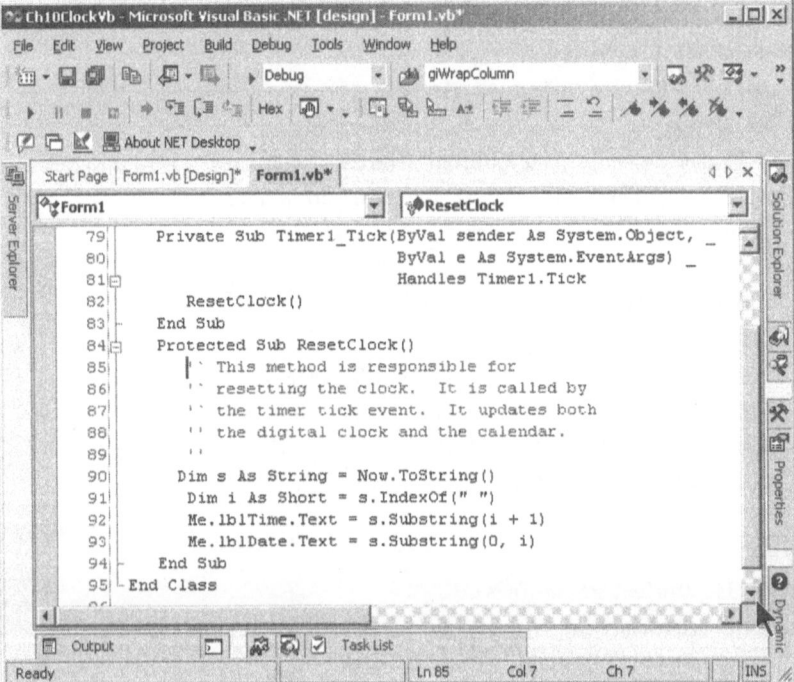

Figure 12-5. Inserted context comments

You will see that there are differing comment characters at the beginning of the comments. I have invented this sequence to tell me whether a line is word wrapped or not. If a line is preceded by '' (two single quotes), it denotes that the line is not word wrapped. In other words, it is terminated by a carriage return and line feed. If the line is preceded by ' ` (a single quote followed by a backward quote), it denotes that the line is word wrapped and the code will concatenate that line to the next line before placing it into the text box in frmGetComments. The two sets of comment characters look so much alike that they should not be a hindrance to reading in the code, and they provide the needed switch to tell the code whether the lines were originally word wrapped or not.

I will not show all of the code for frmGetComments. You can see that code in the code available for download from the Apress Web site (http://www.apress.com). However, I will show the code for the Display method of the form so that you can see how the varying comment characters are being used to "reverse engineer" the word wrapping. Listing 12-9 shows the code for the Display method.

413

Listing 12-9. Display Method of frmGetComments

```vbnet
Public Function Display(ByVal s As String, _
    Optional ByVal sOldText As String = "") _
    As String
    ' If old comments is populated, then if there are
    ' "'`" continuation marks at the start of a line,
    ' concatenate the next line to this one.
    Dim iNL As Long
    Dim i As Long
    Dim sLine As String
    Dim sLine2 As New System.Text.StringBuilder()
    Dim sIn As New System.Text.StringBuilder()
    Dim oUtil As New Utilities(oVB)
    Dim sCmtChars As String

    Try
        If sOldText <> "" Then
            sCmtChars = _
                oUtil.GetCommentCharForDoc(oVB.ActiveDocument)
            iNL = oUtil.MLCount(sOldText, 0)
            For i = 1 To iNL
                sLine = Trim(oUtil.MemoLine(sOldText, 0, i))
                If sLine.StartsWith("'` ") Then
                    ' we have a continuation line so concatenate
                    ' the next line to this one
                    sLine2.Append(Mid(sLine, 4) & " ")
                ElseIf sLine.StartsWith("//` ") Then
                    ' we have a c type continued comment
                    sLine2.Append(Mid(sLine, 5) & " ")
                ElseIf sLine.StartsWith("'' ") Then
                    sIn.Append(sLine2.ToString() & _
                        Mid(sLine, 4) & vbCrLf)
                    sLine2.Remove(0, sLine2.Length)
                ElseIf sLine.StartsWith("//' ") Then
                    sIn.Append(sLine2.ToString() & _
                        Mid(sLine, 5) & vbCrLf)
                    sLine2.Remove(0, sLine2.Length)
                ElseIf sLine.StartsWith("''") Or _
                    sLine.StartsWith("'`") Then
                    sIn.Append(sLine2.ToString() & _
                        Mid(sLine, 3) & vbCrLf)
                ElseIf sLine.StartsWith("//'") Or _
```

```
                sLine.StartsWith("//`") Then
                sIn.Append(sLine2.ToString() & _
                    Mid(sLine, 4) & vbCrLf)
            ElseIf sLine.StartsWith(sCmtChars & " ") Then
                sIn.Append(Replace(sLine, _
                    sCmtChars & " ", "") & vbCrLf)
            ElseIf sLine.StartsWith(sCmtChars) Then
                sIn.Append(Replace(sLine, _
                    sCmtChars, "") & vbCrLf)
            Else
                sIn.Append(sLine & vbCrLf)
            End If
        Next i
        sOldText = sIn.ToString()
    End If
    mbWait = True
    msComments = ""
    mbDirty = False
    Me.Text = s
    Me.txtEnterComments.Text = sOldText
    Me.Show()
    Do While mbWait
        System.Windows.Forms.Application.DoEvents()
    Loop
    Return msComments
Catch e As System.Exception
    MsgBox(e.Message)
End Try
End Function
```

Summary of the Remaining Menus

Let's now move on to creating the other menu forms. Although I do not go into the details of creating all of the forms in the Windows Forms Designer, I do show you the code that is called by them to perform the selected functionality. Most of that code is new.

Because you have seen the frmComment form and its code, you now know how all of the menu forms will work. Only the number and names of the menu items (Label controls) will change, along with the classes and methods that will be called to perform the selected functionality. In other words, once you have seen one of the menu forms in the Windows Forms Designer and the code behind the form, you basically have seen them all.

You will create two more menu forms and the classes or forms that will support them. In this section, I describe the functionality that will be provided by these menus. Most of these menus do not have a large number of features, and one of them has only one feature. This add-in is not only meant to be demonstration of all of the functionality that you have learned, but you can also use it as a skeleton for adding many more features that you would like to see in the add-in.

Windows Menu

This menu will have five items on it that will manipulate windows in the IDE. This menu allows for manipulation of windows in the IDE that are not normally available to the developer. For example, it is not unusual—especially if you have a large monitor, say 19" or 21"—to have many windows open in the IDE. It is really helpful if you can close them all with one click of the mouse. This menu allows you to do that and other things. These five items should spark some creative nerves in your mind and cause you to want to add more features to this particular menu. Table 12-1 gives the names and description of these menu items.

Table 12-1. Windows Menu Items

MENU ITEM	DESCRIPTION
Close And Save All	Closes all Designer and Editor windows. Saves any windows not currently saved.
Close All Saved	Closes all designer and editor windows that are currently saved.
Close And Save (Prompt)	Closes all windows and prompts the user to save if the window is not saved already.
Closes All But Current	Closes all but the currently active window.
Backup Current Window	Makes a backup copy of the active window with a name of fullname.ext.bak.

These menu items will perform their respective functions through the methods of the CWindows class. Listing 12-10 shows this class. Figure 12-6 shows the design of the frmWindowsMenu form.

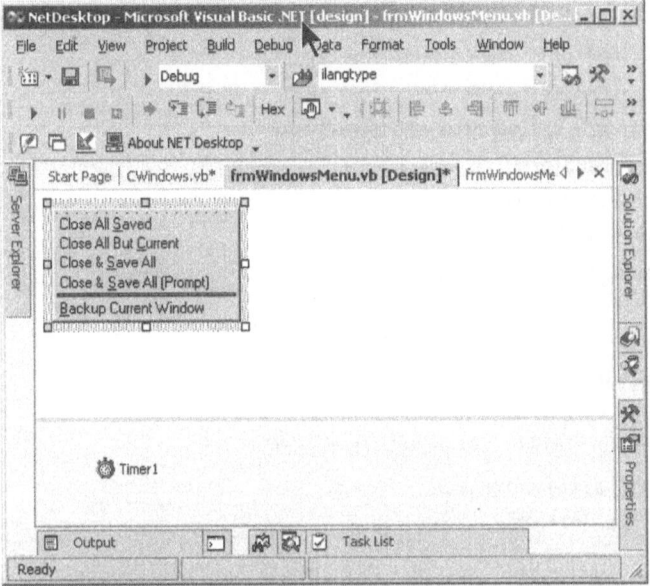

Figure 12-6. The frmWindowsMenu form

The Click events of the frmWindowsMenu will call a method of the CWindows class to perform the desired functionality. Listing 12-10 shows the code for the CWindows class.

TIP *The best way to develop code such as that shown in the CWindows class is to just experiment in the Macros IDE. You will be amazed at the things you can learn by looking through the sample macros and MSDN. Just copy the code from MSDN that you want to test and run it in the Macros IDE. If it doesn't seem to work, as is often the case with MSDN code, keep on playing with it until you figure it out. That will give you a sense of accomplishment when you get some code to work that did not work as it was shown in MSDN. I'm not being critical of MSDN—it is massive, and to expect every code example to work perfectly might be a little optimistic, to say the least.*

Listing 12-10. CWindows Class

```
' This class contains the methods for closing
' and saving windows in the IDE.
' Its methods are called from the frmWindowsMenus
' click event handlers.
Imports Microsoft.Office.Core
Imports Extensibility
Imports System.Runtime.InteropServices
Imports EnvDTE

Public Class CWindows
    Public oVB As DTE
    Public Sub CloseAndSaveWindowsWithPrompt()
        ' Close all documents.
        Dim i As Integer

        With oVB
            For i = .Documents.Count To 1 Step -1
                ' ignore any erors we may encounter in closing a window
                ' so that we continue to next window
                On Error Resume Next
                .Documents.Item(i).Close(vsSaveChanges⏎
                    .vsSaveChangesPrompt)
                Err.Clear()
            Next i
        End With
    End Sub
    Public Sub CloseAndSaveWindows()
        ' Close all documents.
        Dim i As Integer

        With oVB
            For i = .Documents.Count To 1 Step -1
                ' ignore any erors we may encounter in closing a window
                ' so that we continue to next window
                On Error Resume Next
                .Documents.Item(i).Close(vsSaveChanges.⏎
                    vsSaveChangesYes)
                Err.Clear()
            Next i
        End With
    End Sub
```

```vb
Public Sub CloseAllButCurrentWindow()
    Dim i As Integer
    Dim sCurrWin As String = oVB.ActiveDocument.Name

    Debug.WriteLine(sCurrWin)
    With oVB
        On Error Resume Next
        For i = .Documents.Count To 1 Step -1
            If .Documents.Item(i).Name <> sCurrWin Then
                If Not .Documents.Item(i).Saved Then
                    .Documents.Item(i).Close(vsSaveChanges. ↵
                        vsSaveChangesYes)
                Else
                    .Documents.Item(i).Close(vsSaveChanges. ↵
                        vsSaveChangesNo)
                End If
            End If
        Next
    End With
End Sub
Public Sub CloseAllSavedWindows()
    ' Close all saved documents.
    Dim i As Integer

    With oVB
        On Error Resume Next
        For i = .Documents.Count To 1 Step -1
            If .Documents.Item(i).Saved Then
                .Documents.Item(i).Close(vsSaveChanges. ↵
                    vsSaveChangesPrompt)
            End If
        Next i
    End With
End Sub
Public Sub New(ByVal roVB As DTE)
    oVB = roVB
End Sub
Sub BackupCurrentWindow()
    '` This method will make a backup copy of
    '` the active window.  It will be saved as
    '` fullname.bak.  For example a .vb file
    '` will be saved as name.vb.bak.  The file
    '` will be saved and closed.  It will not
```

```
'' be added to the project.
Dim Sel As TextSelection = oVB.ActiveDocument.Selection
Dim sFileName As String = oVB.ActiveDocument.↵
    FullName & ".bak"
Dim epAnchor As EditPoint = Sel.AnchorPoint.CreateEditPoint
Dim epActive As EditPoint = Sel.ActivePoint.CreateEditPoint
Dim txtWin As TextWindow = oVB.ActiveWindow.Object
Dim actPane As TextPane = txtWin.ActivePane
Dim Corner As EditPoint = actPane.StartPoint.CreateEditPoint
Dim Text As String

Sel.SelectAll()
Text = Sel.Text

' Create, save, and close the backup copy of
' the current window
oVB.ItemOperations.NewFile("General\Text File")
oVB.ActiveDocument.Object("TextDocument").↵
    Selection.Insert(Text)
oVB.ActiveDocument.Save(sFileName)
oVB.ActiveDocument.Close(EnvDTE.↵
    vsSaveChanges.vsSaveChangesNo)

' Restore the selection.
Sel.MoveToPoint(epAnchor)
Sel.MoveToPoint(epActive, True)
actPane.TryToShow(Corner, vsPaneShowHow.vsPaneShowTop)
    End Sub
End Class
```

Designer Menu

I have only placed one menu item on the Designer menu form. I expect you to come up with others yourself. I certainly have several in mind, but for the sake of space (and to hopefully get you to look at the .NET version of VBCommander) I do not go any further.

Anyone can write a simple message box command. However, when you start to ask lengthy questions, use different icons, use two or more buttons, and then want to take action on the return from the message box, a designer would be nice. You have probably seen message box designers before. VBCommander has a nice one, even if I did write it. I have converted that feature from VB 6.0 to Visual Basic .NET. Additionally, I have added the capability to handle multiple languages in the generated code. To get the designer started, I needed to create a rather involved form, which is shown in Figure 12-7.

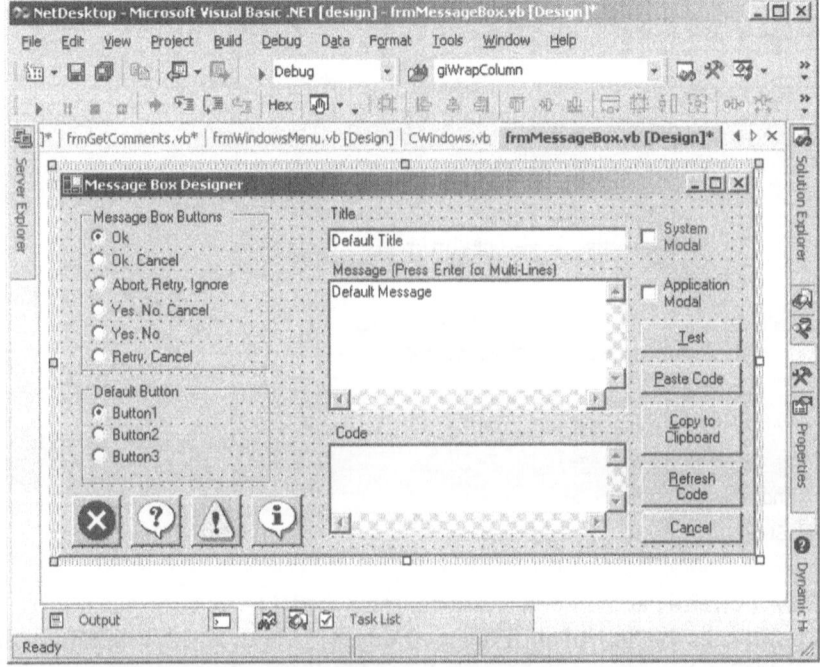

Figure 12-7. MessageBox Designer form

As you can see from the design of the form, the user enters a title and a message. The message can be as long as needed, within reason of course. This type of designer allows the user to place the text of the message box as he or she desires rather than counting on how wide Windows might want to make the message box. Remember that message boxes are an important part of the user interface also.

You can choose the number and type of buttons. If you select any choice other than the OK button, you will receive a return response from the message box. You can choose the icon that you want to display and you can even make the display application or system modal.

Once you have input your message and title and selected the desired options, you can test the message box, view the code that will be generated, copy the code to the Clipboard, or paste the code to the active code editor. I do not show all of the code for the creation of the form here—it is obviously quite lengthy. I do show you the code for the button Click event for pasting the code to the editor in Listing 12-11. You can see that the event code tests to see which type of code is to be generated based on the type of the currently active code window.

Listing 12-11. Button Paste Code Click Event

```
Private Sub btnPasteCode_Click(ByVal sender As System.Object, _
    ByVal e As System.EventArgs) Handles btnPasteCode.Click
    Dim strMBPaintMsg As String
    Dim s As String

    Try
        If iLangType = 8 Then
            strMBPaintMsg = SetUpPaintProc()
        Else
            strMBPaintMsg = SetUpPaintProcForCLang()
        End If

        oUtil.PutCodeBack(strMBPaintMsg)
        Me.Dispose()
    Catch ee As System.Exception
        MsgBox(ee.Message)
    End Try
End Sub
```

If the currently active code editor contains Visual Basic code, the button Click event calls the SetUpPaintProc method (see Listing 12-12) to generate the appropriate code and paste it back to the code editor.

NOTE   *You will see in this method and several others that I am making good use of the StringBuilder object. This object is new to Visual Basic .NET. You should use it for several reasons. It is faster than string concatenation because it does not have to create a new object each and every time you append more characters to the object. If you simply concatenate to a String object, as you had to do in earlier versions of Visual Basic, the old copy of the string is discarded and a new object is created to contain the newly appended characters. You will see the use of the Remove method of the StringBuilder object. Note that the object is zero based and that you must specify the character 0 as the beginning character when you want to remove all characters from the object.*

Listing 12-12. SetUpPaintProc Method

```
Private Function SetUpPaintProc() As String
    Dim intNL As Integer
    Dim i As Integer
    Dim strTemp As String
    Dim strTemp2 As String
    Dim iDefault As Integer
    Dim strM As New StringBuilder()
    Dim oUtil As New Utilities(oVB)

    If strMBType = "F" Then
        strM.Append("Dim sMsg as string" & vbCrLf)
        strM.Append("Dim iRV as integer" & vbCrLf)
    Else
        strM.Append("Dim sMsg as string" & vbCrLf)
    End If

    strTemp = CStr(txtMessage.Text)
    intNL = oUtil.MLCount(strTemp, 0)

    ' we have to build msg lines
    For i = 1 To intNL
        strTemp2 = oUtil.MemoLine(strTemp, 0, i)

        If i = 1 Then
            strM.Append("sMsg = " & Chr(34) & strTemp2 & Chr(34))
        Else
            strM.Append("sMsg = sMsg & " & Chr(34) & _
                    strTemp2 & Chr(34))
        End If

        ' If last line
        If intNL = 1 Then
            strM.Append(vbCrLf)
        ElseIf i < intNL Then
            strM.Append(" & Chr(10)" & vbCrLf)
        ElseIf i = intNL Then
            strM.Append(vbCrLf)
        End If
    Next i
```

```vb
' now build the options
If rbButton1.Checked Then
    iDefault = CType(vbDefaultButton1, Integer)
ElseIf rbButton2.Checked Then
    iDefault = CType(vbDefaultButton2, Integer)
Else
    iDefault = CType(vbDefaultButton3, Integer)
End If

strTemp = Format$(intMBOptions + _
    iDefault + _
    intMBSystemModal + _
    CType(IIf(intMBSystemModal = 0, intMBIcon, 0), _
        Integer), "####")
If Trim(strTemp) = "" Then
    strTemp = "0"
End If

' now build the MsgBox call
If strMBType = "S" Then
    ' build a statement
    strM.Append("MsgBox sMsg, " & strTemp & ", ")
    strM.Append(Chr(34) & Trim(CStr(txtTitle.Text)) & ⤸
        Chr(34) & vbCrLf & vbCrLf)
Else
    ' build a function call
    strM.Append("iRV = MsgBox(sMsg, " & strTemp & ", ")
    strM.Append(Chr(34) & Trim(CStr(txtTitle.Text)) & ⤸
        Chr(34) & ")" & vbCrLf)
    strM.Append(vbCrLf)

    ' now set up the analysis code
    Select Case intMBOptions
        Case 0
            ' Ok button
        Case 1
            ' OkCancel
            strM.Append("If iRV = 1 Then" & vbCrLf)
            strM.Append("    ' Ok Code goes here" & vbCrLf)
            strM.Append("Else" & vbCrLf)
            strM.Append("    ' Cancel code goes here" & vbCrLf)
            strM.Append("End If" & vbCrLf)
```

```
        Case 2
            ' Abort, Retry, Ignore
            strM.Append("If iRV = 3 Then" & vbCrLf)
            strM.Append("   ' Abort Code goes here" & vbCrLf)
            strM.Append("ElseIf iRV = 4 Then" & vbCrLf)
            strM.Append("   ' Retry code goes here" & vbCrLf)
            strM.Append("Else" & vbCrLf)
            strM.Append("   ' Cancel code goes here" & vbCrLf)
            strM.Append("End If" & vbCrLf)
        Case 3
            ' Yes, No, Cancel
            strM.Append("If iRV = 6 Then" & vbCrLf)
            strM.Append("   ' Yes Code goes here" & vbCrLf)
            strM.Append("ElseIf iRV = 7 Then" & vbCrLf)
            strM.Append("   ' No code goes here" & vbCrLf)
            strM.Append("Else" & vbCrLf)
            strM.Append("   ' Cancel code goes here" & vbCrLf)
            strM.Append("End If" & vbCrLf)
        Case 4
            ' YesNo
            strM.Append("If iRV = 6 Then" & vbCrLf)
            strM.Append("   ' Yes Code goes here" & vbCrLf)
            strM.Append("Else" & vbCrLf)
            strM.Append("   ' No code goes here" & vbCrLf)
            strM.Append("End If" & vbCrLf)
        Case 5
            ' RetryCancel
            strM.Append("If iRV = 4 Then" & vbCrLf)
            strM.Append("   ' Retry Code goes here" & vbCrLf)
            strM.Append("Else" & vbCrLf)
            strM.Append("   ' Cancel code goes here" & vbCrLf)
            strM.Append("End If" & vbCrLf)
        End Select
    End If
    Return strM.ToString
End Function
```

If you execute the MessageBox Designer, you will see it displayed as shown in Figure 12-8. There I have filled in a message and shown the code. It is ready to be pasted back to the form.

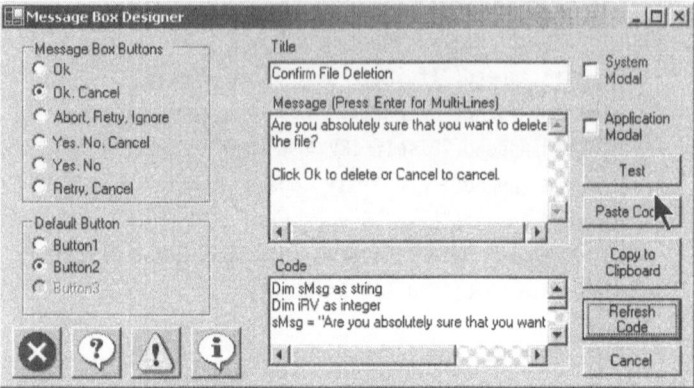

Figure 12-8. The MessageBox Designer in action

In Figure 12-9 you will see the Visual Basic code for displaying the message box pasted to the editor. You will see that the MessageBox Designer also generated code for taking action based on the return from the message box.

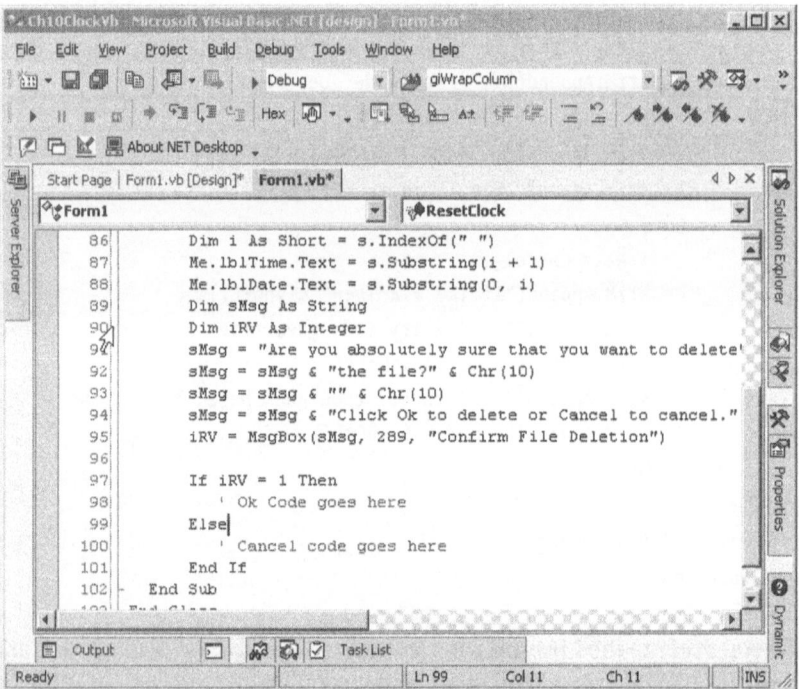

Figure 12-9. MessageBox Designer–generated Visual Basic code

One of the options of the MessageBox Designer is to allow you to test the MessageBox before you paste the generated code into the code editor. Figure 12-10 shows the Designer with the tentative message box displayed. If you do not like the appearance of the message box, you can change it and test it again and again until you get it exactly the way you want it. At that point, you can paste the code to the editor.

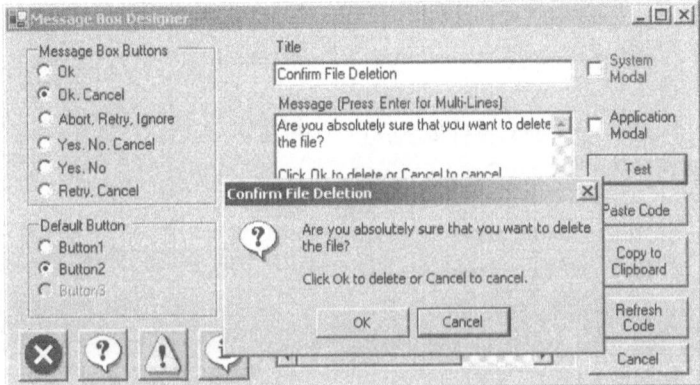

Figure 12-10. Testing the MessageBox Designer

If the Click event of the Paste button determines that the user is developing in C# or C++, it will call the SetUpPaintProcForCLang method, which is shown in Listing 12-13.

NOTE *Because the code for C# and C++ are not exactly the same for all of the message box constants, it would take a different code generator for C++. I have not bothered to do that in this demonstration. If you try to use the Designer in C++ code, a message will be displayed when you attempt to load the MessageBox Designer telling you that the Designer will not work for C++. The Designer will not load in that case.*

Listing 12-13. SetUpPaintProcForCLang Method

```
Private Function SetUpPaintProcForCLang() As String
      Dim intNL As Integer
      Dim i As Integer
      Dim strTemp As String
      Dim strTemp2 As String
```

```
                    Dim sDefaultBtn As String
                    Dim strM As New StringBuilder()
                    Dim oUtil As New Utilities(oVB)
                    Dim sButtons As String
                    Dim sIcon As String
                    Dim sTitle As String = Chr(34) & Me.txtTitle.Text & Chr(34)

                Try
                    If strMBType = "F" Then
                        strM.Append("string sMsg;" & vbCrLf)
                    Else
                        strM.Append("string sMsg;" & vbCrLf)
                    End If

                    strTemp = CStr(txtMessage.Text)
                    intNL = oUtil.MLCount(strTemp, 0)

                    ' we have to build msg lines
                    For i = 1 To intNL
                        strTemp2 = oUtil.MemoLine(strTemp, 0, i)

                        If i = 1 Then
                            strM.Append("sMsg = " & Chr(34) & _
                                strTemp2 & "\n" & Chr(34) & ";" & vbCrLf)
                        Else
                            strM.Append("sMsg = sMsg + " & Chr(34) & _
                                strTemp2 & "\n" & Chr(34) & ";" & vbCrLf)
                        End If
                    Next i

                    ' now build the options
                    ' Create the default button string
                    If rbButton1.Checked Then
                        sDefaultBtn = "MessageBoxDefaultButton.Button1"
                    ElseIf rbButton2.Checked Then
                        sDefaultBtn = "MessageBoxDefaultButton.Button2"
                    Else
                        sDefaultBtn = "MessageBoxDefaultButton.Button3"
                    End If

                    ' create the buttons string
                    Select Case True
```

```vb
        Case Me.rbOkCancel.Checked
            sButtons = "MessageBoxButtons.OKCancel"
        Case Me.rbOk.Checked
            sButtons = "MessageBoxButtons.OK"
        Case Me.rbAbortRetryCancel.Checked
            sButtons = "MessageBoxButtons.AbortRetryIgnore"
        Case Me.rbRetryCancel.Checked
            sButtons = "MessageBoxButtons.RetryCancel"
        Case Me.rbYesNo.Checked
            sButtons = "MessageBoxButtons.YesNo"
        Case Me.rbYesNoCancel.Checked
            sButtons = "MessageBoxButtons.YesNoCancel"
End Select

' create the icon string
Select Case intMBIcon
    Case vbQuestion
        sIcon = "MessageBoxIcon.Question"
    Case vbExclamation
        sIcon = "MessageBoxIcon.Exclamation"
    Case vbInformation
        sIcon = "MessageBoxIcon.Information"
    Case vbCritical
        sIcon = "MessageBoxIcon.Stop"
    Case Else
        sIcon = "MessageBoxIcon.Information"
End Select

' now build the MsgBox call
' build a statement
strM.Append("DialogResult iRV = _
            MessageBox.Show(sMsg, " & _
            sTitle & ", " & _
            sButtons & ", " & _
            sIcon & ", " & _
            sDefaultBtn & ");" & vbCrLf)

If strMBType = "F" Then
    ' now set up the analysis code
    Select Case intMBOptions
        Case 0
            ' Ok button
```

```
Case 1
    ' OkCancel
    strM.Append("switch (iRV)" & vbCrLf & _
                "{" & vbCrLf & _
                "    case DialogResult.OK:" & _
                vbCrLf & _
                "        // Ok code goes here" & _
                vbCrLf & _
                "        break;" & vbCrLf & _
                "    default:" & vbCrLf & _
                "        // cancel code goes here" _
                & vbCrLf & _
                "        break;" & vbCrLf & _
                "}" & vbCrLf)
Case 2
    ' Abort, Retry, Ignore
    strM.Append("switch (iRV)" & vbCrLf & _
                "{" & vbCrLf & _
                "    case DialogResult.Abort:" _
                & vbCrLf & _
                "        // Abort code goes here" _
                & vbCrLf & _
                "        break;" & vbCrLf & _
                "    case DialogResult.Retry:" _
                & vbCrLf & _
                "        // retry code goes here" _
                & vbCrLf & _
                "        break;" & vbCrLf & _
                "    default:" & vbCrLf & _
                "        // Ignore code goes here" _
                & vbCrLf & _
                "        break;" & vbCrLf & _
                "}" & vbCrLf)
Case 3
    ' Yes, No, Cancel
    strM.Append("switch (iRV)" & vbCrLf & _
                "{" & vbCrLf & _
                "    case DialogResult.Yes:" & _
                vbCrLf & _
                "        // Yes code goes here" _
                & vbCrLf & _
                "        break;" & vbCrLf & _
                "    case DialogResult.No:" & vbCrLf _
```

```
                                  & _
                              "        // No code goes here" & vbCrLf
                              & "          break;" & vbCrLf & _
                              "    default:" & vbCrLf & _
                              "        // Cancel code goes here" _
                              & vbCrLf & _
                              "          break;" & vbCrLf & _
                              "}" & vbCrLf)
            Case 4
                ' YesNo
                strM.Append("switch (iRV)" & vbCrLf & _
                              "{" & vbCrLf & _
                              "    case DialogResult.Yes:" & _
                              vbCrLf & _
                              "        // Yes code goes here" _
                              & vbCrLf & _
                              "          break;" & vbcrlf & _
                              "    default:" & vbCrLf & _
                              "        // No code goes here" & _
                              vbCrLf & _
                              "          break;" & vbCrLf & _
                              "}" & vbCrLf)
            Case 5
                ' RetryCancel
                strM.Append("switch (iRV)" & vbCrLf & _
                              "{" & vbCrLf & _
                              "    case DialogResult.Retry:" & _
                              vbCrLf & _
                              "        // Retry code goes here" & _
                              vbCrLf & _
                              "          break;" & vbCrLf & _
                              "    default:" & vbCrLf & _
                              "        // cancel code goes here" & _
                              vbCrLf & _
                              "          break;" & vbCrLf & _
                              "}" & vbCrLf)
        End Select
    End If
    Return strM.ToString
Catch e As System.Exception
    MsgBox("Error in SetupPaintforCLang: " & e.Message)
End Try
End Function
```

Once the user designs and pastes the code for a message box to be used in a C# program, the code will appear as shown in Figure 12-11. Because this display is from a running application, the code is shown and the displayed message box is displayed also.

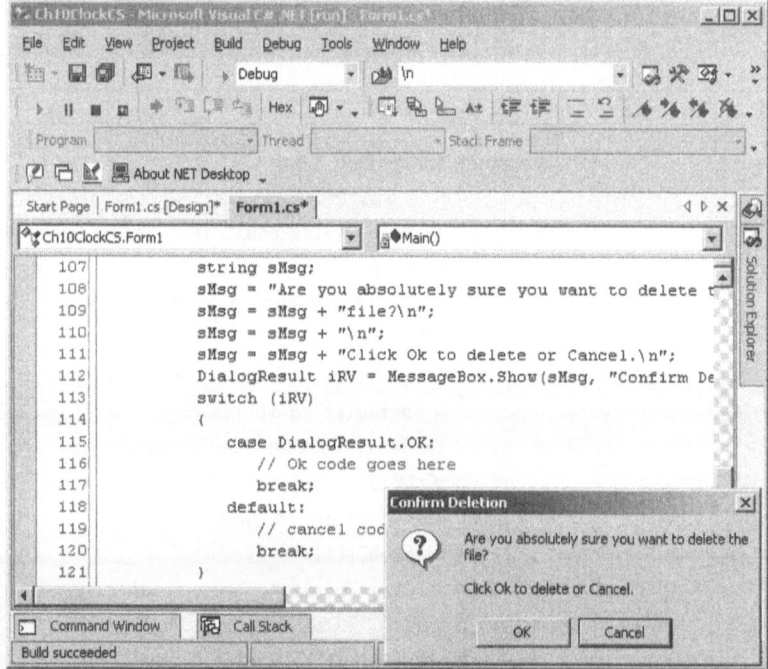

Figure 12-11. MessageBox Designer–generated C# code

About Box

Until now you haven't placed an About box in any of your add-ins. Because this is a real production add-in, you'll want to say who is responsible for its development. You do that with the About box, which you'll learn about in this section.

I also want to do something else in this section: I want to illustrate how simple it is to create a UserControl in Visual Basic .NET. This is not a book on creating UserControls, but then this is not going to be a complex UserControl. It will be just a little flash for the audience.

When you click the NET Desktop tool button, the About box will display. It is fairly standard, with just a few labels and a single UserControl that displays an animated logo for my company. The form is shown in Figure 12-12. You will see that the light in the lighthouse is rotating. Obviously, this is the UserControl and it is simply dropped on the form. Because a UserControl is always running, even in design mode, the light will rotate as soon as the control is dropped onto a form at design time.

Figure 12-12. The About NET Desktop box

Building the UserControl

To build a UserControl, go to the start page of Visual Studio .NET. Click the New Project button and the New Project dialog box will display. Click the Visual Basic Projects folder and click the Windows Control Library icon. Enter the name for your control's project and select a path where you want the project stored. Click OK to create the project.

In Figure 12-13, you will see that I have placed four picture boxes, one on top of the other, in the UserControl's designer. I have dropped down the list of properties so that you can easily see that there are more images than just the one that appears on the Designer. Each of the four picture boxes has a picture of the lighthouse and the fog light is rotated 90 degrees in relation to the previous image. If I then alternately show and hide the four different images, it makes the lighthouse fog light appear to rotate.

I have also placed a Timer control on the form and set the Interval property to 500. This will cause the timer to fire every half second.

The only code required in the control is code to consecutively hide and show the four images as the timer fires. Listing 12-14 shows the code for the Timer1_Tick event. This code will be activated every half second. The code is very simple. It determines which picture box is currently visible. It then makes the next picture in line for showing visible and makes the other three invisible.

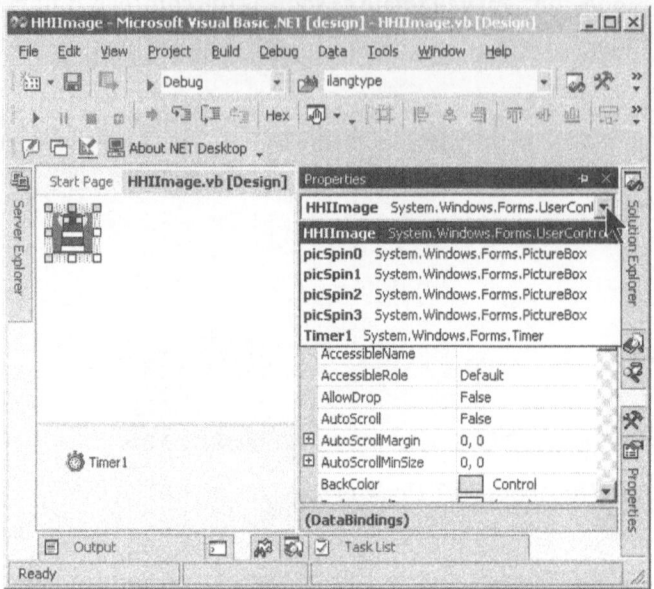

Figure 12-13. The UserControl's designer

Listing 12-14. Timer1_Tick Event

```
Private Sub Timer1_Tick(ByVal sender As Object, _
    ByVal e As System.EventArgs) Handles Timer1.Tick
    Select Case True
        Case Me.picSpin0.Visible
            picSpin1.Visible = True
            picSpin2.Visible = False
            picSpin3.Visible = False
            picSpin0.Visible = False
        Case picSpin1.Visible
            picSpin1.Visible = False
            picSpin2.Visible = True
            picSpin3.Visible = False
            picSpin0.Visible = False
        Case picSpin2.Visible
            picSpin1.Visible = False
            picSpin2.Visible = False
            picSpin3.Visible = True
            picSpin0.Visible = False
        Case picSpin3.Visible
            picSpin1.Visible = False
            picSpin2.Visible = False
```

```
        picSpin3.Visible = False
        picSpin0.Visible = True
    End Select
End Sub
```

Once the code is in place, you must build the project before the control will appear in the Toolbox. After the project is built, the control's icon will be in the Toolbox and you can drag it onto a form in another project of the solution.

Event Handling

There is one last area that I want to cover with this add-in. In Chapter 11, I covered the use of events. In a couple of those events, I inserted some useful functionality. The first was a reminder to notify you when you have failed to change the default name of a form, class, or module. The second was to cause the Task List to open automatically when an error item is added to the Task List. I have added these two events to the Connect class. In the declaration section of the class, I have placed the following code snippet. This code declares the events for the two items mentioned previously.

```
' declare DTE events we want to handle
Public WithEvents eventWindows As EnvDTE.WindowEvents
Public WithEvents taskListEvents As EnvDTE.TaskListEvents
```

In the OnConnection method of the class, I have placed the code shown in Listing 12-15, which will associate the events with their handlers. This code will also create an instance of the CReminders class that will be called by the event handlers to process the information from the events. If you need a more thorough explanation of what happens in these events, please refer back to Chapter 11.

Listing 12-15. Linking the Events to Event Handlers

```
' link DTE events we want to handle
Dim events As EnvDTE.Events
events = oVB.Events
eventWindows = CType(events.WindowEvents(Nothing), _
    EnvDTE.WindowEvents)
taskListEvents = CType(events.TaskListEvents(Nothing), _
    EnvDTE.WindowEvents)
oRemind = New CReminders(oVB)
```

Listing 12-16 shows the code for the event handlers that are linked to the events by the code in Listing 12-15.

Listing 12-16. Task List and Windows Event Handlers

```
' Event handlers for DTE events we are handling
Private Sub eventWindows_WindowActivated(ByVal -
    GotFocus As EnvDTE.Window, _
    ByVal LostFocus As EnvDTE.Window) _
    Handles eventWindows.WindowActivated
    ' Let's do something useful
    ' if the window name is a default name, e.g, Form(n),
    ' Module(n) or Class(n)
    ' suggest to the user that they need to rename it
    oRemind.CkForRemindOfDefaultName(GotFocus.Caption)

    ' task item removed does not always fire because of
    ' multiple events firing, so place the calls in this
    ' event to kludge the closing of the task list
    If GotFocus.Caption.StartsWith("Task List") Then
        oRemind.CkForClosingTaskList()
    End If
    If LostFocus.Caption.StartsWith("Task List") Then
        oRemind.CkForClosingTaskList()
    End If
End Sub
Private Sub taskListEvents_TaskAdded(ByVal _
    TaskItem As EnvDTE.TaskItem) _
    Handles taskListEvents.TaskAdded
    ' activate the task window
    oRemind.ActivateTaskList()
End Sub
```

Figure 12-14 shows what happens when a project opens and a form still having a default name comes up in the active window. The developer is immediately reminded that the form's name should be changed. The developer will continue to be reminded once per instance of the IDE to do so until he or she changes the name.

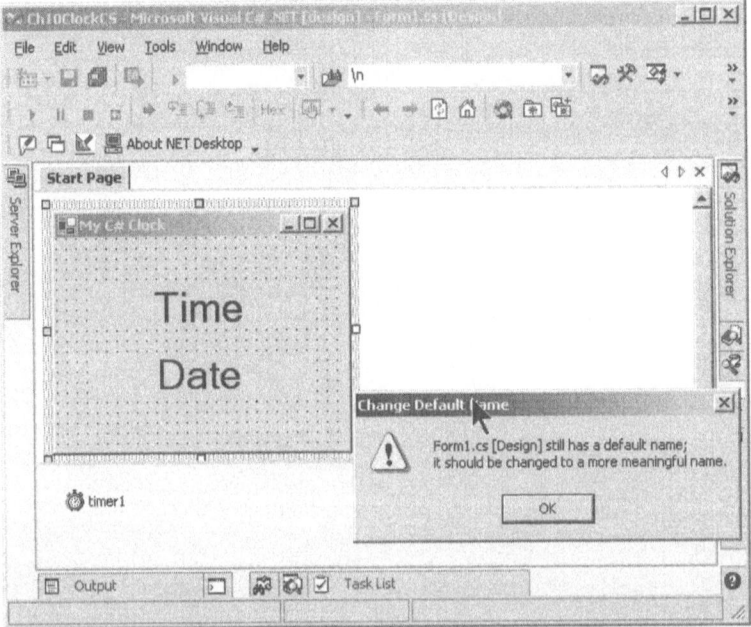

Figure 12-14. Default form name detected

Summary

In this chapter I have tried to combine functionality from almost every chapter. You saw several examples of code manipulation, manipulation of windows, and generation of code. You saw code generation in both Visual Basic and C#.

In this chapter, you built what I hope you consider to be a useful add-in. It should be just the start from which you continue to build additional features. The methods and classes contained in the project form a framework for future development. The project for the add-in contains all of the reusable objects that you have created in the book.

In Chapter 13, you will see how to migrate a VB 6.0 add-in to Visual Basic .NET. You will see that the way you have built your add-ins in VB 6.0 will determine the amount of code that you will be able to migrate without changes as you move to .NET.

CHAPTER 13

Migrating VB 6.0 Add-ins to .NET

"Success supposes endeavour."
—Jane Austen

IN CHAPTER 1, I SAID that VB 6.0 add-ins are, for all practical purposes, broken by .NET. There is good news and bad news in that statement. The good news is that you have a more powerful model to upgrade to. The bad news is that VB 6.0 compiled add-ins that implement IDTExtensibility will not load in the .NET IDE. The message shown in Figure 13-1 displays when you try to connect to the add-in. Although the message does not bother to tell you the name of the interface that is unsupported, my educated guess is that it is the IDTExtensibility (VB 6.0 automation) interface, simply because that is the only interface implemented in the add-in.

 **NOTE** *I could be wrong about this being the problem. However, the terms "VBIDE" and "IDTExtensibility" do not appear in MSDN. From that standpoint, I am left to believe that the interface is not supported by Visual Studio .NET.*

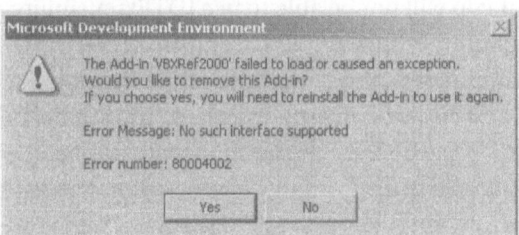

Figure 13-1. Error message encountered when trying to load a VB 6.0 add-in

Before I go further into the subject of upgrading your VB 6.0 add-ins, there is some additional disappointing news. If you run your old VB 6.0 add-ins through the Migration Wizard, you probably will find that not all of your code upgrades successfully. The misleading thing is that once the upgraded add-in has been brought into Visual Studio .NET, none of the extensibility object references will be marked in error. The upgrade tool recognizes that your program is an add-in and adds a COM interoperability reference to your project for the VBIDE.DLL, which is the automation DLL for VB 6.0.

This would imply that you could still use the automation object that you used in VB 6.0 if you do not have to have any of the new functionality of the new .NET automation object. I say this with reservations, however, because this does not mean that you will be able to use your add-ins without modification, even if they make it through the Migration Wizard fairly unscathed.

Having run the upgrade tool on your add-in, you are faced with several tasks. First, you must clean up any errors unresolved by the upgrade tool. Second, you must register the add-in manually using Regasm.exe. Finally, you have to make the entries in the registry so that the Add-in Manager will list your add-in in its dialog box. Having performed these tasks, you would expect that your add-in would now load. That's where the disappointment comes—it will not. In fact, after you upgrade a very simple add-in that basically does nothing except add an Office CommandBar menu, the same message shown in Figure 13-1 will display. You are once again met with the message "No such interface supported."

NOTE   *Having worked on this problem for several days with no success, I am left with the conclusion that the upgrade tool thinks that IDTExtensibility is supported, but Visual Studio .NET does not. It would be extremely helpful if Microsoft either corrected this situation or, if it is a matter of "user error," provided documentation as to how it is supposed to work.*

Assuming that you will not be able to use IDTExtensibility, you can still get a lot of mileage out of running your VB 6.0 add-ins through the Migration Wizard. Here again, the amount of usability that you retain in migrating any type of application, especially add-ins, will be proportional to the applicability of the VB 6.0 functionality upgrading to .NET. For example, there has been a paradigm switch in the way the Windows Forms Designer works. A large percentage of the properties on forms, controls, and their respective events have changed. Therefore, if your VB 6.0 add-in was manipulating properties on a VB 6.0 form and/or some of the controls on the form, the probability is extremely high that the code will require a rewrite in .NET, for two reasons. First, the extensibility model has changed. Second, the properties that you are trying to manipulate have changed. That may or may not be catastrophic to your add-in functionality. In some cases, you may simply need to change the names of the properties that you were manipulating. In other cases, a property may no longer exist. However, it may have been replaced by some other property. There are many more properties in .NET forms than there were in VB 6.0 forms.

In this chapter, I take you through the process of migrating a VB 6.0 add-in. It is not a large one, but I discuss some of the problems that I have encountered in migrating some larger and more extensive add-ins. I tell you some things you can do before migrating your application, and I point out the most obvious areas (not individual code) that will not upgrade. You can get more detailed information by searching MSDN on the subject of migrating applications.

Preparing to Migrate an Add-in

There are several major areas that simply will not upgrade from VB 6.0 to .NET. The first thing you must do is make sure that the application you want to migrate will compile correctly and completely in VB 6.0. The .NET Migration Wizard will not accept any application from an earlier version of Visual Basic except VB 6.0. If you have an application that is from an earlier version of Visual Basic, you must bring it into VB 6.0 and clean up any errors before attempting to migrate to .NET.

> **NOTE** *You should not have any problems moving a VB 5.0 application to VB 6.0. However, you do have to do it. Also, you should have a copy of VB 6.0 on the machine that you want to use to migrate the application. You should compile the VB 6.0 application to ensure that all components, including third-party components, can be found on that machine. Otherwise, the wizard will not be successful in upgrading your application.*

Table 13-1 is a brief summary of the major areas that you should be aware of before upgrading. You may or may not decide to do anything in these areas, but if you do not, you will likely see a lot of "not upgraded" messages in the code output from the wizard.

Table 13-1. Preparing to Upgrade to .NET

AREA	DESCRIPTION
Data	.NET introduces an advanced version of ADO called ADO.NET. Although DAO and RDO can still be used, .NET does not support bound controls that use these data access packages. If you are using DAO and data binding, you should consider converting to ADO or leaving the application in VB 6.0. In the case of an add-in, you will have to convert to ADO.
Graphics	Several of the graphics objects, such as Line and Shape controls, are not supported by .NET.
Printer object	The Printer object is not supported by .NET. All printing operations will have to be rewritten.
Clipboard object	This object is still in .NET, but the SetData method has been changed to SetDataObject, and a cursory glance at the diagnostic might cause you to think Microsoft has taken out the Clipboard.
Drag and drop	The drag-and-drop operations of your applications will have to be rewritten.
Variants	All variants will be converted to Object, and that can cause some subtle problems.
APIs	Some API calls may need to be revised or replaced with .NET Framework classes.
GoSub	The GoSub statement is no longer supported in .NET. You must rewrite code that uses GoSub.
Option Base	The Option Base statement has been removed from the language. Arrays must be based at zero. This was done to maintain compatibility between Visual Basic .NET and other .NET languages. Code using arrays with a base other than zero need to be examined.
Dates	Dates are not stored as Doubles in .NET. If you have been doing calculations counting on the storing of dates as Doubles, you will have to rewrite the code.
Legacy keywords	The use of such legacy keywords as LSet, VarPtr, ObjPtr, StrPtr, Def, and computed GoTo are not supported in .NET.

Running the Migration Wizard on an Add-in

To run the Migration Wizard, open a VB 6.0 project (.vbp) in Visual Studio .NET. The following list describes the various steps of the wizard and tells you what to do in each step.

Step 1 is simply an outline of what the wizard will do for you. There is nothing for you to do but click the Next button.

Step 2 allows you to pick what type of application to produce, DLL or EXE. If you are converting a DLL or add-in, you will have no choice but to create a DLL. The EXE option will be disabled.

In Step 3, you must select a path and directory in which to save the converted application.

Step 4 allows you cancel or proceed with the migration; all selections are complete.

Step 5 displays a progress bar as well as the objects that are being processed as the wizard progresses through your application.

NOTE *Do not be alarmed if your application migration seems to take a long time. One of my add-ins with 10 forms and about 8,000 lines of actual code took 20 minutes on a 650MHz computer.*

Migration Wizard Diagnostics

When the wizard completes the upgrade process, you will see that it has placed diagnostic comments around the lines of code with which it had trouble or could not upgrade. The diagnostics take the form of those shown in Listing 13-1. When the wizard encounters a line of code that cannot be upgraded, a comment will be placed after the line of code that reads "UPGRADE_ISSUE...not upgraded." After the description of the object or statement that could not be upgraded, a link to MSDN describing the problem will be inserted at the end of the diagnostic comment. If there is some doubt as to the validity of what the wizard has done with a particular line of code, it places a diagnostic beginning with "UPGRADE_WARNING...". In the case where the wizard has upgraded a line of code but you should be told about it because of possible side effects, it will place an "UPGRADE_NOTE..." comment. In Listing 13-1, you will see that some of the comments are underlined. These are the links to MSDN.

NOTE *The diagnostic is generated all on one line, but I have made two lines of the diagnostics in the following code so they will fit on the book's pages.*

Listing 13-1. Upgraded Code with Diagnostics

```
Sub ErrHandler(ByRef Func As String, _
                Optional ByRef SubFunc As Object = Nothing)
    ' Display a Trappable Error in a Standard Format.
    Dim sMsg As String

    'UPGRADE_NOTE: IsMissing() was changed to IsNothing(). ↵
     Click for more:
    'ms-help://MS.VSCC/commoner/redir/redirect.↵
      htm?keyword="vbup1021"'
    'UPGRADE_WARNING: Couldn't resolve default property ↵
      of object SubFunc.
    ' Click for more:
    'ms-help://MS.VSCC/commoner/redir/redirect.↵
      htm?keyword="vbup1037"'
    If IsNothing(SubFunc) Then SubFunc = ""

    'UPGRADE_WARNING: Couldn't resolve default property of ↵
     object SubFunc.
    ' Click for more:
    'ms-help://MS.VSCC/commoner/redir/redirect.↵
      htm?keyword="vbup1037"'
    sMsg = "The Following Error: " & Trim(Str(Err.Number)) _
      & Chr(10) & _
      "Desc: " & ErrorToString() & Chr(10) & Chr(10) & _
      "Occured in Proc: " & Trim(Func) & Chr(10) & _
      "SubProc: " & SubFunc
    frmPleaseWait.DefInstance.Display(↵
      "CodeMgr: System Error", sMsg)
    Exit Sub
End Sub
```

When the newly upgraded add-in is opened in the IDE, the Task List will display a list of errors that it found during the upgrade process. After running a very small add-in through the Migration Wizard, the list of errors shown in Figure 13-2 was displayed in the Task List.

 **NOTE** *It is highly unlikely that you will run an application of any size through the Migration Wizard without it finding some things that will not upgrade.*

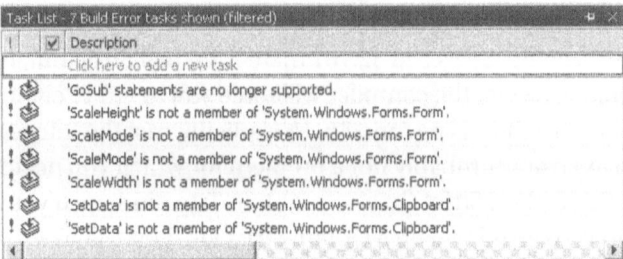

Figure 13-2. Upgrade errors shown in the Task List

If you double-click any error line in the Task List, the module containing the specified line of code will be loaded into the active window and the cursor will be positioned on the line in question.

Concerning Option Strict

When the Migration Wizard upgrades your application, it will insert the following directive at the top of each module:

```
Option Strict Off
```

Option Strict is a new compiler directive in Visual Basic .NET. It is like the VB 6.0 directive Option Explicit, but it serves a different purpose. Option Strict can be turned on or off by changing the last word to On or Off. If you turn it on, as many experts recommend, you are likely to see a lot more compiler errors in your code. All of them will be useful, but many of them can become quite frustrating. One of the things the upgrade process does for you is convert Integer variables to Short. This is because in .NET an Integer is now 32 bits rather than 16 bits as in

VB 6.0. The problem is that intrinsic functions such as InStr return a .NET Integer. Consider the following VB 6.0 code snippet:

```
Dim iPtr As Integer
iPtr = InStr("ABCDEFG", "A")
```

When upgraded by the Migration Wizard, the code snippet will look as follows:

```
Dim iPtr As Short ' changed by the upgrade
iPtr = InStr("ABCDEFG", "A")
```

With Option Strict Off, there is no problem. If you change to Option Strict On, the second line of code will immediately be marked in error with a diagnostic that reads "Option Strict disallows implicit conversion from Integer to Short." If the value of iPtr can never exceed 32,767 there is no real error. But, because you have set Option Strict On, the compiler will force you to either change the type of iPtr to Integer or use the CType function to explicitly cast the Integer to Short.

This type of error is probably not a problem for which you need to leave Option Strict On. Option Strict On also prohibits late binding. If you have used late binding in VB 6.0 and you turn Option Strict On, you will have to change the code to make it compile. Sometimes it is difficult, if not impossible, to use early binding in every situation. If you have such a case, Option Strict On will prevent a successful compile and you will not be able to build an executable. Again, Option Strict On is a good thing assuming that you can change the code to early binding. Late binding not only causes a performance hit, but it can also generate runtime exceptions if the Just-in-Time (JIT) compiler cannot resolve the late binding at runtime.

VB 6.0 Add-in Code No Longer Needed

In a VB 6.0 add-in you had to write an entry to the vbaddin.ini file in the Windows or Winnt directory. When an add-in was placed in the .ini file, it caused the Add-in Manager to list the add-in in its dialog box. This code is no longer needed in .NET.

Listing 13-2. AddToIni Method

```
Sub AddToINI()
        'this sub should be executed from the Immediate window
        'in order to get this app added to the VBADDIN.INI file
        'you must change the name in the 2nd argument to reflect
         'the correct name of your project
```

```
    Dim ErrCode As Integer
    ErrCode = WritePrivateProfileString("Add-Ins32", _
        Name & ".Connect", "0", "vbaddin.ini")
End Sub
```

.NET Replacement for VBAddin.ini

Once a VB 6.0 add-in has been through the Migration Wizard and you have
cleaned up any errors, including the conversion to the new extensibility model,
the add-in must still be registered and entries must be made to the registry to
cause the add-in to be listed in the Add-in Manager dialog box. There are two
ways to accomplish these two processes. First, you can manually set a start-up
project, create a setup project, manually register the add-in, and manually
create the registry entries to cause the add-in to be listed in the Add-in Manager
dialog box.

When the migration tool processes your VB 6.0 add-in, the output will be the
project for the add-in. Although it will be included in a solution (.sln), there will
be no setup project created and the add-in project itself will not be ready for execution. If you attempt to execute the project, you will probably receive the error
message shown in Figure 13-3.

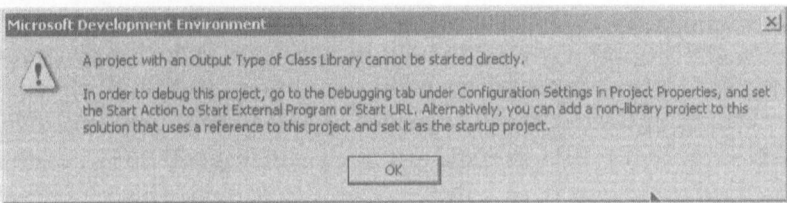

Figure 13-3. The no start-up project error message

An add-in (DLL) project cannot be debugged by itself. You must have a start-
up project that can be started, which will be the client application. This client
application will connect to the add-in (server application). When you use
the Add-in Wizard to create a .NET add-in, it does all of this for you behind the
scenes. However, the migration tool does none of it. The error message shown in
Figure 13-3 tells you how to get a start-up project configured. To perform this
process, right-click the add-in project in the Solution Explorer window. Select the
Properties option and the Project Properties dialog box will display, as shown in
Figure 13-4. Click the Configuration Properties folder. Click the Start External
Program radio button. Browse to the copy of devenv.exe on your computer. Click
the OK button to close the dialog box. What you are doing is telling your add-in
project to start another instance of the Visual Studio IDE as your start-up project.
Next, you must register your add-in manually.

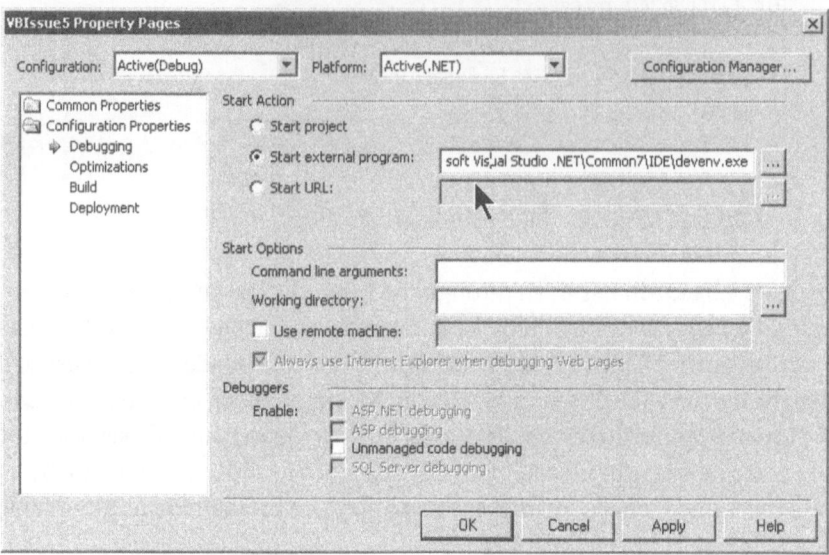

Figure 13-4. Setting a start-up project in the Project Properties dialog box

Registering the Add-in

This is a task that you would not have to worry about if you were creating the add-in via the Add-in Wizard. Because you are upgrading the add-in via the migration tool, you must now get the add-in registered. To do this, you must use Regasm.exe. This is a command line utility that comes with Visual Studio .NET. You use it to manually register DLLs created in .NET that are written in either Visual Basic or C#. C++ DLLs are still registered with Regsvr32.exe. The command window displayed in Figure 13-5 shows a typical execution of Regasm.exe and its output notification of a successful registration.

TIP *If you still want to attempt to make an upgraded VB 6.0 add-in work using IDTExtensibility, be aware that Regasm.exe does not create the registry string entry named CodeBase. This is the entry that tells the path and file name of the add-in DLL. A missing CodeBase string entry for the add-in will result in an "Unknown Error" display. You can pull your hair out over that one. You can look up a CodeBase entry in the registry and enter one manually in the area where your add-in was registered. This anomaly appears to be related only to upgraded VB 6.0 add-ins and not .NET add-ins that were created on another machine.*

![Command Prompt window showing regasm.exe registration output]

Figure 13-5. Using Regasm.exe to register an add-in

Creating Registry Entries for the Add-in

One last task that must be accomplished is the creation of the registry entries for the Add-in Manager. You could type them in manually using Regedit, but I recommend that you use a .REG file like the one shown in Listing 13-3. Place the lines shown below into a file with a .REG extension. Replace the ProgID with the one from the Connect class of your add-in. The ProgID is shown in boldfaced font in Listing 13-3.

Listing 13-3. Registry File for Add-in Manager Registry Entries

```
REGEDIT4
[HKEY_LOCAL_MACHINE\SOFTWARE\Microsoft\VisualStudio\7.0\Addins]
[HKEY_LOCAL_MACHINE\SOFTWARE\Microsoft\VisualStudio\7.0\Addins\⤸
Connect_NET.Connect]
"FriendlyName"="VBIssue"
"Description"="Log changes to project files."
"LoadBehavior"=dword:00000003
"CommandLineSafe"=dword:00000000
```

> **NOTE** *"Connect_NET.Connect" was generated by the upgrade tool and can be found as the ProgID on the class declaration line of the Connect class. In a wizard-generated Connect class, the ProgID would be ProgIDAttribute and would contain a GUID value instead of "Connect_NET.Connect."*

Once you have created the registration file, you simply double-click the file in the Windows Explorer and your add-in will be registered with the Add-in Manager.

Building a Setup Project

A second way of registering your migrated add-in is to add a setup project to your solution, build it, and install it. This process will not only register your add-in, but it will also create the registry entries that will cause the add-in to be listed in the Add-in Manager dialog box.

NOTE *If you are attempting to run an add-in in the IDE and you do not have a setup project, you can follow the procedure outlined in this section to create one. This procedure is applicable regardless of whether you are dealing with an upgraded VB 6.0 add-in or a .NET add-in that was not created by the Add-in Wizard on your computer. The latter will be the case if you download an automation sample from the Microsoft Web site. You will get the add-in project, but it probably will not have a setup project associated with it.*

To create a setup project, go to the start page and click the New Project button. When the New Project dialog box opens, click the Setup and Deployment Projects folder. Next, click the Setup Project icon and enter the name of the project and the path where you want the project stored. Click the OK button to create the setup project.

Once the setup project is created, it will probably be empty. To build the setup project, right-click the setup project and click the Build option on the pop-up menu. Once the project has been built, you can right-click the setup project and click the Install option on the pop-up menu. This will cause the Install Wizard to run and lead you through the installation process. After the installation has completed, the add-in will be registered and it will be listed in the Add-in Manager dialog box.

Should I Go All the Way with .NET?

Having gone through the process of upgrading an existing VB 6.0 add-in, you must now convert your references to the automation objects from the old IDTExtensibility (VB 6.0) interface to IDTExtensibility (.NET). Once you do that, several questions arise: Should I go all the way with .NET? In other words, should I move from DAO or ADO to ADO.NET? Should I convert to the use of the new functionality provided by the .NET classes? With respect to add-ins, should I rearrange my code so that I can isolate the references to extensibility objects in a central location as much as possible?

In my opinion, the answer to all of these questions is yes! Obviously, Visual C# is a new language. If you plan to take advantage of the new classes in the .NET Framework, then Visual Basic .NET is like a new language. In some cases, such as the Clipboard object, graphics objects, and the Printer object, you have no choice but to rewrite the code. You can't reference the Clipboard exactly as you've been used to. The Printer object no longer exists. Graphics objects have changed. WinForms aren't structured like VB 6.0 forms were. API calls may require modification or replacement with usage of .NET classes. Once you start to look at the differences, there seems to be no place to stop. In the next few sections, I discuss some of the major areas for conversion and give you a suggested outline for upgrading your add-ins to Visual Basic .NET.

Begin with the Migration Wizard

You could possibly bring code files into a .NET project, one at a time, and correct the obvious errors. Notice that I said "code files." If your add-in has forms, most of them will survive the Migration Wizard. It would be very time consuming to re-create all of the forms from scratch in Visual Studio .NET. In VBCommander for VB 6.0, for instance, I have over 40 forms. You can imagine the work that it would take to recreate those forms. I do have one very complex form in an add-in that came through looking really weird! While looking at the properties for the form, I found that the Migration Wizard had set the BackgroundImage property to some System.Drawing image. Once I set that to Nothing, the problem disappeared and my form looked fine. Figure 13-6 shows this fairly complex form that has been upgraded to a .NET form.

> **NOTE** *If you examine the code behind the form, you will note some extra code in the initialization code that you would not normally find in a form that is generated by the .NET Windows Forms Designer. It appears to be related to the difference in the way VB 6.0 forms are initialized as opposed to WinForms initialization. Also, VB 6.0 forms could be instantiated directly. In Visual Basic .NET you have to instantiate an instance of a form instead of the form itself.*

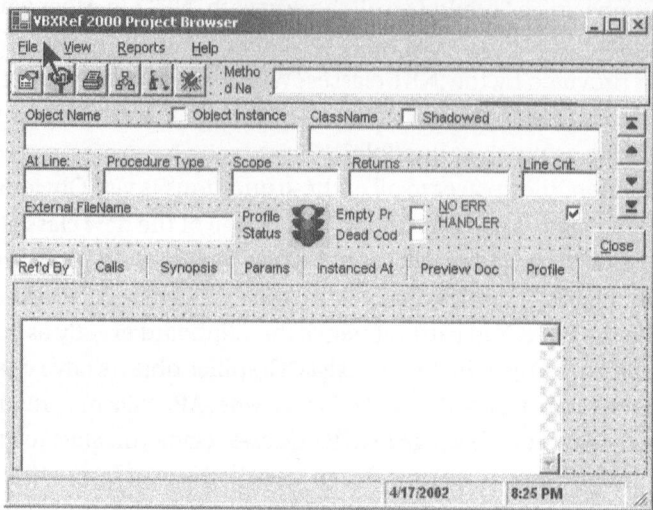

Figure 13-6. VB 6.0 form upgraded to a .NET form

Even the code modules would be a frustrating exercise to convert manually. The upgrade tool seems to run for an inordinate length of time, but it is doing a lot of work that would take you a lot longer if you did it manually.

> **TIP** *If you are upgrading a large application using the Migration Wizard, you may encounter hundreds of errors, especially if you have made many separate references to some nonexistent object such as the Printer object. When the caption of the Task List shows "102 Errors," that may not represent all of the errors. The Task List will only show 102 errors at one time.*

Use the Add-in Wizard to Create a New Add-in Framework

Because you have to move to the new extensibility model, IDTExtensibility2, you should use the Add-in Wizard to create the basic add-in framework, or Connect class. The methods, parameters, Imports, and Implements are all different in a .NET extensibility Connect class than in a VB 6.0 upgraded Connect class. Also, in using the wizard, you will not have to worry about any of the registration issues.

After you have the Connect class, it is a fairly simple matter to copy the code modules and forms from your upgraded add-in to your new add-in framework created by the wizard. Basically, you are replacing the upgraded VB 6.0 Connect class with a new .NET Connect class. But my recommendation is to copy all of the files from the upgraded add-in to a new directory where you have created the new add-in with the wizard. You can then go to the Windows Explorer, select all of the files that you want to add to the new add-in project, and drag and drop them on the project folder in the Visual Studio .NET IDE. They will be automatically added to the project.

Centralize the References to the Extensibility Object

Throughout this book, I have stressed the need to keep the references to the extensibility objects concentrated in one class where possible. I have shown you how to use such functions as GetCodeFromWindow, GetWholeProc, AddMethodToEndOfDocument, and PutCodeBack to make the references to the extensibility objects. Using this approach limits your exposure to change if you have to make changes to the code that uses the extensibility objects. I realize that this is not always possible, but you should try to do this wherever possible. You should use the Utilities class from the Chapter 12 code as a basis for developing other functions such as the ones just named to perform common, often used functionality for you.

Upgrade to IDTExtensibility2 Objects

Once you add your upgraded add-in files to the new add-in created by the Add-in Wizard, you will have no problem locating code that needs to be changed. The errors will be listed in the Task List. You will have to tackle them one at a time by looking for replacement functionality within the .NET Framework.

> **NOTE** *I have tried to cover the most practical automation objects in the course of the various chapters of this book. However, I am sure that I have not covered every object and method that you could possibly desire to use or need. There are some 3,400 objects in the .NET Framework and many of them are related to extensibility. I am sure that you will have to do some digging on your own, especially in the area of the Windows Forms Designer. The objects related to manipulation of forms and their associated components are extremely complex and abstract.*

Upgrade to ADO.NET

I confess that a couple of my VB 6.0 add-ins are still using DAO. The problem is not that I do not know ADO. I have been programming in ADO, developing corporate applications, for over 2 years. The problem is that the add-ins worked fine and Les' law number one is "If it ain't broke, don't fix it!" That law is spawned from expediency and from seeing too many programmers try to "fix" code that is working and wind up breaking it.

Now that we're in .NET, DAO has a problem. Bound controls using DAO aren't supported by .NET. So the obvious answer is to upgrade to ADO. And while you're at it, convert to ADO.NET. ADO.NET is so much more powerful; it's the next generation of data access from Microsoft. It is where Microsoft is devoting its time and money with relation to data access.

NOTE *If you upgrade an application that uses ADO, the upgrade tool will wrap the ADO COM objects and you can use the code as is. Even so, it is still good to consider upgrading to ADO.NET if you have the time.*

If you are not already familiar with ADO.NET, MSDN has lots of examples and there are many books on the market on the subject. Many of the books that are written on the more general subjects of .NET will have a chapter or two on ADO.NET.

Printing in Visual Basic .NET

As I mentioned earlier in the chapter, the VB 6.0 Printer object is no longer supported. Visual Basic .NET provides greatly improved support for printing through classes that control the printing of documents. These new classes allow you to modify print settings and choose printers, and they even allow print preview. The Printer object is replaced in Visual Basic .NET with the PrintComponent. Although the behavior of the two objects is quite different, in most cases the functionality of the old Printer object can be duplicated.

In order to learn how the printing capabilities have changed in Visual Basic .NET, refer to the PrintComponent in MSDN. There are also several examples available on the Microsoft Web site.

Use the .NET Framework Classes

The .NET Framework provides a rich set of classes that will be new to you. I am still learning the ramifications of the statement "Everything is an object in .NET." I constantly see new methods on a simple String object. Take time to explore the options afforded by IntelliSense to a simple String object. You will be amazed at the new and easy ways of doing things. For example, the use of the InStr, Mid, and Left functions can often be replaced with the use of the IndexOf, LastIndexOf, StartsWith, and EndsWith methods of the String object.

Learn to use the new StringBuilder class. It is faster than the String object and is not a resource hog when you are concatenating strings. This is just one example of the great new functionality of the .NET classes.

Use the Macros IDE

Chapter 8 was devoted entirely to the use of macros, the Macro Explorer, and the Macros IDE. At the risk of repeating myself, I cannot overemphasize the power of the Macros IDE in developing and testing code that can ultimately be used in an add-in. By simply substituting DTE for the application object, you can develop and test most add-in code related to extensibility objects in the Macros IDE.

 **CAUTION** *There is at least one notable exception to the interchangeability between the Macros IDE and add-ins. You cannot create an instance of IDesignerHost in the Macros IDE. You can still move and resize controls in a macro, but you must use the DTE.ExecuteCommand statement rather than use an IDesignerHost object.*

Explore the code that comes in the macro samples. There is a world of ideas and practical working sample code in the samples provided by Microsoft.

Examine the Automation Samples

In Chapter 1, I mentioned that the third CD from Beta 2 contained automation samples. There were many add-ins covering a wide range of subjects in that sample set. If you do not have the Beta 2 CDs, you can find the automation samples on Microsoft's .NET Web site. There are sample add-ins written in Visual Basic, C#, and C++. They will provide a world of information related to add-ins in .NET.

Summary

In this chapter you saw how to use the Migration Wizard to upgrade a VB 6.0 add-in to Visual Basic .NET. You learned that you need to move from the older extensibility model to the new model in .NET. You also saw an outline of a procedure for upgrading your old add-ins from VB 6.0 to .NET, along with suggestions for continuing the learning process of developing add-ins in .NET.

As I said previously, it would not be possible to cover all of the objects, methods, properties, events, classes, and interfaces that are provided by the extensibility model. That would require me to know the intricacies of practically every object listed in MSDN. From the outset, that was not the stated goal of this book. I do hope that I have helped provide you with a jump start in the major areas that you might want to create add-in functionality.

Remember, add-ins are limited only by the creativity and ingenuity of the developer. However, in Visual Studio .NET, with more power comes the requirement for more research. In many cases, you will become frustrated by the abstract nature of the various objects and the lack of adequate documentation and examples in MSDN. But perseverance will be rewarded with success in most cases. From personal experience in doing the research for this book, the old adage "If at first you don't succeed, try, try again" is the best advice I can give you. Sometimes you will be tempted to give up. Let me encourage you to try it another way, again and again, until you succeed.

Appendixes

Appendixes

APPENDIX A
Extensibility Objects

THIS APPENDIX LISTS the major extensibility (automation) objects that you need to use to write fairly complex add-ins. The extensibility object model is extremely large in .NET. It is very probable that some objects have been overlooked or missed in this compilation.

I group the objects by functionality type and then alphabetically within the type. I don't attempt to list all of the properties, methods, or events associated with the respective objects. This appendix is simply an attempt to provide a quick reference to extensibility objects and a summary of their functionality. It is meant to provide you with a place to start to find what you need in MSDN. MSDN is very large and covers approximately 3,400 classes. This appendix extracts a small subset of those objects to provide you with a springboard into MSDN for information related to extensibility.

I have created some fairly complex add-ins through the course of this book. At the same time, I have used only a small number of the objects, collections, and interfaces from the very large extensibility model. This should illustrate that you do not need to concern yourself with all of functionality of the extensibility model in order to automate most of the everyday tasks you encounter in the development process.

Build Objects

You can programmatically build projects and solutions from an add-in or macro by using the Build object.

BuildDependency (Object)

The BuildDependency object represents all of the projects that the specified project depends on.

BuildDependencies (Collection)

This collection contains all of the BuildDependency objects in the solution.

BuildManager (Object)

To manage portable executable files produced by custom tools, third-party developers can use the BuildManager object. For more information, refer to the "Introduction to the BuildManager Object" page in MSDN.

Configuration (Object)

The Configuration object relates to all of a project or project item's properties that are dependent on Build Configuration objects.

ConfigurationManager (Object)

The ConfigurationManager object is a matrix of project and platform configuration names. Configuration objects comprise the elements of the matrix. Check the "Properties, Methods, and Events" link for this object in MSDN for a full description of the usage of this object. Also, be aware that not all languages are supported by configuration objects.

Configurations (Collection)

The Configurations collection contains the Configuration objects. Each configuration object relates to the properties for a project's configuration name and platform.

CodeModel

The objects and collections included in this section all relate to the CodeModel object. The CodeModel object and its associates allow you examine the structure of a source code file without programmatically parsing the code. This set of objects is fairly complex to use and many of the objects, methods, or properties work only for Visual C# and are not supported for VB .NET. These objects provide read-only access to the structure of the source file. In my opinion, they are of limited value, except for the function of documenting your code, and therefore I did not cover them in the main body of this book.

NOTE *I have included a small example of the use of the CodeModel in Appendix B.*

The CodeModel object and its associated objects are for use by the C# and VB .NET languages. There is a corresponding set of objects that is for use with Visual C++. The same objects are available, except that they are prefixed by "VC" (as in "VCCodeModel").

CAUTION *If you are using VB .NET to write your add-in, you should look up the desired object, method, or property in MSDN to ensure that it is supported for Visual Basic before you spend time trying to use it. For example, methods such as AddVariable and AddFunction are not supported for VB .NET.*

CodeAttribute (Object)

The CodeAttribute object defines the attributes of a CodeElement object in the CodeModel object. It represents one attribute related to a code element. You can add new attributes with the AddAttribute method.

CodeClass (Object)

The CodeClass object relates to a class in source code. It is part of the CodeElement object. The CodeElement object is a member of the CodeModel object.

CodeDelegate (Object)

The CodeDelegate object represents a delegate in source code.

CodeElement (Object)

The CodeElement object relates to a code element or construct in a source file. A code element can be any fragment of code. In general, this means that there is a CodeElement object for each definition or declaration statement in the source code.

CodeElements (Collection)

The CodeElements collection contains all of the code elements in a source file. You should check MSDN if you are programming your add-in in Visual Basic.

CodeEnum (Object)

The CodeEnum object relates to an enumeration in source code. Look at the "Properties, Methods, and Events" link for this object in MSDN for a more detailed description of what the object does.

CodeFunction (Object)

The CodeFunction object defines a function construct in a source file.

CodeInterface (Object)

The CodeInterface object represents an interface in source code. See the "Methods, Properties, and Events" link related to this object in MSDN for a complete definition of this object.

CodeModel (Object)

The CodeModel object is an alternative to the complex task of parsing text in a code file. However, the CodeModel object is not only very complex itself, but also many of the methods are not supported for VB .NET. The CodeModel object offers read-only access to your code structure. You can use the CodeModel object to analyze the structure of your code. In Visual C#, you can also use methods such as AddVariable and AddFunction to add code to the source file. These methods are not available to Visual Basic developers.

CodeNameSpace (Object)

The CodeNameSpace object relates to namespace declarations in a source file.

CodeParameter (Object)

The CodeParameter object relates to parameters of a function definition.

CodeProperty (Object)

The CodeProperty object relates to a property method in a source code file and determines how properties are defined in the respective languages in Visual Studio .NET.

CodeStruct (Object)

The CodeStruct object relates to a structure in a source code file. See the "Properties, Methods, and Events" link for this object in MSDN for more information on this object.

CodeType (Object)

The CodeType object relates to a class construct in a source file in the IDE. You can determine if a CodeElement implements a CodeType object with the IsCodeType property of the CodeElement object.

CodeTypeRef (Object)

The CodeTypeRef object defines the type of a construct in a source file.

CodeVariable (Object)

The CodeVariable object defines a variable construct in a source file.

FileCodeModel (Object)

The FileCodeModel and CodeModel objects provide the functionality to access the structure of the code in a project in the IDE.

Commands

Command objects can be executed both from a macro and from an add-in. They normally represent menu commands that you can find on the various menus of the IDE.

Command (Object)

The Command object relates to a command in the IDE. You can reference the Command object by using DTE.Commands.Item(index). You can invoke any command in the IDE by using DTE.ExecuteCommand in the Macros IDE. You can do the same thing in an add-in by using appObj.ExecuteCommand.

Commands (Collection)

The Commands collection contains all of the Command objects in the IDE.

Debugger

The objects related to the debugger are used in the debugging process.

Breakpoint (Object)

The Breakpoint object allows you to programmatically manipulate a breakpoint by using its properties and methods.

Breakpoints (Collection)

The Breakpoints collection contains a list of Breakpoint objects in the IDE.

Debugger (Object)

You can use the Debugger object to explore and manipulate the state of the debugger and the program being debugged. You can reference the Debugger object through the DTE object.

Expression (Object)

The Expression object contains properties used to examine items returned by an expression evaluation.

Expressions (Collection)

The Expressions collection is a collection of Expression objects.

Language (Object)

The Language object contains properties used to examine the language specified by the debugger.

Languages (Collection)

The Languages collection is a collection of Language objects.

Process (Object)

You use the Process object to examine and manipulate processes.

Program (Object)

You use the Program object to examine and manipulate programs. You can use this object to check if a program is being debugged, and you can examine a program's process and threads managed by the program.

Programs (Collection)

The Programs collection is a collection of Program objects.

StackFrame (Object)

You can use the StackFrame object to examine and manipulate stack frames. A stack frame is the same as a function call.

StackFrames (Collection)

The StackFrames collection contains all of the current StackFrame objects.

Thread (Object)

The Thread object allows you to examine and manipulate threads from an add-in.

Threads (Collection)

The Threads collection contains the currently extant Thread objects.

Documents

Documents are the open editor or designer files in the IDE. They are nontool windows, and they contain text that can be edited or designers that can be manipulated.

Document (Object)

A Document object represents a document or designer that is open for editing in the Visual Studio .NET IDE. The Document object only represents documents that have an area to edit text.

Documents (Collection)

The Documents collection contains all of the Document objects currently open in the Visual Studio .NET IDE. You can reference the collection by DTE.Documents.

EditPoint (Object)

The EditPoint object provides the functionality to manipulate text as data in a buffer. There is a text buffer shadowing the text in a document editor. EditPoint operates on the text buffer while TextSelection is related to the text displayed in the editor.

TextPane (Object)

You can split a Text Editor window into two panes. The TextPane object gives you access to the text selected in each pane, as well as the pane's properties, such as height, width, and so on.

TextPanes (Collection)

The TextPanes collection contains one or more of the TextPane objects for a Text Editor window.

TextPoint (Object)

TextPoint objects operate on text displayed in a code editor. A TextPoint object differs from an EditPoint object in that the EditPoint object operates on code in the text buffer that shadows the text editor.

TextSelection (Object)

The TextSelection object provides access to view-based editing operations and selected text.

DTE

The Development Tools Environment (DTE) is the root object of the .NET automation object. It has numerous objects that are related directly to it. Those objects are listed in this section.

AddIn (Object)

The AddIn object represents an add-in registered in the Add-in Manager dialog box. The AddIn object provides information to other add-ins. It is also used to pass to the Microsoft Office CommandBar object model methods to identify the add-in requesting to create CommandBar objects.

AddIns (Collection)

The AddIns collection contains all of the add-ins listed in the Add-in Manager dialog box.

BuildEvents (Object)

The BuildEvents object fires events before and after the build starts and completes.

CommandBarEvents (Object)

This object causes a Click event to occur when a control on the command bar is clicked.

DebuggerEvents (Object)

The DebuggerEvents object defines events supported by the debugger.

DocumentEvents (Object)

This object provides document events when documents close and open.

DTE (Object)

DTE is the root object of the Visual Studio .NET automation object model. It is provided to add-ins as the applicationObject parameter to the OnConnection method. It is also known as the application object. You must use the applicationObject in an add-in to reference any of the automation objects in the environment. You can also use DTE in macros to reference the automation objects in a macro.

Events (Object)

The Events object gives you access to all events in the IDE.

Find (Object)

The Find object allows you to execute find operations on documents and files in the IDE. It allows you to search for and replace text in the code editor programmatically.

FontsAndColorsItems (Collection)

The FontsAndColorsItems collection contains details related to the color, appearance, and other font-related attributes of an item.

Globals (Object)

The Globals object is a cache for storing data while an instance of the IDE is extant. You can also persist data between sessions of the IDE using the Globals object.

IDesignerOptionService (Interface)

The IDesignerOptionService object allows you to access the Options dialog box, which is available through Tools ➤ Options in the IDE. You can retrieve and update settings in the dialog box through the use of the GetOptionValue and SetOptionValue methods.

IDTCommandTarget (Interface)

The IDTCommandTarget interface allows you to implement named commands in the environment. It also allows you to define the status of a command or execute it.

If you enter a command that was added with the AddNamedCommand method into the Command window, the Command window first checks to see if the command is enabled or not using the IDTCommandTarget interface's QueryStatus method. The same applies if you call the ExecuteCommand method.

IDTToolsOptionsPage (Interface)

The IDTToolsOptionsPage interface allows you to create your own custom Tools Options pages. When implemented, it provides five methods that act as events within the environment.

IDTWizard (Interface)

The IDTWizard interface allows you to create wizards that can appear in the Add Project and Add Item dialog boxes. When implemented, it provides one method, Exec, whose code executes when the wizard is activated.

IExtenderProvider (Interface)

The automation extenders portion of the Visual Studio .NET automation model provides the ability to add or filter properties that are displayed in a specified project type.

IFilterProperties (Interface)

IFilterProperties should be implemented by an automation extender if it wants to filter one or more Extender properties.

ItemOperations (Object)

This object performs common file actions.

Macros Object

The Macros object allows you to control the macro recorder from an add-in. You can detect when macros are recording. You can also insert lines of code into a macro and resume recording.

OutputWindowEvents (Object)

The OutputWindowEvents object provides events for changes to the Output window.

Properties (Collection)

The Properties collection allows you to iterate through the properties of the DTE object.

Property (Object)

The Property object relates to a property in a generic collection of properties for a specified object.

SelectionContainer (Object)

The SelectionContainer object is a generic selection-tracking object. There is one global selection object for the environment: DTE.SelectedItems.SelectionContainer. SelectedItems is a collection that represents individual ProjectItem objects from which you can get the Project object. Because an item can offer a selection of an arbitrary object within its context, however, the SelectionContainer can represent any type of selected object.

SelectionEvents (Object)

This object provides events when a selection changes.

SolutionEvents (Object)

This object fires an event when a solution item is added, removed, or renamed.

StatusBar (Object)

The StatusBar object represents the status bar in the IDE. The IDE has only one status bar and it is created by the IDE. You can update the progress and text panels of the status bar by using the methods of the StatusBar object.

TextEditorEvents (Object)

The TextEditorEvents object fires an event when the cursor is moved to a new line in the TextEditor.

WindowConfiguration (Object)

The WindowConfiguration object contains all named window configurations created for the environment. You can save your current window layout in the Visual Studio environment as a named window configuration.

WindowConfigurations (Collection)

The WindowConfigurations collection contains all such configurations. It is possible to save your current window layout in the Visual Studio environment as a named window configuration. The WindowConfigurations collection is the repository for these configurations.

WindowEvents (Object)

This object fires an event when the active window changes.

Project

The items in this topic are related to a project in a .NET solution. Projects consist of properties and ProjectItem objects.

Imports (Object)

The Imports object contains a collection of all imports for a Visual Basic project. It determines the namespaces to import for the project. Importing a namespace allows you to reference members of the namespace without having to fully qualify the object or method.

ImportsEvents (Object)

The ImportsEvents object gives you access to the events that are raised when a project Imports statement is added or deleted from a Visual Basic project. This object can be referenced from both the VSProject and DTE objects.

OutputGroup (Object)

Each project in the IDE has a group of files. These files form an output group. They are marked as the outputs for the project. An OutputGroup contains the files that are built by the project.

OutputGroups (Collection)

The OutputGroups collection contains the OutputGroup objects for the project. See the "OutputGroup (Object)" section for more information.

ProjectEvents (Object)

The ProjectEvents object forms the base interface from which projects derive their specific events.

ProjectItem (Object)

The ProjectItem object represents an item in a project. These items can take the form of classes, forms, modules, icons, bitmaps, resource files, text files, and so forth.

ProjectItems (Collection)

The ProjectItems collection contains all of the ProjectItem objects in the project. The collection will be a flat list of items unless one of the ProjectItem objects itself is a collection. An example would relate to a Windows form that has both a file with an extension of .vb and a file with an extension of .resx. Both of these files together comprise the form. The form is incomplete without both of the files.

Projects (Collection)

The Projects collection contains all of the projects of the same kind in the IDE.

Solution

The Solution object represents all projects and solution properties in the IDE. It is a collection of all projects in the IDE. It also contains solution properties such as build configurations and references.

Reference (Object)

The Reference object represents one reference in the project. When you include a reference to a .NET project, .NET assembly (DLL), or COM object, you can reference the public members of the reference.

References (Collection)

The References collection contains all of the references to external components in a Visual Basic or C# project. To reference a member of an external component, you must add a reference to the component to your project's References object.

SolutionBuild (Object)

This object represents the root of the build automation model at the solution level.

SolutionConfiguration (Object)

The SolutionConfiguration object relates information about a specific way to build a solution.

SolutionConfigurations (Collection)

The SolutionConfigurations collection contains all the SolutionConfiguration objects in the solution.

SolutionContext (Object)

The SolutionContext object represents all projects in the solution. You can use this object to determine whether a project is built or deployed.

SolutionContexts (Collection)

The SolutionContexts collection contains all of the SolutionContext objects in a solution configuration.

VSProject (Object)

This applies only to Visual Basic and C# projects. The VSProject object contains information that is specific to the Visual Basic or C# project.

VSProjectItem (Object)

The VSProjectItem object contains information relating to a Visual Basic or C# project item. An item can be a class, form, module, text file, bitmap, or icon.

Window Objects

There are several tool windows within the IDE, including Output, Command, Task List, and ToolBox. Each of these windows has one or more objects and collections associated with them. This section briefly describes those objects and collections.

CommandWindow (Object)

The CommandWindow object allows you to get to the Command window in the IDE. You can reference the Command window by using DTE.Windows.Item(vsWindowKindCommand).Object. You can send output text to the CommandWindow object through the use of the OutputString method. You can also clear the window by using the Clear method of the CommandWindow object.

ContextAttribute (Object)

The ContextAttribute object relates to a single attribute for a window's context. See the "Properties, Methods, and Events" link for this object in MSDN for a full explanation of the usage of this object.

ContextAttributes (Collection)

The ContextAttributes collection contains all of the attributes related to the solution context or a window context.

OutputWindowPane (Object)

The OutputWindowPane object represents a pane in the Output window of the IDE. The Output window normally has a default Output pane. When in debug mode, it also has a Debug pane. You can add panes to the Output window by using the Add method. Once you have created a new pane, you can use the OutputString method to write text to the pane. Once you have created a pane, it cannot be deleted until the IDE is closed. It will not persist between sessions of the IDE.

OutputWindowPanes (Collection)

The OutputWindowPanes collection contains all of the Output window panes in the IDE.

TaskItem (Object)

The TaskItem object relates to a single task item in the Task List. Compiler errors are automatically placed in the Task List by the code editor for the respective language. Double-clicking an item will position the code editor at the offending line of code. You can programmatically add task items to the Task List window.

TaskItems (Collection)

The TaskItems collection contains all the items in the Task List window. Usually, a TaskItem is an error message placed into the task list by the code editor when it encounters a line of code that will not compile.

TaskList (Object)

The TaskList object allows you to navigate through the Task List. There is only one Task List in the IDE and it is created by the IDE.

TextDocument (Object)

The TextDocument object represents the text file in the active editor.

TextWindow (Object)

The TextWindow object represents a window containing a text document. A TextWindow object is returned by the Object property of a Window object if the window is a Text Editor window.

Toolbox (Object)

The Toolbox object represents the Toolbox in the IDE. The Toolbox is a Windows object. When a WinForms Designer is the active document in the IDE, the active ToolBox tab contains the components available for use on the form. If a code editor is the active window, the ToolBox tab represents the Clipboard Ring.

ToolBoxItem (Object)

A ToolBoxItem object can be a component in the case that the active window is a WinForms Designer. It is a text item in Clipboard Ring in the case where the active window is a code editor.

ToolBoxItems (Collection)

The ToolBoxItems collection contains all items in the ToolBox tab.

ToolBoxTab (Object)

The ToolBoxTab object relates to a tab in the ToolBox, including the objects that the tab contains.

ToolBoxTabs (Collection)

The ToolBoxTabs collection contains all tabs in the ToolBox object.

UIHierarchy (Object)

The UIHierarchy object provides a common object model for standard tool windows that use tree views to present their contents. You can programmatically select data in these windows by using the UIHierarchy object.

Window (Object)

This object represents an open window in the IDE.

Windows (Collection)

The Windows collection contains all of the open windows in the IDE.

WinForms

Forms within .NET can no longer be manipulated behind the scenes as they could in VB 6.0. The forms are still text files, but the code that creates components cannot be manipulated directly in the text file as it could in VB 6.0. The extensibility objects for programmatically manipulating forms within the IDE are available. They are complex and abstract. The objects listed in this section are the basic starting objects with which you must work.

IComponent (Interface)

The IComponent interface allows you to create and manipulate components on a form.

IDesignerHost (Interface)

The IDesignerHost interface allows you to manage designer transactions and components. You must use this interface to manipulate forms and their contained components.

ObjectExtenders (Object)

The ObjectExtenders object gives you access to automation extenders. See the MSDN topic "Implementing and Using Automation Extenders" for more information on automation extenders.

PropertyDescriptor (Object)

The PropertyDescriptor object allows you to reference and change properties on a form or a component on a form.

PropertyDescriptorCollection (Collection)

The PropertyDescriptorCollection collection contains a set of PropertyDescriptor objects. It allows you to select a specified property from the collection of properties of the component or form.

SelectedItem (Object)

The SelectedItem object represents a selected project item or items in the IDE.

SelectedItems (Collection)

The SelectedItems collection contains the SelectedItem objects in the IDE.

TypeDescriptor (Object)

The TypeDescriptor object provides information about the properties and events of a component, including a form.

APPENDIX B

Quick Reference: How Do I ...?

THIS APPENDIX CONTAINS frequently asked questions (FAQs) by add-in developers. Specifically, it addresses FAQs that begin with "How do I." Obviously, this is not an exhaustive list of subjects. It is simply an attempt to provide answers, either in text, code samples, pointers to material covered in the book, or all three, that relate to the most frequently implemented functionality in add-ins.

You will also find some answers to questions on some of the more complex issues that may have not been covered in the course of the book. You can assume that each section is prefaced by "How do I" and followed by a question mark.

 **NOTE** *Some of the code examples that follow use the DTE object, and some reference oVB (application object). The use of DTE means that the code has been tested in the Macros IDE and will work in an add-in by changing to reference from DTE to oVB. You can execute the add-in examples in a macro by switching from oVB to DTE. There are a few cases where code has been tested in an add-in but it will not work in a macro. Specifically, any use of IDesignerHost in a macro will fail.*

Because most of the code examples are short or can be found in the code already provided in the code samples for the respective chapters, no downloadable code is available for this appendix.

Get Code from a Code Editor Window

The following code shows the GetCodeFromWindow method of the Utilities class. It uses only the TextSelection object. It assumes that the user has selected a block of text on which to perform some functionality.

```
Public Function GetCodeFromWindow() As String
    Dim s As String
    Dim selCodeBlock As TextSelection
    Dim oUtil As New Utilities(oVB)

    Try
        selCodeBlock = _
            CType(oVB.ActiveDocument.Selection(), _
            EnvDTE.TextSelection)
        GetCodeFromWindow = selCodeBlock.Text
    Catch e As System.Exception
        MsgBox("Error: " & e.Message, MsgBoxStyle.Critical, _
            "GetCodeFromWindow")
    End Try
    oUtil = Nothing
End Function
```

Retrieve a Whole Procedure from a Code Editor Window

The following code retrieves a whole procedure from a module. The function expects that the cursor lies somewhere within the procedure to be retrieved. You can find this code in the Utilities class in the code for Chapter 12. It uses the TextSelection and EditPoint objects. It will retrieve any comments that immediately precede the procedure definition line.

```
Public Function GetWholeProc() As String
    Dim ts As TextSelection = oVB.ActiveWindow().Selection
    Dim ep As EditPoint = ts.ActivePoint.CreateEditPoint
    Dim sLine As String
    Dim i As Integer
    Dim sCommentChar As String

    Try
        sCommentChar = Me.GetCommentCharForDoc(oVB.ActiveDocument)
        sCommentChar = Left(sCommentChar, 1)
        If sCommentChar = "/" Then
            If Len(ts.Text) = 0 Then
                MsgBox("For a C#/C++ project you must select ⏎
                    the whole proc.")
                Return ""
```

```
            End If
        End If


        ' if the user has selected the whole proc,
        ' then just return it
        ' otherwise select it for them...
        If Len(ts.Text) > 0 Then
            If (InStr(1, ts.Text, "Sub ", 1) > 0 Or _
               InStr(1, ts.Text, "Function ", 1) > 0) And _
               (InStr(1, ts.Text, "End Sub", 1) > 0 Or _
               InStr(1, ts.Text, "End Function", 1) > 0) _
               Then
                Return ts.Text
            End If
            GoTo SelectTheProc
        Else
SelectTheProc:
            '' Get the start of the proc
            ep.MoveToPoint(ep.CodeElement(EnvDTE.vsCMElement. ↵
                vsCMElementFunction).GetStartPoint↵
                (vsCMPart.vsCMPartWhole))

            ' move selection start point to top of proc
            ts.MoveToPoint(ep, False)

            ' back up to previous line looking for comments
            i = 0
            Do
                ep.LineUp()
                ts.MoveToPoint(ep, False)
                ts.SelectLine()
                sLine = ts.Text
                If Left(Trim(sLine), 1) <> sCommentChar Then
                    ep.LineDown()
                    ts.MoveToPoint(ep, False)
                    Exit Do
                End If
                i = i + 1
            Loop

            ' if the count of comment lines > 0  the
            ' ts point is set properly
            ' else we must move it back to the original
            ep.LineDown(i + 1)
```

```
                        ' move to bottom of proc
                        ep.MoveToPoint(ep.CodeElement(EnvDTE.vsCMElement. ⏎
                            vsCMElementFunction).GetEndPoint( ⏎
                            vsCMPart.vsCMPartWhole))


                        ' select the proc
                        ts.MoveToPoint(ep, True)
                        Return ts.Text
                End If
        Catch e As System.Exception
            System.Windows.Forms.MessageBox.Show( ⏎
                "You must either select " & _
                "the whole procedure or your cursor must be ⏎
                within the procedure " & _
                "to be selected.  " & e.Message)
            Return ""
        End Try
    End Function
```

Put Code Back into a Code Editor Window

The PutCodeBack method shown in the following code will replace a selected
block of code in a module. It uses only the TextSelection object. You can find this
code in the Utilities class in the code for Chapter 12.

```
    Public Sub PutCodeBack(ByVal s As String)
        Dim selCodeBlock As TextSelection
        'Dim datobj As New System.Windows.Forms.DataObject()

        Try
            selCodeBlock = CType(oVB.ActiveDocument.Selection(), _
                EnvDTE.TextSelection)
            'datobj.SetData(System.Windows.Forms.DataFormats.Text, s)
            'System.Windows.Forms.Clipboard.SetDataObject(datobj)

            'selCodeBlock.Paste()
            selCodeBlock.Delete()
            selCodeBlock.Insert(s, 1)
        Catch e As System.Exception
            MsgBox("Could not put code back in window.", _
                MsgBoxStyle.Critical, _
                "PutCodeBackInWindow")
        End Try
    End Sub
```

Add a New Method to the End of a Module

The AddMethodToEndOfDocument method shown in the following code uses
the TextDocument and EditPoint objects to place a new method at the end of the
module in the active window. The module can be a class, module, or code for
a form. Cursor position is of no consequence.

```
Public Sub AddMethodToEndOfDocument(ByVal NewMethod As String)
    Dim objTD As TextDocument = oVB.ActiveDocument.Object
    Dim objEP As EditPoint = objTD.EndPoint.CreateEditPoint

    ' We are past the end of the last line of the document
    ' move back in front of the End Module/Class
    objEP.LineUp(1)

    ' if a c# file, we must get within the namespace and
    ' the class braces
    If Me.GetFileType(oVB.ActiveDocument) = 9 Then
        objEP.LineUp(1)
    End If
    objEP.Insert(NewMethod)
End Sub
```

Reference Properties of a Form

Properties of a form are referenced through the IDesignerHost object. It is actually complex and abstract, but once you learn how to reference one property, you
can then reference any property the same way.

The following code snippet references the Size property of a form. The Size
property was chosen because a System.Drawing.Size object must be used, which
is a little more involved than a simple String property. Note that the active window must contain a WinForms Designer. The comments in the code describe
what is taking place in the code.

```
' Get a forms designer host object
Dim fdHost As IDesignerHost
If applicationObject.ActiveWindow.Caption. ⤸
    EndsWith("[Design]") Then
    Dim sName As String, sText As String
    fdHost = CType(applicationObject.ActiveWindow.Object, _
        IDesignerHost)
```

```
        ' get property descriptor collection object
        ' properties of a form are referenced through
        ' the RootComponent
        ' of the designer host object
        Dim pdc As PropertyDescriptorCollection
        pdc = TypeDescriptor.GetProperties(fdHost.RootComponent)
        ' get property descriptor object
        Dim pd As PropertyDescriptor
        ' display size of form
        ' set property descriptor to point to size
        pd = pdc("Size")
        Dim sSize As String = _
            pd.GetValue(fdHost.RootComponent).ToString()
        MsgBox("Default Form Size = " & sSize)
    End If
```

Change a Property on a Form

Properties of components on a form are referenced through the IDesignerHost object, in much the same way that properties on a form are referenced.

The following code snippet references the Size property of a form. The Size property was chosen because a System.Drawing.Size object must be used, which is a little more involved than a simple String property. Note that the active window must contain a WinForms Designer. The comments in the code describe what is taking place in the code.

```
    ' Get a forms designer host object
    Dim fdHost As IDesignerHost
    If applicationObject.ActiveWindow.Caption. ⏎
        EndsWith("[Design]") Then
        Dim sName As String, sText As String
        fdHost = CType(applicationObject.ActiveWindow.Object, _
            IDesignerHost)

        ' get property descriptor collection object
        ' properties of a form are referenced through
        ' the RootComponent
        ' of the designer host object
        Dim pdc As PropertyDescriptorCollection
        pdc = TypeDescriptor.GetProperties(fdHost.RootComponent)
        ' get property descriptor object
        Dim pd As PropertyDescriptor
```

```
' display size of form
' set property descriptor to point to size
pd = pdc("Size")
Dim sz As System.Drawing.Size
sz = New Size(250, 400)
pd.SetValue(fdHost.RootComponent, sz)
End If
```

Reference Properties of a Control on a Form

The IDesignerHost object is used to reference properties of a form, as well as the properties of any of the components on the form.

The following code snippet demonstrates how to reference a property of the form. In this code, the Size property is referenced because it is a little different from a simple String property. To reference the Size property or the Location property, you must use the System.Drawing.Size object. The following code snippet assumes that the active window contains a WinForms Designer. The code is commented well enough to describe what is taking place in the code. For more details on manipulating controls, see Chapter 6 and the code for that chapter. Note that you must always have an IDesignerHost object to reference anything on a form, including the form's properties or component properties.

```
' Get a forms designer host object
Dim fdHost As IDesignerHost
If applicationObject.ActiveWindow. ⤶
    Caption.EndsWith("[Design]") Then
    Dim sName As String, sText As String
    fdHost = CType(applicationObject.ActiveWindow.Object, _
        IDesignerHost)
    '' Get and set the value of the size proeprty,
    '' showing values
    '' before and after.
    Dim pd As PropertyDescriptor
    pd = pdc("Size")
    MsgBox("Default Button size = " + _
        pd.GetValue(btn1).ToString())
    Catch e As System.Exception
        MsgBox(e.Message)
    End Try
End If
```

Change a Property of a Control on a Form

The following code snippet uses the IDesignerHost, the PropertyDescriptor, and PropertyDescriptorCollection to demonstrate changing the Size and Location properties of a button on a form. The code assumes that the active window contains a WinForms Designer. For additional details on manipulating controls and forms, see Chapter 6 and the code for that chapter.

```
' Get a forms designer host object
Dim fdHost As IDesignerHost
If applicationObject.ActiveWindow.Caption. ↵
    EndsWith("[Design]") Then
    Try
        Dim sName As String, sText As String
        fdHost = CType(applicationObject.ActiveWindow.Object, _
            IDesignerHost)
        '' Get and set the value of the size proeprty,
        '' showing values
        '' before and after.
        Dim pd As PropertyDescriptor
        Dim pdc As PropertyDescriptorCollection
        pd = pdc("Size")
        MsgBox("Default Button size = " & _
            pd.GetValue(btn1).ToString())

        ' resize the button
        Dim sz As System.Drawing.Size
        sz = New Size(100, 60)
        pd.SetValue(btn1, sz)
        MsgBox("custom Button size = " & _
            pd.GetValue(btn1).ToString())

        '' reposition the button
        pd = pdc("Location")
        Dim loc As System.Drawing.Point
        loc = New Point(30, 30)
```

```
        pd.SetValue(btn1, loc)
        MsgBox("New button location = " & _
            pd.GetValue(btn1).ToString())
    Catch e As System.Exception
        MsgBox(e.Message)
    End Try
End If
```

Reference All of the Selected Controls on a Form

Components on a form are referenced through the use if IComponent objects, along with PropertyDescriptor and PropertyDescriptorCollection objects. Assuming that the user has selected one or more components on a form, the following code lists the Name property of each component:

```
' loop through the selected component collection
' listing properties
Dim pd As PropertyDescriptor
Dim pdc As PropertyDescriptorCollection
Dim ic As IComponent
Dim c As Component
For Each c In sel.GetSelectedComponents
    ic = CType(c, IComponent)
    pdc = TypeDescriptor.GetProperties(ic)
    pd = pdc("Text")
    s = pd.GetValue(ic).ToString
    pd = pdc("Name")
    s2 = pd.GetValue(ic).ToString
    MsgBox("Component Text = " & s & Chr(10) & _
            "Component Name = " & s2)
Next
```

Create a Windows Application Project from an Add-in

Projects are created through the use of templates. See the WinFormsAutomation add-in in Chapter 6 for a description and code for creating a new solution and a Windows application project.

Add an Item to a Project

You can add an item to a project through the use of the AddFromFile method of the ProjectItems object. The following code snippet creates a solution, adds a Visual Basic console application, and finally adds a file to the project:

```
' This function creates a solution and adds a Visual
' Basic .NET Console
' project to it.
Dim sln As Solution
Dim prj As Project
Dim prjitems As ProjectItems

' Create a reference to the solution.
sln = DTE.Solution

' Create a new solution.
sln.Create("c:\temp2", "TestSolution")

' Create a new VB Console application project.
' Adjust the save path as
' needed.
prj = sln.AddFromTemplate(⤶
    "C:\Program Files\Microsoft Visual Studio⤶
    .NET\Vb7\VBWizards\ConsoleApplication\Templates\1033\⤶
   ConsoleApplication.vbproj", "c:\temp2", "TestProjectt", True)
prjitems = prj.ProjectItems

' Add a project item from a file.
Prjitems.AddFromFile("C:\temp\Test.bas")
```

Delete an Item from a Project

A project item can be deleted from the project by use of the Delete method of the ProjectItems collection.

Add a Menu Item to the IDE

Chapter 7 deals with all facets of several types of user interfaces. See Chapter 7 and its code for help in adding a menu item to the IDE.

Add an Add-in Toolbar to the IDE

Chapter 7 demonstrates how to add a Microsoft Office toolbar (CommandBar) to the IDE. The Chapter 7 code provides the complete code for this task.

Add Tool Buttons to a Toolbar

Chapter 7 demonstrates how to add Microsoft Office (CommandBarControls) tool buttons to the IDE. The Chapter 7 code provides complete code for this task.

Add Multilevel Menus to the IDE

Chapter 7 demonstrates how to add multilevel Microsoft Office CommandBarControls to the IDE.

Capture Events in the IDE

Chapter 11 contains code demonstrating how to capture DTE events.

Add a New Class, Form, or Module

You can add classes, forms, and modules to a project through the use of templates in the same way you add a project to a solution. You can use the AddFromTemplate method of the ProjectItems object.

Persist My Own Clipboard Ring

You can create and persist your own Clipboard Ring. See the discussion of the ToolBox object in Chapter 9.

Access the Tool Options Dialog Box Programmatically

You can use the IDesignerOptionService interface to access the properties and settings in the Options dialog box available through Tool ➤ Options in the IDE. Chapter 6 provides an example under the "Accessing Designer Options" section.

Manually Register an Add-in Not Created with the Add-in Wizard on My Computer

Refer to the "Registering the Add-in" section in Chapter 13. You can also do this by building and installing the application if you have the add-in solution.

Manually Make the Registry Entries for the Add-in Manager Dialog Box for Add-ins Not Created by the Wizard on My Computer

Refer to the "Creating Registry Entries for the Add-in" section in Chapter 13.

Create a Setup Project for an Add-in Not Created on My Computer

Refer to the "Building a Setup Project" section in Chapter 13.

Debug an Add-in When I Only Have the Add-in Project

Chapter 13 covered this subject in detail, but basically you must perform the following steps:

1. Create a setup project in the solution.

2. Set a start-up project in the configuration section of the Project Properties dialog box.

3. Register the add-in.

4. Make the registry entries for the Add-in Manager.

Recognize When a Form Has Been Added to the Project

I have found that many of the events that I would expect to fire when I add a form or a component do not fire. The ProjectItemsEvents ItemAdded event does not appear to fire when a new item is added to a project. Assuming this is the case, it then becomes more difficult to determine if a form has been added to the project.

One event that does fire without fail is the WindowActivated event of the DTE.WindowEvents object. With a little bit of creativity, you can examine the window to see if it is a Form Designer window and, if so, you can take further action to examine the form. For example, you can check to see if the name has been changed from its default name. You can implement a Form Property Prompter and prompt the user to set certain basic properties such as the Name and Text properties, FormBorderStyle, and so forth. If you do this, then when you encounter a form that still has a default name such as "Form1," you can assume that the form has just been added or that the user has not yet changed the default name. Of course, you should give the user a way to turn off the prompting, unless of course you intend to enforce some type of naming convention for all forms. Be aware that the WindowActivated event is firing every time you click a new window, so do as little coding as possible to determine if you are looking at the window that you want to manipulate.

Recognize When a Component Has Been Added to a Form

There is a very complex methodology for doing this. You must create a "Listener" class. The Listener must implement the IComponentChangeService interface. The following listing shows the code for a sample Listener class. You will notice that the code to associate all event handlers except ComponentAdded has been commented out. I did this because I am only interested in knowing when a component has been added.

 **NOTE** *The code in this topic is provided only in the book, for example purposes. No downloadable code is provided for the appendix examples. I have tested the code in this topic in an add-in and it works.*

```
Imports System.ComponentModel.Design
Imports System.ComponentModel.Component
Imports System.ComponentModel
Imports System.Windows.Forms
Imports Microsoft.Office.Core
Imports EnvDTE
Imports Extensibility

'` To set up a listener, first dim a fdHost in the connect
'` class.  Next, instance the Listener Class.  Put a public
```

```
'' variable of IDesignerHost (fdHost) in it.
'` When a windowActivated event fires, check the document
'` caption for .vb*|.cs* [Design], indicating that we have a
'` Windows form designer window activated.  If so, set the
'` fdHost object variable to the new window, and set the
'` fdHost variable in the Listener class.
' '
'` This will set the listener events so that when a component
'` is added to the designer, we will be notified.  The
'` ComponentChangedEventArgs parameter will have the component
'' that is being added.
' '
'` Pass the componenet and the designerhost to the property
'' prompter form.
' '
'` This should work in theory; let's see how it works in
'` practice.
' '
Public Class CDesignerListener
    Public FDHost As IDesignerHost
    Private m_changeService As IComponentChangeService
    Friend oVB As DTE

    ' Object constructor
    Public Sub Activate() 'ByVal host As IDesignerHost)
        ' m_host = host
        If FDHost Is Nothing Then Exit Sub

        m_changeService = FDHost.GetService(GetType(⏎
          IComponentChangeService))

        If Not (m_changeService Is Nothing) Then
            ' Clear the old component change events to prepare
            ' for re-siting.
            'RemoveHandler m_changeService.ComponentChanged, _
            '     AddressOf OnComponentChanged
            'RemoveHandler m_changeService.ComponentChanging, _
            '     AddressOf OnComponentChanging
            RemoveHandler m_changeService.ComponentAdded, _
                AddressOf OnComponentAdded
            'RemoveHandler m_changeService.ComponentAdding, _
            '     AddressOf OnComponentAdding
            'RemoveHandler m_changeService.ComponentRemoved, _
```

```vb
'        AddressOf OnComponentRemoved
'RemoveHandler m_changeService.ComponentRemoving, _
'        AddressOf OnComponentRemoving
'RemoveHandler m_changeService.ComponentRename, _
'        AddressOf OnComponentRename
    End If


    ' Adds an event handler for the ComponentChanged event
    ' if an IComponentChangeService was obtained.
    If Not (m_changeService Is Nothing) Then
        'AddHandler m_changeService.ComponentChanged, _
        '     AddressOf OnComponentChanged
        'AddHandler m_changeService.ComponentChanged, _
        '     AddressOf OnComponentChanged
        'AddHandler m_changeService.ComponentChanging, _
        '     AddressOf OnComponentChanging
        AddHandler m_changeService.ComponentAdded, _
            AddressOf OnComponentAdded
        'AddHandler m_changeService.ComponentAdding, _
        '     AddressOf OnComponentAdding
        'AddHandler m_changeService.ComponentRemoved, _
        '    AddressOf OnComponentRemoved
        'AddHandler m_changeService.ComponentRemoving, _
        '     AddressOf OnComponentRemoving
        'AddHandler m_changeService.ComponentRename, _
        '     AddressOf OnComponentRename
    End If
End Sub 'New
' The IComponentChange calls this right after
' a component has been changed.
Private Sub OnComponentChanged(ByVal sender As Object, _
    ByVal e As ComponentChangedEventArgs)
    ' If the host is loading, this event was not
    ' caused by a user, and can be ignored.
    If FDHost.Loading Then
        Return
    End If
    ' If a transaction is in progress,
    ' wait for a TransactionClosed
    ' event which indicates when it's finished.
    If FDHost.InTransaction Then
        AddHandler FDHost.TransactionClosed, _
```

```vb
                    AddressOf OnDesignerTransactionClosed
            Return
        End If
        ' This is a valid UserChange event, so process it.
        OnUserChange("OnComponentChanged: " & _
            e.Component.ToString & " Type: " & _
            e.Component.GetType.ToString)
    End Sub 'OnComponentChanged


    ' This is the OnComponentChanging handler method.
    ' This method calls
    ' OnUserChange to display a message that indicates
    ' the name of the
    ' handler that made the call and the type of the
    ' event argument.
    Private Sub OnComponentChanging(ByVal sender As Object, _
        ByVal ce As ComponentChangingEventArgs)
        OnUserChange("OnComponentChanging")
    End Sub 'OnComponentChanging


    ' This is the OnComponentAdded handler method.
    ' This method calls
    ' OnUserChange to display a message that indicates
    ' the name of the
    ' handler that made the call and the type of the
    ' event argument.
    Private Sub OnComponentAdded(ByVal sender As Object, _
        ByVal ce As ComponentEventArgs)
        'OnUserChange("OnComponentAdded " & ce.Component.Site.Name)
        System.Windows.Forms.Application.DoEvents()
        If Connect.gbPropertyPrompter Then
            Dim oFH As New CFormHandler(oVB)
            oFH.PromptNewComponent(FDHost, ce.Component)
        End If
    End Sub 'OnComponentAdded


    ' This is the OnComponentAdding handler method.
    ' This method calls
    ' OnUserChange to display a message that indicates the
    ' name of the
    '    handler that made the call and the type of
    ' the event argument. */
    Private Sub OnComponentAdding(ByVal sender As Object, _
```

```vb
    ByVal ce As ComponentEventArgs)
    OnUserChange("OnComponentAdding")
End Sub 'OnComponentAdding


' This is the OnComponentRemoved handler method.
' This method calls
' OnUserChange to display a message that indicates
' the name of the
' handler that made the call and the type of
' the event argument. */
Private Sub OnComponentRemoved(ByVal sender As Object, _
    ByVal ce As ComponentEventArgs)
    OnUserChange("OnComponentRemoved")
End Sub 'OnComponentRemoved


' This is the OnComponentRemoving handler method.
' This method calls
' OnUserChange to display a message that indicates the
' name of the
' handler that made the call and the type of the
' event argument.
Private Sub OnComponentRemoving(ByVal sender As Object, _
    ByVal ce As ComponentEventArgs)
    OnUserChange("OnComponentRemoving")
End Sub 'OnComponentRemoving


' This is the OnComponentRename handler method.
' This method calls
' OnUserChange to display a message that indicates the
' name of the
' handler that made the call and the type of the
' event argument. */
Private Sub OnComponentRename(ByVal sender As Object, _
    ByVal ce As ComponentRenameEventArgs)
    OnUserChange("OnComponentRename")
End Sub 'OnComponentRename


' The program began listening to the TransactionClosed
' event in OnComponentChanged().
Private Sub OnDesignerTransactionClosed(ByVal sender As Object, _
    ByVal e As DesignerTransactionCloseEventArgs)
    ' To stop listening to transaction messages,
    ' remove the handler.
```

```
        RemoveHandler FDHost.TransactionClosed, _
           AddressOf OnDesignerTransactionClosed
        OnUserChange("OnDesignerTransactionClosed")
    End Sub 'OnDesignerTransactionClosed

    ' Called in response to a change made by the user.
    Private Sub OnUserChange(ByVal s As String)
        MsgBox(s)
    End Sub 'OnUserChange
End Class
```

Once the class is coded, it must be instantiated and supplied with an object of type IDesignerHost. That causes the Listener to monitor events taking place in the Windows Forms Designer. The way that I have implemented the Listener class is by following the steps described in the following subtopics.

Create an Object Variable of IDesignerHost (fdHost) and an Instance of the Listener Class in the Connect Class of the Add-in

The code for this is shown in the following code snippet. These variables should be declared at the module level of the Connect class:

```
    Dim fdHost As IDesignerHost
    Dim oListener As New CDesignerListener()
```

Register for the DTE Windows Events

In the WindowActivated event, check the caption of the window that was activated. If the caption ends with "[Design]", you know that a Windows Forms Designer is the active window. If that is the case, you will set the fdHost object to the ActiveWindow.Object and then set the fdHost into the Listener class. Finally, you call the Activate method of the Listener object to cause it to associate the event handlers with the new fdHost object. The code for doing so is as follows:

```
    If oVB.ActiveWindow.Caption.EndsWith("[Design]") Then
        fdHost = CType(oVB.ActiveWindow.Object, IDesignerHost)
        If fdHost.RootComponent.Site.Name <> sFDHostName Then
            oListener.FDHost = fdHost
            oListener.Activate()
        End If
    End If
```

Reload a Component

Many times you will make changes to a component and then, before you save the changes, determine that you would like to reload the component from its original state in order to cancel the changes. It may be that the changes are too numerous or complex, in the case of a form, and you just want to restore the module, class, or form without having to unload and reload the project. The following macro command will do that for you. Make sure the component that you want to reload is the active window. When the window prompts you to save the changes, click the No button.

```
Sub ReloadComponent()
    Dim projs As System.Array
    Dim proj As Project
    Dim sln As String = DTE.Solution.Item(1).Name
    Dim pn As String
    Dim s As String
    Dim s2 As String = DTE.ActiveDocument.FullName
    Dim awn As String = DTE.ActiveDocument.Name
    projs = DTE.ActiveSolutionProjects()
    proj = CType(projs.GetValue(0), EnvDTE.Project)
    pn = proj.Name
    s = sln & "\" & pn & "\" & awn
    DTE.Windows.Item(Constants. ⏎
        vsWindowKindSolutionExplorer).Activate()
    DTE.ActiveWindow.Object.GetItem(s) ⏎
        .Select(vsUISelectionType. ⏎
            vsUISelectionTypeSelect)
    DTE.ExecuteCommand("Project.ExcludeFromProject")
    System.Windows.Forms.Application.DoEvents()
    DTE.Windows.Item(Constants. ⏎
        vsWindowKindSolutionExplorer).Activate()
    System.Windows.Forms.Application.DoEvents()
    DTE.ItemOperations.AddExistingItem(s2)
    DTE.Windows.Item(Constants. ⏎
        vsWindowKindSolutionExplorer).Activate()
    DTE.ActiveWindow.Object.GetItem(s). ⏎
        Select(vsUISelectionType. ⏎
            vsUISelectionTypeSelect)
    DTE.ActiveWindow.Object.DoDefaultAction()
End Sub
```

Close All Saved Windows in the IDE

The following procedure will close all open windows in the IDE that currently have not been changed since they were saved. It uses the Documents collection to access the open windows. It uses the Saved property of the Document.Items() object to determine if a document is saved or "dirty."

```
Public Sub CloseAllSavedWindows()
    ' Close all saved documents.
    Dim i As Integer
    With oVB
        On Error Resume Next
        For i = .Documents.Count To 1 Step -1
            If .Documents.Item(i).Saved Then
                .Documents.Item(i).Close(vsSaveChanges⏎
                    .vsSaveChangesPrompt)
            End If
        Next i
    End With
End Sub
```

Close and Save All but the Active Document

Sometimes it would be nice just to clear the desktop by closing all windows but the active window. The following procedure will do that for you. It uses the Documents collection and compares the names of the documents to the name of the current document before determining whether or not to close the window.

```
Public Sub CloseAllButCurrentWindow()
    Dim i As Integer
    Dim sCurrWin As String = oVB.ActiveDocument.Name

    Debug.WriteLine(sCurrWin)
    With oVB
        On Error Resume Next
        For i = .Documents.Count To 1 Step -1
            If .Documents.Item(i).Name <> sCurrWin Then
                If Not .Documents.Item(i).Saved Then
                    .Documents.Item(i).Close(vsSaveChanges⏎
                        .vsSaveChangesYes)
                Else
                    .Documents.Item(i).Close(vsSaveChanges⏎
```

```
                .vsSaveChangesNo)
            End If
        End If
    Next
  End With
End Sub
```

Make a Backup Copy of the Current Window

Before you make massive changes to a source file, you might want to make
a backup copy of the file. If you later decide that you want to restore the copy of
the source code before you made the changes, you will have a copy to restore.
Obviously, you could do this manually through the Windows Explorer, but you
can do it very easily within the IDE with the following procedure:

```
Sub BackupCurrentWindow()
    '` This method will make a backup copy of
    '` the active window.  It will be saved as
    '` fullname.bak.  For example, a .vb file
    '` will be saved as name.vb.bak.  The file
    '` will be saved and closed.  It will not
    '' be added to the project.
    Dim Sel As TextSelection = oVB.ActiveDocument.Selection
    Dim sFileName As String = oVB.ActiveDocument.FullName & _
        ".bak"
    Dim epAnchor As EditPoint = Sel.AnchorPoint.CreateEditPoint
    Dim epActive As EditPoint = Sel.ActivePoint.CreateEditPoint
    Dim txtWin As TextWindow = oVB.ActiveWindow.Object
    Dim actPane As TextPane = txtWin.ActivePane
    Dim Corner As EditPoint = actPane.StartPoint.CreateEditPoint
    Dim Text As String

    Sel.SelectAll()
    Text = Sel.Text

    ' Create, save, and close the backup copy of the
    ' current window
    oVB.ItemOperations.NewFile("General\Text File")
    oVB.ActiveDocument.Object("TextDocument").↵
        Selection.Insert(Text)
    oVB.ActiveDocument.Save(sFileName)
    oVB.ActiveDocument.Close(EnvDTE.vsSaveChanges.↵
        vsSaveChangesNo)
```

```
' Restore the selection.
Sel.MoveToPoint(epAnchor)
Sel.MoveToPoint(epActive, True)
actPane.TryToShow(Corner, vsPaneShowHow.vsPaneShowTop)
End Sub
```

Open All Code and Designer Windows

If, for some reason, you would like to open all of the code and designer windows
in the project, the following procedure will do that for you. It does not open the
AssemblyInfo.vb file because you would not normally change this file.

```
Sub OpenAllWindows()
    Dim pi As ProjectItem
    Dim prj As Project
    Dim sln As String = DTE.Solution.Item(1).Name

    On Error Resume Next
    For Each prj In DTE.ActiveSolutionProjects
        For Each pi In prj.ProjectItems
            'Debug.WriteLine(pi.Name)
            If pi.Name.ToUpper.EndsWith(".VB") And _
                pi.Name.ToUpper <> "ASSEMBLYINFO.VB" Then
                Dim pn As String = prj.Name
                Dim s As String = pi.Name.ToString
                ' GetType(Sln.Name\proj.name\prjItem.name)
                Dim s2 As String = sln & "\" & pn & "\" & s
                DTE.Windows.Item(Constants.↵
                    vsWindowKindSolutionExplorer).↵
                    Activate()
                DTE.ActiveWindow.Object.GetItem(s2).Select(↵
                    vsUISelectionType.vsUISelectionTypeSelect)
                DTE.ActiveWindow.Object.DoDefaultAction()
                'System.Windows.Forms.Application.DoEvents()
                Dim doc As Document = DTE.ActiveDocument()
            End If
        Next
    Next
End Sub
```

Use the CodeModel Object to Analyze Code

To get a list of all variables and methods in your project, you can call the GetMembersList method shown in the following code. It will loop through all of the CodeElement objects in the project. It calls the GetMembers function, which is also shown in the following code, to append members to the string. You do not have to have any code windows open while this code is executing. The CodeModel is scanned behind the scenes and is actually quite fast.

```
Public Function GetMembersList(ByVal PI As Integer, _
    Optional ByVal rsCompName As String = "") _
    As String
    ' this method and its helper sub GetMethods
    ' will list all of the members in the project.
    Dim cm As CodeModel
    cm = oVB.Solution.Projects.Item(PI).CodeModel

    ' Look for all the namespaces and classes in the
    ' project.
    Dim list As String
    Dim ce As CodeElement
    On Error Resume Next
    For Each ce In cm.CodeElements
        If (TypeOf ce Is CodeClass) Then
            ' See if that namespace or class contains
            ' other classes.
            If rsCompName = "" Or _
                ce.Name.ToUpper = rsCompName.ToUpper _
                Then
                GetMembers(ce, list)
            End If
        End If
    Next

    Return list
End Function

Sub GetMembers(ByVal ct As CodeElement, _
    ByRef list As String)
    ' ct could be a namespace or a class.
    ' Add it to the list
    ' if it is a class.
    Static sClass As String
```

```vb
        Dim sp As Integer
        Dim ep As Integer

        On Error Resume Next
        If (TypeOf ct Is CodeClass) Then
            list &= "Class: " & ct.Name & " Kind: " & _
                ct.Kind.ToString & vbCrLf
            sClass = ct.Name
        ElseIf (TypeOf ct Is CodeFunction) Then
            sp = ct.StartPoint.Line
            ep = ct.EndPoint.Line
            list &= "Class: " & sClass & _
                ", Method: " & ct.Name & _
                ", Start: " & sp.ToString & _
                ", Lines: " & _
                (ep - sp + 1).ToString & vbCrLf
        ElseIf (TypeOf ct Is CodeVariable) Then
            sp = ct.StartPoint.Line
            list &= "Class: " & sClass & _
                ", Variable: " & ct.Name & _
                ", Start: " & sp.ToString & vbCrLf
        Else
            sp = ct.StartPoint.Line
            list &= "Class: " & sClass & _
                " Element: " & ct.Name & _
                " StartLine: " & sp.ToString & vbCrLf
        End If

        ' See if there are any nested namespaces or
        ' classes that might
        ' contain other classes.
        Dim ce As CodeElement
        For Each ce In ct.Members
            If (TypeOf ce Is CodeNamespace) Or _
                (TypeOf ce Is CodeClass) Or _
                (TypeOf ce Is CodeFunction) Or _
                (TypeOf ce Is CodeVariable) Then
                GetMembers(ce, list)
            End If
        Next
    End Sub
```

Display a Variable or Method Declaration Line in a Code Window

If you have a window name and a line number, you can display the desired line in the window by calling the DisplayCodeSelection method shown in the following code. You can get window names and line numbers of all CodeElement members by using the CodeModel object as shown previously. You will notice that this code method will automatically open the desired window for you and then select the specified line. The window name parameter (rsWinName) is a concatenation of the solution name, the project name, and the file name separated by backward slashes.

```
Public Sub DisplayCodeSelection(ByVal rsWinName As String, _
    ByVal riLine As Integer)
    ' Open the specified window, move to specified line,
    ' and select the line.
    ' This method can be called by features such as search
    ' program, project browser, and track changes.
    ' rsWinName="SlnName\PrjName\modulename.vb"
    Dim s As String

    Try
        's = Mid(rsWinName, InStrRev(rsWinName, "\") + 1)
        oVB.Windows.Item(Constants. ⤶
            vsWindowKindSolutionExplorer).Activate()
        oVB.ActiveWindow.Object.GetItem⤶
            (rsWinName).Select(vsUISelectionType. ⤶
            vsUISelectionTypeSelect)
        'oVB.ActiveWindow.Object.DoDefaultAction()
        oVB.ExecuteCommand("View.ViewCode")
        System.Windows.Forms.Application.DoEvents()
        Dim objTextDoc As TextSelection = _
            oVB.ActiveDocument.Selection
        objTextDoc.StartOfDocument()
        objTextDoc.MoveToLineAndOffset(riLine, 1, False)
        objTextDoc.MoveToLineAndOffset(riLine + 1, 1, True)
        oVB.ActiveDocument.Activate()
    Catch ex As System.Exception
        MsgBox("DisplayCodeSelection: " & ex.Message)
    End Try
End Sub
```

Index

books for professionals by professionals™

apress™

About Apress

Apress, located in Berkeley, CA, is a fast-growing, innovative publishing company devoted to meeting the needs of existing and potential programming professionals. Simply put, the "A" in Apress stands for *"The Author's Press™"* and its books have *"The Expert's Voice™".* Apress' unique approach to publishing grew out of conversations between its founders Gary Cornell and Dan Appleman, authors of numerous best-selling, highly regarded books for programming professionals. In 1998 they set out to create a publishing company that emphasized quality above all else. Gary and Dan's vision has resulted in the publication of over 50 titles by leading software professionals, all of which have *The Expert's Voice™*.

Do You Have What It Takes
to Write for Apress?

Apress is rapidly expanding its publishing program. If you can write and refuse to compromise on the quality of your work, if you believe in doing more than rehashing existing documentation, and if you're looking for opportunities and rewards that go far beyond those offered by traditional publishing houses, we want to hear from you!

Consider these innovations that we offer all of our authors:

- **Top royalties with *no* hidden switch statements**
  Authors typically only receive half of their normal royalty rate on foreign sales. In contrast, Apress' royalty rate remains the same for both foreign and domestic sales.

- **A mechanism for authors to obtain equity in Apress**
  Unlike the software industry, where stock options are essential to motivate and retain software professionals, the publishing industry has adhered to an outdated compensation model based on royalties alone. In the spirit of most software companies, Apress reserves a significant portion of its equity for authors.

- **Serious treatment of the technical review process**
  Each Apress book has a technical reviewing team whose remuneration depends in part on the success of the book since they too receive royalties.

Moreover, through a partnership with Springer-Verlag, New York, Inc., one of the world's major publishing houses, Apress has significant venture capital behind it. Thus, we have the resources to produce the highest quality books *and* market them aggressively.

If you fit the model of the Apress author who can write a book that gives the "professional what he or she needs to know™," then please contact one of our Editorial Directors, Gary Cornell (gary_cornell@apress.com), Dan Appleman (dan_appleman@apress.com), Peter Blackburn (peter_blackburn@apress.com), Jason Gilmore (jason_gilmore@apress.com), Karen Watterson (karen_watterson@apress.com), or John Zukowski (john_zukowski@apress.com) for more information.